Y0-EZC-846

The Ancients and the Moderns

Studies in Continental Thought

John Sallis, general editor

Consulting Editors

Robert Bernasconi
Rudolf Bernet
John D. Caputo
David Carr
Edward S. Casey
Hubert L. Dreyfus
Don Ihde
David Farrell Krell
Lenore Langsdorf
Alphonso Lingis
William L. McBride
J. N. Mohanty
Mary Rawlinson
Tom Rockmore
Calvin O. Schrag
†Reiner Schürmann
Charles E. Scott
Thomas Sheehan
Robert Sokolowski
Bruce W. Wilshire
David Wood

The Ancients and the Moderns

Edited by Reginald Lilly

INDIANA UNIVERSITY PRESS
Bloomington and Indianapolis

JA
81
A57
1996

© 1996 by Indiana University Press

All rights reserved

No part of this book may be reproduced or utilized in any form or by any means, electronic or mechanical, including photocopying and recording, or by any information storage and retrieval system, without permission in writing from the publisher. The Association of American Univeristy Presses' Resolution on Permissions constitutes the only exception to this prohibition.

The paper used in this publication meets the minimum requirements of American National Standard for Information Sciences—Permanence of Paper for Printed Library Materials, ANSI Z39.48-1984.

Manufactured in the United States of America

Library of Congress Cataloging-in-Publication Data

The ancients and the moderns / edited by Reginald Lilly.
p. cm. — (Studies in Continental thought)
Papers originally delivered at the New School for Social Research at the semiannual symposia in honor of Hannah Arendt.
Includes bibliographical references and index.
ISBN 0-253-33041-6 (cl : alk. paper)
1. Political science—History—Congresses. 2. Political science—Philosophy—History—Congresses. I. Lilly, Reginald. II. Series.
JA81.A57 1996
320.1'01—dc20 95-31887

1 2 3 4 5 01 00 99 98 97 96

In memory of Reiner Schürmann

Contents

PART II: Contemporary Τόποι: Nihilism and Subjectivity

Preface

The texts comprising the present volume were originally delivered at the New School for Social Research at the semiannual symposia in honor of Hannah Arendt that were organized by Reiner Schürmann beginning in 1980. However, the papers only occasionally took Arendt's work as their principal theme; rather, like Arendt's own work, they covered a broad range of topics. Schürmann discerned a possible common ground among several of them, and he initially selected these for inclusion in the present volume, whose title, *The Ancients and the Moderns*, was given by him. Owing to illness and his tragically early death, Schürmann was unable to finish editing these papers, a task that he asked the editor to complete.

As those familiar with the grace and depth of his work would expect, Schürmann invited individuals to the Hannah Arendt Symposium who were serious and estimable thinkers; it is a privilege to be able to collect and offer their essays in honor of the memory of Reiner Schürmann: a friend, a philosopher, and a friend of all who love philosophy.

Acknowledgments

I would like to thank the *Graduate Faculty Philosophy Journal* for permission to include the following essays: "In Search of a Civic Union: The Political Theme of European Democracy and Its Primordial Foundation in Greek Philosophy" and "Paradigm Evolution in Political Philosophy: Aristotle and Hobbes" by Manfred Riedel, "The Greek Πόλις and the Creation of Democracy" by Cornelius Castoriadis, and "'The First Times' in Rousseau's *Essay on the Origin of Languages*" by Victor Gourevitch. Several of the texts contained Greek written in the Latin alphabet; I thank Jeff Taylor for the lion's share of work expended in retranscribing this back into the original.

The Ancients and the Moderns

Introduction: Fault Lines

Reginald Lilly

To many, perhaps most, philosophers and students, the phrase "the ancients and the moderns" conjures up vague images of an old dispute of uncertain nature that must have long since become irrelevant, more a matter for intellectual historians than germane to issues at the heart of contemporary philosophical discourse. That the ideological episode named by this phrase has been all but forgotten by philosophy, consigned to its inert past, seems to be an unavoidable conclusion if one surveys current philosophical book lists, journals of philosophy, and philosophy convention programs. Indeed, "the ancients and the moderns" is a locution coined in an era and in response to specific circumstances which in important respects are no longer ours. The French of the seventeenth century seem to have been the first to give the name *la querelle des anciens et des modernes* (referred to as "the Battle of the Books" by the English and here as "the *Querelle*") to that constellation of disputes in which the basic contours of intellectual life were being refigured and recast as what we now recognize as "modernity."[1] Attention is lavished on modernity and its destiny pro or con; little note is taken of its founding battle. If the birth of modernity is thought of at all—whether by its defenders or by its critics—it seems more often than not to be thought of oedipally, that is, as a fledgling era that came into its own by finally laying low a tradition that was already flagging from loss of vitality.

The reader of this volume will discover, however, that as the designation for a theme of philosophical reflection, "the ancients and the moderns" names a farrago of relations that not only constitutes a moment in our Western European past but also conditions philosophical reflection at the close of the twentieth century. Those who thoughtfully reflect on the *Querelle* may see that the oft-heralded vanquishing of the ancients by the moderns is perhaps not only overdrawn but is a decidedly self-serving monochromatic modernist representation of what in fact was a much more nuanced and ambiguous affair; and inasmuch as modernity faces new challenges today, an appreciation of the historical emergence of modernity will help its critics not to be duped into attacking straw figures of modernity (which is often the case) and may reveal in the *Querelle* many lights that illuminate contemporary critical assessments of modernity.[2] It is within the context of such contemporary reflections on modernity that this collection of essays is situated. Laying out the horizon within which these reflections take place will help us understand more clearly the significance of "the ancients and the moderns" for today and to appreciate the contributions made by the essays in this volume.

The story of modernity is familiar enough. Philosophical reflection from Descartes to Kant and Hegel subjected premodern (medieval, Renaissance) thought to a critique of its traditionally metaphysical and dogmatic foundations and thereby opened up the space for a positive accomplishment: the construction of a body of knowledge that could definitively rejoin that virulent skepticism that harbors the seeds of nihilism. Nietzsche and, later, Heidegger challenged both the secure foundation in subjectivity that modern philosophy claims to have established and, a fortiori, the conception of history as a teleological progression to its (promised) consummation in a scientific metaphysics. If the modern conception of subjectivity and the program based on it have thereby been disrupted, this disruption has also opened up a site—or perhaps one should say "sites," τόποι—in which the tradition can be examined and questioned anew.

Of course the experience of disruption was definitive of modernity (which finds its absolute representation in Hegel); it not only constituted the inaugural gesture of modernity in its backward-glancing repudiation of the tradition but also came to be seen as a necessary moment in the continuing cycle of modern historical progress. The reflections on, even the critiques of, the disruption by and of modernity found in the essays in this volume do not, however, reject our modernist past outright; nor do they reassert or attempt to reform or correct the modern conception of subjectivity and history or prepare them for their sublation in a future—all very "modern" approaches to this past. These essays require us to rethink the nature of "the subject," of "history," and of "human πρᾶξις," and they call on us to rethink what has, in fundamental ways, been obscured and even obliterated by that modernist reading of history which endeavored—with awe-inspiring consistency—to assign a determinate meaning and significance to all historical things, events, ideas. (It is of no small significance for contemporary thought that the moderns have seemingly succeeded in utterly devaluing the philosophy of their Renaissance precursors and opponents—the "ancients".) These essays should also serve as a caution to critics of modernity who have relied too heavily on the moderns' own self-representation rather than take account of the quarrel in which they staked their claim to philosophy. These essays, in an exemplary manner, show us that a return to historical materials is indispensable for "modernity" is, if anything, a historico-critical term. And unlike the heated disputes over historical materials found in the Renaissance and the *Querelle*, the recursions to the past found here are not defined by the struggle over whether the site of truth lies in an antediluvian or pre-Christian paradise subsequently buried under the rotting corpus of Western European culture from which it must be rescued or whether it lies in a future that must be delivered from Greco-Christian mystagogues. Rather than a linear trajectory of either decay or ascension, these essays reveal the past to be a site of multiple origins and sources for the revisioning of what history is, what sense subjectivity can have, and how we might think of philosophical activity and human πρᾶξις. And as the historical thinking of modernity here is also often marked by a πόλεμος, it should be no surprise that revisiting and rethinking that πόλεμος, that *Querelle*, which engendered modernity is more compelling today than ever before. Each in its own way, the essays collected in this volume summon us to think modernity through "the ancients and the moderns."

With the exception of those by John Sallis and Klaus Held, the essays found here were not originally presented under the heading of "the ancients and the moderns." And though they were all given under the auspices of the semiannual Hannah Arendt Memorial Symposium founded and organized by Reiner Schürmann at the New School for Social Research, neither do they all take Arendt's philosophy as their focus. Those who knew Schürmann would not be surprised that he selected and collected symposium presentations under the heading "the ancients and the moderns." A German by birth, educated in France, and a lifelong teacher in the United States, Reiner Schürmann displayed interests and expertise that were legendary. A master of ancient and modern languages with a profound knowledge of and involvement in art, an award-winning novelist, a scholar extraordinaire of the history of philosophy, a tireless supporter of the New School, a redoubtable interlocutor, he had the sort of cultivation and civility that truly justifies the appellation "Renaissance man." Like Renaissance thinkers—and this characteristic he certainly shared with Arendt—he had a passion for thinking, for *débat*, for matters of human πρᾶξις and history. These are the passions that gave birth to the various themes of the symposia, and they were the passions of the *Querelle*. Offering several of the best symposia presentations in a volume entitled *The Ancients and the Moderns* expresses Schürmann's profound sense of the historical conditions of our contemporary situation, a sense that is present in all the essays, even where it is not the explicit theme.

The New School for Social Research became known in the second third of this century as a home for many great European intellectuals, and this tradition continued with Schürmann's direction of the Arendt symposia. Schürmann hosted the finest scholars of philosophy, politics, literature, and history from Germany, France, Italy, and elsewhere at these semiannual symposia. Given the historical and cultural diversity of the Renaissance and the *Querelle*, these essays by some of the brightest lights of Europe offer an unprecedented opportunity to gain insight into the formation and destiny of those issues that "the ancients and the moderns" brings into view.

Schürmann envisioned the present collection as demonstrating thematically and *in actu* that a return to the Greeks and to modernity, to the *Querelle*, is an indispensable rite of passage for thinking, whether it seeks to develop, extend, transform, or call into question the tradition; a better homage to Arendt could not be imagined. Accordingly, the essays comprising the first part of the volume, each in its own way, revisit Greek thought and especially the Greek experience of the πόλις and the crisis into which this experience eventually entered. In the light of this, essays in the second part explore possibilities and difficulties of thought and πρᾶξις within this tradition. More specifically, in the first part, "Initial Figures, Emergent Crises," Manfred Riedel, Cornelius Castoriadis, John Sallis, and Christian Meier examine basic structures and issues constitutive of the Greek πόλις and Greek politics. One will find among these essays quite different methods of approaching (and even conflicting interpretations of) the Greeks; but it is no longer an issue of either the idealization or the depreciation of the Greeks but of the multiplicity and consequences of the possible determinations of our contemporary world that are given to us in a reflection on the Greeks. Rüdiger Bubner, Riedel, Klaus Held, Paul Ricoeur, Reinhart Koselleck, Castoriadis, and Wolfgang Hardtwig focus on that historical crisis out of which modernity first emerges. As becomes evident in these essays, the very nature of crisis and modernity does not, perhaps as the founders of modernity would require, call for partisanship but for a retrieval of possibilites of thinking and acting. These essays should disabuse us of many clichés of "modernity" and "the ancients."

In the second part, "Contemporary Τόποι: Nihilism and Subjectivity," the essays are situated in that space opened up by the contemporary critical questioning of modernity, especially that accomplished by Martin Heidegger, certainly one of the most important and influential critics of modernity. Jean-Luc Marion, Jacques Taminiaux, Giorgio Agamben, and Rémi Brague find in him not simply a compelling thinker of the legacy of Greek and modern philosophy but a figure whose understanding of philosophy and its history is itself something that must be questioned. Finally, Victor Gourevitch, Frank Ankersmit, Heinrich Mohr, and James Mensch explore problems and possibilites of thinking about the subject within the context of a world in which one of the schisms that shaped modernity and continues to be an issue—between philosophy and literature—is itself thought through from the standpoint of the twentieth century.

If a philosophical sense of the *Querelle* has diminished in favor of an increasing awareness of the ascendancy of modernity, it is safe to say that the Renaissance is one of the most neglected, misunderstood, even maligned periods in the history of philosophy, ostensibly having failed either to contribute to the grand theological architecture constucted by medieval Scholasticism or to recognize the indefeasibility of the scientific rationality shaping modernity.[3] When one takes a closer look, however, it seems far more likely that the contentious discourse carried out by Petrarch, Ficino, Pico, Lorenzo Valla, Erasmus, Machiavelli, Bruno, and other Renaissance thinkers, born out of medieval intellectual life, opened up the space and gave initial shape to the terrain on which Francis Bacon, Vico, Descartes, and modern philosophy could find a footing, a terrain on which the battle royal of the ancients and the moderns was to be waged. And indeed, considering the conflicts informing philosophy today, these Renaissance thinkers might appear rather kindred spirits to some. What is needed are genealogies of the epoch-founding *Querelle* which would place it back on the

Renaissance soil on which the endgame of medieval culture was played out and in which the seeds of modernity sprouted and flourished. Nonetheless, it would be absurd in the present context to attempt anything like a summary of Renaissance thought; such would contradict the very spirit of the present undertaking.[4] Therefore, it is my intention only to sketch in rough outline several related issues important to Renaissance thought that are relevant to the seventeenth and eighteenth century *Querelle* as well as to the reflections carried out here under the aegis of "the ancients and the moderns." These issues are the development of textual criticism as a central philosophical endeavor, the emergence of the concept of history, and the multiplication of authority.

It is common to characterize contemporary, so-called postmodern philosophy as hypercritical or as being parasitic on the texts of the tradition, hence as being commentary or literary criticism—the latter amounting to a condemnation, especially when voiced by those who conceive of philosophical practice as more or less a continuation of modern philosophy. When Bacon exhorts, "Down with antiquities and citations or supporting testimonies from texts; . . . down with everything philological,"[5] or Descartes repeatedly expresses thinly veiled contempt for the literary character of "learned discourse,"[6] we could easily mistake these statements directed against Renaissance humanists as a part of the contemporary polemic over the role of texts and textual criticism in philosophy. This debate, however, is original to the Renaissance and in at least this one respect the Renaissance offers an historical precedent for contemporary controversies over what philosophy is and does. This "critical dispute" merits our attention.

Regardless of what one's philosophical sensibilities may be, all contemporary philosophers find in the Greeks, above all in Socrates and Plato, the first practitioners of philosophy; yet the visions of who Socrates was and what he was doing are as diverse as the contemporary philosophical spectrum. For example, some find in Socrates a dramatic and highly contextualized discourse to be read for its λόγος-shaping legacy, while others find exemplified in him a valuable if sometimes crude method of subjecting a series of propositions to a logical examination that seeks their truth value.[7] The vision of philosophical practice as logical dialectic happens to have been the one that inspired medieval Scholasticism. As bequeathed by the Romans, medieval education was generally divided into theology and the liberal arts, the latter comprising the *quadrivium* (arithmetic, music, geometry, and astronomy) and the *trivium* (the "lower," less scientific arts—grammar, logic and rhetoric);[8] these secular disciplines subordinated to theology were often synonymously referred to as "philosophy." Though there were developments in the disciplines and content of the liberal arts over the six hundred years after Augustine, its basic structure remained for the most part unaltered; and because of the lack of any thematic coherency and philosophy's clear separation from the font of wisdom, theology, Paul O. Kristeller, for instance, suggests that one should not speak of there being anything called medieval philosophy before the early twelfth century. It was Peter Abelard and, later, Peter Lombard, Peter of Spain, Ockham, et al. who helped raise logic and dialectics from its "lowly" association with grammar and rhetoric to a preeminent status among the philosophical disciplines and make it a central tool for dealing with theological issues; in the guise of logic, philosophy became the handmaiden of theology. Theological discourse took on a formulaic character: typically one or more theses were proposed, objections thereto acknowledged, and replies given. As medieval thought increasingly gave pride of place to propositional reasoning and logic, texts functioned within a philosophical context as they had within a theological context, namely, as unproblematic vehicles for communication or, where authority was in question, as *pièces justificatives.* Apart from matters of biblical or theological concern, there was relatively little interest in the ancients per se, much less any concern for the actual production, dramatic content, or historicity of ancient texts. Texts were but a corruptible site where eternal truth could come, if waveringly, to light (though even this would suggest more of a theory of textuality than seems to have been present). Theological and philosophical criticism was almost purely a matter of a logic that found in Scripture and other hallowed texts premises and expected conclusions.

The very nature of philosophical discourse and the significance of written documents underwent a fundamental transformation due in large part to two events—the discovery and introduction of classical Greek texts into Western philosophical discourse from the twelfth to the sixteenth century and the invention of movable type in the fifteenth century. The printing press facilitated the uniform and widespread distribution of both primary and secondary materials (the latter, in particular, having been extremely scarce because of the human costs of reproduction), which in turn enabled individual collectors and scholars to amass personal libraries of several thousand books, whereas previously the accumulation of several dozen was an accomplishment.

This twofold archival formation engendered what we might call today textual and intertextual problematics and eventually helped bring about a shift in focus away from Scholastic logistics to questions of textual composition and validity, a shift fundamental to the Renaissance conception of intellectual activity and a future issue in the *Querelle.* These literary critical methods were developed in large part in response to philosophical problems encountered in the process of translating newly acquired Greek texts into Latin and comparing existing Latin translations with the Greek. An important moment in this process was provided by the early Renaissance translator of Aristotle, Leonardo Bruni (1369–1444), whose controversial treatise *On Correct Translation* was based on a new conception of language, textuality, and thought: since all languages (including Latin) are historically and culturally contingent, the proper reading and translation of a text requires one to take account of broader cultural formations. In conceiving of a text as part of a cultural phenomenon to which it must be related, he was perhaps the first to anticipate important features of nineteenth and twentieth century hermeneutics, though, unlike a later hermeneutics, he conceived of there being a comparability between languages and cultures that could be negotiated by "perfect" translations.[9] Later, Lorenzo Valla (1407–57) produced a notoriously critical comparison of the Latin Vulgate with the Greek (an exercise that would earn him an appearance before the Inquisition). He also brought a hermeneutically informed philology to bear in his devastating debunking of the so-called Donation of Constantine, thereby providing one of the earliest examples of using principles of philology to invalidate a revered historical document, a practice that was raised to an epochal passion in the Renaissance. Though there clearly was no one method that Renaissance scholars used in their treatment of texts, all of their methods—whether philological, imitative, systematic, or synthetic—took λόγος in all its textuality as the point of departure.[10]

Because the Renaissance experienced a massive influx of cultural materials challenging the very underpinnings of the medieval European world and making the development of methods of textual criticism almost inevitable as a coping strategy, it is important to draw attention to the order of appearance of the texts, even if somewhat schematically. The sequence of ideologies is central to the development of the modern and even the contemporary sense of philosophical criticism.

As has been well documented, the flourishing of the Roman Empire, with its educational emphasis on rhetoric, whose focus was on public speaking and written communiqués (especially letters), went hand in hand with the eclipse of Greek culture and philosophy. Only as assimilated to Roman culture was the Greek philosophical tradition preserved in the Middle Ages. By the seventh century only a few short works—significantly, they were logical works—of Aristotle and half of Plato's *Timaeus* were extant in Greek and available in Latin translation. What knowledge of or interest there was in Greek philosophy was filtered through Cicero, Augustine, and Boethius; in other words, it was radically Latinized, bent toward pragmatic, especially rhetorical, ends. Cicero in the liberal arts and Augustine in theology communicated what little there was of Plato in the early and middle medieval Age. Aristotle's presence was similarly insignificant. From the beginning of the twelfth century to the end of the thirteenth, virtually the entire corpus of Aristotelian texts, along with a mass of its Arabic commentaries, was discovered and translated.[11] In addition to assisting the concomitantly increased prestige of logic and the *quadrivium* already noted, Aristotle's natural philosophy supplemented what could be derived solely from sacred documents. It also provided medieval thought with the tools needed for critical reasoning and the conceptual resources that made systematic philosophy and theology possible for the first time. In Aristotle the medievals found a means to "transform Christian doctrine from scattered pronouncements of Scripture, the Councils, and the Church Fathers into a coherent and systematic body of statements,"[12] and in this regard medieval theology imitated the scientific systematicity that was already being developed in the liberal arts.

If Aristotle provided the means for the transformative systematization of theology and its rapprochement with the nontheological, scientific arts, he likewise represented the encounter with a non-Christian, philosophical view of the world, which had the effect of disturbing that very theology which his works served to develop. Thus, given the generation of a body of literature and the requirement, faced by all systematic thought, of assembling it into a *unified* whole, scholars not only had to reconcile the diverse and often conflicting interpretations of Aristotle that became apparent through comparative practices but also found it necessary to reconcile these interpretations with Christian theology. Scholasticism experienced systematic requirements necessitating that text-critical methods be developed to deal with lacunae and conflicting interpretations. The Greek straining of the Latin grammar and vocabulary, which had been the basis for the unity of theological discourse, is but one example of the impact that linguistic and textual issues had on cultural and ideological matters.[13]

Aristotle was, then, something of a Trojan horse for medieval thought, for though he offered philosophers tools (e.g., the *Organon*) for developing arguments to construct and defend the edifice of theology, he simultaneously offered a basis for thinking systematically and independently of Christian theology. Hence, as early as 1210 Aristotle was simultaneously a subject to appropriate and to censor, itself a measure of the emerging centrality of textuality for questions of authority and ideology.

For two hundred years Aristotle was virtually the sole representative of Greek philosophy in the medieval world, so much so that Thomas Aquinas could fondly refer to him in the Averroistic manner as "the Philosopher." Even by the beginning of the fifteenth century virtually the only access to Plato was fragmentary and was filtered through Augustine and the Church Fathers. Francesco Petrarch (1304–74), something of a founding father of the Renaissance who never had the advantage of extensive access to Platonic texts or of mastering the Greek language, was the leader of the first generation to advance Plato against the hegemony of Aristotle and the Scholastics. The fifteenth century saw a dramatic development in the accumulation of philosophical texts: thanks to Marsilio Ficino (1433–99) and others, most all of Plato's presently extant Greek works were rediscovered and appeared in Latin translations that were widely read, as were a number of Stoic, Epicurean, and Skeptical philosophers.

Though it would be oversimplistic to equate medieval thought with Aristotle and the humanist thought of the Renaissance with Plato (for there were medieval Platonists and Renaissance Aristotelians), certainly the Platonists exercised the greater influence over the Renaissance and indisputably the manner of appropriating antiquity took a decisive turn with the Platonists of the fifteenth and sixteenth centuries, as did the treatment of philosophical texts; it would be especially against the Platonists and, even more, against the centrality they accorded to texts in philosophy that the moderns would exercise their greatest invective. If Renaissance Platonists did not invent the practice of textual criticism, they were the first to genuinely problematize what had been ignored by the logicism of the Scholastics, namely, the historical-cultural horizon and linguistic construction of texts. Georgios Plethon (1360–1452) seems to have been the first to find camouflaged in the dialogues of Plato something like a systematic theology, and, opposing Plato to Aristotle in this and other matters, he raised pagan thought generally, and especially Plato's, almost to an equal footing with Christian theology. His student, John Bessarion (1403–72), advocated a reading of Platonic texts which may seem today a commonplace but at the time certainly was a great novelty: texts are not to be read in a literal, propositional manner but with a philologically educated eye which sees them as "sacred" messages clothed in every manner of literary trope. Imbued with the rhetorical sensibility conveyed over the ages by Cicero's legacy, Bessarion experienced a certain linguistic "thickness" or literary opacity belonging to texts, and, unlike Plethon, he sought a way of reading Platonic and Christian texts that would establish a virtual conceptual identity among them, a manner of reading that accounted for differences or conflicts in terms of the historically conditioned age and linguistic world within which the texts were composed. Bessarion's student Ficino—perhaps the most influential Platonist of the Renaissance—saw the pagan philosophers as struggling with the same eternal issues as Christianity and, through an allegorically minded reading of Plato and Neoplatonism, developed a metaphysics at least parallel to if not inchoately rivaling Christian theology. In deriving a hierarchy of being and conjoining it with a Platonic doctrine of love, he presented a systematic view of life and spiritual edification that represented a critical alternative to prevailing church doctrine and its Scholastic theology. One of the many crucial developments we have with Ficino is the "literary critical turn" in philosophy, which increasingly seems irrevocable (even in proportion to the modernist rejection of it) and whose moral and theoretical significance is undeniable.

The rebirth of Platonism through Petrarch, Ficino, and others signified a conception of culture, marked by epochal shifts, in which the moral and religious well-being of humanity was seen as at risk and in need of a fundamental renovation; above all it required a reconception of language and reading that gives the allegorical, ironic, and poetic character of texts an unprecedented centrality. It is within the context of this textual polysemy that one must understand the critical and ambitious works of Valla, who, seeing the decline of the Roman Empire as responsible for the pathetic state of the Latin language, understood language itself to be conditioned by historical processes and attempted in his *Dialectical Disputations* a comprehensive reformation of the Latin language and philosophical methodology. As has been shown,[14] Valla provides perhaps the best-known instance in the early Renaissance of a more general debate over the precision and rhetorical resources of ancient Latin, vulgate Latin, and the vernacular, an issue which would become central in the quarrel of the ancients and the moderns with, for example, Descartes's deep suspicion of "speech devised by the common crowd" and "the ways of speaking"[15]—be they Latin or vernacular—and his advocacy of the superiority of the ahistorical language of certitude: mathematics. The didactics of Petrus Ramus, the skeptical spirituality of Erasmus, and the eloquent despair of Montaigne are important extensions not only of the Renaissance encounter with the linguisticality and textuality of thought and culture but also of the historical relativism of these factors.[16] It is against this background that mid-seventeenth-century modernists embarked upon the project of constructing ideal languages, that is, languages stripped of every historical contingency or poetic ambiguity.[17]

One ought not forget that the proliferation of texts that necessitated the devising of new methods of reading, writing, even thinking represented a challenge to the Renaissance mind, which always sought within this diversity of materials a unity; though reflexivity is often associated with Descartes and the moderns, it became an important feature of Renaissance thought in its quest for methods to deal with the hyperdissemination of texts. This, of course, is not to deny that reflexivity clearly had a different end and value in the Renaissance than it would come to have in modernity.[18] The Renaissance methodical reflexivity sought unity in the face of proliferation of texts of various sorts and origins. This is one reason, I suggest, why it was de rigueur among Renaissance intellectuals to begin their studies by situating them within a "catalogue" of activities and domains of investigation, a catalogue itself only conceivable given the presumption that all domains of study amount to various categories of discourse.[19] It was within the general effort to define one's own sort of discourse vis-à-vis the universe of discourse that Renaissance thought came to consider history as a form of narrative discourse and to raise the first questions concerning the nature of history and historical writing.[20] This revisioning of philosophy around the practices of reading and writing rather than disputation and around rhetoric and discourse rather than logical deduction is a Renaissance development whose significance can hardly be overemphasized, especially in light of its relevance for contemporary thought. Of course the "bookishness," the literary character, of Renaissance thought, of "the ancients," would become a *cause célèbre* for the modernist rejection of the tradition in favor of the "book of the world," i.e., observation, experimentation, scientific verification. In a manner somewhat reminiscent of the medieval conception of the text qua vehicle, the moderns did not view language and the text as a primordial if somewhat provisional site for the disclosure of truth but as a medium, much in need of reformation, in which universal and clearly grasped truths find expression. Whereas, for example, Descartes used reflexive doubt to absolutely sever the connection between language or "text" and truth—indeed, to sever truth from everything historically contingent—the reflexive doubt of the Renaissance thinker served to remove the thinker from the medieval *universum* and to bring individuals back to their own place within the scheme of things, back to their own culture, their own language, and their own position within the course of history—that position or perspective in terms of which they understood the whole. Here we can see a methodological basis for the growing nationalism and regionalism that was fundamental to Renaissance politics.

So the amassing of cultural artifacts not only spurred the development of literary critical methods but also went hand in hand with the development of a specifically "modern" sense of history, one that necessarily involved a consciousness of perspective. Whereas the medieval schema of history characteristically was a tableau of three to seven "ages of man" statically juxtaposed next to one another, the Renaissance experienced history increasingly as a complex dynamic whole.[21] As Anthony Grafton points out, "Renaissance readers certainly developed a form of historical awareness that had few precedents in their immediate environment. The humanists realized that any classical text was not just the product of a single intellect but a subordinate part of an organic cultural and historical whole. Accordingly, they set out to eliminate from the corpus of genuine antiques all works that used a vocabulary, employed concepts, or referred to events that their supposed authors could not have known."[22] Arnaldo Momigliano writes that "the sober and fastidious scholarship of the great antiquarians of the sixteenth century . . . improved on Varro because they combined literary, archaeological and epigraphical evidence, their preference being for literary and epigraphical texts. They slowly pieced together Roman chronology, topography, law and religion: they discovered *Roma sotterranea*."[23] So intimately associated are the literary and the historical for the formation of Renaissance thought that one is not surprised to find Petrarch, discoverer of the Greek literary legacy, also acknowledged as the first to develop a "modern" conception of history and bring it to bear on the organization and correction of extant literary and cultural antiquity.[24] Emphasizing the proximity of historical and literary discourses, one commentator claims that "fifteenth-century writers were usually unwilling and largely unable to make a clear distinction between fact and fiction, either in theory or in practice (though they sometimes attempted it), and that their various methods of reconstructing the past produced a history very different from our own," adding that the fifteenth-century writer Caxton, "and his contemporaries accepted and embroidered an elaborate body of legend, both sacred and secular, and did not seek to differentiate between romance and chronicle or between past and present."[25] But we should not take this as denying that some, such as Flavio Biondo (1392–1463) and other antiquarians, clearly distinguished between fictions and historical facts even if they did so unsystematically and idiosyncratically; nor should it lead us to ignore the increasing appreciation for questions of evidence and source authority.[26] It does, however, indicate that historical truths were seen as serving higher moral truths, truths which cut across the boundary of historical fact and literary invention, and here one must acknowledge the presence and function of the preponderantly practical concerns—moral, ethical, political, philological, scientific—that were central to Renaissance life. Renaissance historiographers seemed convinced that historical fact would reveal in the particulars what was becoming increasingly obvious in large through the production of an ancient *Weltanschauung*, namely, that compared with pre-Christian culture, fifteenth and sixteenth century culture seemed relatively crude, decadent, and anachronistic. History and wisdom became more intimately related than they had been since antiquity.

Though Renaissance thinkers such as Valla seem to have made the distinction between original and derivative authorities that Momigliano finds basic to the modern conception of historiography,[27] it also seems clear that the Renaissance concept of history was long in development, for despite the advances made by Biondo and Valla, important but subtle distinctions such as this remained fallow for some time, at least in Italy.[28] As the past was not initially conceived of as a domain of scientific knowledge to be studied for its own sake, it represented—and one need merely mention the name of Machiavelli (1469–1527) as an exaggerated example—an indispensable practical resource, be it for imitation or exploitation. That, by one account, it was sixteenth-century French legal scholars, such as Estienne Pasquier, who brought a sophisticated sense of textual interpretation and concern for authority and evidence to bear on both legal and historical documents and artifacts testifies to the essential confluence of textuality, historicality, and practicality in Renaissance thought.[29]

To come to grips with the Renaissance understanding (or understandings) of history is a complicated task made no simpler by the fact that it has clearly been all too easy to take modernist perspectives on the *Querelle* as a point of departure.[30] One can see how, for instance, Renaissance humanism has successfully been caricatured as conservative, authoritarian, intellectually sloppy, pessimistic about the future, and nostalgic for the past by a modernist intellectual culture that favored the univocal over the poetic, the clear over the ambiguous, the impersonal over the idiomatic, *mathesis* over traditions. Clearly, history conceived along Cartesian lines as a teleologically progressive movement from a foundational moment to a definitive elaboration of scientific truth was not the experience of history found in the early or mid-Renaissance; nor, strictly speaking, was it Descartes's conception of history. Indeed, as central as history was to the Renaissance consciousness, the modernist rejection of Renaissance epistemology would necessarily be tantamount to what one scholar describes as the "massive abuse"[31] of history as an intellectual discipline from the middle of the seventeenth to the middle of the eighteenth century—it was simply ignored if not reviled in that century during which modernity was securing its foundations. It would be possible and worthwhile to track the intellectual tenor of the seventeenth and early eighteenth centuries in terms of the transformed conception of history from that of literature to science. Fontanelle, Vico, Voltaire, D'Alembert, and their contemporaries are pivotal in this transformation. And if the sense of proper historiography continued to be unsettled and unsettling during and after the high point of the *Querelle*, it was so along familiar lines: Condillac and Montesquieu found history ennobling if inevitably speculative, while Voltaire, Fontanelle, and D'Alembert sought to make historical knowledge scientific knowledge that could serve not only or even primarily moral interests but every human endeavor. For them, history should aspire to logic. One can see the fault lines of the *Querelle* in the very conundrum that D'Alembert faced; in lieu of a scientifically founded system of principles that would allow for the precise and systematic ordering of historical knowledge, D'Alembert made use of a literary device: the encyclopedia, whose unity is a new catalogue of discourses, a "book."

If anything should be clear from this admittedly cursory presentation of Renaissance thought, it is that the proliferation of texts and text-critical methods and the profusion of cultural artifacts and concomitant historical perspectives are symptoms of an epochal movement: the multiplication of authority. As the relation of authority and *ancienneté* became less of a *donnée* and more of a complex question, the hegemonic institutions of church and monarchies underwent radical transformations that brought with them new horizons of thinking and acting. A world that once took its bearings from a monolithic and seemingly sempiternal church experienced an accelerating decentralization, secularization, and regionalization; conflicting methods of scientific practice were advanced, as were diverse literary canons; power was disseminated through sometimes overlapping and often disjunctive political institutions; historical relativism with all its theoretical and practical problems increasingly became a "fact of life." So when Brian P. Copenhaver and Charles B. Schmitt write that "the prospect of *choosing* among metaphysical claims or among attitudes towards metaphysics as diverse as those put forward by Valla, Ficino, Suárez, and Campanella was a terrible freedom for a culture so well-integrated in its beliefs,"[32] they could be characterizing the intellectual climate of the Renaissance from the thirteenth century to the beginning of the seventeenth and beyond. If, in looking back to the tradition, we can see that the rather paradoxical notion of "choosing an authority" played into the hands of the founders of modern philosophy and their voluntarism, if we can understand the polemical character of modernity along with its strategic advantages and ideological limitations, we can also see that the issues the moderns struggled with in the *Querelle* and the questions they claim to have answered are, at this late date in the age of modernity, still pressing. We should now be able to begin to see that in returning to the tradition, to the "quarrel of the ancients and the moderns," we recover a multiplicity of resources for our own thinking and acting.

NOTES

1. The classic scholarly study of the *Querelle* is Hyppolyte Rigault's *Histoire de la querelle des anciens et des modernes* (Paris: Hachette, 1856). On the problems of determining the nature of the *Querelle*, see Hans Baron, "The *Querelle* of the Ancients and the Moderns as a Problem for Renaissance Scholarship," *Journal of the History of Ideas*, 20, no. 1 (January 1959), pp. 3–22. Though more programmatic and partisan, see also Stanley Rosen, *The Ancients and the Moderns: Rethinking Modernity* (New Haven, 1989). See also various works by Jean-François Lyotard, esp. *The Postmodern Condition*, tr. Geoff Bennington and Brian Massumi (Minneapolis, 1984), and "Re-writing Modernity," *Substance*, 16, no. 3, pp. 3–9, for contemporary thematizations of this subject. Robert Black claims that Benedetto Accolti, a mid-fifteenth century Italian, was the first to discuss the ancients and the moderns. See Black, "Ancients and Moderns in the Renaissance: Rhetoric and History in Accolti's *Dialogue on the Preeminence of Men of His Own Time*," *Journal of the History of Ideas*, 43, no. 1, p. 8 (January–March 1982).

2. Anthony Grafton's lively and compelling *Defenders of the Text: The Tradition of Scholarship in the Age of Science, 1450–1800* (Cambridge, Mass., 1991) goes a long way toward dispelling the clichés about the Renaissance propagated by modernists such as Bacon and Descartes and showing the importance of the Renaissance for contemporary intellectual life. In particular, Grafton is concerned to show that the view of the Renaissance as lacking scientificity and as immersed in the fabulous is a misrepresentaion on the part of the moderns.

3. Paul Oskar Kristeller has been a tireless advocate of Renaissance studies and constantly reminds his readers of the vast areas of scholarly neglect. For an overview of this neglect, see Brian P. Copenhaver and Charles B. Schmitt, *A History of Western Philosophy*, vol. 3: *Renaissance Philosophy* (Oxford, 1992), ch. 6, esp. p. 339 ff.

4. Several excellent books can serve as introductions to Renaissance thought. See Copenhaver and Schmitt, *Renaissance Philosophy*; Ernst Cassirer, *The Individual and the Cosmos in Renaissance Philosophy*, tr. M. Domandi (Oxford, 1963); P. O. Kristeller, *Renaissance Thought: The Classic, Scholastic and Humanist Strains* (New York, 1961), and *Renaissance Thought and Its Sources* (New York, 1979); C. Trinkaus, *The Scope of Renaissance Humanism* (Ann Arbor, 1983); R. Weiss, *The Renaissance Discovery of Classical Antiquity* (Oxford, 1969).

5. Quoted from Grafton, *Defenders of the Text*, p. 2.

6. Part 1 of Descartes's *Discourse on Method* is an extended obloquy against the philological, historicist, and poetic character of philosophy.

7. This characterization of the Platonic corpus is one that often conceives of the dialogues as a series of propositional statements whose truth value is to be tested. Candid representatives of this approach to Plato are Gail Fine and Terrence Irwin. An alternative approach to the Greeks—one that could be described as hermeneutical—approaches the Platonic dialogues as textual compositions that require an appreciation of the dramatic, contextual, and dialogical character of the texts in order to fairly render their meaning. See, among others, Hans-Georg Gadamer, *Dialogue and Dialectic*, tr. P. Christopher Smith (New Haven, 1980), and John Sallis, *Being and Logos: The Way of Platonic Dialogue* (Atlantic Highlands, 1986).

8. By the beginning of the thirteenth century the difference between theology and philosophy, which was committed to reason as opposed to faith and to mundane matters rather than spiritual ones, was becoming ambiguous enough that Pope Gregory IX was forced to address an ominous letter to the Theology Faculty of the University of Paris warning against dabbling in philosophy, though it is clear that he also recognized the invaluable resources to be found in Aristotle. See Fernand Van Steenberghen, *Aristotle in the West: The Origins of Latin Aristotelianism* (Louvain, 1965), p. 80 ff.

9. See *Leonardo Bruni Arentino. Humanistisch-philosophische Schriften*, ed. Hans Baron (Leipzig, 1928), pp. 70–81. Heidegger, in many of his later texts, especially *The Principle of Reason*, goes so far as to say that translation is the way in which history epochalizes itself.

10. Bernard Weinberg, in *A History of Literary Criticism in the Italian Renaissance*, vol. 1 (Chicago, 1961), discusses both the diversity among and the similarity between the different methods of treating literary texts in the Renaissance.

11. See Van Steenberghen, *Aristotle in the West*.

12. Kristeller, *Renaissance Thought and Its Sources*, p. 117.

13. For example, the term *esse* was used to cover more than thirty Greek terms.

14. Sarah Stever Gravelle, "The Latin-Vernacular Question and Humanist Theory of Language and Culture," *Journal of the History of Ideas*, 49, no. 3 (1988), pp. 367–86.

15. The relation of perception, silence, and language is central to Descartes's second Meditation.

16. On the sixteenth-century experience of the historical mutability of language in France, see George Huppert, *The Idea of Perfect History* (Chicago, 1970), pp. 156–58.

17. See, for instance, J. R. Knowlson, "The Ideal of Languages of Veiras, Foigny, and Tyssot de Patot," *Journal of the History of Ideas*, 24, no. 2 (1963), pp. 269–78.

18. For a survey of the question of method in the Renaissance, see Neal W. Gilbert, *Renaissance Concepts of Method* (New York, 1960).

19. See Weinberg, *A History of Literary Criticism*, ch. 1.

20. The image of Renaissance historians as concerned with the form of historical discourse to the disadvantage of scientific validity has been challenged by Grafton and by E. B. Fryde, *Humanism and Renaissance Historiography* (London, 1983).

21. The exact "shape" of history is irrelevant here—there were circular and more or less linear visions of history.

22. Grafton, *Defenders of the Text*, pp. 29–30.

23. Arnaldo Momigliano, "Ancient History and the Antiquarian," *Studies in Historiography* (New York, 1966), p. 6.

24. Peter Burke, *The Renaissance Sense of the Past* (New York, 1969), p. 20.

25. Joseph M. Levine, *Humanism and History: Origins and Modern English Historiography* (Ithaca, 1987). See also Huppert, *The Idea of Perfect History*, esp. ch. 2.

26. See Fryde, *Humanism and Renaissance Historiography,* chs. 1 and 2.

27. Momigliano, "Ancient History and the Antiquarian," p.2.

28. Huppert, *The Idea of Perfect History,* p. 23.

29. Ibid, pp. 28–71.

30. See Baron, "The *Querelle* of the Ancients and the Moderns."

31. Judith N. Shklar, "Jean D'Alembert and the Rehabilitation of History," *Journal of the History of Ideas*, 42, no. 4 (1981), p. 644.

32. Copenhaver and Schmitt, *Renaissance Philosophy*, p. 349.

PART I.

Initial Figures, Emergent Crises

ONE

In Search of a Civic Union: The Political Theme of European Democracy and Its Primordial Foundation in Greek Philosophy

Manfred Riedel

Democracy—what is it? A slogan in political dispute or a term of political science? A way of life or a complex of laws and institutions? In our present-day language it seems to express all these alternatives at once. We are familiar with the slogan that "democracy" is understood as the government of the people by the people or, as the Marxists tell us, the "people's democracy." But nobody knows exactly who the people are. We use the term in political science to designate a form of government. But in the meantime we have experienced the ungovernability of modern society. We prefer the way of life offered by democracy, the possibility of free choice to satisfy our human needs. But while enjoying an incomparably high level of liberty we live more than ever before in privacy. Every generation is brought up under democratic laws and institutions. But each new one doubts their political wisdom. Each asks very plainly and very radically as well: democracy—to what end?

This question should be taken seriously. Asking "why democracy" not only includes putting its legal and institutional existence aside; it also questions its justification, asks what the ends of democratic laws and institutions are. What has been put into question is the *spirit of democracy*—whether its real existence in modern European society is justifiable or not. Posed this way, the question might allude to what social scientists call a "legitimacy crisis." I do not believe that we can speak of a crisis of legitimacy as such. We have to speak about the crisis of modern European democracy, because the so-called legitimacy crisis indicates the dissolution of what I will call the *political theme of democracy*. What is also at issue here is the search for a civic union (*Bürgerbund*), i.e., a civility (*Bürgerlichkeit)* possible for men, and its meaning for democracy. This search originates in European philosophy and runs through European history. In present times we see it at work in both Western and Eastern societies, dominated by different social systems and ideologies, last but not least, in Poland's Solidarity movement. If we follow this guiding thread through European history, we can redisclose the lost spiritual shape of modern democracy—*the original political theme of democracy as a life-form of citizens* instead of a political slogan or a term of political science, a way of life or a complex of laws and institutions.

Every spiritual shape exists essentially within a universal historical continuity or in a particular unity of historical space and time. It has its *history* constituted by an *object*. If we pursue the objective continuity in the perspective of historical science, it leads us further and further away from our own nation to neighboring nations, and thus from one historic period to the next: in modernity from the European Enlightenment back to Italian Renaissance Humanism and to medieval Scholasticism, in antiquity from the Romans to the Greeks and further back to the Egyptians, the Persians, and so on. Clearly, there is no end to this progression.[1] We can move back into prehistoric times or move out into another historical realm, for example, the Indian, Chinese, or Mexican historical sphere. But if we ask about the spiritual shape of democracy, our question is limited. It has its *tradition* marked by a theme.

If we pursue this theme in the perspective of philosophy, it will lead us to a primordial basis. In contrast to objects which can be discovered by scientific methods (observation, experiments, theoretical frameworks), themes have to be posed by philosophical discourse: by the interplay of question and answer in the search for a meaning. Philosophy's birthplace is the Greek city-state, the first political entity of democracy in time. It is true that philosophical discourse is not oriented toward the legal and institutional entity of "democracy" because this term in connection with the political theme acquires a negative meaning very early on. Its guiding thread is the form of civility possible for men or, to use the language of Plato, the *idea of a civic union*. This idea breaks through the historical space and time of the Greek city-state. It is, indeed, the *breakthrough of the political theme of democracy in European history,* which happens in individual men and in human groups united by an inner kinship of spirit, that encompasses the laws and institutions or their city-states, transcending local boundaries and national differences.

If we consider the origin of the political theme posed in Greek philosophy, we find confirmation of an *entelechy* inborn in European history. It holds sway throughout all the changing movements of the European spirit and accords to them the sense of development toward an ideal shape of *being political* as an eternal pole. According to Husserl, who has constrained this τέλος to phenomenological philosophy in the sense of *universal science*, the supranational unity of Europe does not have a mature shape that has ever been reached or could ever be reached as a shape that recurs again and again. Indeed the spiritual τέλος of European humanity, in which the particular τέλος of particular nations and of individual men is contained, is an infinite idea toward which, in concealment, the whole spiritual becoming aims, so to speak. It has to be *interpreted,* as hermeneutic philosophy argues, and interpretation includes the *application of universals.* As soon as it becomes consciously recognized in its development as τέλος, i.e., by interpreting ideas, it necessarily also becomes practical as a goal of the will; and thereby a new, higher stage of development is reached, one which is under the guidance of normative ideas.[2]

I

In order to retrieve these ideas we have to bring into focus the primordial basis of the political theme in Greek philosophy. It cannot be understood without reference to the eidetic constitution of communality and governability revealed in the Aristotelian *formula of political identity.* Its arguments will be introduced later. At this point it is enough to summarize the essential ideas of the political theme.

What is essential to the primordial foundation of the political theme? First, the direction from questions of facts to questions of values posed by the search for meaning in philosophical discourse. Starting with *political being in time*, the πόλις, philosophical discourse constantly asks what "being political" *means*, that is, to govern and be governed as man and citizen, as a member of the city-state. Second, what is essential is the direction of every *particular concept* to *conceptual universals*—what we have called *normative guiding ideas.* After their first breakthrough in Plato they reach a final state of development in Aristotle. The establishment of the identity formula at the beginning of the *Politics* is primary. Observing the datum of history, i.e., a political being in time, Aristotle discovers the *civic union* which has remained as an idea for all political reasoning ever since then.

The Greek city-state is based on the concept of *communality* in Aristotelian terms: the πόλις is a species (εἶδος) of the genus κοινωνία, "communication." Communality, however, is a mode of being political, i.e., both the possibility and the necessity for man to become a citizen by searching for the civic union, in Aristotelian terms: the πόλις is a κοινωνία πολιτική, "civil society." The Greek expression designates what I would like to call the *eidetic constitution of communality.* It is indeed the εἶδος of the πόλις which is outlined in the Aristotelian definition. The significance of the eidetic constitution of communality gets its evidence from the complementary basis of the city-state which consists in governability. In Aristotelian terms: the πόλις is a species (εἶδος) of the genus ἀρχή, "governance." Governability, again, is a mode of being political which conditions political being in time, that is, the πόλις. We shall have to explain the relationship between these concepts later on. They are necessary to establish what might be called the *eidetic constitution of government.*

Philosophical discourse, we should remember, cannot be divided properly into the kinds of objects it investigates, but merely comprises a group of disciplines like economics, legislation, strategies. In its primordial foundation it relates to *practical philosophy*, gaining the meaning of the all-encompassing theory of human πρᾶξις that belongs to human life-forms.[3] A more incisive survey of the life-forms inherent in reason and choice—worthy for man— must be launched, unfettered by myth and the appeal to tradition. Practical philosophy refers not only to the life-forms characteristic of philosophers but to what is essentially human—*man's humanity.* According to the guiding idea of the civic union, political philosophy concerns a theme pertaining to the modes of being political, together with political being in time of πολιτική κοινωνία itself. What is properly human cannot be understood in reference to man's life outside of communality and governability. On the contrary it is contained in it because humanity is just as little a natural characteristic of man as communality or governability is. They need, so to speak, an eidetic constitution. This idicates the original εἶδος of τὰ πολιτικά, i.e., πολιτική κοινωνία belonging to the life-form of man's humanity as both ζῷον λόγον ἔχον and ζῷον πολίτικον.

Instead of taking these formulae for granted we must interpret them in the context of the primordial basis of the political theme. The eidetic constitution of communality is, at the same time, a linguistic one. The appeal of language is connected with the primordail basis of the political theme. It starts as early as the Socratic-Platonic insight into the changeability and manifoldness of meaning which distinguishes political concepts so conspicuously from everyday language or scientific modes of speaking about natural and artificial objects.[4] Through political language, the πρᾶξις which is articulated in it becomes accessible. Philosophical discourse continues and reveals what is already actualized in linguistic preconceptions about politics. To this extent it is close to an empirical science; it not only describes particular modes of the political being in time but also compares and distinguishes them; it generalizes political experience and thereby reveals political universals. It describes the life-form of the πόλις in concepts which are constantly directed toward universality.

With reference to the parts of the civic union, i.e., the modes of being political by acting and speaking citizens, Greek philosophy distinguishes a threefold unity of political universals: (1) freedom, (2) equality, and (3) independence. This constant direction pervading philosophical discourse breaks through in Plato and Aristotle. The life-form of the Greek city-state is articulated in ideas detachable from it and transferable to other life forms. This detachment and transferal process began at the end of Hellenism with the appropriation of Greek political language by Cicero, began anew during the High Middle Ages with the scholastic translations and commentaries, continued in Renaissance Humanism, and molds the language of modern philosophy up to the threshold of the Enlightenment and the French Revolution. What characterizes classical political language and is, in the long run, decisive, is the idea of the *civic union*, the fundamental presumption of civility. It runs through European history and thus appears as the connecting link betweek Antiquity and Modernity. Civility, the characteristic of a citizen, is based on *partnership* in the sense of *participating in a common good* and *initiating a common being-at-work*, the capacity among citizens as free, equal, and independent communicating men to govern and be governed. Together these modes of being political regulate the search for the civic union in Greek philosophical discourse.

These aspects of the political theme are linguistically articulated in the classical idea of civil society (πολιτική κοινωνία) and its identity with the city-state (πόλις). It comes into the open at the beginning of the Aristotelian *Politics*.[5] The first general statement that every πόλις represents a κοινωνία is followed by a second one which claims that every κοινωνία is formed for an end (τέλος) in the sense of a common good. Assuming that all κοινωνία seek to achieve an end, it is further stated (based on the assumption made by Aristotle that all human endeavor and activity can be construed in terms of ends and means) that one accomplishes this in an exceptional manner (μάλιστα). The "supreme" or "highest" good is sought by that society which is the supreme or highest one and encompasses all others: this is the so-called city-state or civil society αὕτη δ' ἐστίν ἡ καλουμένη πόλις καὶ ἡ κοινωνία ἡ πολιτική. Translated into Latin the formula becomes *civitas sive societas civilis res publica*.

II

The Aristotelian idea contains the essential acquisition of the primordial basis of the political theme in Greek philosophy. In its original meaning it circumscribes *communality* which connects freedom with equality and independence and for this reason actualizes the *political participation* of the citizens, civility (πολίτευμα). How these concepts are related to each other is a unique question demanding careful interpretation. We answer it by explaining the function of the formula of political identity.

The concepts πόλις and πολιτική κοινωνία, *civitas* and *societas civilis*, mean the same thing in classical and modern political philosophy: namely, they identify the civic union, i.e., the unity between communality and governability, civil society and government. Although that which is "identical," in Latin "*idem*," is in Greek ταὐτόν, translated "the same," the political identity formula does not express a tautology similar to the customary principle of identity: A = A. It contains two different conceptual elements, the genus κοινωνία and the species πολιτική, and as such it corresponds to a *politological relation*. Both concepts belong together, that is, their relation determines the mode of being political in time. What has to be related are the different parts of political being as κοινωνία (society) and πολίτης (citizen) into the unit of one and the same concept. The "how" of this relation is a unity caused by neither one nor the other. Therefore I use the term *participatory unity*, which characterizes the idea of the civic union. It is linguistically expressed in the Aristotelian concept of "civil society," πολιτική κοινωνία. Πόλις and πολιτική κοινωνία, however, are not the "same," but "identical" in the sense of "belonging together."[6] The identity formula thus determines the understanding of the political theme underlying the different forms of government.

The *prooemium* to the *Politics* reminds one of the introduction to the *Nicomachean Ethics* and the beginning of the *Metaphysics*. The first book of the *Metaphysics* begins with the general statement that all men by nature desire to know (980 a 1). The first book of the *Nicomachean Ethics* begins with the statement—again a general one—that every action is value-oriented, i.e., aims at some good, whereby the expression "good" is defined as the goal or end "at which all things aim" (1094 a 1–3). This statement can be understood as the principle of Aristotle's theory of actions which we may call *praxeology*. It defines the various concepts of end at the beginning of the *Politics*, as well as that kind of purposeful and value-oriented human endeavor common to all three books (the theory of knowledge, action, and the development of society): it is for the sake of what appears to be good that all people do what they do (1252 a 2–3).[7] According to the first principle of the praxeology, technical and scientific activity as well as craftsmanship and artistic work are all examples of particular goals, each of which is based on the other and taken altogether form a single complex of actions and goals. This complex is analyzed in the prooemium of the *Politics* under the title of "πόλις" and "κοινωνία πολιτική." The hierarchy of particular goals terminating with a "supreme" and "comprehensive" goal corresponds to the ascent, explained in terms of communality, to a "civil" or "political" society which contains within itself all of the lesser communal modes. As the "supreme" and "comprehensive" *communality* it is introduced by the concept which terminates the succession of practical ends by its universality. The universal goal, explained as the "good life" (εὖ ζῆν), is the same for both individuals and the society. It appears, however, that the end of the good life can only be fully attained in civil society so that—in the *prooemium* of both books—it is defined as the highest political good.

The doctrine of the universal goal describes as aspect of the classical political *theme* which refers to the *eidetic* constitution of government. In order to understand its function we have to prove another argument in the *prooemium* of the *Politics*.

The definition of the πόλις in terms of πολιτική κοινωνία arises out of a controversy carried on by Aristotle (in the Socratic School as well as in Plato's Academy) concerning *governability*. Without specifically mentioning Plato by name, the assault on the provisions of the *Republic* and the *Statesman* begins here and is then intensified in the second book with an incisive criticism of Plato's search for political unity.[8] What justifies the exposition of πολιτική κοινωνία is Plato's metaphorical manner of speech about the civic union, according to which the πόλις must be united as "one man." This provokes the dispute about the concept of governance (ἀρχή). Aristotle begins by raising an objection to the thesis that ἀρχή in polity, kingship, despotism, and household is "the same" and not distinguishable qualitatively or according to the mode of ἄρχειν, but only quantitatively on the basis of the number of governors and governed.[9] This can be called the *thesis of the homogeneity* of governance which reflects one of the prevailing opinions about the political theme. To refute the empty generality of the thesis, Aristotle starts with the definition of the πόλις in terms of κοινωνία and the presupposition that the form of ἀρχή connected with it should be differentiated according to the individuals living in the respective κοινωνία. In this context Aristotle approaches a clarification of the three *practical universals* which constitute *praxeology*: (1) governance, (2) participation, and (3) communication.

The term *governance* designates what the Greek word ἀρχή means: namely, that there must be an *initiative* or *beginning* in every individual or social action. And in the same way there has to be a goal in the sense of good. No good can be achieved by an action without κοινωνία. This word can be rendered as both "participation" and "communication." In the primordial basis of the political theme it describes the communicative relations between acting individuals striving for and bringing about a communal work. At the same time it signifies the participative relation to the communal work which is bound by laws and institutions for actions, the enduring order of communality. The word κοιυωυία accordingly means two different things: the communal work of acting individuals united by a common good and the communality itself which has come to exist in particular κοινωνίαι, including the πόλις itself as πολιτική κοινωνία. This term, to state it more clearly, indicates the core of the political theme. Were political philosophy merely a discourse about initiatives or beginnings of action, it would have to be based exclusively on the concept of governance (ἀρχή). On a primordial basis, however, it is a discourse about ends or common goods shared by acting individuals. Therefore it is based on the complementary concepts of communication and participation. The threefold unity of these practical universals—governance, communication and participation—conditions the type of civility possible for men. They shape what may be called the societal condition.

In our present-day language this unity has vanished. According to theories of modern democracy the societal condition is constituted in terms of communication excluding governance. This constituent of the societal condition is replaced by *domination* which is opposed to both communication and participation. In order to grasp how they are originally related in the political theme we refer to the middle term *participation*. Although this problem plays a prominent role in the horizon of the classical theme, there is no Greek equivalent. We try to retranslate it into the original context of citizen partnership which mediates the classical with the modern theme of political philosophy.

The Greek expression for citizen partnership is πολίτενμα, the sphere of public speaking and acting which describes civility as the life-form of citizens. Its meaning was grounded in Plato on the principle that it is man who possesses the skillful πρᾶξις of governing and being governed. Hegel quite correctly explained the Platonic understanding of πολιτεύειν as "living in and with and for one's people, leading a general life wholly devoted to the public interest."[10]

In the *Politics* of Aristotle, πολίτευμα also circumscribes the πόλις as a *determinate kind of* πρᾶξις—political practice not only of a particular institution, but of being political in a citizen partnership. This corresponds to the transformation of political realtionships—in this special case, to the identity of πόλις and πολιτική κοινωνία articulated in the different forms of πολιτεία.

The modern word usually used for πολιτεία is "government." It describes the institutional framework of governing and thereby denotes a more technical meaning than we can find in Plato and Aristotle. This inadequacy is quite clear when we bear in mind the identity formula in the first book of the *Politics*. The third book returns to the concept of civil society, but with a fresh starting point.

What the πόλις is will now be answered in terms of participation—a term which explains the given answer and differentiates the isolated concept of governance.

The original meaning of civility—participating in political practice and public life—is implied in the basic role which the idea of civil society plays in the primordial basis of the political theme. In Plato's famous *doctrine of ideas*, κοινωνία is synonymous with μέθεξις—participation of the "parts" in a whole, the totality of *dialectical thought* (κοινωνία τῶν εἰδῶν). Aristotle explains the political sense of this conception and he does so in his search for the civic union. The argument against the thesis of homogeneity—that the most important question is what governing qualifies—arises with the presupposition that there must be a specific concept between the two class concepts κοινωνία and ἀρχή, to use modern terms: between the realm of communication on the one hand, and that of "domination" on the other. Accordingly, a different criterion is needed in order to differentiate the homogeneity theses. The quantitative criterion—how many govern—is unsatisfactory. Aristotle therefore introduces a second criterion, the argument of participation, which makes governing legitimate and constitutes governability. Government is not only determined by who is governing a society, but also by the particular policy of the governors, which can either be concerned with everyone's ends (a common good) or the private ends of the one, the few, or the many. Due to the consideration given to the *ends of governance*—the criterion of political quality—the *number of governments* in the traditional clarification is doubled, with a table of three "legitimate" forms (monarchy, aristocracy, polity) which reflect the ends of all contrasted with a table of "illegitimate" forms which have been "perverted" by the private ends of the *governors*.[11] In this latter table "democracy" is located as "deviant" *polity*—that exemplary government where the search for the civic union has reached its goal. In contrast to democracy, which is based on the governance of the many in their own interests (e.g., acquiring more property) and thereby creating disunion, polity has instituted both communality and governmentality. It is exemplary because this particular kind of political government actualizes political universality, i.e., the civility possible for men, men's humanity.

The distinction between legitimate and illegitimate governments is the fundamental question of the political theme that has to be answered for our present political involvement. Clearly it is not a question of fact but one of value which can only be answered on a normative basis. The normative meaning of the Aristotelian political theme is reinforced for democracy by an argument that has often been mistakenly considered a revision of the original eidetic constitution of government or even the muddling of its different forms.[12] In truth, however, the argument merely introduces an additional distinction with which—as exemplified by the deviant ("illegitimate") government—the systematically restricted importance of the first (empirical) criterion of quantity can be shown.

Once again the argument begins with the inaccuracy of the traditional political language in which the word "democracy" means "the rule of the many in the interests of all" and would therefore belong to the legitimate forms. Aristotle's scheme of classification departs from this usage. "Democracy" together with "oligarchy" represents a form of government which is exercised in search of property by different classes, namely either by the "rich" or the "poor." According to Aristotle it is merely coincidental that the rich—in accordance with the Greek word ὀλιγαρχία—actually represent a minority and the poor a majority. In any event, "facts" cannot decide a question of principles and values. Even if there were a government, Aristotle says, in which the rich were numerically stronger and the poor were conversely the weaker, the governance of the "many" rich would have to be called "oligarchy" and analogously the governance of the "few" poor, "democracy." Governability is not defined by the number of rulers, but by the choice of ends common to all citizens, the "good life."[13]

It is only with the classification under the heading of "common" ends that the fundamental question of the political theme is finally ready to be answered. Whereas evidence about property only allows empirical ("coincidental") statements to he made,[14] the standard of goals results in statements founded on a normative basis and with which the ambiguous word "governance" can be differentiated and specified in detail. Fundamental here is the distinction between "just" and "unjust" government. It can be called "just" when it is exercised not in the interest of goals arbitrarily chosen by governors but according to a goal which is "good" for all, since it can be expected that everyone can participate in it.[15]

Only in this case is governability eidetically constituted. Conversely, an "unjust" government would then have to be defined as one that excludes participation, i.e., the common choice of goal made by the governors and the governed together. This general statement of Marxist theory that all government is based on the interests of the ruling class or group does not lie entirely outside the distinction that I have drawn according to Aristotle; however, it refers only to the division of "deviant" governments and possesses therefore *only partial, not universal, validity*. What the idea of justice presupposes is precisely participation: the possibility of both communality and governability in which the rulers govern in accordance with the common "interest" or the ends of all citizens. This argument, I believe, is the primordial basis of the political theme. Radiating from Greek philosophy to contemporary philosophical discourse, it is valid for modern democracy. The dissolution of the political theme of democracy during the last hundred years has been motivated by the struggle for or against property in European society. In our times the search for the civic union has begun again. Running through the opposing social systems of capitalism and communism, it can and will reshape the spirit of European democracy.

NOTES

This essay originally appeared in the *Graduate Faculty Philosophy Journal*, vol. 10, no. 2, pp. 101–112.

1. See E. Husserl, *Die Krisis der europäischen Wissenschaften und die transzendentale Phänomenologie, Husserliana*, vol. 6, ed. W. Biemel (The Hague, 1954), p. 319 f.

2. This conclusion of an essential practical philosophy is the last one Husserl has drawn for himself. See ibid., p. 321.

3. Aristotle, *Nicomachean Ethics*, X, 10, 1181 b 15.

4. See Plato, *Phaedrus*, 263 a–b.

5. Aristotle, *Politics*, I, 1, 1252 a 1–1252 b 30; *Nicomachean Ethics*, VIII, 11.

6. Cf. the interpretation of "identity" in M. Heidegger, *Identity and Difference*, tr. Joan Stambaugh (New York, 1974), pp. 23–29.

7. Cf. Aristotle, *Nicomachean Ethics*, I, 1, 1093 b 18–1094 a 11, with *Politics* I, 1, 1252 a 4–5; 2, 1252 b 27–1253 a 1.

8. See Xenophon, *Memorabilia*, III, 4, 12; Plato, *Politicus*, 259 b ff.

9. Plato, *Republic*, I, 1, 125 a 7–16.

10. Plato, *Politicus*, 263 b.

11. Aristotle, *Politicus*, III, 7, 1279 a 32–1279 b 10.

12. For example, most recently by Robert A. Dahl, *Modern Political Analysis* (Englewood Cliffs, N.J., 1963), p. 27.

13. Aristotle, *Politics*, III, 8, 1279 b 20–1280 a 5; similarly IV, 4, 1290 a 30–1290 b 19.

14. Aristotle, *Politics*, III, 8, 1279 b 36.

15. Aristotle, *Politics*, IV, 8, 1278 b 15–30; 1279 a 17–21; 1279 a 25–31. Cf. R. Spaemann, "Die Utopie der Herrschaftsfreiheit," in M. Riedel, ed., *Rehabilitierung der praktischen Philosophie*, vol. 2 (Freiburg, 1974), p. 213 f.

TWO

The Greek Πόλις and the Creation of Democracy

Cornelius Castoriadis

How can we orient ourselves in history and politics? How can we judge and choose? It is from this political interest that I start—and in this spirit that I ask: in ancient Greek democracy is there anything of political relevance for us?

In a sense, Greece is obviously a presupposition of this discussion. The reasoned investigation of what is right and wrong, of the very principles that are the basis of our ever being able to say, beyond trivialities and traditional preconceptions, that something is right or wrong, arises for the first time in Greece. Our political questioning is, ipso facto, a continuation of the Greek position, although of course we have transcended it in many important respects and are still trying to transcend it.

Modern discussions of Greece have been plagued by two opposite and symmetrical—thus, in a sense, equivalent—preconceptions. The first, and most frequently encountered over the last four or five centuries, is Greece as eternal model, prototype, or paradigm.[1] (One contemporary outlook merely inverts this preconception: Greece as antimodel, as negative model.) The second and more recent preconception involves the complete "sociologization" or "ethnologization" of the examination of Greece. Thus the differences between the Greeks, the Nambikwara, and the Bamileke are only descriptive. No doubt this second attitude is formally correct. Not only, needless to say, is there not nor could there be any difference in "human value," "worthiness," or "dignity" between different peoples and cultures, but neither could there be any objection to applying to the Greek world the methods—if there be any—applied to the Arunta or to the Babylonians.

The second approach, however, misses a minute and decisive point. The reasoned investigation of other cultures and the reflection upon them does not begin within the Arunta or the Babylonian cultures. Indeed, one could show that it could not have begun with them. Before Greece and outside the Greco-Western tradition, societies are instituted on a principle of strict closure: our view of the world is the only meaningful one, the "others" are bizarre, inferior, perverse, evil, or unfaithful. As Hannah Arendt has said, impartiality enters this world with Homer.[2] This is not just "affective" impartiality. It is the impartiality of knowledge and understanding. The keen interest in the other starts with the Greeks. This interest is but another side of the critical examination and interrogation of their own institutions. That is to say, it is a component of the democratic and philosophical movement created by the Greeks.

That the ethnologist, the historian, or the philosopher is in a position to reflect upon societies other than his own and, indeed, even upon his own society becomes a possibility and a reality only within this particular historical tradition—the Greco-Western tradition. Now, on one hand, this activity may have no theoretical privilege over any other—say, poison divination by the Azanda. Then, for example, the psychoanalyst is but a Western variety of shaman, as Lévi-Strauss has written, and Lévi-Strauss himself, along with the entire society of ethnologists, is but the local variety of sorcerer within this particular group of tribes exorcising, if you will, the alien tribes. The only difference is that rather than fumigating them out of existence, they structuralize them out of existence. Or, on the other hand, we may postulate or posit a qualitative difference between our theorizing about other societies and about "savages" and attach to this difference a specific, limited but firm, positive valuation.[3] Then a philosophical discussion starts. *Then*, and not before. To start a philosophical discussion is to imply that one has already affirmed that for oneself unrestricted thinking is the way of entering upon problems and tasks. Thus, since we know that this attitude is by no means universal but extremely exceptional in the history of human societies,[4] we have to ask how, under what conditions, in which ways, human society was capable, in one particular case, of breaking the closure in virtue of which it generally exists?

In this sense, though describing and analyzing Greece is equivalent to describing and analyzing any other randomly chosen culture, thinking and reflecting about Greece is not and cannot be. For in this latter case, we are reflecting and thinking about the social and historical conditions of thought itself—at least, thought as we know and practice it. One has to eliminate these twin attitudes: there was, once upon a time, a society which remains for us the inaccessible model; *or*, history is essentially flat, there are no significant differences between cultures other than descriptive ones. Greece is the social-historical *locus* where democracy and philosophy are created, thus, of course, it is our own origin. Insofar as the meaning and the potency of this creation are not exhausted—and I firmly believe that they are not—Greece is for us a *germ*, neither a "model," nor one specimen among others, but a germ.

History is creation: the creation of total forms of human life. Social-historical forms are not "determined" by natural or historical "laws." Society is self-creation. "That which" creates society and history is the instituting society, as opposed to the instituted society. The instituting society is the social imaginary in the radical sense.

The self-institution of society is the creation of a human world: of "things," "reality," language, norms, values, ways of life and death, objects for which we live and objects for which we die—and of course, first and foremost, the creation of the human individual in which the institution of society is massively embedded.

Within this wholesale creation of society, each particular, historically given institution represents a particular creation. Creation, as I use the term, means the positing of a new εἶδος, a new essence, a new form in the full and strong sense: new determinations, new norms, new laws. The Chinese, the classical Hebrew, the ancient Greek, or the modern capitalist institution of society each means the positing of different determinations and laws, not just "juridical" laws but obligatory ways of perceiving and conceiving the social and "physical" world and acting within it. Within, and by virtue of, this overall institution of society emerge specific creations: science, for example, as we know and conceive it, is a particular creation of the Greco-Western world.

There follows a series of crucial questions, about which I can only sketch some reflections here.

First, how can we understand previous or "foreign" institutions of society? (For that matter, how and in what sense can we say that we understand our own society?) We do not have, in the social-historical domain, "explanation" in the same sense the physical sciences do. Any "explanation" of this sort is either trivial or fragmentary and conditional. The innumerable regularities of social life—without which, of course, this life would not exist—are what they are because the institution of this particular society has posited this particular complex of rules, laws, meanings, values, tools, motivations, etc. And this institution is nothing but the socially sanctioned (sanctioned formally or informally) magma of social imaginary significations created by this particular society. Thus to understand a society means, first and foremost, to penetrate or reappropriate the social imaginary significations which hold this society together. Is this at all possible? We have to take into account two facts here.

The first, indisputable fact is that *almost all* of the people in a given society do not and cannot understand a "foreign" society. (I am not speaking, of course, about trivial obstacles.) This points to what I have called the cognitive closure of the institution. The second (which can be and is disputed, but to which I nevertheless hold) is that under some very specific social, historical, and personal preconditions, some people can understand something about a foreign society. This points to some sort of "potential universality" in whatever is human for humans. Contrary to inherited commonplaces, the root of this universality is not human "rationality' (if "rationality" were at stake here, nobody would ever have understood anything about the Hebrew God, or, for that matter, about any religion whatsoever), but creative imagination as the core component of nontrivial thinking.[5] Whatever has been imagined strongly enough to shape behavior, speech, or objects can, in principle, be reimagined (rerepresented, *wiedervorgestellt*) by somebody else.

Two significant polarities have to be stressed here.

In this social-historical understanding, there is a distinction between "true" and "false"—and not just in the trivial sense. One can talk sense about "foreign" societies, and one can talk nonsense—of which there is no dearth of examples. The "true" cannot be subjected in this case (as, more generally, it never can in matters of thought) to the banal "verification" or "falsification" procedures which are currently (platitudinously and wrongly) considered to demarcate "science" from "nonscience." For instance, Burckhardt's realization of the importance of the agonistic element in the Greek world (which looms so large in Hannah Arendt's thinking about Greece), is *true*—but not in the same sense as $E = mc^2$ is true. What does "true" mean in this former case? That the idea of the agonistic brings together an indefinite class of social and historical phenomena in Greece that would otherwise remain unconnected—not necessarily unconnected in their "causal" or "structural" relation but unconnected in their *meaning;* and that its claim to possess a "real" or "actual" referent (i.e., that is not just a delusion, or convenient fiction, or even an *Idealtypus*, an observer's limiting rational construction)[6] can be discussed in a fecund way, though this discussion may be and, in the decisive cases, *has* to be interminable. In brief, it *elucidates* and initiates a process of elucidation.

The situation is different, at first glance, when we are speaking about our own history or tradition, about societies which though "other" are not "foreign" since there is a strong genealogical connection between their imaginary significations and ours, since we still somehow "share" the same world, since there is still some active, intrinsic relationship between their institutions and our own. It would seem that since we succeed this creation but fall within the same concatenation, since we find ourselves, so to speak, downstream, since we live, at least partly, within the mental framework and the universe of beings which is posited, our understanding of our "ancestral" societies would present no mystery. But of course, other problems arise. This "common belonging" is by necessity partly illusory, but often tends to be taken as fully real. Projective "value judgements" become important and interfere with understanding. The proper distance between ourselves and "our own past" is very difficult to establish; the attitudes toward Greece cited earlier are examples. The illusion of the *Selbstverständlichkeit* can be catastrophic: thus, people today consider democracy or rational inquiry to go without saying, naively projecting onto the whole of history the exceptional situation of their own society, and are unable to understand what democracy or rational inquiry could mean for the society where they were created for the first time.

The second question is: if history is creation, how can we judge and choose? It is to be stressed that this question would not arise if history were simply and strictly a causal concatenation, or if it did contain its φύσις and τέλος. It is precisely because history is creation that the question of judging and choosing emerges as a radical, nontrivial question.

The radicality of the question stems from the fact that despite a widespread naive illusion, there is not and cannot be a rigorous and ultimate foundation of anything—not of knowledge itself, not even of mathematics. One should remember that this foundational illusion has never been shared by the great philosophers: not by Plato, not by Aristotle, not by Kant, not by Hegel. The first outstanding philosopher who was under the delusion of "foundation" was Descartes, and this is one of the respects in which his influence has been catastrophic. Since Plato, it has been known that every demonstration presupposes something which is not demonstrable. Here I want to stress one other aspect of the question: the judgments and choices we make belong to the history of the society in which we live and depend upon it. I do not mean that they depend upon particular social-historical "contents" (though this is also true). I mean that the sheer fact of judging and choosing in a nontrivial sense presupposes not only that we belong to that particular history, to that particular tradition where judging and choosing first become effectively possible, but that we have already, before any judgment and choice of "contents," judged affirmatively and chosen this history and this tradition in this respect. For this activity of judging and choosing, and the very idea of it, is a Greco-Western activity and idea—it has been created within this world and nowhere else. The idea would not and could not occur to a Hindu, to a classical Hebrew, to a true Christian, or to a Muslim. Classical Hebrews have nothing to choose. They have been given the truth and the Law once and for all by God, and if they started judging and choosing about that, they would no longer be Hebrew. Likewise, true Christians have nothing to judge or choose: they have to believe and to love. For it is written: "Judge not, that ye be not judged" (Matt. 7: 1). Conversely, Greco-Westerners ("Europeans") who produce rational arguments for rejecting the European tradition confirm eo ipso this tradition and that they belong to it.

But neither does this tradition offer us repose. For while it has produced democracy and philosophy, both the American and the French Revolutions, the Paris Commune and the Hungarian Workers' Councils, the Parthenon and *Macbeth*, it has produced as well the massacre of the Melians by the Athenians, the Inquisition, Auschwitz, the Gulag, and the H-bomb. It created reason, freedom, and beauty—and it also created massive monstrosity. No other animal species could ever create Auschwitz or the Gulag; to create that you must be a human being. These extreme possibilities of humanity in the field of the monstrous have been realized par excellence in our own tradition. The problem of judging and choosing thus also arises within this tradition, which we cannot validate for a moment en bloc. And of course, it does not arise as a simple intellectual possibility. The very history of the Greco-Western world can be viewed as the history of the struggle between autonomy and heteronomy.

It is well known that the problem of judging and choosing is the object of Kant's third *Critique*, and that Arendt in her later years turned toward the third *Critique* in her search for some grounding for these activities of the mind. I feel a form of illusion is spreading among some of Arendt's followers or commentators (1) that somehow or other Kant "solved" this problem in the third *Critique*, and (2) that his "solution" could be transposed to the political problem or at least facilitate the latter's elaboration. Facilitate, indeed, it does—but in a negative way, as I will try to show briefly.

I submit that the whole affair is a strange (but philosophically commonplace) *chassé-croisé* of correct insights arrived at for the wrong reasons. It begins with Kant himself. Why is Kant, nine years after the first edition of the *Critique of Pure Reason*, driven to the question of *Urteil* and *Urteilskraft*?[7] The apparently watertight answers given to this question in the preface and introduction to the third *Critique* I consider to be rational reconstructions or rationalizations, Kant's dressing up in systematic and systematizing garb deeper and not fully conscious philosophical motivations.

First among these, no doubt, is the realization that the whole edifice of the *Critique of Pure Reason* stands on air, that any "given" just is not sufficient to produce *Erfahrung* (experience), that the organization of a "world" out of the *Mannigfaltigkeit* (diversity) of the given entails that this *Mannigfaltigkeit* already be intrinsically organized to a minimal degree, since it must be at least *organizable*. No category of causality could ever legislate a *Mannigfaltigkeit* which would follow this law: if *y* once succeeded an *x*, never again will a *y* succeed an *x*.[8] Of course, in such a "fully chaotic" world the existence of an actual, effective "knowing subject" would be impossible—but this is a second and equally strong argument against the monocracy of subjective transcendentalism. The object of the legislation has to be forthcoming as "legislatable," and the legislator actually has to "exist" as well. Both entail a world that is not completely chaotic.

A worthy philosophical answer is not supplied to this question by the "happy accident" (*glücklicher Zufall*), the "contingent" character of the "systematic unity" of the laws of nature and of their capacity to fulfill the requirements of *Verstand*—which is indeed, in a sense, the truth of the matter. Hence the turn to a reflective and not constitutive teleology of nature: though we cannot "prove" it, nature works as if it were organized according to ends. For these workings of nature, the human work of art provides an analogy, since in it we can see "imagination in its freedom as determinable by the understanding according to ends" (§59).

The second motivation is precisely the recognition of the specificity of the work of art.[9] Kant has to bring together his desire (or need) to provide an "aesthetics" in the usual sense, a philosophy of the beautiful and philosophical *locus* for it, and his dim realization of the ontological specificity of art as *creation*. This is, of course, where Kant transcends the classical tradition and its ontology. The great work of art does not follow rules but posits new rules—it is *Muster* and *exemplarisch*. The artist, the genius, is not able to "describe" or "scientifically explain" his product, but posits the norm "as nature" (*als Natur*, §46). Nature of course is here *natura naturans*, not *natura naturata*, not the nature of the *Critique of Pure Reason*, but a "living" power of emergence, bringing together matter under form. The genius is *Natur*—and *Natur* is genius!—*qua* free imagination determinable according to finality.

The third motivation is Kant's increasing preoccupation with the questions of society and history. This is manifest in his numerous writings of the period related to these subjects and expressed in the third *Critique* through the ideas of a *sensus communis* and of the distinction between objective and subjective universal validity (*Allgemeingültigkeit*).

Between addressing the questions arising from the frequent contemporary recourse to the third *Critique* in connection with the activities of judging and choosing, it is necessary to point to a paradox of the first magnitude: Why should one have recourse to the *Critique of Judgement* when the whole of Kant's *practical* philosophy is explicitly directed towards supplying rules and maxims of judgment and choice in "practical" matters?[10] Why is the apparently firm ground offered by Kant's practical philosophy in matters of ultimate political judgment neglected in recent discussions while it abundantly inspired, eighty years ago, neo-Kantian socialists and Austro-Marxists, for example? If the categorical imperative as such is an empty, simple form of abstract universality, as Schiller and Hegel rightly saw, if Kant's attempts to derive substantive injunctions and interdictions from the principle of contradiction are flawed, certainly the same cannot be said about Kant's maxims. "Be a person and respect others as persons"; "respect humanity in every human being"; "treat others as ends and never simply as means"—if these principles hold, one may certainly still be shocked by Eichmann and what he represents, but one will not wonder about the possibility of judging him. Then Hans Jonas would not have to worry about being able to say to a Hitler "I will kill you," but not "you are wrong."[11]

But of course the matter does not end here. First, Hitler would be right in answering: you cannot *demonstrate* to me the validity of your maxims. Second, he would answer nothing of the sort. Nazis and Stalinists do not discuss, they just draw their guns. Third, the maxims escape the flaw of indeterminacy only because we are used to giving a more or less determinate content to the terms "person," "humanity," etc. This is not philosophical hairsplitting. Not so long ago, the Church was burning people at the stake in order to save their "humanity"—their souls. Maxims (or any similar rules) are of value only within and for a community where (1) reasonable (not "rational") discussion is accepted as a means of overcoming differences, (2) it is recognized that everything cannot be "demonstrated," and (3) there is a sufficient (even if tacit) degree of consensus beyond logical definition about the meaning of terms like "person," "humanity"—or for that matter, "liberty," "equality," and "justice." It will be noted that these terms refer to social imaginary significations par excellence.

The similarities between these prerequisites and those of any discussion about art are obvious. This of course does not mean that political and aesthetic judgments are species of the same genus—but that it is not, prima facie, unreasonable to explore the conditions under which a community can discuss and agree upon matters beyond those accessible through procedures of strict demonstration.

It is equally obvious, however, that these conditions are so restrictive as to be of no use when we come to ultimate questions. Kant's third *Critique* in fact presents a description of rather than a "solution" to the problem of judging. Significant as this description is, it offers no help in the search for "foundations." As a "solution," from a logician's point of view, it only begs the question; in terms of my framework, it describes the primitive circle of social-historical creation without actually understanding it. To this I now turn briefly.

Let us note from the outset that, as far as I know, the invocation of the *Critique of Judgment* in regard to the issue of social-historical creation refers only to the idea of "taste" and "reflective judgment," and not at all to the idea that the great work of art is creation. In this way, a central and fatal *aporia* in Kant's work is ignored or concealed.

For Kant, the aesthetic "reflective judgment" possesses a *subjektive Allgemeingültigkeit* (a subjective universal validity)—as opposed to the objective universal validity of, e.g., determinative judgments in the theoretical field. It appeals to *taste* and is founded upon the possibility of the subject's placing itself "in the other's place." No such condition is required for judgments of objective universal validity. Where "the other" is, from the point of view of *quid juris*, is irrelevant.

Where does this subjective universal validity of the judgment of taste derive from? From the fact that in aesthetic judgment I do not say "It pleases me" or "I find this beautiful," but "This *is* beautiful." I claim universality for my judgment. But this of course will not do. It is perfectly possible that I give (or that I am bound to give) the form of universality to a class of my judgments without any content corresponding to this form in a valid way. It is perfectly possible that I formulate a claim to universality, and that this claim remain frustrated and vacuous. The logical-transcendental trap does not work here. When I say not "I believe P to be true," but "P is true," the question of the objective universal validity of my judgment can be settled in principle by rules and procedures. And if someone tells me, "nothing is ever true," or "truth is a matter of whim," he walks, de jure, out of the room of rational discussion. I need not worry about him, and more generally (in Kant's eyes), in theoretical matters I do not even need the approval of "the other," nor need I look at things "from his point of view."[12] Not so for the reflective judgment, where I *do* need to introduce the other's point of view. Now, if the other were "pure taste"—if such a thing as "pure taste" exists, *even* "transcendentally," that is, in the same way *reiner Verstand* must "exist"—the judgment would be mere wordplay. The other would be just another concrete instance of the same "universal" (though of course not a logical or "discursive" universal) of which I would also be an instance. For if "pure taste" exists, this would entail that it owe nothing to the "empirical particularities" of the subjects concerned nor be affected by them (just as in the cases of knowledge and ethics). But in the domain of the aesthetic judgment, the other has to be taken into consideration precisely qua other. He does not differ from me "numerically," as the scholastics would say, but substantively. Despite the connotations of the term "reflective," in reflective judgment the other is not a mirror. It is *because* he is other (nontrivially different) that he can function where Kant locates him. It is because *different* people *can* agree on matters of beauty that the aesthetic judgment exists and is of a nature other than theoretical or pure practical (ethical) judgments. In the latter cases, the agreement is both necessary and superfluous. Universality, there, is identity through or across indefinite and indifferent numerical "instantiations." But the "subjective universal validity" of the aesthetic judgment is commonality through or across nonidentity. The other has to find—or does find—the *Nightwatch* beautiful even though he is nontrivially different from me.

But different how, to what extant, up to what point? Different just enough, not too much, and not too little. Would my judgment of *Oedipus Rex* become shaky if a throng of very refined Tang, Song, or Ming mandarins found the play repugnant? Should I think of Hokusai's point of view when looking at *Les demoiselles d'Avignon?* Kant speaks repeatedly, of course, about the "education of taste." But education of taste gives rise to two intractable philosophical problems (intractable at least from *this* perspective). First, education of taste is impossible unless (1) beauty is already there, and (2) it is rightly recognized as such. Whence, by whom, and on what basis? Who shall educate the educators? Either education of taste is a meaningless expression, or beauty is a historical *Faktum* (as, indeed, *Erfahrung* also is) and its "recognition" or "reception" cannot be "explained" or "understood" (let alone *be* founded) any more than its creation (Kant says "production," *Erzeugung*) can. What we discover here again is the primitive, originary circle of creation: *creation presupposes itself.* Second, if we think of historically effective education, then we would have (as indeed we do) the *imposition* of a given "taste" in a particular culture. Uniformity of taste will then be more or less "obligatory," and reflective judgment will provide no more input than that already injected into the historical subjects.

Now if beauty is a historical *Faktum*, there is not only one history of this *Faktum*, but a vast plurality of such histories—and thus also of tastes. We have been educated and continue educating our offspring in and through the creations of our own particular history. It is also our own history—*and this history alone*—that has educated us so that we find beauty in the sculpture of the Mayas, the painting of the Chinese, or the music and dance of the Balinese, while the reverse is not true. To be sure, some of the best interpreters of Mozart today are Japanese. But they attain to this insofar as they have been "Westernized"—not so much in that they have learned the piano, Mozart, and so forth, but in that they have accepted this very opening, this movement of acculturation, with its corollary: that the music of some barbarians is not to be rejected beforehand but may be worth the effort of appropriation.[13]

If the other is not a shadow or a mannequin, he belongs to a definite and concrete social-historical commonality. Concrete means particular: a particular community, and its particular "education"—that is, tradition. But then, the appeal to the other's point of view floats uneasily between vacuousness and tautology. It is vacuous if the addressee is supposedly to be found in each and every particular community. It is tautologous if it is an appeal to our own community: for then it is an appeal to go on judging as beautiful what has already been so judged.

That this should be so is, of course, the consequence of what I called the cognitive closure between the different social-historical worlds. This applies to art as well as to "science," to sufficient reasons for dying as well as to table manners. To be sure, there is a distinction to be drawn between "science" and the rest, or at any rate between science and art. Even if we disdain pragmatic arguments of the sort "the universal validity of our science over against savage magic is 'proven' by the fact that we kill savages much more effectively than their magic can kill us," it remains that the chances for effective "universal validity" in science are much greater than those in art. For in the case of science, the component that supplies the identity among its variations (λέγειν and τεύχειν) is paramount, and this component is less variable among different cultures.[14] For instance, insofar as causality is recognized everywhere (magic itself operates on some sort of causality postulate), you can convince any savage with a few operations that X causes Y. The chances that you could bring him to love *Tristan und Isolde* are immeasurably less: for this you would have to educate him in and through several centuries of European culture. This is of course no accident: "art"—which has never been just "art," except for a short and recent historical period—is much more strongly and deeply linked to the kernel of a society's imaginary significations than is "knowledge of things."

Of course, to all this there is a Kantian answer, and it is at least a threefold one. First, the work of art addresses itself "to the subjective element, which one can presuppose in all men (insofar as it is required for possible knowledge in general)" (§38). This is to be found in the combination of the free play of imagination with the legality (*Gesetzmässigkeit*) of understanding (§35), in a proper proportion (§21). Second, the foundation of the "necessity" of the judgment of taste must lie in an "indeterminate concept," the concept "of a supersensible substratum of phenomena" (§57). Third, there exists a historical process, equivalent to a progress in education of taste—and certainly to an actualization of effective universality through convergence—and this is a manifest in the development of civilization in general and in *Aufklärung* in particular (§41).

It is neither possible nor necessary to discuss these points here. I will only note regarding the first one that it implies much more than it initially appears to do. One can easily grant that imagination, understanding, and a "productive" interplay of the two are present in all humans. But the question of taste entails much more than such abstract universal "faculties"; it pertains to their concrete historical specification (and Kant is well aware of this, as the third point shows; cf. also the Remark to §38). Of much greater importance, however, these ideas imply the whole of Kant's philosophy—both "pure philosophy," and "philosophy of history." Without it, the third *Critique* hangs in the air. I find it puzzling that those who today advocate recourse to the third *Critique* do not seem to realize that they have to take into the bargain as well the idea of a "supersensible substratum of phenomena," and of "humanity" (in the *Kantian* sense of "supersensible"). Nor do they seem to realize that beauty is "the symbol of the moral good" (59). I find it even more puzzling that they are able to disregard the essential link between Kant's theory of taste and judgment and the historical world, which is Kant's unequivocal and firm position on the *Aufklärung*. If all the human tribes, after long wanderings in the wild forests of precivilization, were to gather now in the glades of the *Aufklärung* where we, the first comers, were to greet them as they arrive, the problems would surely be quite different. But have we not been told that it was precisely because of the shattering crisis within the *Aufklärung*'s ideas and standards that the whole discussion began?

Consider now the other kernel of the third *Critique*. The fine arts are arts of genius, and the work of genius is a *creation*—though Kant does not use the term.[15] It is new, not "numerically," but essentially, in that it posits new norms: it is a new εἶδος. Thus it is a "model" or "prototype" (*Muster*).

But a model of what, and for what? The term is strange, since one would naturally expect it to be a model for imitation—and Kant rejects and severely and rightly condemns imitation and insists strongly on essential originality as the distinctive character of the work of art, that is, of genius.

The work of genius is a prototype of nothing and for nothing—if we take "prototype" in the formal sense.[16] Yet it is indeed a prototype in two other ways. It is a prototype of the "fact" of creation: it proposes itself as an "example" not for imitation (*Nachahmung* or *Nachmachung*), but for "succession" or "continuation" (*Nachfolge*), for the fact and feat of creation to be reenacted. And it is a model for the education of taste. In both respects, however, the circle of historical creation is present, and no "logical," "analytical" construction allows us to escape this paradoxical situation. The *chef d'oeuvre* can only be a model for taste if there is already taste enough to recognize it as a *chef d'oeuvre*. And it is a model for the reenactment of the creative act if it is already recognized as the embodiment of such an act.

Behind Kant's apparently watertight construction and beyond the realization of its precariousness, we find a deep intuition of the truth of the matter. Art as creation cannot be "explained." Nor can the reception of the great work of art be "explained." The "educative" function of the new, of the original, is both a fact and a paradox.[17] It is an instance of the fact and the paradox of each and every historical creation.

Kant's theory of aesthetics is the only part of his fundamental writing in which he is forced to go beyond his strictly dualistic approach and to consider what later neo-Kantians (e.g., Rickert) would call *das Zwischenreich des immanenten Sinnes* (the in-between realm of immanent meaning). It is also the part in which he comes closest to recognizing creation in history—at least in substance, though he does not and could not name it. Beauty is created. But it is characteristic, first, that Kant have an "exceptionalist" view of creation: only genius creates, and it does so "as nature." (This "nature" of course has nothing to do with the "nature" of his theoretical philosophy. It is easy to see that it is an uneasy pseudonym for God; "genius" is a fragmented offshoot of the creative intelligent power that reflection on the teleology of "nature" must posit.) Second, that creation has to be restricted to the ontologically weightless domain of art. What Kant has to say about scientific work in the third *Critique* shows that it is intrinsically necessary for him to trivialize and reduce it to a cumulative process. In the domain of art, the effective validity, recognition, and reception of the norms (meanings, or "values" in neo-Kantian parlance) must take on decisive importance. Hence the move from "objective" to "subjective universal validity," and from "determinative" to "reflective": determination does not depend upon the opinion of the other, while reflection does indeed involve it. Thus, the irreducible character of creation and the commonality/community of humans acquire, however halfheartedly, some philosophical status, even if only as problems.

Kant believes that he answers the question of the essence of beauty (of what beauty *is*) and of the "necessity" of its common recognition. Of course he does no such thing. We have to recognize the decisive importance of the third

Critique, *not* for the question of judging but for its insights into creation and human commonality. We also have to recognize the limitations of these insights—and the necessary origin of these limitations in the "main body" of Kant's philosophy (the two other *Critiques*). To remove these limitations, this main body must be exploded, but then the insights of the third *Critique* gain a completely different meaning, and lead in unexpected directions. Because of these limitations—which are, in fact, common to the mainstream of the inherited philosophical tradition—it is not possible for Kant to think the radical social imaginary or instituting society; he cannot really think the sociality of history, even the historicity of society.[18] Hence the restriction to "genius" and to "art": the creation of institutions is ignored, or, at best, has to be presented as a purely "rational" affair (cf. the "nation of devils" in *Zum ewigen Frieden*). This is why the primitive circle of creation (that creation presupposes itself) can only loom confusedly and indistinctly between the lines and behind the aporias of Kant's treatment: beauty is recognized because there is taste, and taste is there because men have been educated, and men have been educated because they have already been in touch with beauty—in other words, because they recognize beauty before being, in principle, capable of doing so.

In the field of art, the social-historical consists in self-institution. "Genius" is here both a particular case of, and a pseudonym for, historical creation in general. The reception of the work of art is a particular case of the active and self-creative participation and cooperation of human communities in the institution of the new—in the institution *tout court*. "Reception" is no less paradoxical—and no less creative—than creation. And, of course, nothing in all of this brings us any closer to deciding how to judge and choose. The generalization and radicalization of Kant's insights can only bring about a generalization and radicalization of the aporias involved. For everybody always judges and chooses not only within but by means of the particular social-historical institution—the culture, the tradition—which formed him. Indeed, without this he would not be *able* to judge and choose anything. That Kant is both capable of knowing this and ignoring it is typical of his essential stand as an *Aufklärer*: in truth, there is but *one* history—and for all that really matters, this one history coincides with our own (or, our own history is the "transcendentally obligatory" meeting point of all particular histories). One might be tempted to treat this stand as "empirical" and dispensable, but that would be a mistake. For this postulate—the "transcendentalization" of the historical fact of the *Aufklärung*—is necessary, if the semblance of an answer is to be given in "universal" terms to the original question. If all of us belonged substantially to the same tradition—or if one tradition was, de jure, the "true" one—we could appeal to the "same" taste (but even then, only on the counterfactual supposition that creative breaks within that tradition remain within some sort of undefinable bounds).

We can now conclude on the *chassé-croisé* of correct insights and wrong reasons which occur within the contemporary invocation of the third *Critique*. Kant's theory of judgment is appealed to because of the delusion that it could contribute an answer to the question of judging and choosing—which it does not. And the third *Critique* is *not* appreciated for what is, in truth, its most precious germ: the insight into the fact of creation. But this is no accident. For contemporaries repudiate (at least tacitly) the main body of Kant's philosophy; if they did not, there would be no need to resort to the third *Critique* in matters of practical-political judgment. Now, when liberated from the transcendental scaffolding, and from the postulates referring to the supersensible, the idea of creation becomes uncontrollable. If norms themselves are created, how is one to escape the abhorrent thought that Right and Wrong themselves are social-historical creations? Consequently, refuge is taken instead in some vaguely perceived *sensus communis* regarding matters of Right and Wrong—forgetting again that it was the actual breakdown of this *sensus communis* that initiated the very discussion in the first place.

Can we go further than stating the obvious facts—that judging and choosing always take place within and by means of an already existing social-historical institution or else spring out of a new creation in the face of which no criteria are available except the ones this new creation establishes for the first time? And how can we confront reasonably, if not "rationally," the question of judging and choosing between different institutions of society—the political question par excellence?

I will not discuss this problem here. I will only repeat: the absolute singularity of our Greco-Western or European tradition lies in its being the only tradition wherein this problem arises and becomes thinkable. (This does *not* mean that it becomes "soluble"—*pace* Descartes and Marx.) Politics and philosophy *and* the link between them have been created here and only here. Of course, this *does not* mean that this tradition can be "rationally" imposed upon—or defended against—another tradition that ignores or rejects this setting. Any rational argumentation presupposes the common acceptance of rationality as a criterion. It is not so much pragmatically ineffectual as it is logically absurd to argue "rationally" with Hitler, Andropov, Khomeini, or Idi Amin Dada. Indeed, "pragmatically," such argumentation can be defended as a political ("pedagogical") activity: there is always a chance that some followers of these men may be or become inconsistent and thus permeable to "rational" arguments. But to take a more dignified example, can argumentation invoking rationality, the equal value of all humans qua humans, for example, carry any weight against a deeply held belief that God has revealed himself and his will—the latter entailing, for instance, the forced conversion and/or extermination of the infidels, sorcerers, heretics, etc.? Silly, modern parochialism is capable of laughing at this idea as "exotic"—even though it was central to all "civilized" societies as recently as two centuries ago.

Judging and choosing, in a radical sense, were created in Greece, and this is one of the meanings of the Greek creation of politics and philosophy. By politics I do not mean court intrigues or fighting among social groups over interest or position (both of which existed elsewhere), but a collective activity whose object is the institution of society as such. In Greece we have the first instance of a community explicitly deliberating about its laws and changing those laws.[19] Elsewhere laws are inherited from the ancestors or given by gods or by the One True God; but they are not posited as created by men after a collective confrontation and discussion about right and wrong law. This position leads to other questions, which also originated in Greece: not only "Is *this* law right or wrong," but "What is it for a law to be right or wrong, that is, what is justice?" Just as in Greek political activity the existing institution of society is called into question and altered for the first time, similarly Greece is the first society where we find the explicit questioning of the instituted collective representation of the world—that is, where we find philosophy. Further, just as political activity in Greece leads to the question not merely of whether this particular law is right or wrong, just or unjust, but of what justice is in general, so philosophical interrogation leads rapidly to the question not only of whether this or that representation of the world is true, but of what truth is. Both questions are genuine questions—that is, they must remain open forever.

The creation of democracy and philosophy and the link between them has its essential precondition in the Greek vision of the world and human life, the nucleus of the Greek imaginary. This can perhaps best be clarified by the three questions in which Kant summarizes the interests of man. About the first two: What can I know? What ought I to do? an endless discussion begins in Greece, and there is no "Greek answer" to them. But to the third question: What am I allowed to hope? there is a definite and clear Greek answer, and this is a massive and resounding *nothing*. And evidently it is the true answer. "Hope" is not to be taken here in the everyday trivial sense—that the sun will again shine tomorrow, or that a child will be born alive. The hope to which Kant refers is the hope of the Christian or religious tradition, the hope corresponding to that central human wish and delusion that there be some essential correspondence, some consonance, some *adequatio*, between our desires and decisions, on the one hand, and the world, the nature of being, on the other. Hope is the ontological, cosmological, and ethical assumption that the world is not just something out there, but *cosmos* in the archaic and proper sense, a total order which includes us, our wishes, and our strivings as its organic and central components. The philosophical translation of this assumption is that being is ultimately good. As is well known, the first one who dared to proclaim this philosophical monstrosity clearly was Plato—after the classical period had ended. This remained the fundamental tenet of theological philosophy in Kant, of course, but in Marx as well. The Greek view is expressed as early as the myth of Pandora. For Hesiod hope is forever imprisoned in Pandora's box. In preclassical and classical Greek religion, there is no hope for an afterlife: either there is no afterlife, or if there is one, it is worse than the worst life on earth—as Achilles reveals to Odysseus in the Land of the Dead. Having nothing to hope from an afterlife or from a caring and benevolent God, man is liberated for action and thought in *this* world.

This is intimately linked with the fundamental Greek idea of χάος. For Hesiod, in the beginning there is chaos. In the proper, initial sense, χάος in Greek means void, nothingness. It is out of the total void that the world emerges.[20] But already in Hesiod, the world is also chaos in the sense that there is no complete order in it, that it is not subject to meaningful laws. First there is total disorder, then order, κόσμος, is created. But at the "roots" of the world, beyond the familiar landscape, chaos always reigns supreme. The order of the world has no "meaning" for man: it posits the blind necessity of genesis and birth, on one hand, of corruption and catastrophe—death of the forms—on the other. In Anaximander, the first philosopher for whom we possess reliable testimony, the "element" of being is the ἄπειρον, the indeterminate, indefinite—another way of thinking chaos. Form, the particularized and determinate existence of the various beings, is ἀδικία, injustice—one may well call it ὕβρις. That is why the particular beings have to render justice to one another and pay compensation for their injustice through their decay and disappearance.[21] There is a strong though implicit connection between the two pairs of opposite terms, χάος/κόσμος and ὕβρις/δίκη. In a sense, the latter is the transposition of the former into the human domain.

This vision conditions, so to speak, the creation of philosophy. Philosophy, as the Greeks created and practiced it, is possible because the world is not fully ordered. If it were, there would not be any philosophy, but only one, final system of knowledge. And if the world were sheer chaos, there would be no possibility of thinking at all. But this vision of the world also conditions the creation of politics. If the human world were fully ordered, either externally or through its own "spontaneous operation," if human laws were given by God or by nature or by the "nature of society" or by the "laws of history," then there would be no room for political thinking and no field for political action and no sense in asking what the proper law is or what justice is (cf. Hayek). But furthermore, if human beings could not create some order for themselves by positing laws, then again there would be no possibility of political, instituting action. If a full and certain knowledge (ἐπιστήμη) of the human domain were possible, politics would immediately come to an end, and democracy would be both impossible and absurd: democracy implies that all citizens have the possibility of attaining a correct δόξα *and* that nobody possesses an ἐπιστήμη of things political.

I think it is important to stress these connections because a great many of the difficulties of modern political thinking are related to the persisting dominant influence of theological (that is, Platonic) philosophy. The operative postulate that there is a total and "rational" (and therefore "meaningful") order in the world, along with the necessary implication that there is an order of human affairs linked to the order of the world—what one could call unitary ontology—has plagued political philosophy from Plato through modern liberalism and Marxism. The postulate conceals the fundamental fact that human history is creation—without which there would be no genuine question of judging and choosing, either "objectively" or "subjectively." By the same token, it conceals or eliminates the question of responsibility. Unitary ontology, in whatever guise, is essentially linked to heteronomy. The emergence of autonomy in Greece was conditioned by the nonunitary Greek view of the world that is expressed from the beginning in the Greek "myths."

A curious but inevitable consequence of the "model/antimodel" mentality employed when examining Greece, and in particular Greek political institutions, is that these are taken, so to speak, "statically," as if there were *one* "constitution," with its various "articles" fixed once for all, that could and must be "judged" or "evaluated" as such. This is an approach for people who seek recipes—whose number, indeed, does not seem to be on the decrease. But, of course, what is important in ancient Greek political life—the *germ*—is the *historical instituting process:* the activity and struggle around the change of the institutions, the explicit (even if partial) self-institution of the πόλις as a permanent process. This process goes on for almost four centuries. The annual election of the θεσμοθέται in Athens is established in 683/2 B.C., and it is probably around the same time that the citizens in Sparta (9,000 of them) are instated as ὅμοιοι ("similar," i.e., equals) and the rule of νόμος (law) affirmed. The widening of democracy in Athens continues well into the fourth century. The πόλις—at any rate Athens, about which our information is most complete—do not stop questioning their respective institutions; the δῆμος goes on modifying the rules under which it lives. This is, of course, inseparable from the hectic pace of creation during this period in all fields beyond the strictly political one.

This movement is a movement of explicit self-institution. The cardinal meaning of explicit self-institution is autonomy: we posit our own laws. Of all the questions arising out of this movement, I will briefly survey three: "Who" is the "subject" of this autonomy? What are the limits of his action? What is the "object" of autonomous self-institution?[22]

The community of citizens—the δῆμος—proclaims that it is absolutely sovereign (αὐτόνομος, αὐτόδικος, αὐτοτελής, self-legislating, self-judging, self-governing, in Thucydides' words). It also affirms the political equality (equal sharing of activity and power) of all free men. This is the self-position, self-definition, of the political body, which contains an element of arbitrariness—and always will. *Who* posits the *Grundnorm*—in Kelsen's terminology, the norm ruling the positing of norms—is a *fact*. For the Greeks, this "who" is the body of adult, male, free citizens (which means, in principle, those men born of other citizens, though naturalization is known and practiced). Of course, the exclusion of women, foreigners, and slaves from citizenship is a limitation we do not accept. This limitation was never lifted in practice in ancient Greece (at the level of ideas, things are less simple, but I will not discuss this aspect here). But indulging for a moment in the absurd "comparative merits" game, let us remember that slavery was present in the United States until 1865 and in Brazil until the end of the nineteenth century. Further, in most "democratic" countries, voting rights were granted to women only after World War II; no country today grants political rights to foreigners, and in most cases naturalization of resident foreigners is by no means automatic (a quarter of the resident population of very "democratic" Switzerland are μέτοικοι).

Equality of the citizens is of course equality in respect of the law (ἰσονομία), but it is essentially much more than that. It is not the granting of equal passive "rights," but active general participation in public affairs. This participation is not left to chance, but actively promoted both through formal rules and through the general ἦθος of the πόλις. According to Athenian law, a citizen who will not take sides while the city is in civil strife becomes ἄτιμος—deprived of political rights.[23]

Participation materializes in the εκκλησία, the Assembly of the people, which is the acting sovereign body. All citizens have the right to speak (ἰσηγορία), their votes carry the same weight (ἰσοφεφία), and they are under moral obligation to speak their minds (παρρησία). Participation also materializes in the courts. There are no professional judges; virtually all courts are juries with their jurors chosen by lot.

The εκκλησία, assisted by the βουλή (Council), legislates and governs. This is *direct democracy*. Three of its aspects deserve further comment.

1. *The people versus "representatives."* Direct democracy has been rediscovered or reinvented in modern history every time a political collectivity has entered a process of radical self-constitution and self-activity: town meetings during the American Revolution, *sections* during the French Revolution, the Paris Commune, the Workers' Councils, or the Soviets in their original form. Hannah Arendt has repeatedly stressed the importance of these forms. In all these cases, the sovereign body is the totality of those concerned; whenever delegation is inevitable, delegates are not just elected but subject to permanent recall. One should remember that for classical political philosophy, the notion of "representation" is unknown. For Herodotus as well as for Aristotle, democracy is the power of the δῆμος, unmitigated in matters of legislation, and the designation of magistrates (not "representatives"!) by sortition or rotation. Scholars merely repeat today that Aristotle's preferred constitution, what he calls πολιτεία, is a mixture of democracy and aristocracy, and forget to add that for Aristotle the "aristocratic" element in this πολιτεία is the *election* of the magistrates—for Aristotle clearly and repeatedly defines election as an aristocratic principle. This is also clear for Montesquieu and Rousseau. It is Rousseau, not Marx or Lenin, who writes that Englishmen believe that they are free because they elect their Parliament, but in reality are only free one day every five years. When Rousseau says that democracy is a regime too perfect for men, suitable only for a people of gods, what he means by democracy is the identity of the *souverain* and the *prince*—that is, there are no *magistrates*. Serious modern liberals in contradistinction to contemporary "political philosophers"—knew all this perfectly well. Benjamin Constant did not glorify elections and "representation" as such; he defended them as lesser evils on the grounds that democracy was impossible in modern nations because of their size *and* because people were not interested in public affairs. Whatever the value of these arguments, they are based upon the explicit recognition that representation is a principle alien to democracy. This hardly bears discussion. Once permanent "representatives" are present, political authority, activity, and initiative are expropriated from the body of citizens and transferred to the restricted body of "representatives," who also use it to consolidate their position and create the conditions whereby the next "election" becomes biased in many ways.
2. *The people versus the "experts."* Linked to the principle of direct democracy is the Greek view of "experts." Not only legislative decisions but important political ones—on matters of *government*—are made by the εκκλησία after it has listened to various speakers, possibly including those who claim some

specific knowledge about the affairs at hand. There are not and cannot be "experts" on political affairs. Political expertise—or political "wisdom"—belongs to the political community, for expertise, τέχνη, in the strict sense is always related to a specific, "technical" occupation, and is, of course, recognized in its proper field. Thus, Plato says in the *Protagoras*, the Athenians will listen to technicians when the building of proper walls or ships is discussed, but will listen to anybody when it comes to matters of politics. (The popular courts embody the same idea in the domain of justice.) War is, or course, a specific field entailing a proper τέχνη, and thus the war chiefs, the στρατηγοί, and elected—as are the technicians in other fields charged by the πόλις with a particular task. So Athens was, after all, a πολιτεία in Aristotle's sense, since some (and very important) magistrates were elected.

Now the *election* of the experts entails another principle central to the Greek view, clearly formulated and accepted not only by Aristotle but, despite its massive democratic implications, even by that archenemy of democracy, Plato. The proper judge of the expert is not another expert, but the *user*: the warrior and not the blacksmith for the sword, the horseman and not the saddler for the saddle. And evidently, for all public (common) affairs, the user, and thus the best judge, is the πόλις. From the results—the Acropolis, or the tragedy prizes—the judgment of this user appears to have been quite sound.

One can hardly overemphasize the contrast between this view and the modern one. The dominant idea that experts can be judged only by other experts is one of the conditions for the expansion and the growing irresponsibility of the modern hierarchal-bureaucratic apparatus. The prevalent idea that there exist "experts" in politics, that is, specialists of the universal and technicians of the totality, makes a mockery of the idea of democracy: the power of the politicians is justified by the "expertise" they would alone possess, and the, inexpert by definition, populace is called upon periodically to pass judgment on these "experts." It also—given the emptiness of the notion of a specialization in the universal—contains the seeds of the growing divorce between the capacity to attain power and the capacity to govern—which plagues Western societies more and more.

3. *The community versus the "State."* The Greek polis is *not* a "State" in the modern sense. The very term *State* does not exist in ancient Greek (characteristically, modern Greeks had to invent a word, and they used the ancient κράτος, which means "sheer force"). Πολιτεία (e.g., in the title of Plato's work) does not mean *der Staat* as in the standard German translation (the Latin *respublica* is less opposed to the meaning of *politeia*). It means both the political institution/constitution and the way people go about common affairs. It is a scandal of modern philology that the title of Aristotle's treatise Ἀθηναίων Πολιτεία is everywhere translated "The Constitution of Athens," both a straightforward linguistic error and the inexplicable sign of ignorance or incomprehension on the part of very erudite men. Aristotle wrote *The Constitution of the Athenians.* Thucydides is perfectly explicit about this: Ἄνδρες γὰρ πόλις, "for the πόλις is the men." For example, before the Battle of Salamis, when Themistocles has to resort to a last-ditch argument to impose

his tactics, he threatens the other allied chiefs that the Athenians will take their families and their fleet and found anew their city in the West. This notwithstanding the fact that for the Athenians—even more than for the other Greeks—their land was sacred and they took pride in their claim to autochthony.

The idea of a "State" as an institution distinct and separated from the body of citizens would not have been understandable to a Greek. Of course, the political community exists at a level which is not identical with the concrete, "empirical" reality of so many thousands of people assembled in a given place at a given time. The political community of the Athenians, the πόλις, has an existence of its own: for example, treaties are honored irrespective of their age, responsibility for past acts is accepted, etc. But the distinction is not between a "State" and a "population"; it is between the continuous corporate body of perennial and impersonal Athenians and the living and breathing ones.

No "State" and no "State apparatus." There is, of course, in ancient Athens a technical-administrative mechanism, but it does not possess any political function. Characteristically, this administration, up to and including its higher echelons—police, keepers of the public archives, public finance—is composed of slaves (possibly Treasury Secretary Donald Regan and certainly Federal Reserve Chairman Paul Volcker would have been slaves in Athens). These slaves were supervised by citizen magistrates usually drawn by lot. "Permanent bureaucracy," the task of *execution* in the strictest sense, is left to the slaves.

The designation of magistrates through lot or rotation in most cases ensures participation by a great number of citizens in official tasks—and knowledge of those tasks. That the εκκλησία decides all important governmental matters ensures the control of the political body over elected magistrates, as does the fact that they are subject to what amounts in practice to the possibility of recall at any time: conviction in a judicial procedure entails inter alia that they lose their office. Of course all magistrates are responsible for their performance in office as a matter of routine (εὔθυνα); accounts are given, in the classical period, to the βουλή.

In a sense, the unity and very existence of the political body is "prepolitical," at least insofar as explicit political self-institution is concerned. The community "receives itself," as it were, from its own past, with all that this past entails. (In part, this is what the moderns call the question of "civil society" versus the "State.") Elements of this given may be politically irrelevant or nontransformable. But *de jure*, "civil society" is itself an object of instituting political action. This is strikingly exemplified by some aspects of Cleisthenes' reform in Athens (506 B.C.). The traditional division of the population among tribes is superseded by a redivision having two main objects. First, the number of tribes is changed. The traditional (Ionian) four φυλαὶ become ten, each subdivided into three τρίττυης, all sharing equally in all magistratures through rotation (which entails what is in fact the creation of a new, "political" year and calendar). Second, each tribe is formed by a balanced composition of agricultural, maritime, and urban people. Thus the tribes—which henceforth have their "headquarters" in the city of Athens—become neutral as to territorial or professional particularities; they are clearly political units.

What we have here is the creation of a properly political social space, founded on social (economic) and geographical elements, but not *determined* by these. No phantasm of "homogeneity" here: an articulation of the citizen body within a political perspective is created and superimposed on the "prepolitical" articulations without crushing them. This articulation obeys strictly political imperatives: equality of power sharing on the one hand, unity of the body politic (as against "particular interests") on the other.

The same spirit is exemplified by a most striking Athenian disposition (Aristotle, *Politics*, 1330 a 20): when the εκκλησία deliberates on matters entailing the possibility of a conflict, such as a war with a neighboring πόλις, the inhabitants of the frontier zone are excluded from the vote. For they could not vote without their particular interests overwhelming their motives, while the decision must be made on general grounds only.

This again shows a conception of politics diametrically opposed to the modern mentality of defense and the assertion of "interests." Interests have, as far as possible, to be kept at bay when political decisions are made. (Imagine the following disposition in the U.S. Constitution: "Whenever questions pertaining to agriculture are to be decided, senators and representatives from predominantly agricultural States cannot participate in the vote.") At this point one may comment on the ambiguity of Arendt's position concerning what she calls "the social." She rightly saw that politics is destroyed when it becomes a mask for the defense and assertion of "interests." The political space is then hopelessly fragmented. But *if* society is, in reality, strongly divided along conflicting "interests"—as it is today—insistence on the autonomy of politics becomes gratuitous. The answer, then, is not to ignore the "social," but to change it so that the conflict of "social"—that is, economic—interests ceases to be the dominant factor in shaping political attitudes. If this is not done, the present situation among Western societies results: the decomposition of the body politic and its fragmentation into lobbies. In this case, as the "algebraic sum" of opposing interests is very often zero, the consequence is political impotence and aimless drift, such as is observed today.

The unity of the body politic has to be preserved even against extreme forms of *political* strife. This is, to my mind, the meaning of the Athenian law on ostracism (not the usual interpretation, which sees in it a safeguard against would-be tyrants). In Athens political division and antagonism should not be allowed to tear the community apart; one of the two opposing leaders must go into temporary exile.

General participation in politics entails the creation for the first time in history of a *public space*. The emphasis Arendt has put on this, her elucidation of its meaning, is one of her outstanding contributions to the understanding of Greek institutional creation. I will confine myself, therefore, to a few additional points.

The emergence of a public space means that a political domain is created which "belongs to all" (τὰ κοινά)[24] The "public" ceases to be a "*private*" affair—of the king, the priests, the bureaucracy, the politicians, and the experts. Decisions on common affairs have to be made by the community.

But the essence of the public space does not refer only to "final decisions"; if it did, it would be more or less empty. It refers as well to the presuppositions of the decisions, to everything that leads to them. Whatever is of importance has to appear publicly. This is, for example, effectively realized in the *presentation* of the law: laws are engraved in marble and publicly exposed for everybody to see. But much more importantly, law materializes in the discourse of the people, freely talking to each other in the ἀγορά about politics and about everything they care about before deliberating in the εκκλησία. To understand the tremendous historical change involved, one only has to contrast this with the typical "Asiatic" situation.

This is equivalent to the creation of the possibility—and actuality—of free speech, free thinking, free examination and questioning without restraint. It establishes λόγος as circulation of speech and thought within the community. It accomplishes the two basic traits of the citizen already mentioned: ἰσηγορία, the right for all equally to speak their minds, and παρρησία, the commitment for all to really speak their minds concerning public affairs.

It is important to stress here the distinction between the "formal" and the "real." The existence of a public space is not just a matter of legal provisions guaranteeing rights of free speech, etc. Such provisions are but conditions for a public space to exist. The important question is: what are the people actually doing with these rights? The decisive traits in this respect are courage, responsibility, and shame (αἰδώς, αἰσχύνη). Lacking these, the "public space" becomes just an open space for advertising, mystification, and pornography—as is, increasingly, the case today. Against such development, legal provisions are of no avail, or produce evils worse than the ones they pretend to cure. Only the education (παιδεία) of the citizens as citizens can give valuable, substantive content to the "public space." This παιδεία is not primarily a matter of books and academic credits. First and foremost, it involves becoming conscious that the πόλις is also oneself and that its fate also depends upon one's mind, behavior, and decisions; in other words, it is participation in political life.

Equally important, hand in hand with the creation of a public space goes the creation of a *public time*. By this I do not mean just "social," "calendar" time, a system of sociotemporal benchmarks, which, of course, already exists everywhere. I mean the emergence of a dimension where the collectivity can inspect its own past as the result of its own actions, and where an indeterminate future opens up a domain for its activities. This is the meaning of the creation of historiography in Greece. It is a striking fact that historiography properly speaking has existed only during two periods of human history: in ancient Greece, and in modern Europe—that is, in the cases of the two societies where questioning of the existing institutions has occurred. In other societies, there is only the undisputed reign of tradition, and/or simple "recording of events" by the priests or the chroniclers of the kings. But Herodotus starts with the declaration that the traditions of the Greeks are not trustworthy. The disruption of tradition and critical inquiry into "true causes" of course go together. Moreover, this knowledge of the past is open to all. Herodotus, for example, is reported to have read his *Histories* to the Greeks assembled for the Olympic games (*si non e vero, e ben trovato*). And the Funeral Speech of Pericles contains a survey of the history of the Athenians from the viewpoint of the spirit of the activities of the successive generations—a survey leading up to the present and clearly pointing toward new things to be done in the future.

What are the limits of political action—the limits of autonomy? If the law is God-given, or if there is a philosophical or scientific "grounding" of substantive political truths (with Nature, Reason, or History as ultimate "principle"), then there exists an extrasocial standard for society. There is a norm of the norm, a law of the law, a criterion on the basis of which the question of whether a particular law (or state of affairs) is just or unjust, proper or improper, can be discussed and decided. This criterion is given once and for all and, *ex hypothesi*, does not depend upon human action.

Once it is recognized that no such ground exists, either because there is a separation between religion and politics, as is, imperfectly, the case in modern societies, or because, as in Greece, religion is kept strictly at bay by political activities, and once it is also recognized that there is no "science," no ἐπιστήμη or τέχνη, of political matters, the question of what a just law is, what justice is—what "the proper" institution of society is—opens up as a genuine, that is, interminable, question.

Autonomy is only possible if society recognizes itself as the source of its norms. Thus society cannot evade the question: why this norm rather than that?—in other words, it cannot evade the question of justice by answering, for example, that justice is the will of God, or the will of the tsar, or the reflection of the relations of production. Neither can it evade the question of *limits* to its actions. In a democracy, people *can* do anything—and must know that they *ought not* to do just anything. Democracy is the regime of self-limitation; therefore it is also the regime of historical risk—another way of saying that it is the regime of freedom—and a tragic regime. The fate of Athenian democracy offers an illustration of this. The fall of Athens—its defeat in the Peloponnesian War—was the result of the ὕβρις of the Athenians. Ὕβρις does not simply presuppose freedom; it presupposes the absence of fixed norms, the essential vagueness of the ultimate bearings of our actions. (Christian sin is, of course, a heteronomous concept.) Transgressing the law is not ὕβρις; it is a definite and limited misdemeanor. Ὕβρις exists where self-limitation is the only "norm," where "limits" are transgressed which were nowhere defined.

The question of the limits to the self-instituting activity of a community unfolds in two moments. Is there any intrinsic criterion of and for the law? Can there be an effective guarantee that this criterion, however defined, will not be transgressed?

With the move to fundamentals, the answer to both questions is a definite *no*. There is no norm of norms which would not itself be a historical creation. And there is no way of eliminating the risks of collective ὕβρις. Nobody can protect humanity from folly or suicide.

Moderns have thought—have pretended—that they have found the answer to these two questions by fusing them into one. This answer would be the "Constitution" as a fundamental Charter embodying the norms of norms and defining particularly stringent provisions for its revision. It is hardly necessary to recall that this "answer" does not hold water either logically or effectively, that modern history has for two centuries now in all conceivable ways made a mockery of this notion of a "Constitution"; or that the oldest "democracy" in the liberal West, Britain, has no "Constitution" at all. It is sufficient to point to the shallowness and duplicity of modern thinking in this respect, as exemplified both in the field of international relations and in the arena of changes in political regimes. At the international level, despite the rhetoric of professors of "International Public Law," there is in fact no law but the "law of force," that is, there is a "law" as long as matters are not really important—as long as you hardly need a law. The "law of force" also rules concerning the establishment of a new "legal order" within a country: "a victorious revolution creates right" is the dictum which almost all teachers of international public law avow, and all countries follow in practice. (This "revolution" need not be, and usually is not, a revolution properly speaking; most of the time, it is a successful *Putsch*.) And, in the European experience of the last sixty years, the legislation introduced by "illegal" and even "monstrous" regimes has always been maintained in its bulk after their overthrow.

The very simple point here is of course that in the face of a historical movement which marshals *force*—be it by actively mobilizing a large majority or a passionate and ruthless minority in the forefront of a passive or indifferent population, or be it even just brute force in the hands of a group of colonels—legal provisions are of no avail. If we can be reasonably certain that the reestablishment of slavery tomorrow in the United States or in a European country is extremely improbable, the "reasonable" character of our forecast is *not* based on the existing laws or constitutions (for then we would be simply idiotic), but on a judgment concerning the active response of a huge majority of the people to such an attempt.

In Greek practice and thinking the distinction between "constitution" and "law" does not exist. The Athenian distinction between laws and decrees of the εκκλησία (ψηφίσματα) did not have the same formal character and in fact disappeared during the fourth century. But the question of self-limitation was dealt with in a different (and, I think, more profound) way. I will consider only two institutions related to this problem.

The first is an apparently strange but fascinating procedure called γραφὴ παρανομόν (accusation of unlawfulness).[25] The procedure can be briefly described as follows. You have made a proposal to the εκκλησία, and this proposal has been voted for. Then another citizen can bring you before a court, accusing you of inducing the people to vote for an unlawful law. You can be acquitted or convicted—and in the latter case, the law is annulled. Thus you have the right to propose anything you please, but you have to think carefully before proposing something on the basis of a momentary fit of popular mood and having it approved by a bare majority. For the action would be judged by a popular court of considerable dimensions (501, sometimes 1,001 or even 1,501 citizens sitting as judges), drawn by lot. Thus, the δῆμος was appealing against itself in front of itself: the appeal was from the whole body of citizens (or whichever part of it was present when the proposal in question was adopted) to a huge random sample of the same body sitting after passions had calmed, listening again to contradictory arguments, and assessing the matter from a relative distance. Since the source of the law is the people, "control of constitutionality" could not be entrusted to "professionals"—in any case, the idea would have sounded ridiculous to a Greek—but only to the people themselves acting in a different guise. The people say what the law is; the people can err; the people can correct themselves. This is a magnificent example of an effective institution of self-limitation.

Tragedy is another institution of self-limitation. People usually speak of "Greek tragedy," but there is no such thing. There is only *Athenian* tragedy. Only in the city where the democratic process, the process of self-institution, reached its climax, only there could tragedy (as opposed to simple "theater") be created.

Tragedy has, of course, many layers of signification, and there can be no question of reducing it to a narrow "political" function. But there is certainly a cardinal political dimension to tragedy, not to be confused with the "political positions" taken by the poets, not even with the much commented upon (rightly, if insufficiently) Aeschylean vindication of public justice against private vengeance in the *Oresteia*.

The political dimension of tragedy lies first and foremost in its ontological grounding. What tragedy, not "discursively" but through *presentation*, gives to all to see, is that Being is Chaos. Chaos is exhibited here, first, as the absence of order *for* man, the lack of positive correspondence between human intentions and actions, on one hand, and their result or outcome, on the other. More than that, tragedy shows not only that we are not masters of the consequences of our actions, but that we are not even masters of their *meaning*. Chaos is also presented as Chaos *in* man, that is, as his ὕβρις. And the ultimately prevailing order is, as in Anaximander, order through catastrophe—a "meaningless" order. From the universal experience of catastrophe stems the fundamental *Einstellung* of tragedy: universality and impartiality.

Arendt has rightly said that impartiality enters this world through the Greeks. This is already fully apparent in Homer. Not only can one not find in the Homeric poems any disparagement of the "enemy," the Trojans, for example, but the truly central figure in the *Iliad* is Hector, not Achilles, and the most moving characters are Hector and Andromach. The same is true for Aeschylus's *Persians*—a play performed in 472 B.C., seven years after the battle at Plataea, with the war still going on. In this tragedy, there is not a single word of hatred or contempt for the Persians; the Persian queen, Atossa, is a majestic and venerable figure, and the defeat and ruin of the Persians is ascribed exclusively to the ὕβρις of Xerxes. And in his *Trojan Women* (415 B.C.), Euripides presents the Greeks as the cruelest and most monstrous beasts—as if he were saying to the Athenians: this is what you are. Indeed, the play was performed a year after the horrible massacre of the Melians by the Athenians (416 B.C.).

But perhaps the most profound play, from the point of view of tragedy's political dimension, is *Antigone* (442 B.C.). The play has been persistently interpreted as a tract against human and in favor of divine law, or a least as depicting an unsurmountable conflict between these two principles (or between "family" and "State," as in Hegel). This is indeed the manifest content of the text, repeated again and again. Since the spectators cannot fail to "identify" with the pure, heroic, helpless, and desperate Antigone against the hard-headed, authoritarian, arrogant, and suspicious Creon, they find the "thesis" of the play clear. But the meaning of the play is multilayered and the standard interpretation misses what I think is most important. A full justification of the interpretation I propose would require a complete analysis of the play, which is out of the question here. I will only draw attention to a few points. The insistence on the obvious—and rather shallow—opposition between human and divine law forgets that for the Greeks to bury their dead is *also* a human law, as to defend one's country is *also* divine law (Creon mentions this explicitly). The chorus oscillates from beginning to end between the two positions, always putting them on the same plane. The famous hymn (v. 332–75) to the glory of man, the builder of cities and creator of institutions, ends with praise for the one who is able to *weave together* (παρείρειν) "the laws of the land and the justice of gods to which he has sworn" (cf. also v. 725: "well said from both sides"). Antigone's upholding of "divine law" is remarkably weakened by her argument that she did what she did because a brother is irreplaceable when one's parents are dead, and that with a husband or a son the situation would have been different. To be sure, neither the divine nor the human law regarding the burial of the dead recognizes such a distinction. Moreover, what speaks through Antigone, here and throughout the play, more than respect for the divine law, is her passionate love for her brother. We need not go to the extremes of interpretation and invoke incestual attraction, but we certainly must remember that the play would not be the masterpiece it is if Antigone and Creon were bloodless representatives of principles and not moved by strong passions—love for her brother in Antigone's case, love for the city *and* for his own power, in Creon's case. Against this passionate background, the characters' arguments appear additionally as rationalizations. Finally, to present Creon as unilaterally "wrong" goes against the deepest spirit of tragedy, and certainly of Sophoclean tragedy.

What the final verses of the chorus (v. 1348–55) glorify is not divine law, but φρονεῖν, an untranslatable word, unbearably flattened in its Latin rendering by *prudentia*. The chorus lauds φρονεῖν, advises against impiety, and reverts again to φρονεῖν, warning against "big words" and the "ὑπέροχοι," the excessively proud.[26] Now the content of this φρονεῖν is clearly indicated in the play. The catastrophe is brought about because *both* Creon *and* Antigone insist on their own reasons, without listening to the reasons of the other. No need to repeat here Anitgone's reasons; let us only remember that Creon's reasons are irrefutable. No city can exist—and therefore, no gods can be worshipped—without νόμοι; no city can tolerate treason and bearing arms against one's own country in alliance with foreigners out of pure greed for power, as Polynices did. Creon's own son, Aimon, clearly says that he cannot prove his father wrong (v. 685–6); he voices the play's main idea when he begs Creon not to μόνος φρονεῖν, "not to be wise alone" (v. 707–9).

Creon's is a political decision, taken on very solid grounds. But very solid political grounds can turn out to be very shaky, if they are only "political." To put it in another way, precisely because of the totalistic character of the domain of politics (in this case, inclusive of decisions about burial and about life and death), a correct political decision must take into account all factors, beyond the strictly "political" ones. Even when we think, on the best of rational grounds, that we have made the right decision, this decision may turn out to be wrong, and catastrophically so. Nothing can guarantee a priori the correctness of action—not even reason. And above all, it is folly to insist on μόνος φρονεῖν, "being wise alone."

Antigone addresses itself to the problem of political action in terms which acquire their acute relevance in the democratic framework more than in any other. It exhibits the uncertainty pervading the field, it sketches the impurity of motives, it exposes the inconclusive character of the reasoning upon which we base our decisions. It shows that ὕβρις has nothing to do with the transgression of definite norms, that it can take the form of the adamant will to apply the norms, disguise itself behind noble and worthy motivations, be they rational or pious. With its denunciation of the μόνος φρονεῖν, it formulates the fundamental maxim of democratic politics.[27]

What is the "object" of autonomous self-institution? This question may be rejected at the outset if one thinks that autonomy—collective and individual freedom—is an end in itself, or that once significant autonomy has been established in and through the political institution of society, the rest is no more a matter of politics but a field for the free activity of individuals, groups, and "civil society."

I do not share these points of view. The idea of autonomy as an end in itself would lead to a purely formal, "Kantian" conception. We will autonomy both for itself and in order to be able *to do*. But to do what? Further, political autonomy cannot be separated from "the rest," from the "substance" of life in society. Finally, a very important part of that life concerns common objectives and works, which have to be decided in common and therefore become objects of political discussion and activity.

Arendt did have a substantive conception of what democracy—the πόλις—was about. For her, the value of democracy derived from the fact that it is the political regime in which humans can reveal who they are through deeds and speech. To be sure, this element was present and important in Greece—but not only in democracy. Arendt (after Jacob Burckhardt) rightly emphasized the agonistic character of Greek culture in general—not only in politics but in all spheres, and one should add, not only in democracy but in all cities, Greeks cared above all for κλέος and κῦδος and the elusive immortality they represented.

However, the reduction of the meaning and purposes of politics and of democracy in Greece to this element is impossible, as the foregoing brief account, I hope, makes clear. Moreover, it is surely very difficult to defend or support democracy on this basis. First, though of course democracy more than any other regime allows people to "manifest" themselves, this "manifestation" cannot involve everybody—in fact not even anybody apart from a tiny number of people who are active and deploy initiative in the political field as narrowly defined. Second, and more importantly, Arendt's position defers the crucial question of the content, the substance, of this "manifestation." To take it to extremes, surely Hitler and Stalin and their infamous companions have revealed who they were through deeds and speech. The difference between Themistocles and Pericles, on the one hand, and Cleon and Alcibiades on the other, between the builders and the gravediggers of democracy, cannot be found in the sheer fact of "manifestation," but in the content of this manifestation. Even more so, it is precisely because for Cleon and Alcibiades, the only thing that mattered was "manifestation" as such, sheer "appearance in the public space," that they brought about catastrophe.

The substantive conception of democracy in Greece can be seen clearly in the entirety of the *works* of the πόλις in general. It has been explicitly formulated with unsurpassed depth and intensity in the most important political monument of political thought I have ever read, the Funeral Speech of Pericles (Thuc. 2, 35–46). It will always remain puzzling to me that Arendt, who admired this text and supplied brilliant clues for its interpretation, did not see that it offers a *substantive* conception of democracy hardly compatible with her own.

In the Funeral Speech, Pericles describes the ways of the Athenians (2, 37–41) and presents in a half-sentence (beginning of 2, 40) a definition of what is, in fact, the "object" of this life. The half-sentence in question is the famous φιλοκαλοῦμεν τε γὰρ μετ᾽ εὐτελείας καὶ φιλοσοφοῦμεν ἄνευ μαλακίας. In "The Crises of Culture" Arendt offers a rich and penetrating commentary of this phrase. But I fail to find in her text what is, to my mind, the most important point.

Pericles' sentence is impossible to translate into a modern language. The two verbs of the phrase can be rendered literally by "we love beauty . . . and we love wisdom . . . ," but the essential would be lost (as Arendt correctly saw). The verbs do not allow this separation of the "we" and the "object"—beauty or wisdom—external to this "we." The verbs are not "transitive," and they are not even simply "active": they are at the same time "verbs of state." Like the verb *to live*, they point to an "activity" which is at the same time a way of being or rather *the* way by means of which the subject of the verb *is*. Pericles does not say we love beautiful things (and put them in museums), we love wisdom (and pay professors or buy books). He says we *are* in and by the love of beauty and wisdom and the activity this love brings forth, we live by and with and through them—but far from extravagance, and far from flabbiness.[28] This is why he feels able to call Athens παίδευσις—the education and educator—of Greece.

In the Funeral Speech, Pericles implicitly shows the futility of the false dilemmas that plague modern political philosophy and the modern mentality in general: the "individual" versus "society," or "civil society" versus "the State." The object of the institution of the πόλις is for him the creation of a human being, the Athenian citizen, who exists and lives in and through the unity of these three: the love and "practice" of beauty, the love and "practice" of wisdom, the care and responsibility for the common good, the collectivity, the πόλις ("they died bravely in battle rightly pretending not to be deprived of such a πόλις, and it is understandable that everyone among those living is willing to suffer for her," 2, 41). Among the three, there can be no separation; beauty and wisdom such as the Athenians loved them and lived them could exist only in Athens. The Athenian citizen is not a "private philosopher" or a "private artist" but a citizen for whom philosophy and art have become ways of life. This, I think, is the real, materialized, answer of ancient democracy to the question about the "object" of the political institution.

When I say that the Greeks are for us a germ, I mean, first, that they never stopped thinking about this question: what is it that the institution of society ought to achieve? And second, I mean that in the paradigmatic case, Athens, they gave this answer: the creation of human beings living with beauty, living with wisdom, and loving the common good.

Paris and New York, March 1982–June 1983

NOTES

The principal ideas found in this article were presented for the first time in a lecture given on October 29, 1979, to a seminar at the Max Planck Institute in Starnberg led by Jürgen Habermas. Johann Arnason, Ernst Tugendhat, and Albrecht Wellmer were among the participants. Since then these ideas have been at the center of my work in my seminar at the Ecole des Hautes Etudes en Sciences Sociales in Paris, and they provided the substance for a course in August 1982 at the University of São Paulo, a seminar in April 1985 at the University of Rio Grande do Sul (Porto Alegre), and several other presentations. The text published here is that of a lecture read on April 15, 1982, in New York, during one of the Hannah Arendt Memorial Symposia in Political Philosophy organized by the New School for Social Research which dealt with the origins of our institutions. The original English version was published in the *Graduate Faculty Philosophy Journal* of the New School, 9, no. 2 (Fall 1983), pp. 79–115. A French translation appeared in my *Domaines de l'homme. Les carrefours du labyrinthe II* (Paris, 1986), pp. 261–306.

1. Karl Marx wrote in the *Introduction to a Critique of Political Economy* that Greek art presented an *inaccessible* model, not insuperable or insurmountable but *inaccessible.*

2. Hannah Arendt, "The Concept of History," *Between Past and Future* (New York, 1968), p. 51.

3. Perhaps needless to add, this in itself does not allow any "practical" or "political" conclusions.

4. Linguists seem to recognize and register some four thousand languages extant today. Though there is of course no one-to-one correspondence between language and total institution of society, this gives a rough indication of the order of magnitude of different types of society that have existed in the recent past.

5. Relying on "rationality" alone has led, e.g., to the nineteenth-century characterizations of primitive religion and myth as sheer nonsense (or "junk," as Marx and Engels wrote)—or to contemporary structuralism and other procrustean beds.

6. A "central limit," one would say in mathematics. (Note added in 1986.)

7. It is true that Kant, in his initial plans dating back to 1771, when he projected writing a work entitled "Limits of Sensibility and Reason," proposed to treat in the same framework theoretical reason, ethics, and taste; but the way in which the last of these objectives was realized in his 1790 book and especially in connection with the "teleology of nature" seems to me to justify the remarks in the text. (Note added in 1986.)

8. The problem is already stated in the *Critique of Pure Reason*, A 653–54. See *Critique of Judgment*, Introduction, V, and VI, where the expression "happy accident" (*glücklicher Zufall*) occurs.

9. A useful and informative recent survey of the widespread preoccupation of that period with the work of art and imagination is given by James Engell, *The Creative Imagination* (Cambridge, Mass., 1981).

10. Richard Bernstein rightly and clearly stressed this point in "Judging—the Actor and the Spectator," a paper delivered at the Conference on the Work of Hannah Arendt in New York in October 1981.

11. See Michael Denneny, "The Privilege of Ourselves: Hannah Arendt on Judgment," in *Hannah Arendt: The Recovery of the Public World*, ed. M. A. Hill (New York, 1979), pp. 259 and 273. See also the exchange between Hans Jonas and Hannah Arendt, pp. 311–15.

12. In fact, even in the theoretical field this is not so; but I cannot enter here into the question of the social-historical conditions of thought. Suffice it to say that "objective universal validity," as Kant conceives of it, is virtually equivalent to the perfect isolation or disembodiment of "theoretical consciousness," and thus to some sort of solipsism. For instance, Kant completely ignores the inseparability of thought and language as a *theoretical* (not "psychological") problem. At the same time, he asserts (in the third *Critique*)—strangely enough, from the "transcendental" point of view—that without communication there is no knowledge.

13. A well-known story reports that two centuries ago the Chinese emperor turned down the proposal of an English embassy for a trade treaty with the remark, "I can well see why the barbarians would wish to have our products, but I do not see how they could offer a worthwhile equivalent."

14. On these terms and the problem itself, see Cornelius Castoriadis, *Imaginary Institution of Society*, tr. Kathleen Blamey (Cambridge, Mass., 1987), ch. 5.

15. Only once (§ 49) does Kant speak of *schöpferische Einbildungskraft*, "creative imagination." As this expression was current in the eighteenth century, Kant's insistence on always calling the imagination *productive* cannot be fortuitous.

16. Of course, the work of art is also a "presentation" of the ideal of morality. But in the present context, this notion is irrelevant. Moreover, it can be taken into consideration only if one accepts Kant's metaphysics. This follows from the supersensible character of that which is to be presented (*dargestellt*). Finally, we have an apparent *aporia*: any *Darstellung* (by artistic genius) is adequate; any *series of Darstellungen* is insufficient, since it never "exhausts," so to speak, that which is to be presented. One can see here another important ground of the dependence of Kant's aesthetics (and theory of judgment) on his metaphysics—comparable to the one in the *Critique of Practical Reason*: the infinite or insuperable distance between humanity and the Idea—and the (vain) attempt at once to maintain *and* cover it through some sort of infinite walk. In the *Critique of Practical Reason* this leads, inter alia, to the nonsensical argumentation on the immortality of the soul. In the *Critique of Judgment* (where an "imminent" historical progression is clearly envisaged) it leads to the idea of an unending series of *Darstellungen*. The difference is that in the first case (moral action) we are permanently deficient (nobody is ever a saint, says the *Critique of Practical Reason*); in the second case (art) the work of genius is certainly not deficient. The point bears further elaboration, which

should take into account Kant's *Anthropologie*, and which cannot be given here. Let me add that, in truth, the absolute adequacy of the *chef d'oeuvre* is nothing but its presentation of the Abyss (the Chaos, the Groundless), and that the inexhaustibility of art is rooted in the ontological character of the Abyss as well as the fact that each culture (and each individual genius) creates its own way into the Abyss—the second being again a manifestation of the first.

17. See also Cornelius Castoriadis, "The Sayable and the Unsayable," *Crossroads in the Labyrinth*, tr. Martin H. Ryle and Kate Soper (Cambridge, Mass., 1984), in particular pp. 137–38.

18. This is also why he has to confine his insights on imagination to its strictly "individual-subjective" dimension. See Cornelius Castoriadis, "La découverte de l'imagination," *Libre* 3 (1978); reprinted in *Domaines de l'homme. Les carrefours du labyrinthe II* (Paris, 1986), pp. 327–63.

19. I cannot agree with Arendt's idea that in Greece legislative activity was a secondary aspect of politics. This would hold only in a limited sense of the term *legislative*. Aristotle counts thirteen "revolutions" in Athens, that is, changes in the fundamental ("constitutional") legislation.

20. Olof Gigon clearly established this in *Der Ursprung der griechischen Philosophie von Hesiod bis Parmenides* (Basel, 1945). (Note added in 1986.)

21. The meaning of Anaximander's fragment (Diels, B, 1) is clear, and "classical" historians of philosophy have, for once, interpreted it correctly. Heidegger's "interpretation" of it ("Der Spruch des Anaximander," in *Holzwege*) is, as usual, Heidegger dressed up as Anaximander.

22. Given the constraints of space, I will have to speak "statically" myself, ignoring the movement and considering only some of its most significant "results." I beg the reader to bear in mind this inevitable limitation.

23. Aristotle, *Constitution of the Athenians*, VIII, 5.

24. Something similar can be found in some savage societies, but it is confined to the handling of "current" affairs, since in these societies the (traditional) law cannot be called into question.

25. M. I. Finley stressed the importance and elucidated the spirit of this procedure in *Democracy, Ancient and Modern* (New Brunswick, 1973). See also V. Ehrenberg, *The Greek State*, 2d ed. (London, 1969), pp. 73, 79, 267, where two other important procedures or provisions similar in spirit are also discussed: ἀπάτη τοῦ δήμου (deceit of the δῆμος) and the exception τῶν νόμον μὴ ἐπιτήδειον εἶναι (inappropriateness of a law).

26. I must leave open here the question raised by Arendt's (and Hölderlin's) interpretation of these last verses (*The Human Condition*, p. 25, n. 8), which does not, in any case, create difficulties for my comment. Curiously, Michael Denneny in his excellent paper does not mention the translation offered in *The Human Condition* and supplies instead a different (oral) rendering by Arendt, which is totally unacceptable, both philologically and from the point of view of the play's whole meaning. See Denneny, pp. 268–69 and 274.

27. An additional support for my interpretation can be found at the end (v. 1065–75) of Aeschylus's *Seven against Thebes*. This is certainly an addition to the initial text, probably dating from 409–405 B.C. (Mazon, in the Budé edition, p. 103). This addition has been inserted to prepare for the performance of *Antigone* immediately afterward. It makes the *Seven* end with the two halves of the chorus divided, the one chanting that they will support those who are united with their blood (γενεά) because what the πόλις holds to be right is different at different times (i.e., the laws of the πόλις change though blood right is perennial), the other asserting their support for the πόλις and δίκαιον (i.e., right): a nonnegligible testimony of how Athenians at the end of the fifth century viewed the matter and the meaning of *Antigone*.

28. I follow the usual translation of εὐτέλεια. Arendt's rendering of this word, ending with the interpretation "we love beauty within the limits of political judgment," while not strictly impossible, is extremely improbable.

THREE

The Politics of the Χώρα

John Sallis

It belongs to the exemplary role accorded the Greeks in Hannah Arendt's work that she discovers in their political institutions and thought not only certain essential moments of political life that have subsequently been obscured but also the very operations that first obscured such moments and drove them to the margin of Western political thought. One such moment is action (πρᾶξις), which, according to Arendt's interpretation, Plato's thought submits to a fateful substitution. The substitution involves both a reduction and a subordination of action. It is a matter, first of all, of distinguishing knowledge from action in a way that gives knowledge primacy over action, substituting for a knowledge operative within action a knowledge that would precede action and determine it in advance. This shift is, in turn, supported by a referral of political action to the paradigm of making (ποίησις), in which a certain knowledge, a vision of what is to be made, always precedes the actual fabrication. Making is, then, in effect substituted for action—that is, action is reduced to a subordinate phase within making. It is the paradigm of making—that is, the very orientation to a paradigm to be held in view in such a way that one might fabricate a product that looks like the paradigm—it is this that comes to determine the orientation of subsequent political thought.

Arendt points to two effects of this orientation to making: first, it renders political thought essentially uptopian, directed primarily to the vision and elaboration of the paradigm; second, it produces a degradation of politics into a means by which to achieve a higher end, namely, the making or remaking of the πόλις in the image of the paradigm. Arendt draws special attention to the way in which such a portrayal of the realm of human affairs as a sphere of making can acquire a connection with violence: within such a purview violence can come to be glorified as the necessary means for remaking the πόλις or the state. Thus she recalls Marx's dictum that "violence is the midwife of every old society pregnant with a new one."[1]

No doubt Arendt is correct in tracing such effects back to Plato's thought and, specifically, to the prominent role that making (ποίησις) plays in that thought. And yet, when one returns to the Platonic text with these effects in mind, one cannot but be surprised at how openly that text also goes about limiting the hegemony of ποίησις. For example, in Book 10 of the *Republic* one finds a discussion in which Socrates introduces a certain differentiation: for each thing these are, he says, three arts, one that will use the thing, one that will make it, and one that will imitate it. Socrates insists also on a hierarchical ordering of these arts and, in particular, on the superiority of using over making:

> It is quite necessary, then, that the man who uses each thing be more experienced and that he report to the maker what are the good or bad points, in actual use, of the instrument he uses. For example, about flutes, a flute player surely reports to the flute-maker which ones would serve him in playing, and he will prescribe how they must be made, and the other will serve him. (601d–e)

Making is thus interrupted, limited, by a certain knowledge that can only come to it from outside its own sphere, a vision that only the user, not the maker himself, can provide. In most instances of course the using is itself, in turn, a kind of making: the flute player, who instructs the flute-maker as to how the flute is to be made, uses the flute in order, in turn, to produce music, to make beautiful sounds. Nonetheless, the knowledge that the flute player provides to the maker is not the same as that operative in his own production of beautiful sounds, even though he will indeed have learned through the practice of his music-making art how flutes ought to be made. The structure of making thus undergoes considerable complication: not only is it limited from above, receiving from the user its vision of the paradigm, but also within making as such there is a doubling of the operative forms of knowledge: each artisan is both maker and user and must both possess the vision of what is to be made and also have acquired through the practice of his art the vision to be communicated to the artisan below him in the hierarchy.

Yet, it is not only through the analysis of the order connecting different arts that the Platonic text exposes an operation that limits ποίησις. Nor is it a matter only of extending the hierarchies of arts up to their point of convergence in the statesman so as to reopen at that level the question of πρᾶξις, to reopen it by considering whether the statesman's action could ever be reappropriated once and for all to the sphere of ποίησις and statecraft submitted, without remainder, to the philosophical vision of the good. It is not only from within and from above that the Platonic text shows ποίησις to be subject to the operation of limits but also, indeed most powerfully and unretractably, from below. It is not only the freedom of action and use that interrupts and limits ποίησις but also, indeed first of all, a force of necessity to which ποίησις will always already have been submitted. The necessity is not that of a ruling paradigm and its law, but rather a necessity opposed to art and hence more like chance. It can be called the errant kind of cause, *errant* in various senses ranging from "wandering" to "straying," to "going astray," to "erring." Within a certain kind of discourse, so-called εἰκὼς λόγος, likely discourse in the sense of discourse on likenesses, on images—within such discourse this errant necessity is called mother, nurse, receptacle. But in the discourse that calls it by its proper name, it is called χώρα. That discourse—what I shall call Plato's chorology—occurs near the center of the dialogue *Timaeus*. Within that dialogue the chorology follows two other discourses: first, the extended introductory discourse in which Socrates and Critias, in turn, speak of politics; and then Timaeus' long discourse on the making of the cosmos. I shall undertake to show, at least in broadest outline, that in these discourses what may appear to be an unlimited affirmation of ποίησις is instead an interrogation of the limits of ποίησις. I want to show also that the chorology gathers what is disclosed in the discourses that precede it, that in thinking and saying the χώρα Plato thinks and says the limits of ποίησις and, hence, the limits that govern and in a sense threaten any political discourse oriented to ποίησις. I want thus to show that the *Timaeus* broaches a politics of the χώρα.

Yet, what about the appearance of unlimited affirmation, the semblance that the history of Western thought has almost continuously translated into reality, into an allegedly Platonic origin of utopian political thought? What about Arendt's account of this history? If the Platonic texts indeed pose the limits of ποίησις, limits from within, from above, and especially from below, how can Plato's thought have had the effect described so accurately and convincingly in Arendt's discussions? How is it that ποίησις can have determined *without limit* the basic orientation of political thought in the lineage of Plato's *Republic*?

The utopian effect of the Platonic texts was a determined result, determined by a certain way of reading those texts, which is to say also a way of *not* reading, of refusing to read. The way of reading and not reading that produced the utopian effect was itself, in turn, determined by an orientation to a certain restricted economy, that is, by a demand that everything exposed by the reading be situated within that economy, appropriated to it. Even such submission to an economy has its Platonic precedent, at least if one grants with Arendt that Platonic thought extends the law of the household to the regulation of the πόλις at large.[2] But what is decisive in the economy that comes to regulate the history of the reading and nonreading of the Platonic texts is the reduction of the χώρα that it enforces. By reducing the χώρα , by excluding its power to limit ποίησις and to disrupt every unlimited affirmation of ποίησις, the operation of the economy serves to preclude the commencement of a politics of the χώρα.

It goes almost without saying that here I can hardly even begin the immense task of tracing the reading of the *Timaeus* and of marking the economic operation in that reading. For there is no text in the Western philosophical tradition that has been more continuously read or that has been more interwoven in the fabric of Western metaphysics. The *Timaeus* was a subject of debate among Plato's early successors in the Academy and of course for Aristotle. It was a subject of commentary by Plutarch, Plotinus, and Proclus, and it was widely known during the Middle Ages in the Latin translation by Chalcidius. The dialogue continued to be discussed up through Schelling and Hegel, and even quite recently by Heidegger and Derrida.

Let it suffice here merely to note a single passage from Aristotle and its remote echo in Hegel. In Book 4 of the *Physics* Aristotle writes:

> This is why Plato says in the *Timaeus* that matter and the χώρα are the same; for the receptive and the χώρα are one and the same. Although the manner in which he speaks about the receptive in the *Timaeus* differs from that in the so-called *Unwritten Teachings*, nevertheless he declares that place and the χώρα are the same. (209b11–16)

The passage is remarkable for its lack of correspondence with the text of the *Timaeus.* It poses three identifications: that the receptive (μεταληπτικόν) and the χώρα are the same; that matter (ὕλη) and the χώρα are the same; and that place (τόπος) and the χώρα are the same. Of these three identifications, only the first has any justification in the text of the *Timaeus* and then only if one erases any difference that might be connoted between μεταληπτικόν and the Platonic words δεχόμενον and ὑποδοχη. For the identification of the χώρα with matter (ὕλη) there is little textual warrant and certainly none that could justify a simple, straightforward identification: for though one of the images presented of the χώρα is that of the gold on which all figures may be impressed but which itself is none of these figures and can be none of them if it is to be equally receptive of all, this is only one image among several, to say nothing of that it is an *image of* the χώρα, not an identification of it as such. One cannot but suspect that the identification posed by Aristotle serves precisely to transpose into the economy of Aristotle's thought a moment of the Platonic discourse that would otherwise either simply escape or else disrupt that economy.

The third of the identifications is less obviously unjustified: one can indeed find numerous passages in the dialogues where χώρα is used in a sense closely allied to that of τόπος, and it is not surprising that English translators of the *Timaeus,* from Thomas Taylor on, have most often rendered χώρα as "place." The difficulty here is that the chorology—the scant half-page near the center of the *Timaeus*—insists on the differentiation between χώρα and τόπος. Speaking of the χώρα as itself withdrawing from speech, touching upon it as to be touched without sense and only by a sort of bastard reckoning, Timaeus says: "and looking toward which we are absorbed in a dream and affirm that it is necessary that all that is be somewhere in some place [τόπος] and occupy some χώρα" (52b). Whatever identification of χώρα and τόπος this passage may suggest is vigorously retracted as Timaeus continues: "Under this dreaming, we are not able to awaken and to distinguish all of these and others akin to them . . . and so to say the truth." In the dream, then, we conflate precisely what it is necessary in truth to differentiate; it is only in the dream that we identify χώρα and τόπος and believe that to think the χώρα is simply to affirm that everything that is is somewhere, in some place. The Aristotelian text too remains absorbed in this dream, appropriating the χώρα to τόπος, dreaming of a place that has a place within the economy of the *Physics,* offering only the slightest hint that matters might be somewhat different in the *Unwritten Teachings.*

Hegel, too, translates χώρα into place, the place (*Ort*) in which things are produced. Hegel uses the word *erzeugt*: "produced, fabricated" but also "procreated, begotten"—Hegel thus reinscribing in his text an oscillation that runs throughout the *Timaeus* and that reflects at the level of semantics one of the primary ways in which the dialogue brings ποίησις into question. Nonetheless, Hegel essentially repeats the Aristotelian reduction of the χώρα, translating it into "place" and even identifying it with "passive matter."[3] Little wonder that in reading the *Timaeus* Hegel can so easily recognize there what his *Logic* calls the concept, the idea—most notably in the world-soul's gathering of the cosmos into a whole.[4]

The enforcement of the reduction of the χώρα, the forcing of it into the economy of metaphysical thought, is thus carried out especially in and through translation, for example, in Chalcidius's translation of it as *locus* and in Thomas Taylor's rendering of it as "place." What is decisive is that translating χώρα—either within Greek or from Greek to another language—functions also as a way of saying what χώρα means. It serves as an instrument by which to forge, even if indirectly, a connection of the χώρα to a meaning, that is, to an intelligible εἶδος. To translate χώρα, for instance as "place," is to say that both words have the same semantic correlate, the same meaning, translation consisting in the move from one word to the other by way of the common meaning. To grant the possibility of translation is, then, to grant the legitimacy of bringing an eidetic determination to bear on the χώρα. But the χώρα, says Timaeus, is a third kind, distinct from the intelligible εἴδη and equally distinct from those things that are sensible and generated and that, sharing both name and looks with the intelligible, are subject to eidetic determination, that is, have meaning. The χώρα has no meaning, and to translate it, to submit it to eidetic determination, is to appropriate it to an economy of meaning, to violate it. Can it be that the entire history of the reading of the *Timaeus* has been haunted by this specter of violence?

In order to show how the *Timaeus* broaches a politics of the χώρα, one must reread outside all eidetic economy not only the chorology but also the other discourses insofar as they serve to expose the limits gathered into the χώρα. Let me turn, then, to the Platonic text and begin rereading it. Where is one to begin? Presumably at the beginning—following the injunction given in the *Timaeus*, though not at the beginning, the injunction: "With regard to everything it is important to begin at the natural beginning" (29b). But where is the natural beginning? Where is the beginning of nature, of the cosmos? Is it a beginning in time or a beginning of time? Or even a beginning that would precede the beginning of time? *What* is the natural beginning? Is the beginning, the ἀρχή, a *what* at all? Is the χώρα not also a beginning? Is it not indeed *the* natural beginning, the beginning of nature, the mother? The question of beginning thus leads directly into the thick of the questioning that the dialogue pursues. In the *Timaeus* nothing is more vigorously interrogated than the question of the beginning.

But it is a question, first of all, of the beginning *of the text*. One ought to begin reading at the beginning of the text, at its natural beginning. But can one ever be certain where a text begins? Can one ever establish with assurance its *natural* beginning, bringing the concept of nature to bear upon discourse, to which one usually opposes it. Is there anything natural about discourse, about a text? Is even its linearity something that would allow one to establish its natural beginning? Can one be certain that the beginning of the text does not require a retrospective activation by what comes later in the linear order of the text? Are there not texts that begin only after having already begun? Is the *Timaeus* perhaps such a text? Is it perhaps only in doubling back to the beginning that one can finally read with understanding those opening words by Socrates, that enigmatic counting: one, two, three . . . ? Can one ever be assured of being released from the need for double reading?

There is little assurance, then, in beginning at or near the beginning of the text, though it is here that I shall in fact begin rereading. Even less so in the case of the *Timaeus*: for in the opening remarks by Socrates and the very brief discussion that follows upon them, what seems to be a beginning is collapsed by a reference back to another beginning, the discussion on the previous day, which is to be continued in the present discussion. For purposes of that continuation Socrates complies with Timaeus's request that he recount that previous discussion, that other beginning, that he recount it from the beginning (ἐξἀρχῆς). This structure, a beginning collapsed by reference back to a prior beginning, is one that recurs in virtually every dimension of the *Timaeus*. It is, most notably, the structure by which the discourse comes to open upon the χώρα.

Socrates begins: "The main part of the discourse that I delivered yesterday was about the πολιτεία, what kind seemed to me best and from what kind of men it came" (17c). The discourse preceding the beginning of the *Timaeus* and now to be recounted is thus a discourse on the πολιτεία, a discussion of the constitution, the basic makeup, of the πόλις, a discourse on the political ordering of—let me say, cautiously, with reservations—the city. At least, this political discourse constitutes the main part of the discourse delivered on the previous day. One should note that the word translated as "the main part" (τὸ κεφάλαιον) means literally "what belongs to the head" (κεφάλή). In this regard one should recall the name of a character who speaks very near the beginning of the dialogue actually entitled πολιτεία (translated *Res publica*, *republic*): Cephalus was nothing but head, an old man who had lost all the desires of the body, one on the threshold of death. Especially if a discourse is supposed to have all the parts corresponding to those of a living being—to recall a well-known injunction from the *Phaedrus* (264c)—then one cannot but wonder about the discourse that Socrates is now to recount, since it is *only the head* of the discourse delivered on the previous day. One cannot entirely suppress one's suspicion about the capitalization with which Socrates begins, which is also a decapitating that leaves out of account, that refuses to recount, the rest of the discursive body.

Recounting the head of the discourse, Socrates speaks of the ordering of the city, its ordering according to τέχνη, according to the ποίησις carried out through the practice of the various arts, the τέχναι. As a site for the practice of τέχνη, it is essentially a *technical city*. Each citizen is to practice only his own art, the one to which he is best suited by nature. The best πολιτεία, the best ordering of the city, will be the one according to which each does what is proper to him. Socrates stresses that such propriety is especially imperative for those who are to defend the city. It is thus that they are to have everything in common, to have no private property, the pursuit of which would otherwise distract them from devotion to excellence in their one art, drawing them, for instance, into another, a money-making art that could not but impair their capacity to defend the city. In this best of cities, in order that it be the best of cities, there is to be no regard paid to sexual difference: women are also to be assigned their one sole art, and even those who become guardians are to be treated no differently from the men. Socrates then mentions procreation and, calling attention to the novelty of this proposal, declares that in this regard, too, all are to have all in common. Each should recognize all as his kinsmen, as brothers and sisters, as parents and grandparents, or as children and grandchildren, depending on age. The actual production of children is to be controlled so as to produce the best offspring; this will require that the rulers contrive means to control mating so that good mate with good and bad with bad.

One should note the word that Socrates uses in introducing these novel proposals regarding procreation: he says παιδοποιία, literally "child-production, child-making," as though procreation were a matter of ποίησις, of fabricating one's offspring. Indeed, the ordering of the relations between the guardians is such that what results is a kind of fabricated community. Where the fabrication fails to control fully the product, when, for instance, having contrived that the bad mate with the bad, having sent their offspring off to some other part of the city outside the citadel of the guardians, when it then turns out that, despite all that the art of child-production can do, some such offspring prove worthy, then those worthy ones must be brought back to the citadel and their opposites, those born of the good who have proved undeserving, must be put in their place outside. It is precisely in Socrates' reference to this place outside to which the undeserving will be sent—it is precisely here that the word χώρα occurs for the first time in the *Timaeus*. From the outset it is posed at the margin of what can be fabricated, marking the limit of ποίησις.

The community to be fabricated among the guardians, all having all in common, is to supplement the natural community, the familial community. The fabricated community is to compensate for the ills of the natural community and thus to constitute the citadel around which the best of cities will be built. In compensating for those ills, the supplementary, fabricated community will also tend to replace and displace the natural community, indeed so thoroughly that it will even come to be taken as the natural community, each thus regarding all as his actual kinsmen. The most telling index of this supplemental replacement and displacement of nature is its inevitably introducing into the community what the Greeks regarded as most contrary to nature, namely, incest. According to the fabricated kinship system, one will inevitably mate with one's kin, indeed in every case, since each is the kin of all; all mating will be tainted by incest. Furthermore, since the fabricated kinship system is to efface natural kinship, Socrates remarking explicitly that one is never to recognize one's own offspring, one can—and no doubt some will—happen to mate with a natural kinsman. And if the fabricated system is sufficiently effective in its work of effacement, one can—and no doubt some will—happen to mate with kin without the slightest knowledge that one is doing so. A community fabricated in the image of Oedipus. The best of cities transformed into a scene of tragedy.

Yet, it is not so much as a scene of tragedy that this city is inscribed in the Platonic texts but rather as a subject of comedy. The technical city is to be so rigorously ordered by τέχνη that even mating and procreation would be brought under control, as though these were only matters of the head, as though ἔρως could be brought under technical control and its disruptive power dissolved or at least marginalized, transferred to that place outside to which those are sent who, despite being offspring of the good, turn out to be underserving. In this capital city the eruption of ἔρως across the field of sexual difference would be submitted to technical control and sexual difference effectively effaced along with the natural family. The entire city would be brought under the order of ποίησις and made into a self-enclosed unity in which all needs would be supplied by the organization of the arts. At its center, in the citadel of the guardians who would protect it from any encroachments from outside, the rule of the order of ποίησις would be unlimited.

But it is a matter of decapitation, of a capital city that would be cut off from the erotic necessities of the body. As in a little comedy that breaks out in the course of Timaeus's long discourse on the making of the cosmos: the comedy depicts the prospect of the human head rolling along on the earth, coming upon heights and hollows of all sorts, and being at a loss as to how to climb over the heights and out of the hollows; thus it was, declares Timaeus, that a body was attached to the head as its vehicle of transportation (44d–e).

There is a proliferation of such comedy in the *Republic*. Though it is debatable whether, as Proclus thought, the dramatic dates of the *Republic* and the *Timaeus* are such that the *Republic* can simply be identified with that discourse of the previous day that Socrates recounts in the *Timaeus*, it is manifest that the account given in the *Timaeus* corresponds very closely to that building of the city in discourse that is carried out in Books 2–5 of the *Republic*—in other words, that in both dialogues it is the same city that is being fabricated in λόγος. In the *Republic* that discursive fabrication culminates in an extended comedy that is literally played out by Socrates and Glaucon: imagining the sight of women exercising naked with the men in the palaestras, Socrates refers to the jokes that would be made if gymnastic practices were so altered as to permit such sights; he speaks even of comedies regarding such things. He goes on to lay down a mock standard for comedy: "He is empty who . . . tries to produce laughter looking to any sight as ridulous other than the sight of the foolish and the bad" (452d). Then Socrates and Glaucon openly begin the performance, pretending to carry on a dialogue with those on the other side of the question, generating thus a dialogue within their dialogue. In the course of the comedy one hears, for example, the demand for "a community of pleasure and pain" (462b), a demand that can only be made by disregarding the irreducible singularity of the body and of the pleasures and pains that befall it, that is, by comically disregarding what can never in deed be disregarded. Sexual difference also enters into the play: the difference between men and women is—comically—reduced to something analogous to the difference between bald and long-haired men (454c). What is at issue is perhaps most succinctly expressed when, in response to Socrates' description of the prescribed mating practices, Glaucon insists on the difference between, as he says, geometrical necessities and erotic necessities. What the comedy of the city brings to light is the incapacity of the city—of this fabricated, capital city—to incorporate ἔρως and all that is linked to the erotic, that is, procreation, mating, birth, sexual difference, corporeity itself in its singularity. The comedy exposes this incapacity precisely by playing out the comic disregard for the erotic that such a city involves—that is, by exposing the disregard as comic. What is marked by the comedy and by the recounting of it in the *Timaeus* is the limit of ποίησις with respect to ἔρως.

As Socrates turns from recounting the discourse of yesterday to proposing what he would now like to hear in exchange, his language becomes highly erotic: he speaks of seeing beautiful creatures and being moved by the desire to behold them in motion. His proposal is, then, for a discourse that would depict the city in motion, that is, at war. One cannot help asking why beholding the city in motion means observing it in war. Why could it not be in motion without going to war? Why could it not be in motion simply by having all the arts properly ordered and actually being practiced within the city? At least one reason is that there is one art that can be practiced only in war, namely, that of the guardians. This is to say, then, that the city cannot remain simply a self-enclosed, ordered totality of artisans, that the technical closure of the city will never succeed. The city will always also be related to an outside, an other.

In this regard one should recall that in the *Republic* the only city that is a self-enclosed community of artisans is the first in that series of cities fabricated in λόγος, the simple city of artisans each practicing his art in harmony with the others, the city that the erotic Glaucon calls a "city of sows" (372d). On the other hand, as soon as the so-called "unnecessary desires" come into play, the city can no longer be simply unto itself; it cannot remain self-enclosed, self-sufficient. For in order to satisfy the additional desires, it has to expand, to take some land, some material resources, from another city and so go to war. This transition, one that presumably every city will in deed always already have made, points up the dependence of ποίησις on resources that it does not produce, its dependence on materials that lie outside the order of ποίησις.

In this regard one should also recall how the comedy of the city is briefly resumed at the end of Book 7 of the *Republic*. Likened by Glaucon to a sculptor producing fair men—and women, Socrates adds—Socrates proposes finally that the founding of the new city will require the expulsion of everyone who is more than ten years of age (540e-541a). In order that the ruler-sculptor be able to shape the city in the image of the paradigm constructed in discourse, it is necessary first to make it a city of children, who like the marble used by the sculptor are still sufficiently unformed and can provide the necessary human material for the political ποίησις. As if the citizens to be were raw material, various metals dug up from the earth, as in the noble lie that the rulers are to tell.

Socrates' discourse on the city, even simply as recounted, has the effect of marking three kinds of limits that bear upon political ποίησις: its limitation by ἔρως and all that is linked to the erotic; its limitation by the relation to an outside, to other cities; and its limitation by its dependence on material. Yet, it is not only in the opening discourse that such limits are exposed but also in virtually every discursive phase and level of the *Timaeus*, though of course in various connections and in ways determined by the topology of the dialogue as a whole.

Let me refer to only one other discourse, Timaeus' extended first discourse on the making of the cosmos; even with this discourse I shall have to proceed very schematically, marking only a few nodes of this intricately woven fabric, deferring the patient and careful reading that it by all means requires.

Timaeus tells how the god made the cosmos. The god he calls a δημιουργός, which means an artisan or craftsman, someone who makes things by practicing an art, like those artisans by each of whom a single art is to be practiced, at least according to the prescriptions expressed in the *Republic* and repeated in Socrates' recounting at the beginning of the *Timaeus.* Near the outset of the discourse on the cosmos Timaeus calls the god also τεκταινόμενος; he is a technician, a builder, a maker. It is hardly surprising, then, that Timaeus describes the schema of the god's making of the cosmos in a way that submits it quite precisely to the structure of ποίησις: in producing something an artisan looks to the paradigm and crafts the product according to the model, makes the thing in such a way as to make it look like the paradigm. Likewise with the divine artisan: he looks to the intelligible paradigm and makes a cosmos look like it, makes the cosmos in the image, into an image, of the paradigm.

This orientation to ποίησις governs the entire discourse. Let me, then, simply point to three nodes in the discourse where the limits of this governing schema are marked.

The first comes in Timaeus's account of how the body of the cosmos was made. In this production, Timaeus says, the god used up all the elements, so that nothing was left over from which another cosmos could be made. Thus it was assured that there would be only one cosmos, that the cosmos would be one. Furthermore, by thus leaving nothing outside, the god made the body of the cosmos immune to aging and to illness, which always come upon a body, says Timaeus, "from outside." Though he leaves it unsaid, it follows that the body would also be relieved of the possibility of death. Timaeus says too that the god made the body of the cosmos in the shape of a sphere, because a sphere is similar to itself, self-same, each point equidistant from the center. Thus it was made in the image of intelligible, i.e., utterly self-same, being. Timaeus continues, saying that the body of the cosmos was made smooth all around. Since there was nothing outside it to see or hear, it had no need of those openings to the outside that are called eyes and ears. Since there was no air surrounding it, it had no need of an organ of respiration by which otherwise air would be exchanged between inside and outside. It needed no hands either for grasping or for repelling someone, as in that violent clash with the other that erupts as war. Neither did it need feet with which to venture forth somewhere, to another place. On the contrary, shaping it into a perfectly smooth, uniform surface, the god spun it around uniformly in the same spot. Thus, the body of the cosmos was made self-sufficient, indeed so much so that, as Timaeus says, broaching a bit of comedy, "Nothing went out from it or came into it from anywhere, since there was nothing; it was designed to feed itself on its own waste and to act and be acted upon by itself and within itself" (33c–d). Thus, the body of the cosmos proves to be so self-enclosed that it feeds on its own excrement and affects, feels, only itself. In other words, it is the cosmic analogue of the city of artisans, completely self-enclosed, self-sufficient, lacking all relation to the outside, to an other. The little comedy serves to expose the very limit that has been comically disregarded, the limit constituted by the relation to the outside, to the other.

The second node to which I want to point consists in a certain oscillation in the discourse between the language of making, of fabrication, and that of procreation, of begetting. For example, the δημιουργός is called both the maker (ποιητής) and the father (πατήρ) of the cosmos. And, perhaps most obtrusively, the cosmos, this product of divine ποίησις, is characterized as a living being made in the image of the paradigm of living being—as if Timaeus had forgotten that living beings are, most certainly, begotten and born, not made. Yet, this forgetfulness is only a comic enactment serving to mark the irrepressible reference of the order of ποίησις to that of procreation and birth.

The third node occurs in the transition from Timaeus's first discourse to his subsequent discourse, and the limit marked here is what necessitates this transition. Though it goes unmentioned within the first discourse, what comes to be noted in the transition is that the god, in setting out to make the cosmos, simply uses the four elements that are somehow already there. These elements have to be brought to the order of ποίησις from outside that order. It is precisely this reference back to a precosmic origin that marks again a limit of ποίησις and that, at this point in the dialogue, necessitates the new beginning, the turn back to this beginning before the beginning, the turn that soon leads to the chorology.

In the chorology and the prelude to it, the limits of ποίησις exposed in the preceding discourses are gathered up and thought together in the χώρα. This third kind grants an abode (ἕδρα) to things of the second kind, things that come to be; it lets these phantoms, as Timaeus says, hold "to being in a certain way, on pain of being nothing at all" (52c); it lets them be outside the first kind, outside the sphere of the intelligible εἴδη, yet still hold to being, avoid being nothing at all. One could say—though at the risk of falling into the dream in which the χώρα is conflated with place—that the χώρα is the other, the outside, of being, that which makes externality possible, that which makes it possible for something outside being nonetheless to be. Furthermore, as the discourses immediately surrounding the chorology declare, the χώρα is the outside from which arises the material that must be taken over by the order of ποίησις. The χώρα is a receptacle filled in the beginning with indeterminate powers in flux; it is the mother from whom, then, the elements come to be born. And as mother and receptacle, the χώρα is outside the productive order; it is allied with birth, procreation, and all that is linked to ἔρως. Or rather, it is the outside of the productive order, that which limits ποίησις; it is a third kind that limits and yet also makes possible that circulation between the other two kinds that is called ποίησις.

The chorology would provide, then, a way of thinking the difference between a city built in λόγος and an actual city formed in the image of the paradigm. It would be a matter of thinking this difference, not merely as a gap between fact and ideal that could be gradually narrowed by political means, by employing politics as a productive means, or, as Arendt would say, degrading it into a means; to think this difference by way of the χώρα would be, rather, to think it as displacement to the outside of being, just as, according to the chorology, sensible things come to be outside of being, even if sharing both name and looks with being. It would be a matter of displacement into a place outside being, beyond being, even more, it seems, than the good is beyond being. It is a matter of displacement into place as such, a matter of the displacement engendered by place as such. Or rather, these are some of the things that one cannot but say, struggling to remain wakeful as one falls also back into the dream.

Such a thinking of difference, of displacement, would broach a politics of the χώρα. Is such a politics to be found in the Platonic texts? In the *Laws* perhaps? One cannot but be struck by the very frequent occurrence of the word χώρα in the *Laws*, its occurrence with incomparably greater frequency than in any other dialogue (including the *Timaeus*); and yet, for the most part the word seems to have settled back into its prephilosophical senses, e.g., land, territory, country, rather than calling forth the level of the discourse woven around the word in the chorology. But whether, in any case, the turn that the *Laws* takes to the second-best πολιτεία (739e), along with its insistence on a blending of monarchy and democracy—which the Athenian calls the two mothers of all constitutions (693d, cf. 756e)—whether these moves draw the lines of a politics of the χώρα is a question that could be answered only by a patient and careful reading of this vast text than I can undertake here. It must suffice to have raised the question.

For I want not to conclude without also raising the question of a politics of the χώρα today. If the bearing of thinking today is to be taken from the twisting free of Platonism decisively achieved in Nietzsche's thought and most pointedly expressed, according to Heidegger, in the text from *The Twilight of the Idols* entitled "How the True World Finally Became a Fable," then one cannot but wonder whether, now that the "true" world has finally become a fable, now that the intelligible paradigms have drifted away and become mere stories—one cannot but wonder whether our time is perhaps preeminently the time of a politics of the χώρα. Assuming that one can still think the outside of being after being has proved a vapor and a fallacy. Now there would be only the coming and going of images in the abode granted them by the χώρα. Now there would be only: images taking place—indeed in a place in which all the markers of certainty would have dissolved. Could one, then, begin to rethink the πολιτεία as such a place, withdrawn from the rule of any single, paradigmatic ἀρχή, withdrawn from monarchy—a place not to be possessed, appropriated, and in that sense occupied, an empty place, as, for example, in Lefort's schema of democracy, in which the exercise of power is subject to the procedures of periodic redistribution, so that those who exercise power do not thereby possess power, appropriate it to themselves, like a monarch. Or a dictator.[5]

In any case, a politics of the χώρα will never be a simple linear discourse, one that could be confident of having begun at the beginning, one that could with assurance dispense with all need to double back upon itself, taking back what it has said, even while granting that it will not be able to forgo saying such things again, falling back into the dream. But one thing is certain: a politics of the χώρα will never provide a prescription for making or remaking the πόλις; it will never issue in a paradigm in reference to which that degraded politics of which Arendt writes would then set about fabricating the πόλις, looking to the paradigm so as to make the χώρα in its image. Rather, a politics of the χώρα would look instead to the limits of every such ποίησις and would undertake to think the difference, the displacement, correlative to these limits.

Let me turn back, in conclusion, to Plato and to Arendt, in order not to conclude without having said something about the ancients and the moderns and the famous quarrel between them. In *The Life of the Mind* Arendt describes this quarrel in the following words: "The famous 'quarrel between the ancients and the moderns' actually turns on the question of what the aim of knowledge is; is it 'to save the phenomena,' as the ancients believed, or to discover the hidden functional apparatus which makes them appear?"[6] What I have sought to show is that Plato's *Timaeus* settles the quarrel by replacing its either/or with a both/and, that especially in the chorology Plato both saves the phenomena and discovers what makes them appear, that he does both in a way that undercuts even the traditional understanding of what it means to save the phenomena and to discover the hidden functional apparatus which makes them appear. What I have sought to show is that he saves the phenomena by thinking their displacement into the outside of being, where, even though they share both name and looks with the intelligible, they are utterly differentiated from it, distinctively phenomenal, saved as phenomena from appropriation to the intelligible; and that in thinking the χώρα he discovers the hidden apparatus—Timaeus calls the χώρα an invisible εἶδος—by which phenomena appear, by which they are granted the abode in which they can appear as phenomena distinct from the intelligible.

In the way in which it thus settles the quarrel—or, if you will, displaces it—one can discern the profound affinity that Plato's text has with the bearing of thinking today. Is it perhaps only after the end of Platonism that one can begin to read the *Timaeus*?

NOTES

1. Hannah Arendt, *The Human Condition* (Garden City, 1959), p. 204.
2. Ibid., p. 199 f.
3. G. W. F. Hegel, *Vorlesungen über die Geschichte der Philosophie* II, in *Werke* (Frankfurt, 1971), vol. 19, p. 100 f.
4. Ibid., p. 93.
5. See Claude Lefort, *Democracy and Political Theory*, tr. David Macey (Minneapolis, 1988), esp. 17–19.
6. Hannah Arendt, *The Life of the Mind* (New York, 1981), vol. 1, p. 53.

FOUR

Freedom of Choice and the Choice of Freedom on the Path to Democracy

Christian Meier

Classical antiquity has always played a crucial role in the thought of Hannah Arendt.[1] In it she found the origin of a tradition which, even after its termination in the nineteenth century, still determines our thinking, and whose concepts are still in use, although they are scarcely suited to the description of the phenomena of our times.

At the same time, however, Arendt found a foil in classical antiquity against which the peculiarity of modern thought and modern reality becomes considerably clearer. But she could do this only because she was also aware of the irretrievable peculiarity of classical antiquity, of its different quality, or what we would today call its alien quality. And yet, at the same time she occasionally appears to have been unable to resist the temptation of taking classical antiquity as her standard.

I would like to continue along this path. As a basis I am taking the statement with which Arendt opens her "Tradition and the Modern Age": "Our tradition of political thought has its definite beginning in the teachings of Plato and Aristotle. It came to a no less definite end in the theories of Karl Marx." At the beginning was Plato's allegory of the cave: the sphere of human affairs is dark and confused; only shadows can be detected. The philosopher is therefore compelled to turn away and to search for the light of true knowledge and ideas outside the cave within which everyone else is confined. Only out of such true knowledge can the standards for good politics, which are oriented to the truth, be revealed to him. At the end of this tradition is Marx's decision to turn away from philosophy in order to search for knowledge in the human world only, and above all to "realize" philosophy in politics.[2] Whereas Plato was searching for the one, true, unchanging order, which as an image of the order of the world should be as far removed as possible from the changes of time, Marx wanted to drive history forward. According to Arendt, this urge corresponded to a singular characteristic of the nineteenth century, namely, that it was then no longer possible to develop a political theory. Anyone who attempted one ended up with a philosophy of history.[3] It is as if we are all inescapably embedded, or let us say afloat, in great historical processes, so that it sometimes seems to be less important to know who we are than to know which way we are going. And Marx did indeed write that progress, that is the people, should be made the principle for a constitution: "Progress is then itself the constitution."[4]

I would like to say something about the preconditions for Plato's philosophy, so as to look at it not from the end but from the beginning, to denote its temporal position more precisely and to show more clearly the extent to which it negated the political thought and behavior of the Greeks. From this it may be seen that an attempt to put greater emphasis on the political can still begin with the Greeks—not, however, with Plato but with those before him. Perhaps it is true that after the great period between Plato and Marx, we are today closer to the beginning.[5]

Plato himself describes the impetus behind his philosophy as a feeling of giddiness which overcame him when he was confronted by the abuses of democracy and the attempts to replace it by an oligarchy. The arbitrariness and lack of principles in political activities seemed to him so boundless that he was compelled to search for a truth which must exist even if no one has knowledge of it, a truth to which all manner of politics could be rightly oriented.[6]

Plato's political philosophy is determined in part by an unusual combination of traditional and new, even revolutionary, ideas. Its guiding principle is an extraordinary scope of thoughts and actions, that is, *freedom of choice* between whole constitutions. This is extended to include the freedom to choose a completely different society with completely different people. We should take freedom of choice therefore as our starting point.

It is first testified to by Herodotus[7] in the famous debate between three successful Persian conspirators regarding which form of government their future empire should have: democracy, oligarchy, or monarchy. Herodotus begins with these words: "they discussed περὶ πάντων πραγμάτων," "the whole," the "entirety of things," of "political affairs." Appropriately, the first to speak proposes "to put matters in the midst of the Persians." They should all deliberate and decide. And he justifies this with the words ἐν γὰρ τῷ πολλῷ, ἔνι τὰ πάντα, "the whole is contained within the majority."

This debate certainly never took place among the Persians. It is obviously the product of Greek thinking. The following points are of interest here:

1. There are several forms of government to choose from, apparently as a free choice independent of the prevailing circumstances. Thus it is a question of which of the three is the best.

2. The three forms of government are distinguished according to the criterion of who rules. This does not refer to the qualifications of certain people but to the different number of people—one person, a few people, that is the aristocracy, or many or all the people.

3. When the question of power is put like this it concerns the whole, the "entirety of affairs."

This debate on forms of government is familiar to everyone who has been directly or indirectly concerned with ancient history and political theory. We know, therefore, that the Greeks had at least three forms of government between which to make a free choice. This can also be seen elsewhere than in Herodotus's *Histories*.[8]

Aristotle adopted a much more comprehensive approach. He was concerned not only with the question of which was the best form of government per se, but also with which was the best in the prevailing circumstances. For he knew how much social structure varied in the different cities. This meant that the forms of government have to be, as it were, tailor-made. Not every form of government can be chosen for every city.[9] In this respect, freedom of choice appears to have been limited. But it nevertheless existed in principle. The large numbers of insurrections and changes in government reported by Aristotle and others are singular proof of this.[10]

Yet, however self-evident it might appear to us to choose between forms of government according to the criterion of who rules, it is in fact not so. If it had been self-evident it would have been achieved before the Greeks and before the middle of the fifth century B.C. In fact, it was the outcome of one of the most far-reaching revolutions in world history.[11]

True, it was possible prior to the fifth century to change the political order, but only to a certain extent. A tyrant could, for example, seize power, possibly supported by large sections of the population.[12] Or an oligarchy could take its place. There were various ways of extending the sphere of influence of the people's assembly, or of an advisory body elected by it. But as far as we can tell, these sorts of variations only occurred as modifications within a single given order. Above all, there was no conception of political order determined on the basis of who ruled. Tyranny was a statement about the distribution (or nondistribution) of power. But this was only one of many factors of significance to the city. For the vying noblemen their inclusion or exclusion from power was naturally of crucial importance, but in the eyes of others—and particularly in the eyes of any objective observer—a tyrant might rule just as badly or as well as the aristocracy. The question of how power was wielded depended upon the institutions only to a negligible extent or as a result of chance. Correspondingly, the distribution of power had no connection with many other things which were of importance to the state of the city, such as the economic situation, the principles of law, the scope of action, the limits of arbitrariness, and the extent of the contrast between rich and poor.[13] A difference came to be understood between εὐνομία and δυσνομία, a well-fulfilled order and its opposite. The pattern of the order was by and large given; what was decisive were the modifications in which it found its expression.

In my view it is necessary to draw a clear distinction between the earlier and the later orders. It is not only the question of who rules which is crucial, but also the question of how far the sphere of influence of power, and indeed of politics, extends, and of whether its structure really has a decisive influence on what is thought to be important within a given order. When Aristotle discovers a history leading from monarchy via oligarchy and tyranny to democracy,[14] he overlooks a much more important dimension of change. This is the fact that alongside this development, the ability to determine one's own order grew up gradually and that it was not until democracy was reached that this ability comprised the whole of the order; and it was only then that all the fundamental principles of order were determined by those who ruled. Strictly speaking, Aristotle does not provide a history of the form of government but of the division of power, at the end of which history there is for the first time a form of government determined by who rules.

On the strength of the history of concepts, it would be possible to differentiate between nomistic forms of government (εὐνομία /δυσνομία) and cratistic forms of government (democracy, oligarchy, aristocracy, monarchy, etc.)[15] I would suggest that this should be done for Greek history to emphasize and clarify a decisive fact: in the earlier periods, order could only be understood as a comprehensive framework of conditions, comprising political, economic, ethical, even religious elements. Its prevailing norms were essentially traditional and consisted of customs and conventions, to which several elements of established law were gradually added. The order was essentially outside the sphere of disposal or determination. Besides this an ideal order was thought to preexist, which was a matter of truth and knowledge, not subject to a vote. Decrees and votes could at best serve to come closest to the general ideal.

It is consistent with this type of nomistic order that customs and conventions begin to ease and that society ceases to possess homogeneity of knowledge about what is just or unjust. The order then breaks down, but there is initially no way of replacing it with a new one.

Moreover, replacement will not be possible until, on the one hand, the old order is sufficiently shaken, and, on the other hand, a willingness to create a completely new order has developed in some part of society. The conflict between the rulers and those who are dissatisfied with them must be so serious that it affects the heart of the order and that the latter can and will supersede the former in the position of the ruler. Only the people could do that. In this way an order of the cratistic type emerges: it is usually founded on a sequence of decisions by which people gradually gain control of what becomes the constitution. From then on the ruling group of citizens is responsible for the entire order.

Of course by this time the Greeks understood order in a narrower sense than before: economic and ethical factors were no longer included; rather, it was limited just to political affairs, that is, the question of who has full political rights, how the body politic is organized and how political decisions are to be made. The economic crisis had at that time been overcome, legal security had become a function of the political order, and the range of political topics had been reduced in a process running parallel to the limitation of what was understood as order—and what was to be important as order in the future.[16] So, for example, a social policy in the sense of a molding of society existed before and to some extent after democracy, but not within it.

In the cratistic order, customs, traditions, and conventions were replaced by deliberately created institutions. To a certain extent the Greeks were able to reduce the dependency of the community on existing customs, partly because the institutions themselves were able to enforce a certain type of behavior. Whereas in the nomistic epoch, the execution of power could be extremely arbitrary, it was not until the cratistic epoch that freedom of action could extend to cover the molding of the entire body politic, particularly its core.[17] The extent of the sphere of action spreads. There, in any case, new opportunities of intervention in the established order presented themselves, even if later they would sometimes be overtaxed when faced with new demands.[18]

When a nomistic order is superseded by a cratistic order, there is a breach with far-reaching consequences in those traditional, or what Marx would call *naturwüchsig*, fundamental principles of society which had previously been valid (even if somewhat less effective in the final stages).

In Greece a tremendous rupture took place. Aeschylus felt compelled to reinterpret Zeus and his will: the deep cleft in earthly history made it necessary to create a history for the supreme God, and in an unprecedented manner.[19] At the same time there were completely new openings in art, since the artists gained an entirely new dimension of the portrayal of the human body. The rational system of bringing evidence before court developed out of rhetoric, and since consciousness of the extraordinary scope of methodical actions in all spheres was growing, people believed they had reached the zenith of artistic and scientific skills. Arguments could turn the weaker cause into the stronger one. And one began to believe that chance did not exist and was only an excuse for people whose calculations had gone wrong.[20]

To us the Greeks then still appear to have been restricted in their sphere of action, and we cannot forget that democracies at that time were only of benefit to those who were free citizens and men and not to slaves, noncitizens, and women. But as things stood then, an extremely swift and accelerating process of immense change took place, permitting the scope of human possibilities to multiply within a very short time.

The real turning point toward the cratistic order was the establishment of a consistent democracy in Athens in 461 B.C., a good generation before the birth of Plato. At that time the last political organ of the Athenian aristocracy was done away with. The people's assembly freed itself from the leadership of the aristocracy, even though those who functioned as politicians still continued to be members of the aristocracy or at least well-to-do people.[21]

When the question was no longer whether the mass of the population should have this or that right but rather who should really determine politics—the aristocracy or the people—the entire body politic had to be refounded on a new basis. It was now dependent on institutions to an extent that was completely new. As the phrase indicates, the mass of the people always outnumbers the rest. The reason why they so seldom attain power in world history must have to do with the fact that they usually do not find the institutions to provide a permanent structure for the strength which they virtually possess.

In the time of the Greeks, the masses did attain power. The extent to which this changed everything becomes particularly clear when we consider that the first democracies in world history were able to develop only as direct democracies.[22] Without being able to become professional politicians, the citizens had to participate in politics to an unprecedented degree and regularly, that is, regardless of how interesting the topics were. This was true at least for a large number of citizens. Toward the end of the sixth century a restricted circle, approximately the middle class, had been included in a preliminary stage of democracy, isonomy.[23] About 460 B.C. the circle of active participants was extended to comprise everyone, including the lowest classes.

How did this happen? And to what extent did the peculiarity of this development continue to have an influence on the democracy of the fifth century? One of the particular characteristics of the development of Greek culture is that it is the only culture of its kind which did not originate from a monarchic center. When the democratic process began, the traditional monarchies were on the point of dying out. The tyrants who frequently usurped power during the seventh and sixth centuries may have contributed something to the consolidation of the polity, but they did not establish anything of any permanence in the political sphere. They did not put down any roots and evidently were not prepared to summon up the amount of discipline which would have been needed to establish lasting power. By and large they preferred only to enjoy their power.[24] In this respect they resembled the majority of the Greek aristocracy, who were seldom able to subject themselves to sufficient discipline in the service of the body politic. Thus the crisis of the earlier centuries in Greece, which was originally primarily an economic one, could not be "caught" by the aristocracy or the tyrants. It therefore dragged on and expanded, it spread to society, ethics, and politics. The basic principles of all tradition were shattered. And in spite of many people's efforts, it was not easy to introduce new rules. It was not until an alternative arose out of the mass of the population that in those places where the trouble was greatest, the crisis could be resolved and superseded by a new stable order.

But how could such an alternative be built? The masses who had never before attained power—how did they, in Greece, manage not only to rebel, which cannot lead to the establishment of power beyond the moment, but also to attain the conviction that they had a responsibility, a right to a say, in political matters? How did it come about that they assembled sufficient knowledge, prepared institutions, and combined new opinions with their interests in such a way as to provide the basis for an effective alternative to the existing order?

Within their ranks they developed a new system of ethics, a revaluation of values.[25] This established the demand for active and regular participation in politics, a new identity[26] of the citizen as such, which consolidated this new system by means of high mutual expectations. It led therefore to the development of new structures of personality. If the masses were to gain secure power in the body politic, the people had to undergo a profound transformation. This by no means implies that this was their purpose from the outset. On the contrary, they did not even know that this form of government was possible before they founded it.

In my opinion, this type of change could have been possible only if a trend in political thought had gradually developed a long-term and lasting orientation toward the common people. We have various arguments for this. Since no powerful monarchical centers grew up to draw the intelligentsia to them, since there was on the whole no group in society powerful enough to impose its solution to the crisis or itself as a solution to the crisis on the community, and since hopeless situations also frequently developed, people had to rely to a great extent on intelligent advice. This could be obtained in Delphi, but also from a great number of wise men. It would appear that a whole group of intellectuals formed who specialized in serving the most varied interests with good advice. Their aim was not to gain power (or to serve a particular power) but to find the best solution in each individual case. Greece, with its innumerable cities, at this time resembled a large field of political experiment.[27]

The wise man best known to us from this period is the Athenian Solon.[28] He was of great service to his native city when it furnished him with extensive authority to put things right there. We know of Solon that he perceived that everything which had been previously interpreted as divine punishment ran in fact in accordance with earthly laws. The unjust exploitation of the peasants was harmful to the community because it caused rebellion among them which could lead to civil war. The recognition of this mechanism helped him not only to enlighten the citizens but also to realize that these (earthly) laws could be altered before they had had their full effect. For Solon the responsibility of the citizen for the state of the community ensued from this.[29] He concentrated particularly on those citizens who were not involved in politics (and unjust practices) because they were also affected by the fate of the community.[30] He discovered numerous causalities and publicized his knowledge of them, so that the people's assembly was provided with the requisite knowledge to make the right decisions—and to gain a certain amount of foresight.[31]

But Solon also conveyed a guiding principle for a good order, εὐνομία. His premise was that the gods are just. This could be seen in, among other things, those natural laws which could be empirically observed. If the gods were just, then they must provide a good order. He obviously suspected that such an order lay behind the status quo. Whenever he discovered something that was not in order, such as the high debts of the peasants, which had so many further consequences, he supposed that behind it he would discover the way it ought to be in reality. Thus he came to presuppose the existence of a realizable just order.

In contrast to so many of the conceptions of the pre-Greek cultures, this order was characterized by the fact that no individual power was responsible for it. No god, no king who thought himself particularly favored by the gods.[32] Zeus, insofar as he represented power, was only the embodiment of the law. On the contrary, everyone was responsible for maintaining the order. If necessary, men of outstanding knowledge could be temporarily commissioned with the task of reconstructing the order, but this had to remain an exception.

When someone constructs an order of this type, which functions without his having a regular opportunity to intervene, he must approach it differently than would a monarch, and differently than those who think for him, who are always available if necessary to bring things about which do not happen on their own. Causality and interrelationships must be looked at with more profundity. In my opinion, this type of thinking is to be found at the beginning of Greek philosophy, in views of the κόσμος which are similar to Solon's view of the πόλις. Anaximander can be cited as an example of this.[33] The philosophers were also aware of the problematic questions of the πόλις. And those who were most directly involved with the πόλις needed the analogy with the κόσμος as confirmation of the truth of their assumptions. For in the sixth century B.C., it was truth and the perception of a divine will which were the principle concerns of political thinking; a "religious realism" was applied to understanding the πόλις.[34]

In this way politics and philosophy became intertwined. Political thought thus played a considerable role in the process which finally led to democracy. Its path can be approximately reconstructed. If the purpose of the advice given by the largely independent intelligentsia was to enable the establishment of a good order in the cities, then they must somehow have realized that it was impossible to eliminate the unrest and rebellion among the common people without giving them the right to a certain say in political matters. Otherwise they would have been dependent on the aristocrats and, at the time when prevailing norms were suffering a general breakdown, the aristocrats could not be relied on. The immediate aim of giving the people a say in affairs was presumably to establish legal security. But this was followed by many other things, such as the view that all citizens should have the same political rights. It was only at the very end of this process—and strictly speaking in Athens only as a result of the city's outstanding military successes against the Persians—that a government of the people developed.

There is a lot of evidence supporting the view that the original aim was merely to create a counterbalance[35] to the power of aristocracy within certain institutions, particularly in the people's assembly. Initially no thought was given to the possibility of the community being governed by others than the aristocrats. But there was good reason to endow the majority of citizens with some political rights. The Greeks had no tribunes of the people to protect the poor and those who had no rights. Anyone who took up their case was suspected of aspiring to tyranny. And therefore, to quote Jacob Burckhardt, "for his own protection, the poor man" had to "take part in decisions, be himself judge and councillor."[36] History shows that after the middle of the sixth century the citizens in many Greek towns could no longer be enticed by economic gains but wanted political rights.

The early democracies, however, the isonomies, were more or less governed by the aristocracy, until in 461 the areopag in Athens was deprived of its power. This was the body in which the aristocracy had discussed its policies before using its authority to have them more or less blessed in the assembly.[37] Even after this it was members of the aristocracy who for the most part determined policy in the assembly. But the extent to which they were dependent on it was quite new. Even if they knew how to force it into line they still had to comply with its decisions. In this respect the people really did rate.

I would like to draw a first conclusion. In the case of the Greeks, freedom of choice as regards the whole political order resulted from a severe crisis at the beginning of the development of their culture. Strangely enough it could not be overcome by monarchs. Finally, in the most important and most turbulent community, the only conceivable strength on which a new and legitimate order could be founded was the middle strata of the citizenry, and they could only come to power as a result of a lengthy process of political thinking. In this respect philosophy headed the development of democracy, and the artificial, cratistic order of the Greeks was far more the result of a thought which was not directly focused on power than it was the result of an interest in power or the result of power itself.

To create this alternative, it was necessary for the common people to show themselves extraordinarily willing to become engaged in politics. This had already been the case in various places from the second half of the sixth century; in Athens such an interest increased greatly when democracy reached its full maturity.

It is conspicuous, however, that freedom of choice was not immediately linked to the choice of freedom. It would appear rather that the concept of freedom was not connected with democracy until nearly a generation after its emergence. Kurt Raaflaub has made this seem plausible in his excellent book on the discovery of freedom.[38] Equality and, of course, justice had been striven for. The use of equality as a slogan probably even preceded the emergence of the isonomy. It is very strange that in contrast people became aware of the concept of freedom only as a result of democracy and only after some time. For the Greeks had become only too aware of political freedom, particularly after the Persian wars, when it appeared to them to be virtually their principle characteristic. This was of course freedom from tyranny, freedom from the Persians, a freedom therefore which was then characteristic of most of the Greek city states.[39]

However, things developed quite differently in Greece than they did on the European Continent in the modern age. In Europe the real break with the nomistic order was caused by the absolutist monarchies in which, according to Carl Schmitt, the state even claimed the *ius reformationis*, which finally resulted in the *ius revolutionis*.[40] In Europe the state developed into such a powerful organ that it was able to continue to exist in reality and in the thinking of the democracies. Arendt has demonstrated these characteristics very clearly using the example of the French Revolution and its differences from the American Revolution.[41] In the modern age, therefore, demands for freedom had to be made and realized early and in opposition to the state. In the case of the Greeks, however, it is important that the cratistic orders, the ability artificially to restructure the whole of the body politic, were based on the masses.

This is very clearly demonstrated by the political agitations which directly preceded the areopag's loss of power, which is the beginning of democracy in Athens. Aeschylus gives us insights into these agitations in his tragedy of the period, the *Hiketides*.[42] From this we can reasonably assume that the advocates of reform brought forward one main argument, which was approximately this: "it is all of us who are the πόλις." By this they aimed to put the legitimation of the political order on a completely new basis. The aristocracy's claim to power had been justified by the superior education, experience, and insight of the men of the upper classes, and the special authority of the areopag had been additionally justified by the great success of the city in its foreign policy. The aristocracy maintained, therefore, that they knew best what was good for Athens. This claim could hardly be countered on an intellectual level. For what could have been said in favor of the masses? But the level of argumentation could be changed by claiming, "It is all of us who are the πόλις," that is, we all know what should be done because it concerns us all; we do not need anyone to tell us what to do. Correspondingly we find in the same play the demand that those who are affected by a decision should make that decision. Intelligence is exchanged for identification with the πόλις as the basis for the claim to the highest power, or, in other words, the subject, the citizens, took the place of the object, the πόλις. Herodotus says the same thing: "the whole is contained within the majority."[43] This also answers a new question, that of where the whole is to be found, instead of asking who would be its best administrators. The direct cause of the demands thus made was the suspicion that the aristocrats were acting in their own interests and were corrupt. The fact that the areopag did not convene publicly also raised suspicions. The aristocrats should bring their arguments before the people, then their insights would not be lost. But the people were no longer willing simply to accept these insights in the form of proposals by the leading politicians, supported by the authority of the areopag and hardly able to be questioned. "It is us who are the πόλις" meant that the citizens collectively wanted to decide for themselves freely, publicly, and independently. This was the claim and the justification of democracy.

It can hardly be a coincidence that in the same play by Aeschylus, for the first time, as far as we know, the fact that the people rule is proudly emphasized.[44] So we find the concept of rule detached from the direct holders of the leading positions and transferred to the entirety of the people, most of whom were at first incapable of governing. All that they could do was to make decisions collectively, which means that they could "rule" only to that extent, that is, evidently in a completely new sense of the word. This concept of power corresponds precisely to the identity of the entirety of the citizenry with the πόλις, which was rooted in the political identity of the Athenian citizens. Later on this identity came to be expressed in the strange term πολιτεία, which means citizenship and the citizenry and, at the same time, the political order.[45] This is a manifestation of the fact that the Greeks *were* an order rather than they *had* an order. Incidentally, the members of the δῆμος later laid their own claim to comprehensive political qualifications, particularly to the ability to make right judgments, and therefore to the ability to make right final decisions. As Moses Finley has shown, there was a lot to be said for this claim.[46]

It would therefore appear that apart from the negative arguments against the aristocracy, one particular fact was emphasized in favor of the rule of the people, namely, that the whole is present and inherent in the people; the city is merely the citizenry and therefore undoubtedly capable of acting. The establishment of democracy was probably focused on two aspects. First, it ascertained what was already the case, since the people's assembly was a decision-making body. In this respect it was not a question of shaking off the rule of the aristocracy but of resisting its authority, its undeniable predominance. The other focus resulted from this one in that, as its logical conclusion, the demand was made that the people should rule—and not the aristocracy. This meant that in reality there should be no authority that limited the scope of the people to make decisions. As evidence for the fact that democracy was intended to be understood in such an extreme sense, we have the lengthy periods of political agitation preceding the deprivation of power of the areopag, with which the establishment of popular rule was connected. On the other hand, the aristocracy appears to have claimed that the people wanted to be "unruled" (ἄναρχον) and to have reproached them accordingly.[47] But at first there was no democratic concept of freedom which corresponded to this. In the early stages of democracy, freedom remained restricted to freedom from tyranny.

Perhaps the strange relationship between freedom and equality in this context can be clarified by comparing the Greeks with the Romans. In the Roman Republic, the concept of freedom played a crucial role, whereas that of equality was considerably subordinate.[48] The Roman *libertas* consisted principally in rights of the individual, in their protection, and in safeguarding against force. It was secured in a series of laws. It may also be that forms of equality were at issue in the struggle of the orders, for example, equality before the law or the plebeian aristocrats' demand for equal access to political offices. But this did not result in any demand for the fundamental equality of the political rights of all citizens. It did not go beyond the level of making clear and obvious differentiations between those who could rule and those who were ruled. For the majority of the people, equality with the far superior aristocracy was never conceivable. Politically the concern of the majority could only have been to create special commissioners of opposition and to increase the opportunities for the plebeian assembly to intervene in politics. It is significant that plebeian aristocrats acted for centuries exactly according to their duties without usurping tyrannical power. The essential reason for this must have been the solidarity and superiority of their opponents, which was at the same time a challenge to the plebeian aristocrats to hold together in the political struggle.

The Greeks, on the other hand, were not acquainted with such evident and great superiority and especially with such unity within their aristocracy. It was rather the case that serious conflicts repeatedly emerged in their ranks, and individuals broke away in order to usurp tyrannies. This served at the same time to seal the fate of the opposition in the πόλις. In view of the great number of dissatisfied people who allowed themselves to be mobilized against the aristocracy under these circumstances, wherever opposition originated it always immediately threatened to develop into a tyranny of those who were leading it. It was in this way that the desire—and the opportunity—for regular political commitment of the citizen developed.

This commitment, which then intensified to become that "political identity" which was pursued so far, could hardly be justified otherwise than by the equality of the membership of the polis.[49] A certain equality was already manifested in some common essentials, such as that peasants had a share in the property of the land and that all peasants served as hoplites. But this we also meet in Rome. Far more important was that in view of the shortcomings of the aristocrats, Solon had already allocated a certain amount of responsibility for the order of the city to all its citizens. This aimed at equality with the aristocrats and with the prosperous; when this equality was reached it was supported by a consciousness on the part of the middle and lower stata of a solidarity and community of interests. For them, therefore, the real aim was not the protection of the individual from arbitrariness and force. Such freedoms had to be included in the collective struggle for a say in political affairs.

The demands for equal rights resulted from this: that these rights were necessary for the middle and lower stata to be full-fledged citizens. So it would appear that demands for freedom have to be made especially where there is a superior force to be resisted. On the other hand, equality is of relevance where it is possible to strive for an increasing share in power. This does not exclude the possibility that people initially take it for granted that the positions of leadership are occupied by a group whose personal qualifications make it particularly well suited to rule. But it does prepare the ground for a situation in which this superiority can be superseded by the identity of the citizenry with the πόλις.

Incidentally, it was only a restricted circle of people to whom one had to justify political reforms or revolution. The large number of citizens, relatively uninvolved in domestic and foreign affairs, to which one has to justify oneself today, did not then exists.[50] It was rather a case of everyone being affected, either positively or negatively. Therefore the need for slogans was limited in a special way.

A few decades later, democracy came to understand itself as being determined by freedom. Everyone could live as he pleased within a democracy. And the fact that everyone ruled or was ruled by turns was considered to be the expression of freedom.[51] By then the situation had undergone a fundamental transformation.

First, as new generations grew up taking democracy and particularly the power of the city over its allies for granted, the Athenians got into the habit of deviating from numerous old rules in domestic and foreign matters. They rushed head over heels into high-level politics, had neither the experience nor the standards necessary, and were increasingly tempted to do things that had never been ventured before. As far as we can tell, the Athenians became fully aware of this utterly new freedom around the middle of the 440s, and it became the object of intense dispute. An expression of it can be found in Sophocles' *Antigone*. The Athenians also began to be more aware of their freedom in terms of the contrast between themselves and their Spartan rivals.[52] This comparison may also have been made with greater frequency after the forties of the fifth century.

At this time or soon afterward, the city developed a completely new awareness of power, as we know from Thucydides. In contrast to the Romans, the

Greeks had always sought after and made use of the aspects of power that they could enjoy and not aspects like commitment, service, and care, which cannot be neglected if power is to take root. This can be demonstrated by the lack of duration of the tyrannies, but also by the smallness of the city-states and their inability to control greater territories. Athens was the first city that was able to gain widespread power over the whole of the Aegean. But it also exploited the opportunities power offered without realizing sufficiently its responsibilities or taking those who were being ruled properly into consideration. The Athenians increasingly developed a cynicism resulting from power. And this was linked with a new understanding of freedom: to do what one thought was good, regardless of dependency on, or consideration toward, others.[53] It was precisely this that provoked the criticism of the old aristocrats. In addition it contradicted the values which were still upheld elsewhere in Greece, since the other Greek cities were almost without exception still ruled by the aristocracy. This made it necessary to find an ideological defense for democracy, especially from within democracy. Now at last the slogan of freedom could be produced to counteract the criticism of the way in which the people—and not the aristocracy—were governing the city. This was possible because it was now freedom that would be threatened if the aristocracy were to claim the right to be reinstated in political offices or to make preliminary decisions in a council of aristocrats, regardless of how these claims might have actually been proposed.

It would appear that this was approximately how the claim that democratic freedom consisted in the fact that everyone rules and is ruled in turn was arrived at. The freedom of this citizenry could indeed have been preserved in no other way—the freedom that held such a fascination, not the least because it was at the same time power, the power to rule.[54] By taking advantage of this power, the citizen claimed for democracy what was characteristic of the Greeks. The freedom of Greek democracy was especially the freedom of living, of acting, of ruling—and the freedom of the lower classes within a society whose values were determined now as before by the aristocracy. This attitude can be traced to art, for example, in the policy of building on the Acropolis. The Athenians, including the lower classes, claimed to realize the aristocratic ideal of grace in an unprecedented way.[55]

This Greek freedom is obviously not the same freedom to which we lay claim in the modern tradition. Just as the rule of the δῆμος could only be collective, so its freedom could only be collective; Raaflaub has shown this.[56] This freedom was based on political identity and that meant not only that the citizen regarded himself primarily as a citizen and expected the same of others, but also that the quality of being a citizen drew people closer together, so that solidarity and common interests were of much more importance than differences. Arendt has pointed out the unusual, clear dividing line which the Greeks made between house and city. It was as if the people had to cross a gulf every day in order "to transcend the narrow realm of the household and 'rise' into the realm of politics."[57] In the house the citizen was master of all those who belonged to him; in the city he moved among equals. Specialization of roles within the house and overall responsibility in the πόλις are a part of this division.[58] Incidentally, when the citizens themselves were to such an extent identical with the city, it was not possible for them to consider changing society as a part of politics. Also the "simultaneity of things not simultaneous" (*Gleichzeitigkeit des Ungleichzeitigen*), which has contributed so much to the pluralism of our world, did not develop.[59]

All this left very little room for the development of individuality, except possibly in contrast to the δῆμος. One scarcely hears of anyone, apart from Sophocles' Antigone and Socrates, who retained moral autonomy in the face of the demands of the body politic, although the Athenian community permitted a good deal of freedom to develop and apply criticism and philosophy.

Choices within the political order were limited. There were no factions, no great alternatives within the various forms of government, only between them. The most important conflict was that between those above and those below,[60] the question of whether full political rights should be possessed by everyone or only by a few. This was the alternative between democracy and oligarchy, which can only be clear when one or the other side really does occupy political office and determine policies. This limited choice also enforced severe restrictions on the capacity for freedom, particularly since that *espace privée* from which our notion of freedom derives to such a great extent did not develop, at least not in the fifth century. Burckhardt is right when he says that the Age of Pericles was a state "in which any quiet and thoughtful citizen would refuse to live, in which he would feel desperately unhappy, even if he were not one of the majority, the slaves, but of the freemen."[61]

And yet, even though the freedom which came into being with Greek democracy was not the same as ours, it still led to ours. For, in my opinion, classical philosophy played a crucial role in paving the way for the modern world.

Like the modern, monarchical state, the constitution of Athenian democracy contained a potential explosive made up of specific concentrations of energies. In the case of the monarchical states, this concentration was embodied in the conflict with bourgeois society, which the state at first forced away from politics and then promoted by improving its economic and intellectual conditions. In the case of the Greeks, it was the momentum which, with a certain logical consistency, grew out of the freedom of Athenian democracy, the increasingly unrestrained pursuit of power which finally led to serious constitutional crises and the collapse of Athens.

Because of its old responsibility for politics and for the way out of the crisis of the aristocratic πόλις, with the second crisis philosophy was presented with a renewed challenge. The alternative that had been relied on was played out—the δῆμος had also failed. Some sort of "secondary crisis" began. This resulted in a strange reversal of everything that had been previously valid in Platonic philosophy.

Plato rejects the identity of the citizenry with the city, the comprehensive political responsibility of all those freemen who by descent belong to the city. He replaces it with the rule of philosophers[62] and a conception of the citizen which only concedes full political rights to the "guardians," that is, to the upper class. And he maintains that every person should do only "what he can."[63] The overall political competence of the citizen is therefore replaced throughout by specialization.

Plato rejects at the same time the freedom to choose an individual mode of life and replaces it with the strictest regimentation, going even further than the Spartans. He rejects the freedom to choose between forms of government, since that only leads to party rule,[64] and he replaces it with an orientation to the truth, which knows only one good form of government.

Plato also rejects, as Aristotle shows, the differentiation between house and πόλις, precisely that πόλις, which according to Aristotle, "wants to be made up of equal men."[65] He also, incidentally, disputes the idea that political consultations should be public. In this, Plato pursues with amazing boldness the line of Greek political thought which had unconsciously led to democracy, which had finally culminated in the conviction that unprecedented possibilities are open to mankind, especially those possibilities in methodological action and thought which we encounter in the fifth century.[66] But in Plato this happens under completely altered circumstances and with completely different consequences. The scope available to the changing of political structure was extended to an incredible degree, since it was not only the political but also the entire social world, right down to the question of procreation, sexual intercourse, and the relationship between the sexes, which was to be rebuilt on an entirely new foundation with no conformance to any tradition. And where political thought before democracy was aware of its own weakness, which had been the condition for its extraordinary political influence, Plato reversed this by founding the rule of philosophers. Thus he no longer sought for the truth in concrete politics but outside it, outside the cave. The result of this was that contrary to his own intentions, his philosophy no longer had any chance whatsoever of being translated into reality.

But it has had a profound effect on the intellectual world. Initially it may have induced politicians to be guided by truth and justice. But as soon as the tradition stemming from this philosophy reached the stage of realizing philosophical truths in society itself, totalitarian tendencies easily ensued. For the transformation of society belongs to the state, and continual progress belongs to bourgeois society. And this means, on the one hand, that Marx is following a certain logic when he looks for the truth in the law of history, where for Plato it had lain in ideas. On the other hand, the absoluteness of the two answers to the "secondary crisis" bear comparison. In both cases the political scarcely stands a chance—in Plato, although Platonic philosophy claims to be political, and in the modern age because the potential for change in bourgeois society leads to the philosophy of history, so long as it is instrumental for interpretation.

Perhaps nowadays we should be oriented more to the pre-Platonic thought of the Greeks as it appears, for example, in Aeschylus's Oresteian trilogy.[67] I cannot go into further details here, but the theory, if one may call it that, is obvious. The essence of a good political order is that all essential questions can—or even must—be decided by vote, even if it be with the smallest conceivable majority. But because this is the case, and because it may be that essential questions are at issue, the victors must be conciliatory and the losers must retain a certain position, a certain status in the community. That points to the fact that the truth of democracy is compromise. Aeschylus shows at the same time that the power of intelligence, even the power of the ruler or the ruling class, consists to a considerable extent in the ability to recognize the limits of one's own power, that is, to bring together power and knowledge in a sense that enables orientation to the feasible. It aims at that realism that seeks the truth within the political sphere as it is and not outside it. As Aeschylus shows in the *Prometheus* and the *Oresteia*, such is the will of Zeus. And I presume that that would also have been the wish of Hannah Arendt.

NOTES

This is the text of a lecture given in 1986 as part of the series of the Hannah Arendt Memorial Symposia which Reiner Schürmann wished to collect and edit along with others. Since he was not able to do so, the essay now is contributed to his memory. The text stands essentially as it did in 1986; the notes have been reworked to make reference to English translations that have appeared in the interim. This text was translated by Katherine Tranter, Stuttgart, with revisions by the author.

1. Esp. in Hannah Arendt, *The Human Condition* (Chicago, 1958).
2. H. Arendt, "Tradition and the Modern Age," *Between Past and Future: Eight Exercises in Political Thought* (New York, 1968), p. 17 ff.
3. Ibid., p. 77.
4. K. Marx, *Die Frühschriften,* ed. Siegfried Landshut (Stuttgart, 1904), p. 66.
5. Christian Meier, *The Greek Discovery of Politics* (Cambridge, Mass., 1990).
6. Plato, *Seventh Letter*, 325 c ff.
7. Herodotus, 3, 80 ff.; Meier, *Greek Discovery*, p. 161 ff.
8. J. de Romilly, "Le classement des constitutions d'Hérodote à Aristote," *Revue des Etudes Grecques*, 72 (1959), p. 81 ff.
9. Aristotle, *Politics*, 1288b 10 ff.
10. H.-J. Gehrke, *Stasis: Untersuchungen zu den inneren Kriegen in den griechischen Staaten des 5. und 4. Jahrhunderts vor Christus* (Munich, 1985).
11. Christian Meier, "Die Griechen: Die politische Revolution der Weltgeschichte," *Saeculum*, 33 (1982), p. 133 ff.
12. H. Berve, *Die Tyrannis bei den Griechen* (Munich, 1967), pp. 3 ff., 164 ff.
13. Christian Meier, *Entstehung des Begriffs Demokratie* (Frankfurt, 1970, 1984), pp. 15 ff., 26 ff.
14. Aristotle, *Politics*, 1286b ff., 1297b 16 ff.; V. Ehrenberg, *Der Staat der Griechen* (Zurich, 1965), p. 58.
15. Christian Meier, "Drei Bemerkungen zur Vor- und Frühgeschichte des Begriffs Demokratie," in *Discordia Concors: Festschrift für E. Bonjour* (Basel, 1968), p. 3 ff.; T. Hölscher, "Die Nike der Messenier und Naupaktier in Olympia," *Jahrbuch des Deutschen Archäologischen Instituts*, 89 (1974), p. 101; P. Spahn, *Mittelschicht und Polisbildung* (Frankfurt, 1977).
16. Meier, *Greek Discovery*, p. 140 ff., and *Introduction à l'anthropologie politique de l'antiquité classique* (Paris, 1985), p. 45 ff.; M. I. Finley, *Politics in the Ancient World* (Cambridge, 1983), but see my critical remarks in *Gnomon*, 58 (1986), p. 496 ff.
17. Meier, *Greek Discovery*, p. 144 ff.
18. The best example is Plato's *Republic.*

19. See Christian Meier, *The Political Art of Greek Tragedy* (Cambridge, 1993), p. 137 ff.

20. Meier, *Greek Discovery*, p. 186 ff.

21. Christian Meier, "Der Umbruch zur Demokratie in Athen (462/61 vor Christus): Eine Epoche der Weltgeschichte und was Zeitgenossen daran wahrnahmen," in R. Herzog and R. Koselleck, eds., *Epochenschwelle und Epochenbewußtsein (Poetik und Hermeneutik 12)* (Munich, 1987).

22. Christian Meier, "Entstehung und Besonderheit der griechischen Demokratie," *Zeitschrift für Politik*, 25 (1978), p. 20.

23. Meier, *Greek Discovery*, p. 53 ff.

24. H. Schaefer, *Probleme der alten Geschichte* (Göttingen, 1963), pp. 215, 309, 314 ff.

25. See Tyrtaios 9D; Phokylides 10D; Theognis 145 ff.D; Xenophanes 2D; V. Ehrenberg, *Die Rechtsidee im frühen Griechentum* (Leipzig, 1921), p. 135; G. Steinkopf, "Untersuchung zur Geschichte des Ruhms bei den Griechen," dissertation, Halle, 1937, pp. 42 f., 49 f; W. Jaeger, "Tyrtaios über die wahre Arete," *Sitzungsberichte der Preußischen Akademie der Wissenschaften* (Berlin, 1959), pp. 130 ff., 185 ff. See Also A. W. H. Adkins, *Moral Values and Political Behaviour in Ancient Greece* (London, 1972), p. 46 ff.

26. Christian Meier, "Bürger-Identität und Demokratie," in Christian Meier and Paul Veyne, *Kannten die Griechen die Demokratie?* (Berlin, 1988), p. 47 ff.

27. Christian Meier, "The Emergence of an Autonomous Intelligence among the Greeks," in S. N. Eisenstadt, ed., *The Origins and Diversity of Axial Age Civilizations* (New York, 1986), p. 65 ff.

28. I. M. Linforth, *Solon the Athenian* (Berkley, 1919); Spahn, *Mittelschicht*, p. 139 ff.

29. W. Jaeger, "Solons *Eunomie*," *Sitzungsberichte der Preußischen Akademie der Wissenschaften* (1926); Meier, *Entstehung des Begriffs Demokratie*, p. 143; Meier, "Emergence," p. 82 ff.

30. Spahn, *Mittelschicht*, p. 143 ff.

31. Solon, 3, 5 ff.; 8, 9, 10, 11D.

32. J. P. Vernant, *Les origines de la pensée grecque* (Paris, 1962), p. 119 ff.; Meier, "Emergence," p. 85 ff.

33. Anaximander, Fragment 1, in Vernant, *Les origines.*

34. Meier, *Greek Discovery*, p. 131 ff.

35. Meier, "Emergence," p. 87.

36. Jacob Burckhardt, *Griechische Kulturgeschichte*, vol. 1 (Darmstadt, 1956), p. 206.

37. See n. 20.

38. K. Raaflaub, *Die Entdeckung der Freiheit: Zur historischen Semantik und Gesellschaftsgeschichte eines politischen Grundbegriffs der Griechen* (Munich, 1985).

39. Ibid., p. 71 ff.

40. As far as I know he did not write about this.

41. Hannah Arendt, *On Revolution* (New York, 1963).

42. Meier, *Political Art of Greek Tragedy*, p. 78 ff.

43. Herodotus, 3, 80, 6.

44. Euripides, *Hiketides*, 604, 699; also see Meier, *Political Art of Greek Tragedy*, p. 95 f.

45. Christian Meier, "Politeia," in *Historisches Wörterbuch der Philosophie*, vol. 7 (Basel/Stuttgart, 1989).

46. M. I. Finley, *Democracy Ancient and Modern* (London, 1985).

47. See Aeschylus, *Eumenides*, 526, 696.

48. J. Bleicken, *Staatliche Ordnung und Freiheit in der römischen Republik* (Kallmünz, 1972); K. Raaflaub, ed., *The Struggle of the Orders* (Berkley, 1986).

49. Meier, "Bürger-Identität," p. 67 ff.

50. Finley, *Politics*, p. 122 ff.; Meier, *Gnomon* (see n. 16).

51. Euripides, *Hiketides*, 404 ff., 438 f.; Aristotle, *Politics*, 1317a 40 ff.; Pseudo-Xenophon, *Athenaion Politeia*, 1, 8; Raaflaub, *Entdeckung*, p. 289 ff.

52. Raaflaub, *Entdeckung*, p. 265 f.

53. Ibid., p. 241 ff.

54. Ibid., p. 233 ff.

55. Christian Meier, *Politik und Anmut* (Berlin, 1985).

56. Raaflaub, *Entdeckung*, p. 331 f.

57. Arendt, *The Human Condition*, p. 33.

58. Thucydides, 2, 40, 2.

59. Meier, *Greek Discovery*, p. 152 f.

60. Meier, *Introduction*, p. 45 ff.; Finley, *Politics*, 1 ff.; Meier, *Gnomon* (see n. 16).

61. Jacob Burckhardt, *Über das Studium der Geschichte: Der Text der "Weltgeschichtlichen Betrachtungen" nach den Handschriften*, ed. P. Ganz (Munich, 1982), p. 236.

62. Plato, *Republic*, 473 c/d.

63. Ibid., 423 c/d, 433 a ff.

64. Plato, *Laws*, 832 c.

65. Aristotle, *Politics*, 1261a 18 ff.; D. Sternberger, *Drei Wurzeln der Politik* (Frankfurt, 1978), p. 105 ff.; Aristotle, *Politics*, 1295b 25 f.

66. Meier, *Greek Discovery*, p. 181 ff.

67. Ibid., p. 82 ff.

FIVE

The Modern Dilemma of Political Theory

Rüdiger Bubner

One of the most valuable discoveries bequeathed to us by ancient Greek philosophy is insight into the intimate relation between politics and language. To identify the political with the linguistic might seem puzzling to those who understand politics purely in terms of power and social order and would rank rhetoric, the art of speaking effectively, after strategy, the art of acting effectively. Aristotle was right, however, to observe in the *Politics* that λόγος is the all-important characteristic distinguishing human beings from all other animals.[1] Other "gregarious" animals, endowed with voice, are able to communicate only feelings of pleasure and pain. Humans, however, by means of language are able to disclose and set forth the advantageous and the harmful, the expedient and inexpedient, and, in this way, make clear to one another what is right and wrong, good and evil. In this sense, language, for Aristotle, is a political phenomenon. It is the medium through which mankind seeks to realize the τέλος of its species, that is, through which every generation and every individual participates in giving rational content to those fundamental beliefs constituting the only form of life appropriate to concrete human beings. This is what Aristotle means when he observes that a commonality (κοινωνία) of beliefs constitutes the household and state. In other words, true political unity, for Aristotle, is created where beliefs and values are held in common.

Although for modern thinking it seems self-evident that politics should govern all aspects of everyday life, there is little agreement as to what the general concept of politics means. A wide spectrum of heterogeneous social phenomena, traditionally considered to be outside the pale of politics, is now subsumed within a broad conception of political reality. Even the private sphere can no longer be said to be off-limits to the pressures of public interests, as it is always possible to discover hidden political motives at work in our most mundane dealings with each other. Nature too, now going under the name of "environment," has lost its innocence and become a political issue. In our day-to-day discussions of the people, things, and events constituting our world, it is usual to talk about "political relevance" without bothering to question what *political* really means. We have, it is true, a prolific and influential discipline called political science. But strangely enough, this science takes its fundamental categories for granted and leaves them for the most part vague and undefined. In light of such indifference, we might indeed want to ask whether there still exists, in Aristotle's sense, any understanding at all of those basic beliefs and common goals which bind every member of a political community to every other.

Against the background of this rough sketch of the current level of general political understanding as I believe it to be, I will go on to analyze what I call the modern dilemma of political theory. I will first present four theses and then offer an alternative way of thinking about politics which might help answer this question: what general concept of politics is up to the task of describing in a meaningful way given concrete situations?

My first thesis deals with the reasons for the apparent discrepancy between current discussions about politics and the profound conceptual obscurity characterizing these discussions. It is not enough merely to describe or lament the present situation. Rather it is imperative to lay bare the roots of the problem. A full account, however, would necessitate a long and involved explanation complicated by a mass of historical detail. It is certainly not an easy task to explain how we have come to consider politics such a decisive factor in contemporary life and yet, at the same time, have such a vague understanding of what the political is. Since it is beyond the scope of this essay to recount the entire history leading to this state of affairs, I will attempt to describe the consequences of this development as succinctly as possible.

The community of values Aristotle had in mind dissolved in the course of the development of modern history. This same development witnessed the advent and the ultimate triumph of subjectivity. The substantial political unity of the ancient Greek πόλις, which encompassed all individuals and was essentially prior to them, gradually gave way to this new principle. Modern subjectivity, because it is grounded in the original self-understanding of the ego, cannot be derived from a higher principle and therefore cannot be subsumed under the concept of a quasi-natural organization of society. This is the theoretical basis for today's commonsense notion that the subject must be the starting point of all political discussions.

Subjectivity arises from the structural isolation of the individual's consciousness from the political whole. The intersubjective system of beliefs and values underlying social order thus appears as an abstract and alien structure standing over against the individual and representing objective institutions which restrict subjective freedom. Such a system can be legitimated only if subjects agree to enter political communities by forfeiting their claims to unlimited individuality. This is the modern idea of the social contract, which establishes political unity out of the state of nature, where all individuals are their own masters.

It was Hobbes who, at the beginning of the modern period, was the first to understand politics as an all-powerful instrument at the service of social technology whose purpose is to bring into existence what did not exist before. The figure of the Leviathan, the man-made god, is intended to make social interaction rationally possible among atomized individuals who confront each other as bitter antagonists. The most controversial element of Hobbes's solution to the problem of social order, i.e., the absolute, undisputed power of the sovereign, must be interpreted in the light of this technology. The commonwealth is ingeniously organized to satisfy the desires, needs, and expectations of its isolated and inimical individuals. This artificial, abstract construction, designed to implement a theoretical plan for the most advantageous way to compel people to live together, is certainly a far cry from the ancient Greek conception of the πόλις. For the ancients, the state was just as natural as the people who lived in it.

At the heart of the *Republic*, where the true meaning of the famous and provocative myth of the philosopher king is cautiously revealed, Plato offers an argument of striking simplicity for the origins of political authority, an argument overlooked by many commentators.[2] Plato says here that the wise man is entitled to take over the function of ruling the state because he possesses the knowledge of what everyone strives to attain in life but no one is ever sure of actually acquiring, i.e., the good. Although all πρᾶξις, all human action, aims at a τέλος or a οὗ ἕνεκα, most people do not know what is the best for them. Only the philosopher, who has the political whole in view, is capable of such insight. Despite all his well-known differences with Plato, Aristotle adopts this idea of the natural congruence between everyone's individual interest in the good life and the destiny of the political whole when he claims that the happiness, the εὐδαιμονία, of each citizen and the happiness of the state are one and the same.[3]

These observations elucidate my first thesis: the growing dominance of the modern principle of subjectivity has contributed to the erosion of the substantial political unity characterizing the classical tradition, as epitomized by the ancient Greek πόλις. My second thesis draws upon this conclusion: if the leitmotif of modernity is the preeminence of subjectivity, two opposing theoretical responses are equally conceivable for political thinking. One response can be traced back to Hegel's conception of the modern state as the total reconciliation of political institutions with the dominant principle of subjectivity. The other is a reaction against the glorification of the state in the name of this same principle. In order to elaborate my second thesis, it is necessary to make a short excursus.

Hegel thought himself to be the first philosopher to bring together the ancient Greek idea of political unity with the demands of the modern subject. Even among Hegel's most adamant critics, who denounced the *Philosophy of Right* as an ideological apology for the Prussian monarchy, only a few were willing to deny the fascination of this program. Marx, for example, did not hesitate to subscribe to the Hegelian vision of a unified life-world of political institutions; he merely insisted on a materialistic, demystified horizon from which to determine the true interests of historical subjects. Thus it can be said that communism, at least as Marx originally conceived it, sought a more concrete perspective for the realization of Hegel's intentions. Today, however, it is obvious that this project, which since the nineteenth century has enthralled so many generations, has come to an end.

But let me return more specifically to my main theme. Hegel was right when, in his early writings, he tried to combat the central role the principle of subjectivity plays, above all, in Kant's moral philosophy. The almost exclusive emphasis Kant places on the autonomy of the subject precludes the possibility of a common life-world. Kant should be corrected by Aristotle, while Aristotle's *Politics* should be supplemented by Kantian morality. This was the credo of the young Hegel, a credo which was to take on important systematic dimensions in his last work, the *Philosophy of Right*. There he writes in a famous paragraph: "The principle of modern states has prodigious strength and depth because it allows the principle of subjectivity to progress to its culmination in the extreme of self-subsistent personal particularity, and yet at the same time brings it back to the substantive unity and so maintains this unity in the principle of subjectivity itself."[4] As Hegel here suggests, the modern state has the strength to withstand the influence of the principle of subjectivity, which eroded the integrity of the ancient Greek πόλις, precisely because it is itself based on that very principle. The state no longer stands in radical opposition to its citizens, because they are now comprehended by a political organization embodying their own principle.

This point becomes clearer in the context of the ongoing polemics Hegel waged against Rousseau. According to Hegel, Rousseau's "volonté général," constituted by a social contract, does not provide a political foundation strong enough to support modern society. Because it adheres to the singularity of the will, the social contract precludes the possibility of taking the necessary steps into collectivity. Rousseau's "corps moral et collectif" binds individuals together by a precarious abstraction whose terroristic implications were revealed *in concreto* during the French Revolution. Wherever dissenting individuals must be reintegrated by force into the body politic, constituted by the original contract, Rousseau's sinister maxim is put into practice: "on les forcera d'être libres!" The notion that people are forced to be free is certainly a perverse identification of dominant power with the freedom of the individual. In stark contrast, Hegel's idea that the state, itself the incarnation of the principle of subjectivity and not merely an abstract entity based on an artificial contract, can with impunity allow its members to cultivate their individuality, for conceptually it is impossible for them to break apart. There are no dissident individuals, because the wise state has always taken care to allow for the diversity of subjective interests.

No doubt, Hegel's theory sounds attractive. Nevertheless, many people have resisted its charms and not been inclined to believe it. A good illustration of this is the old dispute over whether the theory represents the speculative ideology of an accommodating philosopher or whether it offers legitimate insights into the structure of the modern state. The axis around which this heated dispute turned was the comparison of Hegel's doctrine with an independently constituted historical reality. But because historical reality is itself the result of interpretation, which by necessity always allows for a multiplicity of other possibilities, historical interpretations give rise to ever new controversies and result in an endless game, an endless turning in circles. Today's discussions about the end of socialism provide yet another example of the bad infinity of historical interpretions. I do not want, however, to take part in this dispute. Instead of putting Hegel's political philosophy to the test from the outside, I will try to analyze it from within the context of its own systematic exposition. The key to understanding

Hegel's astonishing claim that the modern state is based on the principle of subjectivity lies in the proper understanding of this principle.

Hegel's structural analysis of subjectivity is to be found in his *Science of Logic*, in the third and final part entitled "Subjective Logic." I must ask for the reader's indulgence in entering on this complicated subject matter, especially as at first sight it does not seem to have any bearing on political questions. In broad terms, Hegel's logical treatment of subjectivity shows that the concept of the concept and the concept of the self are congruent. Their common dominator is *identity*.[5]

Subjectivity *means being identical with oneself*, where identity is the result of a specific act which negates and preserves all pertaining opposites. What prima facie appears to be opposite turns out to belong to the structure of an identity which mediates all opposites and thereby undermines the relation of opposition. Identity is identification, i.e., the act of integrating into one and the same structure every aspect that might come into play. Where everything belongs essentially to the same, the same shows itself to be through all instances its own identity with itself. This logical analysis of identification, which reveals that the structure of identity is the same throughout, prepares the way for the transition from the *Logic* to the *Philosophy of Right*. This paradoxically abrupt step is plausible because, according to the internal logic of Hegel's dialectic, the identity which knows of no opposite *is* "the realm of freedom." Evidently, the word *freedom* must here be understood metaphorically, indicating a conceptual structure unrestricted by any element which cannot itself be mediated. To transpose this metaphor back into the political realm, however, would seem to be highly problematic.

But this is exactly what Hegel does. He says that the modern state is the true realization of freedom, because all of its elements are integrated without force. Where every aspect of the whole to be differentiated is just another instance of a thoroughgoing identity, the differences between the state and the individual turn out to be only pseudo-differences. Understood as conceptual analysis, philosophical logic is needed to expose the illusory nature of the supposed opposition which dissolves the close bond between politics and autonomous subjects. The opposition is illusory, because the opposites—the state and the individual—in fact belong ineluctably together, and their identity can be proved by means of pure reflection. The step from the logical into the political realm is based on the following argumentation: if the logical core of subjectivity is identity, and if identity is identification or the act of reconciling opposites, then we can call the situation where all is one, where no objective element hinders the development of subjectivity, the realm of freedom.

It goes without saying that such a sophisticated theory cannot be adequately criticized from a so-called realistic standpoint. The problem is not whether the promised realm of freedom is given in historical reality or whether it must wait for better times to be realized. Rather the solution to the problem turns on whether the whole approach of logical analysis is up to the task of determining the nature and function of political institutions.

The danger implicit in substituting a logic of freedom for a politics of freedom is best shown by a different theory based on the same principle of subjectivity, but which at the same time proves to be incompatible with Hegel's glorification of the state. Here traditional liberalism comes on the scene. Liberalism demands that political institutions be measured according to the degree by which they guarantee the unrestricted development of individuality. This demand is the ground for liberalism's far-reaching critique of the state. My third thesis consists then in this: the controversy between the modern state and liberal critique of the state puts into sharp relief the ambiguity of the underlying principle of subjectivity common to both sides of the controversy.

John Stuart Mill's profound distrust of the state offers the best example of the traditional liberal's position. In a way, it can be said that Mill's thought represents the nineteenth-century counterpart to Hegel's étatism. Mills combines convictions typical of the English tradition with skeptical ideas concerning the rightful claims of the state first expressed by Wilhelm von Humboldt. Humboldt's belief that it is imperative to restrict the power of the state grew out of his critique of the postrevolutionary French constitution. It should be added, however, that his critique was far removed from the conservative position of Burke and others, as this position was exemplified in their analyses of the new revolutionary movement. Mill followed Humboldt rather than Burke when, in his brilliant essay *On Liberty* (1859), he laid down the main tenets of classical liberalism, which are still valid today. The hard core of Mill's liberalism consists in a defense of the individual against the state.

What Hegel rejected as obsolete was for Mill of lasting importance and still worth defending. Mill considered the formal concession of freedom to every individual the "vital question of the future."[6] His main argument is that the power of the state conceals the fact that most institutions incorporate a quantitative majority and not a superior rationality.

In Mill's view, modern times have produced the unfortunate phenomenon of people forming themselves into vast conglomerations, then professing to have more worth taken together than when considered separately according to their own merits. This suppression of individuals by individuals, camouflaged behind an institutional facade, is for Mill one of the worst consequences of modern politics. In the light of this de facto censuring of individuality, the state is obligated to guarantee that all its citizens have the right to pursue their own interests, make use of their talents and develop themselves according to their own particular abilities. The liberal understands that "the free development of individuality is one of the leading essentials of well-being."[7] Accordingly, as Mill writes earlier on in the same essay, "The only freedom which deserves the name, is that of pursuing our own good in our own way, so long as we do not attempt to deprive others of theirs, or impede their efforts to obtain it. . . . Mankind are greater gainers by suffering each other to live as seems good to themselves, than by compelling each to live as seems good to the rest."[8]

The modern dilemma of political theory becomes more evident when the principle of subjectivity is seen as the source of two mutually exclusive political concepts. The gap between, on the one hand, the rational state purporting to satisfy the claims of all subjects, and, on the other, the liberal protest against the eclipse of all individuality by institutions, shows exactly how much commonsense understanding of politics has suffered from its overall orientation toward the modern principle of subjectivity. I come now to my fourth and concluding thesis: it is a mistake to make politics subservient to the rule of the abstract principle of subjectivity. The more unanimously philosophers of recent centuries have held the shared conviction as to the preeminence of subjectivity, the more we are given reason to examine this principle in the light of such self-assuredness with an ever more critical eye. Subjectivity may be the conceptual lodestar for theories of mind, and possibly for epistemology and aesthetics, but it does not offer the proper basis for practical philosophy, understood in the broad sense of the term. Political theory goes astray, when it aspires to conform with the principle of subjectivity. Πρᾶξις, not subjectivity, is the fundamental concept for making sense of the political realm. In what follows, I will argue that the ancient Greek concept of πρᾶξις offers contemporary political theory a plausible alternative to the modern principle of subjectivity.

An appeal to πραξις must not necessarily culminate in the retrospective illusion that we can forget about all the complexities of modernity and simply return to a past utopia as represented by the ancient Greek πόλις. Some authors in political philosophy who show sympathy for the classics, for example, Leo Strauss and Eric Voegelin, often give the impression that we are obliged to take sides in the moribund *querelle des anciens et des modernes.*

If my reading of Hegel is correct, this conflict of perspectives was already considered naive at the beginning of the last century and accordingly discounted. After Hegel's dialectical appropriation of the history of thought, we are no longer in a position simply to choose one of two sides, and thereby feel we have carte blanche to exclude the other. To consider both sides, the ancients and the moderns, forces us to become aware of the one-sidedness of each. The concept of πρᾶξις does not by any means afford us an easy way out of the difficult problems raised by modern subjectivity. It does, however, have the important advantage of giving the practical demands of political actors their due without restricting them to the status of self-conscious beings.

Πρᾶξις means: acting under changing and often unforeseeable circumstances in view of aims to be realized in the here and now. Acting is a steady, self-contained process which takes place within the limits of the internal relationship established between aims and actions. Aims are realized by actions and actions are directed toward aims. Without the continuity afforded us by this relationship, our actions would be unable to proceed under the conditions of changing circumstances. Every successive step within the whole process would be in danger of losing its connection with the other necessary steps. The process has its own logic, which can be analyzed only if we do justice to the concrete nature of individual actions. If we follow this logic, we may be able to circumvent the fatal dualism of will, motives, and decisions versus physical movements, their causes and effects, a dualism upon which so many other discussions about human action have foundered. The logic of πρᾶξις is distorted by any attempt to dissociate the subjective from the objective aspects of action which structurally belong together. To put it another way, action should not be regarded as a bridge meant to span the gulf between inner and outer words.

It is obvious that the structural logic internal to the process of action calls for some degree of institutional support. Where most of the factors are unstable, where nothing is absolutely sure, where the course of action cannot be definitely anticipated and the outcome might be influenced by new events, πρᾶξις is in need of a specific orientation. Such an orientation makes sense only if it does not skip over practical concreteness, but instead indicates a secure way for acting within fluctuating circumstances.

This orientation finds its expression in maxims. For various reasons, the term *maxim* is preferable to the more generally accepted but rather vague term *rule*. Rules can pertain to several different things, while maxims function solely to guide our specific, concrete actions. To give two examples: one of my maxims might tell me not to listen to people who tend toward flattery; another maxim might urge me to be honest to my friends. These are instances of the kind of concrete, practical matters for which maxims are suited. Every maxim is established by an individual actor to direct his or her own πρᾶξις. The maxim remains valid for as long as the actor follows it, and it can be immediately given up or replaced by a new one, should πρᾶξις take another direction. Maxims therefore present us with a genuine, positive contribution made by subjectivity to the practical realm of human action.

In contrast to maxims, which prepare the ground for subjective πρᾶξις, intersubjective πρᾶξις requires another kind of orientation which will bind all individual actors into a political whole by prescribing ways of acting to be followed by everyone. Let us call the requirements of intersubjective πρᾶξις the norms of social behavior. Viewed in this way, norms represent a densely woven pattern of interrelated maxims, so that the orientation of πρᾶξις is no longer a matter of private choice but of collective obligation. With regard to determining the quality of concrete actions under changing conditions, norms do not differ from maxims. Rather the difference lies in the unity of diverse actions carried out by diverse actors, a unity made possible by norms.

The prescribing of behavior by norms is indispensable to social organization for relevant aspects of interaction. The task of social organization presents us with the problem of how norms function at the many different levels of interaction, for example: from mere conventions to the "unwritten laws" of tradition, from matters of personal or religious conviction to the positive laws marked out by established legal systems. I am not going to elaborate on the structural origin of norms, their degree of validity, their acceptance and correct implementation by relevant actors, or the manifold historical conditions they reflect. All of these considerations are certainly important for a full-fledged theory of norms, but they need not concern us here.

The next move is to bring us back to the main issue of politics. Norms regulate interaction in important sectors of social organization, but they do not themselves constitute the ground of interaction or the basis for society. When norms are able to perform their appropriate function of making specific ways of acting binding on everyone, interaction must already be institutionalized, and society, as the ultimate horizon for interaction, must already exist. The question is: what then has to be presupposed in order to enable norms to perform their rightful function? The unity of all norms in their totality cannot itself be produced by norms, precisely because there is no norm to prescribe such a unity. This unity, given at a certain time to a certain society, constitutes the general framework of politics. Just as no one maxim alone can adequately designate the point of intersection where all other maxims come together and thereby bring about the transition from subjective responsibility to intersubjective order, there is likewise no one norm obliging us to seek the unity of all norms. Such an integrated unity of norms, however, is a political question whose far-reaching implications extend beyond all the ephemeral controversies and interests of everyday life. This unity, which encompasses the multiplicity of all norms and assigns every norm its place in this multiplicity, is fundamental to any society which understands itself to be a unified and unifying whole. It is the ultimate form which can be given to the coherent actions of members of a society who are both autonomous, acting subjects as well as executors of collective πρᾶξις. To put it succinctly, I consider politics to be the unity of norms in a given society.

As I mentioned at the beginning of this essay, commonly held opinions about issues concerning all members of society are essential for genuine political coherence. I further suggested that language is the medium through which such opinions are meaningfully articulated and exchanged, submitted to corrective criticism and in this way continue to maintain their relevance and efficacy. Linguistic communication forges and strengthens the bonds of community in precisely those matters important to each and every member of a political community. The more people speak openly about what they have in common, the more they feel united when it comes to acting together. In order for norms to function effectively on the various levels of social organization, they must presuppose the unity implicit in such an organization. Since norms alone are unable to establish this necessary unity, we must fall back on language as the only means through which such a unity can find its appropriate, concrete expression.

Language thus proves to be fundamental to politics. But although it is obvious that maxims as well as norms are expressed by means of language, they often do their job of directing subjective and intersubjective actions without necessarily displaying their linguistic force. This is shown by the fact that a great number of unspoken maxims and semiconscious norms are at work in the practical realm without ever being spelled out in words. Nothing comparable can ever be the case for the unity of norms in which the political self-understanding of a given society resides. The unity, which brings together all individual norms, does not exhibit its binding power by tacitly guiding the actions of all members of that society without the possibility of communication by speech. In the absence of language, as the basic medium of communication, a unity of norms would not exist. Since this unity is the mirror in which the political identity of any given historical society is reflected, this identity must be continuously articulated and reinforced by ongoing discussions about common values and convictions.

The political importance of communication through language cannot be overestimated. The members of a given society have as much in common as they are able to say to one another. By means of language, political unity takes shape and finds its substantive corroboration in history. With this point I have reached the end of this essay. Allow me, however, to make one addendum to my argument. The emphasis I have given language should not be identified or confused with the model provided by theories of the so-called ideal dialogue. Habermas and other contributors to communication theory have championed this idea as the cure-all for every social and political malady. In my view, however, all they have in fact produced are refurbished versions of bygone social-contract theories with instruments borrowed from more recent philosophies of language.

In the ideal dialogue, concrete historical conditions, underlying practical interactions, are eliminated with the help of utopian criteria which remain the same for all societies, because no actual society fits such criteria. Through the rose-tinted glasses of the ideal dialogue, the systematic abstractions of classical social contract theories, which presuppose equally atomized individuals, seem to disappear. A closer look, however, reveals that the participants in the ideal dialogue are not members of political communities acting in accordance with maxims and norms, in fact, they are not human at all, but rather indistinguishable representatives of the pure principle of subjectivity. The dialogue's rationality claim depends upon the equality of the participants, which is theoretically guaranteed from the outset. The concept of πρᾶξις, understood as the basis of an adequate theory of politics, surrenders itself to the pseudopractical vocabulary of speech acts. Communication among equal dialogue partners seems to be the model for political life, while the orientation toward the common good, toward shared opinions, values, and beliefs, is considered secondary. The ideal of a dialogue free from repression cannot render, however, a true account of the role language plays in politics, for the simple reason that there is nothing concrete to discuss. The ideal dialogue is an abstract, philosophical substitute for the complex reality of political πρᾶξις. The lesson to be learned from this most recent triumph of the principle of subjectivity is to be cautious with the use of substitutes. As we saw in the case of Hegel's logical dialectic of freedom, although substitutes may exert a certain rational appeal, they can lead concrete, political analysis astray.

In light of the failure of recent theories to provide a coherent concept of politics, it might be fruitful to refer back to Aristotle's insight into the relation between language and politics. Language, as Aristotle saw, is the medium in which commonly shared values at the basis of political unity are established, clarified and stabilized. These values, however, are not something given beforehand and then valid forever. They owe their existence, legitimation, and longevity to the ongoing, day-to-day discussions among members of political communities. The hermeneutical circle, which seems to be at work here, reads something like the following: there is no possibility of political unity without communication, and no possibility of communication, in the ultimate sense of the word, without community.

NOTES

1. Aristotle, *Politics*, 1253 a 7–18.
2. Plato, *Republic*, 505e.
3. Aristotle, *Politics*, VII, 1–3
4. G. W. F. Hegel, *Philosophy of Right*, para. 260.
5. G. W. F. Hegel, *Wissenschaft der Logik*, ed. Georg Lasson, vol. 2 (Hamburg, 1975), p. 240 ff.
6. John Stuart Mill, *On Liberty*, in *Utilitarianism, Liberty, Representative Government: Selections from Auguste Comte and Positivism*, ed. H. B. Acton (London, 1972), p. 65.
7. Ibid., p. 115.
8. Ibid., pp. 76–76.

SIX

Paradigm Evolution in Political Philosophy: Aristotle and Hobbes

Manfred Riedel

I

The question of the relationship of Thomas Hobbes's political philosophy to preceding tradition has always been a matter of debate. The controversy, kindled in Hobbes's time through his polemics with his predecessors, received fresh fuel in our century. The essential counterpoints were set by F. Tönnies and J. Laird, the two patriarchs of recent Hobbes scholarship. The revolutionary element, as Tönnies maintains, is contained in the principle on the state of nature, in the axiom of *homo homini lupus* which discards the classical idea of ζῷον πολίτικον and the associated scholastic-natural right concept of an original community of peace and law among mankind; the traditional element, according to Laird, lies in the principle of citizenship, in the axiom of *homo homini* which is complementary to the first axiom and thereby brings the totality of Hobbes's political philosophy into relief.[1] Laird bases his argument, inter alia, on the thesis with which L. Strauss had further developed the controversy: that his theory does not spring from modern mechanics, as earlier Hobbes interpretations assumed, but from antique sources.[2] The question is what is the nature of these sources; do they in fact, to speak metaphorically, dry up with Hobbes or do they not rather continue to flow underground, emerging into the bed of modern philosophy which he helped prepare?

A clear answer to this question was given—before Strauss—by F. Brandt, an answer which is all the more interesting in that it does not refer to political philosophy but to natural philosophy, i.e., the adoption of Galileo's mechanics. According to Brandt, it can be understood only in the historical context of Aristotelian philosophy.[3] What Brandt demonstrates with the example of the *Theory of the Body*—that its basic concepts, substance and accident, space and time, moment and motion, rely on Aristotelian physics even where these concepts are criticized or expressly rejected as untenable—is also shown by Strauss in another part of the philosophical system, the *Theory of Man*, whose central chapters are based on Aristotle's *Rhetoric*. It would probably be difficult, Strauss observes, to find another classical work whose importance for Hobbes's political philosophy could be anywhere near that of the *Rhetoric*.

Nonetheless, Strauss's thesis remains peculiarly ambiguous. While Strauss attributes the anthropological basis to the Aristotelian tradition, he explains the construction of the third part of the philosophical system, the *Theory of the Citizen*, on the premise of a complete break with the basic political suppositions of just this tradition, the primacy of the concept of law over that of right. The revolutionary element, Strauss agrees with Tönnies, consists in the primacy of the individual's natural right, his subjective claim to self-preservation as against the objective obligation under a universally valid law of reason.[4]

Conversely, M. Oakeshott, with good reason I believe, has brought into relief the conservative element that links Hobbes's philosophy, though not to the original Aristotelian tradition, but to one of its historical variants, the nominalism of the late Middle Ages.[5] As its source, J. W. N. Watkins was able to identify the Aristotelianism of the Padua School.[6] Following on from Oakeshott and Watkins and from the results of the controversy with Strauss, which point in the same direction (a controversy I shall not pursue any further here[7]), Thomas A. Spragens, Jr. has taken up again the question of the relationship of Hobbes's political philosophy to preceding tradition. In contrast to Brandt and Strauss, Spragens does not orient himself solely to natural philosophy or solely to political philosophy; nor does he restrict himself, like most Hobbes scholars who have examined this question,[8] to one or another aspect in the various writings. Instead, Spragens interprets Hobbes's philosophy as a whole on the thesis of a "systematic paradigm transformation"—the critical reference to Aristotle and the then-prevailing Aristotelianism, constantly measuring itself against its conceptualism and still seeking to reconcile itself with this even while radically and dramatically transforming it. It is generally acknowledged, Spragens observes, that Hobbes's political philosophy marks a revolutionary turning point in the history of political thought. What has not been recognized is its systematic structure, which does not simply represent a significant change or a radical break.[9] I agree with this statement, and as I feel that the prospect presents itself of reaching a conclusion to the controversy on the relationship between Hobbes and Aristotle, I should like as my first step here to conduct a more detailed examination of the inquiry.

The term used here, *paradigm transformation*, varies the expression *paradigm change* with which Thomas S. Kuhn circumscribes the relationship between tradition and revolution in the history of science. By *paradigm*, Spragens, like Kuhn, understands complex units of diverse constituent elements which comprise both preconceptual suppositions and generally accepted convictions of a community of scholars as well as conceptual universalities according to which the basic concepts of the respective discipline are structured, empirical data ordered, and solutions to problems sought. While for Kuhn these units are relatively self-contained, so that the emergence of new paradigms from elements of the old appears in the history of science as a not very remarkable case of traditional ("normal") science,[10] Spragens presupposes that they are not mutually exclusive but overlap and influence each other. What the term *paradigm transformation* intends to circumscribe is the concrete unity of the history of science itself, which never proceeds in bounds but moves at all times both heterogeneously and continuously.

Although Spragens takes account of the indisputable fact that every science starts to a certain extent from behind, that is, from existing knowledge, the term cannot deny affinity with the term *paradigm change*. Analogous to Kuhn's original orientation to the change from the Ptolemaic to the Copernican system, Spragens refers to a paradigm which he, invoking Kuhn's introduction of the term to astronomy, calls "cosmological paradigm" and equates with Aristotelian natural philosophy. This "cosmological paradigm" of Aristotle, which served until the seventeenth century as the basic model for the tradition-forming study of nature, for the interpretation of the fundamental realities of the universe and the pattern of their interrelationships, was transformed by Hobbes. According to Spragens, paradigm transformations are more complex than paradigm changes, in which one paradigm is replaced by another and is thereby fundamentally transcended; they do not possess the structure of a scientific revolution as described by Kuhn, for their individual constituent elements—presuppositions, convictions, and basic concepts—change, but the change can only proceed along the lines prescribed by the original paradigm. At the end of such a transformation, Spragens concludes quite consistently, the ensuing paradigm is always a hybrid configuration of new and old elements; the influence of the older paradigm persists, even where its appearance has changed beyond recognition.[11]

This appears to me to define exactly the process that takes place in both the natural and the political philosophy of Hobbes. Only I do not believe that it takes place as the Spragens's thesis presupposes: that the transformation of the cosmological paradigm of nature implicates such a transformation of the political paradigm of society.[12] The transformation of the Aristotelian paradigm—this is my counterthesis—does not inevitably bring with it significant implications for political philosophy; it takes place by itself, independently of natural philosophy, and can be recognized and described from the premises peculiar to it.

Before going on to substantiate this thesis, let me briefly outline it. The question of the relationship of Hobbes's political philosophy to tradition—and on this point I entirely agree with Spragens—is not a question of intellectual origin but of intellectual substance: it concerns both the systematic understanding of his theory and the turning point that it signifies in the history of political thought. I also agree that Hobbes, while dismantling piece by piece the intellectual substance of the paradigm of nature and society established by Aristotle, nonetheless tacitly adopts the supporting structure and the relationship pattern that it embodies.[13] However, to describe this process, the term *paradigm transformation* is, I feel, too broadly formulated. It depicts perhaps the transition at the level of world views but does not encompass adequately what happens at the conceptual level, that is, in philosophizing. I therefore prefer to speak of *paradigm evolution*—a term which is intended first to avoid the assumption of separate paradigms which replace each other or where one is "translated" into the other and secondly to denote the hermeneutic aspect of paradigm formation omitted by Kuhn and Spragens, the level of explicable concepts and their interpretation. For the intellectual substance of the Aristotelian paradigm is nothing other than the force of the concept generated by it, which constitutes what we call *tradition*. Its founder in the realm of philosophy is Aristotle. But the real bearer of the tradition is not the particular *school* that adopts a paradigm but the language, whose universality overlaps the assumedly separate or succeeding paradigms. In using the term *paradigm evolution,* I mean precisely this evolution of concepts, in hermeneutic terms: the history of their influence transmitted through language,[14] which always incorporates both revolutionary and traditional elements, the confrontation of which spurs the development of the intellectual substance of any great philosophy.

In setting ourselves the task of analyzing the evolution of a few basic political concepts in the movement of philosophical thought from Aristotle to Hobbes, that is, from the classical theory of the πόλις to the modern philosophy of the state, three premises are assumed: (1) that paradigms in political philosophy are founded through the overlapping unity of the language and constituted essentially in the concrete unity of the concept; (2) that concepts are not simply terms in the sense of arbitrary conventions for the convenience of discourse and thus not simply an outer mantle of thought, argument, and answer, but prior determinations of possible inquiry and thus conditions for the possibility of any fresh start in philosophy; and (3) that the meaning of concepts follows their usage in that they change, but that this change is tradition forming and so the continuity appears of one and the same movement in which thought itself consists.

II

Language, which embraces all thought, shows, according to Hobbes, a certain similarity with spiders' webs, which was also said at times of the laws of Solon: the weak and delicate minds get caught in the words and entangle themselves therein, but the stronger ones break through the web. Hobbes—and there can be no doubts about this—counted himself among the stronger minds, those who, like the legislators of antiquity, imposed laws on language and a new structure on the web of words by first giving the things their names. But that this self-assessment, which rests philosophically on the position of nominalism, is incorrect can no longer be doubted, either. Most of the scholars already mentioned have established that Aristotelian concepts and inquiries are embodied in Hobbes's thinking. On the other hand, the break from Aristotle is equally apparent through a number of ambiguous statements in Hobbes's writing, so that one has to ask how Hobbes, a philosopher, can think in Aristotelian concepts and at the same time be a firm anti-Aristotelian.

Whoever holds fast to Hobbes's utterances about himself and his place in the tradition will easily find arguments in support of Kuhn's thesis of paradigm change. For the pathos of the innovator, a pathos that animated Machiavelli and others, leads Hobbes to proclaim that his theory of sovereign power differs fundamentally from the practice through most of the world, especially the Western parts, which derived their moral knowledge from the Romans and Athenians.[15]

Yes, and more: he flatly asserts that political philosophy was no older than his book *De Cive*,[16] and that no one before him had sufficient curiosity and method to discover its true rules.[17] The same dogmatism is reflected in his judgment of traditional paradigms, especially those, for instance, associated with the names of Aristotle, Cicero, Thomas Aquinas, and Suárez, whereby Hobbes groups the political philosophy of the Greeks, the Romans, and the Christian Middle Ages into one paradigm. The theory of sovereignty and authority is new, because, as Hobbes stated in his early political work *Elements of Law* (1640), until Hobbes's day no one had demanded to know more on this subject than what Aristotle had observed two thousand years earlier, and all accepted such opinions as principles which were already universally known, without examining their truth or falsity.[18] Similar arguments can be found in *De Cive* (1642) and later in *Leviathan* (1651), where the validity of the classic political paradigm is limited in time and space and associated with past forms of life. Writing about the Germanic and Latin peoples of modern Europe, Hobbes says: "In these western parts of the world we are made to receive our opinions concerning the institution and rights of commonwealths from Aristotle, Cicero and other men, Greeks and Romans, that, living under popular states derived those rights, not from the principles of nature, but transcribed them into their books, out of the practice of their own commonwealths which were popular; as the Grammarians describe the rules of language out of the practice of the time or the rules of poetry out of the poems of Homer and Virgil."[19] And in *Behemoth*, the work which most severely breaks with the tradition, Hobbes even speaks of the "babbling philosophy of Aristotle and other Greeks," which, transmitted through the universities, was the cause of civil wars and revolutions.[20]

This picture is, however, qualified by other statements. Hobbes, like all other philosophers at that time, was familiar with the teachings of Aristotelian philosophy, which he had studied at Oxford. We do not know whether Hobbes read Aristotle in the original or in the version of the scholastic commentators. But it is certain not only that medieval Aristotelianism is present in his work but also that an early modern variation, namely the adoption of Aristotelian philosophy by the humanists, is constantly there.[21] It is not just coincidental that Hobbes occasionally uses the humanistic τόπος of the fallibility of all human beings to defend Aristotle and other ancient philosophers from unwarranted criticism.[22] Even when he was older, Hobbes had, in the manner of the humanists, praise for those few who, like Aristotle and the ancients, carried on scientific work for the sake of the pleasure involved and combined it with the acquisition and mastery of difficult and penetrating theories.[23] The adoption of Aristotle by the humanists differs from medieval Aristotelian philosophy in that the discrepancy between the Latin and the Greek texts was reduced by the greater elegance of the translation and was propagated by conceptual familiarity because of the fidelity of their translations to their experiences of life forms. The humanists were not interested in the entire Corpus Aristotelicum but rather in that part of it which, according to Aristotelian understanding, has as its theme man, his forms of activity, institutions, and goals in life within the total political context.[24] It is Aristotle's political philosophy which forms the center of interest for the humanists, whose adoption of Aristotle was also the starting point for Hobbes. He was, according to his educational background, a humanist. Whereas the humanism of the Renaissance, unenlightened in regard to itself, attempted to apply the tradition of classical forms of life to the modern world and thereby bring both to coincide, Hobbes discovers the undeniable historical difference, retaining nevertheless their rational core. Thus my thesis can be stated more precisely now: Hobbes represents a historically enlightened humanism as opposed to the historically naive (dogmatic) humanism: the classic political idea of the unity of civility and humanity, which had been exaggerated by the forms of life of republican civic humanism during the Renaissance.

III

The key to understanding the evolution of the paradigm is the complementary nature of the axioms about man mentioned at the outset, a fact which was emphasized by Hobbes himself. In the riverbed of modern theories of state prepared by these axioms, there are still ancient sources flowing: "To speak impartially, both sayings are very true: that man to man is a kind of a god; and that man to man is an errant wolf. The first is true if we compare citizens among themselves; and the second if we compare cities. In the one there is some analogy of similitude with the deity, to wit, justice, and charity, the twin sisters of peace. But in the other, good men must defend themselves by taking to them for a sanctuary the twin daughters of war, deceit, and violence that is, in plain terms a more brutal rapacity."[25] The second axiom is not a discovery of Hobbes in regard to the choice of words or the content but is a classical description, originated by Plato and passed on by Aristotle, of man as an emotional and passionate creature who seeks conflict with others and is to that extent similar to animals.[26] Much the same is true for the first axiom, which outlines the idea of a rational and just man who, communicating as a citizen with his fellow citizens, approaches God by being a citizen. Together the two sentences represent the frame of reference for Hobbes's political philosophy. The "theory of the natural condition" is derived from one, the "theory of the civil condition" from the other; and both are related to each other in the same way as passion and reason, animal and man, are related.[27]

In this relationship between the theorems of the modern paradigm there still remains one axiom as it is formulated in Aristotle's *Politics*. This axiom can be summarily characterized accordingly: man's nature, his humanity, is not a natural quality but has something to do with his civility, reason, justice, and freedom, which presuppose as specifically human characteristics the existence of the civic union, or the civil society (πολιτικὴ κοινωνία), as it was called by Aristotle.[28] It is the same assumption which Hobbes makes: that man's humanity is determined by the civility possible for him.

The affinity of these paradigms is usually overlooked because of the impression created by Hobbes's especially harsh judgment of Aristotle's *Politics*, that nothing could be more repugnant to the theory of rule than this book.[29] In addition to that, there is Hobbes's continual polemic against Aristotle's famous formula of man as a ζῷον πολίτικον.[30] This polemic can only be directed at the authors of late antiquity, such as Zeno and Plutarch or Cicero and Seneca, who interpreted this formula as though for man, living together with others satisfied a basic need and was in this sense natural, whereas for Aristotle, men are capable of living in the πόλις not because of their nature but only through coercion. And in the *Leviathan*, where the formula is criticized in connection with Aristotle's reference to living creatures such as bees and ants, Hobbes misunderstands their exemplary function, which is exactly to make clear the difference between animal and human forms of life.[31] In truth, Hobbes maintains the same thing that Aristotle does, according to which everyone possesses a natural desire to live with others, though the πόλις itself as a human form of life is not a natural product but the work of a founder and his skills, laws, and institutions.[32] I do not deny, Hobbes says, that men endeavor to come together in societies (*societates*) because of a kind of natural impulse, but civil societies (*societates civiles*) are not mere gatherings; they are unions (*foedera*), the making of which necessitates trust and covenants.[33]

Tönnies, in his commentary on this part of the text, pointed out that Hobbes, who laid a great deal of worth on definitions, did not in any way define the concept of "society."[34] Does he mean the same thing when he speaks about "society in general" (*societas*) at the beginning of *De cive* and about "civil society" (*societas civilis*) in the footnotes? Apparently not, because Hobbes makes a distinction here similar to the one Aristotle made in the first book of the *Politics*. What is defined is the πόλις, about which it is said that it is a kind of society (κοινωνία), namely the society called "civil" (πολιτικὴ κοινωνία), which encompasses and unifies all other possible kinds of society within itself, beginning with the relationship between master and slave and extending to the complex units of the home, and neighborhood, business and cultural associations, professional and social societies.[35] Whereas the concept of "society" is the supreme kind of union and as such indefinable, the predicate "civil" constitutes its specific difference to other societies. That would explain why the concepts "state" (πόλις, *civilis*) and "civil society" (πολιτικὴ κοινωνία, *societas civilis*) mean the same thing in Aristotle's philosophy and medieval scholasticism: they identify that political paradigm, the civic union.[36] We can speak here of the formula of political identity. "State" and "civil society" are identical and never ambiguous or politically indifferent; logically they are both defined unequivocally and represent the same concept.

Hobbes adopted this conceptual structure and its fundamental formula of political identity, applying it to his problem—the evolution of the civic union to *Leviathan*. With it he counters the formula of political indifference which had taken over the position of the classical formula of political identity in the early modern theory of natural law: that the political concept could be determined in any number of ways, either by a social covenant or by a contract with the ruler or by a mixture of both. The identity formula implies that society and rule are identical and never politically indifferent to one another, because the one concept cannot be determined without the other.[37] The implication of the formula of indifference is exactly the opposite: both concepts are independent from one another, each one for itself exhausts the essence of political reality whereby the determination of their relation to each other, in case it is sought, can be characterized as being "not only—but also."

It is obvious that political theory will therefore remain vague and political practice will be continually in danger of failing. In this situation Hobbes returns to aspects of the classical paradigm, in particular the definition of πόλις as πολιτικὴ κοινωνία, a conceptual structure which he was familiar with from the very beginning through the Latin of the identity formula: *civitas sive societas civilis*, in the humanistic adoption of Aristotle. In the first draft of the new paradigm, the *Elements of Law* (1640), the one side of the formula of indifference, that of "society," appears directly in the definition as the undetermined "multitude of men" seeking to fill the vacuum between the civic union and Leviathan: "This union so made, is that which men call nowadays a Body Politic or civil society; and the Greeks call it πόλις, that is to say, a city; which may be defined to be a multitude of men, united as one person by a common power, for their common peace, defence and benefit."[38] The idea of the civic union, upon which the weight of the definition rests, is not thought of functionally but substantially, despite the concept of a person introduced here for the first time. In reference to Aristotle, Hobbes recognizes democracy as having genetic and political primacy among all the forms of rule, because it originates directly in the contractual union and has freedom as its purpose.[39] It is not without reason that Hobbes refers to contemporary usage of language—the words *state* and *community* do not even appear—and to the primacy of democracy which arises directly from the covenant and is prior to all other forms of rule. And finally it should not be overlooked that Hobbes defines the sovereign's power not as the "highest" but as the "general" or "common" power.

All these traditional political elements go through a phase of evolution in *De Cive* (1642), because Hobbes now interprets the idea of the civic union only functionally. The mere unification of the citizens (*unio civilis*) almost constitutes (*paene eo ipso*) a democracy because they come together as free equals. However, the constitution would immediately return to the state of nature once the council broke up, unless of course it continued in the form of the person of the ruler. The *civitas* is no longer defined only as *societas*, but also as *persona civilis*, whose will represents the will of all persons according to the covenant with the citizens.[40] The political indifference between "rule" and "society" disappears with the inclusion of the concept of the person in the definition of the state. Although Hobbes, as early as the *Elements of Law*, no longer shared the traditional Aristotelian conception dominant in Bodin's writings whereby the civic union existed before all rule in the form of "civil society," and sovereign state power is only adjoined to an association of individuals already existing for itself, as a specific characteristic the idea of union through consensus is still prominent there. What has validity for the civic union is also true for all unions between men, so that the institution of civil society according to covenant is, as it were, perpetuated in the subordinate corporations which are likewise provided with a ruling power.[41] This perpetuation is prevented with the evolution of elements of the Aristotelian paradigm, because the sovereign power, instead of functioning as a specific characteristic of the association, is itself carried by the person who is supplementarily adjoined to the classical identity formula: "Unio autem sic facta, appellatur civitas sive societas civilis, atque etiam persona civilis."[42] The definition still retains the reference to the "multitude of men" who form the real substratum of the body politic. On closer examination, however, the identity formula proves to be just as functional as the idea of the unity of wills on which it is based. The *societas civilis* is the *persona civilis*, because it cannot be identical with itself. The individual with whom the process of constitution began is in the state of nature, a natural person who represents nothing but himself. For that reason, there is no such thing for Hobbes as a society before the existence of the body politic, but only the multitude of men which is not identical, but indifferent, i.e., an indeterminable plurality. But because the will of the many is unable to reach any possible unity of wills as a consequence of the primacy of the natural right of all individual wills to themselves, a supreme power is required to create this unity by coercion and this is called "rule" (*imperium*).[43] The reestablishment of the political identity is accomplished by the concept of rule which enters the identity formula as the other side of the relation of indifference. It is merely a consequence of the evolution of the idea of the civic union when it is completely dropped. This happens in *Leviathan*, where Hobbes no longer speaks of the primacy of democracy but states, in the opposition to Aristotle, that freedom is the same in all forms of rule.[44] Here we find, under the newly introduced title of "Commonwealth," the first definition of the modern state which establishes the connection between the concepts of person and rule. It no longer coincides with civil society but with one person, of whose acts a great multitude, by mutual covenants one with another, have made themselves everyone the author, to the end he may use the strength and means of them all, as he shall think expedient, for their peace and common defense.[45] The idea of the union from which Hobbes in the adoption of the classical paradigm originally began evaporates into the mutuality of a covenant which forms the basis of the state still without being able to establish it. To make oneself the author of the acts of one person and thereby subordinate one's own will and judgment to his will and judgment is indeed more than the mere union by consent. It is the union of all conceived in one and the same person who has concentrated all power in himself. Whoever embodies this person, Hobbes explains, "is called sovereign, and said to have sovereign power (*summa potestas*); and every one besides, his subject (*subditus*)."[46]

IV

Although Hobbes thereby nominally abandons the identity formula, he does not surrender, even in the final version of his political philosophy, the original idea he had in the beginning: the idea of the unity of civility and humanity. Thinking often completely contrary to Aristotle, Hobbes nevertheless remains in touch with the classical problem, because he defends the concentration of power which he advocates with the Aristotelian argument that only the unconditional identification of the subject with the state can guarantee the identity of citizen and man. Man's essence is not a natural characteristic, because it is first formed in the condition of civility and that means, according to Hobbes, by leaving the state of nature. Outside of the state (*civitas*), according to the apparently specific modern apologia which nonetheless uses elements and patterns for argumentation from the classical paradigm, "one defends oneself through one's own strength; within the state through the strength of all. Outside of the state no one is certain of the fruits of his labor; within the state everyone has this security. Finally, outside of the state begins the kingdom of passions, war, fear, poverty, loathsomeness, loneliness, barbarism, ignorance, brutality; on the other hand within the state begins the kingdom of reason, peace, security, wealth, taste, sociability, splendor, science, and charity."[47] The artistic conceptual antithesis contains, if you will, the actual axioms of the evolution of the paradigm: that humanity can be achieved only through civility, that is, the search for peace commanded by the law of nature. It is the same argument Aristotle uses to justify the institution of the πόλις: it originates in order to prevent the war of everyone with everyone and to secure mere existence (ζῆν), but it exists in order to make the good life possible, that is, the just and therefore happy life (εὖ ζῆν).[48] And just as justice is not something good in and for itself for Aristotle, so is peace for Hobbes: the real reason for seeking peace is that without it a prosperous and humane life is impossible.

At this point of their greatest unanimity the acute difference between Hobbes and Aristotle becomes apparent. What we have designated as the evolution of the paradigm and searched for in its origin guided by the political identity formula is nothing other than the development from the classical civic union to the modern state society which Hobbes recapitulates on his way to the *Leviathan*. Factually, it is the transformation of the citizen into the subject who lives only the life of a private person. After overcoming the fear of death by leaving the state of nature, he is preoccupied with the cares of life. Classical political philosophy had conferred them on the class of the subjugated, the slaves and hand workers, and contrasted the cares of life with the pursuit of the good life characterizing the class of the free men or citizens. The happiness of the good life is achieved through civility when a person participates as a citizen in the power of ruling and communicates rationally, justly, and freely with his equals. This happiness is denied to the subjects of the modern state society. But insofar as the sovereign abolishes the political character of the civic union he creates the possibility of a new kind of happiness. He is then responsible for amply providing the citizens with the goods not just for living but also for pleasure.[49] What the subject as a person and a citizen can expect is the satisfaction of all his private human needs. Concerning this satisfaction, however, the idea of the good life is misunderstood as being hedonistic. Hobbes speaks on the one hand about the *bene viveré* of the citizen entirely in Aristotelian sense, on the other hand about the *jucundissime vivere* of man.[50] This ambiguity expresses conceptually what is actually happening historically: that the private person as a human being with needs moves to the forefront of political practice. The sovereign, who must on the one side reduce the citizen to a subject in order to guarantee the lives of the people is on the other required to fulfill the demand of the people for satisfaction of their needs.

The fulfillment of this demand, which for Hobbes is established in accordance with natural right, can be pursued directly by the individuals themselves. They are not literally subjugated, but free within the state—free by virtue of the will of the sovereign within the space remaining *between* the laws. The freedom of the citizen as a subject, and that means civil freedom in the modern sense of the word, refers according to Hobbes to those areas where the laws neither command nor prohibit and which are therefore subject only to the discretion and judgment of the individual: the freedom to buy and sell, enjoy one's property and have it at one's disposal, to enter into contracts with one another, to be free to choose a place of residence, a business, a profession, and so forth. Here the possibility is given to the individuals to dispose at will of the means necessary for the purpose of self-preservation and to produce things for those needs which belong to the *jucundissime vivere.* In acts of this kind the natural state of war of everyone against everyone—although more civil—is reproduced at a higher level, or as Hobbes would prefer to say, that part of natural right which the laws have allowed to remain for the citizens.[51] It is a great achievement of Hobbes's that even while being aware of the fact that his position here contradicted the classical paradigm he defined the concept of "civil freedoms" only negatively. He recognized that the civil liberties of the ancients were not the liberties of the individual citizens, but of the πόλις or *civitas (non civium singularium, sed civitatis libertas est)*.[52] Thus he draws the conclusion from the social and historical development in modern times that was long overdue. Under the conditions of the modern state and the process of eliminating the political character of the civic union begun by the state, the concept of civil freedom can only be defined negatively, because freedom in the traditional political sense of civil action has been taken away from the citizen. What remains is freedom of man as it is secured in natural law, which now becomes the positive content of civil liberty in the sense of rising liberalism. This freedom is restricted to the sphere which has been spared by the sovereign in order to enable the most appropriate use of the individual's pursuit of happiness and the activities associated with it.[53]

One would think that it was only a step from here to Hegel's realization that the state itself is the sphere of civil society and distinct from it. One would thereby be overlooking, however, not only the relatively unimportant position of this aspect in the whole context of Hobbes's system, but also its subordination to the state which corresponds to the historical situation. Hobbes abandons the classical identity formula without discovering the modern formula of difference: that the state and civil society are separate. The two concepts are not distinguished, because the modern civil society for the meantime only exists within a limited sphere of the Leviathan. In contrast to the system of covenants and laws, which, as the basis of Hobbes's construction, are supposed to last for eternity, the contracts which have been made there and the laws of this sphere, which hardly have been recognized, are unimportant. Hobbes does indeed give the activity resulting from the discretion and free judgment of private citizens the title of Roman Law, but not its own proper concept of society, because this remains entangled either in the idea of the body politic or in the concept of the Leviathan.[54] The legal and contractual construction of the natural law theory, which first provides civil liberties for the individual, creates at the same time the illusion of being able to banish them forever to those spheres which the sovereign has left open.

NOTES

This essay originally appeared in the *Graduate Faculty Philosophy Journal,* vol. 9, no. 1 (1982), pp. 109–124.

1. F. Tönnies, "Hobbes und das Zoön Politikon," *Zeitschrift für Völkerrecht,* 12 (1923), pp. 471–88; J. Laird, "Hobbes on Aristotle's Politics," *Proceedings of the Aristotelian Society,* N.S. 4 (1942–43), pp. 1–20.

2. L. Strauss, *The Political Philosophy of Thomas Hobbes: Its Basis and Genesis* (Oxford, 1936), p. 27 ff.

3. F. Brandt, *Thomas Hobbes's Mechanical Conception of Nature* (Copenhagen, 1928), p. 13 ff.

4. Strauss, *The Political Philosophy of Thomas Hobbes,* p. 35.

5. M. Oakeshott, "Dr. Leo Strauss on Hobbes," in *Politica,* 2 (1936–37), pp. 364–79; M. Oakeshott, ed., *Leviathan* (Oxford, 1946), Introduction, pp. xix–xxv.

6. J.W.N. Watkins, *Hobbes's System of Ideas: A Study in the Political Significance of Philosophical Theories* (London, 1965), p. 52 ff.

7. See W. Greenleaf, "Hobbes: The Problem of Interpretation," in R. Koselleck and R. Schnur, eds., *Hobbes-Forschungen* (Berlin, 1969), pp. 9–31.

8. See R. Polin, *Politique et philosophie chez Thomas Hobbes* (Paris, 1953); R. Peters, *Hobbes* (London, 1956, 1967); H. Warrender, *The Political Philosophy of Hobbes: His Theory of Obligation* (Oxford, 1957); F. C. Hood, *The Divine Politics of Thomas Hobbes* (Oxford, 1964); M. M. Goldsmith, *Hobbes's Science of Politics* (New York, 1966).

9. Thomas A. Spragens, Jr., *The Politics of Motion: The World of Thomas Hobbes* (Lexington, Ky., 1973), p. 203.

10. Thomas S. Kuhn, *The Structure of Scientific Revolutions* (Chicago, 1964), p. 148.

11. Spragens, *The Politics of Motion,* p. 45.

12. Ibid., p. 41.

13. Ibid., pp. 41, 203.

14. I refer to H. -G. Gadamer, *Wahrheit und Methode: Grundzüge der philosophischen Hermeneutik* (Tübingen, 1960, 1975).

15. Thomas Hobbes, *Leviathan* (1651), ch. 31.

16. Thomas Hobbes, *De Corpore* (1655), *Ep. ded.*

17. Hobbes, *Leviathan,* ch. 20. Sheldon S. Wolin rightly observes in this connection that Hobbes far outdoes Machiavelli in his endeavors to destroy traditional paradigms. See Wolin, "Paradigma and Political Science," in P. King and C. Parekh, eds., *Politics and Experience: Essays Presented to Professor Michael Oakeshott on the Occasion of his Retirement* (Cambridge, Mass., 1968), p. 139 ff.

18. Thomas Hobbes, *Elements of Law*, pt. 1, ch 13, 3.

19. Hobbes, *Leviathan*, ch. 21; *De Cive, Ep. ded.*

20. Thomas Hobbes, *Behemoth or the Long Parliament,* in *English Works*, ed. Sir William Molesworth, vol. 6, p. 282.

21. See my contribution on Aristotelianism and humanism, "Zur frühzeitlichen Rezeption der Aristotelischen Politik," in *Metaphysik und Metapolitik: Studien zu Aristoteles und zur politischen Sprache der neuzeitlichen Philosophie* (Frankfurt, 1975), pp. 109–28.

22. Thomas Hobbes, *Dialogue of the Common Laws* (1666), in *English Works,* vol. 6, p. 99.

23. Thomas Hobbes, *Decameron Physiologicum*, in *English Works*, vol. 7, p. 72.

24. Aristotle, *Nicomachean Ethics,* X 10, 1181 b 15.

25. Hobbes, *De Cive, Ep. ded.*

26. That was precisely pointed out by Laird, *Hobbes on Aristotle's Politics*, p. 6 f.

27. Thomas Hobbes, *Philosophical Rudiments concerning Government and Society,* II, ch. 7, p. 18.

28. Aristotle, *Politics,* I 2, 1262 b 27–1253 a 5.

29. Hobbes, *Leviathan,* II, ch. 46.

30. Hobbes, *De Cive,* I 2.

31. Hobbes, *Leviathan,* II, ch 17.

32. Aristotle, *Politics,* I 2, 1253 a 29–31.

33. Hobbes, *De Cive,* I 2, footnote.

34. Tönnies, "Hobbes und das Zoön Politikon," p. 476.

35. Aristotle, *Politics,* I 1–2, 1252 a 1–1252 b 30; *Nicomachean Ethics,* VIII 11.

36. See my study *Vom Bürgerbund zum Leviathan. Kategorienlehre und Kategorienwechsel in der politischen Philosophie* (Stuttgart, 1980).

37. See Aristotle, *Politics,* I 1, 1152 a 7–16.

38. Hobbes, *Elements of Law,* I, c. XIX, 8.

39. Hobbes, *Elements of Law,* II, c. VIII, 3.

40. Hobbes, *De Cive,* c. V 9. The functional element is described in *Elements of Law,* I, c XIX 10, simply as the transfer of "the power and the strength" of every individual to the sovereign. In regard to this, see the valuable essay by F. Tönnies, "Die Lehre von der Volksversammlung und die Urversammlung in Hobbes' Leviathan," *Zeitschrift für deutsche Staatswissenschaft*, 89 (1930), p. 17.

41. See Hobbes, *Elements of Law,* I, c. XIX 9.

42. Hobbes, *De Cive,* c. V 9.

43. Ibid., c. V–XIV.

44. Hobbes, *Leviathan,* II, ch. 21. This noteworthy change in Hobbes's relationship to Aristotle is pointed out by David P Gauthier, *The Logic of Leviathan: The Moral and Political Theory of Thomas Hobbes* (Oxford, 1969), p. 145 f., without, however, explaining it more closely.

45. Hobbes, *Leviathan,* II, ch. 17.

46. Ibid.

47. Hobbes, *De Cive,* X, 1; *De Homine,* X, 5; *Leviathan,* ch. 13.

48. Aristotle, *Politics,* I 2, 1252 b 29–30.

49. Hobbes, *De Cive,* c. XII 4. See also XIII 6; 10; 14–15; *Leviathan*, I, c. 11 and 13; *De Corpore*, c. I 6.

50. See Hobbes, *De Cive*, c. XIII 4.

51. Hobbes, *Elements of Law*, II, c. IX, 4; *De Cive*, c. XIII, 15; Oakeshott, ed., *Leviathan*, II, c. 21, p. 139: "The liberty of a subject lieth therefore only in those things, which in regulating their actions, the sovereign hath praetermitted; such as is the liberty to buy, and sell, and otherwise contract with one another; to choose their own abode, their own diet, their own trade of life, and institute their children as they themselves think fit; and the like." The "liberal" elements in Hobbes's theory of natural law were first convincingly worked out by F. Tönnies, *Thomas Hobbes*, 2d ed. (Stuttgart), p. 180 f.

52. Hobbes, *Leviathan*, II, ch. 21.

53. See Hobbes, *De Cive*, c. XIII, 14.

54. It appears to me that C. B. Macpherson completely disregarded that in his thesis that Hobbes oriented himself according to the "possessive market society." See Macpherson, *The Political Theory of Possessive Individualism* (Oxford, 1962), p. 34 ff.

SEVEN

Civic Prudence in Machiavelli: Toward the Paradigm Transformation in Philosophy in the Transition to Modernity

Klaus Held

Key twentieth-century thinkers have diagnosed a crisis of our time, which may indicate that we are leaving the moderns behind and entering a new era. One could assume from this diagnosis that premodern paradigms, which had lost their ability to guide our thinking in the modern period, may now regain their importance in a modified form. This could also be said of "the prudent citizen," a most influential paradigm for the human dimension of a life lived in common that goes back to Aristotle.

Whether or not this paradigm has a new opportunity of affecting the future depends upon the extent to which it still remained foundational for the orientation of human existence in the world during the modern period. One can see especially well how the moderns took up the premodern paradigms in the thinkers of the Renaissance. At first glance this epoch could appear as merely to have had the character of a "rebirth" of antiquity, that is, of a revival of the old paradigms. But decisive, new paradigms of the modern period burst on the scene in the guise of the renewal of antiquity. This can be seen best in the political philosophy of Machiavelli. It is worth mentioning that with respect to the Romans of the republican epoch, Machiavelli himself occasionally used an Italian equivalent of the term *paradigm*: he called it *esemplo*, that is, a shining example and model for his own time.[1] What he had in mind with this expression was political prudence, and according to Machiavelli it is in this sense that we can emulate the Romans.

The decisive paradigms of philosophy are models for the interpretation of our existence in the world, models which were introduced in the context of epoch-founding and sense-instituting ideas. The origin in antiquity of political philosophy as an introduction of such a framework of ideas is intimately connected with the epoch-founding and sense-instituting origin of philosophy in general. In this origin, which we can find in Heraclitus, Parmenides, and Plato, emerges the idea of philosophy as ἐπιστήμη, "science," in opposition to δόξα as the area of "mere opinion." The philosopher understands himself as a critic of δόξα who wants to replace it immediately with ἐπιστήμη.[2] In Aristotle's thought a process begins in which δόξα becomes rehabilitated as political prudence. The prudent citizen defends the δόξα by exercising a self-critique; in this way he preserves the possibility of δόξα's existence.

First I would like to reconstruct the origins of ancient philosophy just sketched here. In the second section of my considerations I want to show how Machiavelli takes up the paradigm of the prudent citizen. With this, political prudence starts to become deeply ambiguous. I will clarify how and why this ambiguity emerges. In the third and final section I would like to draw from this certain implications for the possible situation of philosophy after modernity: does the ambiguous nature of modern political prudence permit us to hope that the process of the rehabilitation of δόξα can continue in the future?

I

In prephilosophical life we can express an opinion with phrases like "it seems to me" or "it appears to me." The equivalent of such expressions in ancient Greek would have been the idiom δοκεῖ μοι. The corresponding noun is the word δόξα. Since Heraclitus, Parmenides, and Plato it has denoted the way the "many," everyday, average human beings think. This way of thinking is based in an attitude which binds human beings to the narrow pregiven horizons of their life-world. The philosophical critique of δόξα attempts to break through this limitedness, so that human beings open themselves to the horizon that goes beyond all limited life-world horizons: the whole as such, *the* world. This task has defined philosophy up to the present day.

Human beings are already familiar with the world prior to all philosophy insofar as they are somehow aware that all limited horizons belong together; they orient themselves in "the" life-world. But they do not make it thematic *as* the one and the whole world. In my view, philosophy, by virtue of its epoch-founding and sense-instituting origin, undertakes to convince human beings of the possibility of such an openness to the world *as* world.

Under the spell of δόξα human beings only have opinions. Their thinking and acting is determined by the limitedness of their horizons in terms of the δοκεῖ μοι. Philosophy in its initial form is a radical break with δόξα. Therefore philosophy generally rebukes having opinions. But such a critique of having opinions can only appear as a mere opinion to the many who live under the spell of opinion. The frontal attack against δόξα cannot motivate them to open themselves to the world as world. For this reason, Aristotle inaugurates a fundamental change of the philosophical attitude toward δόξα. Accordingly the self-understanding of the philosopher changes: he must and can work on the presupposition that δόξα itself is capable of inaugurating the openness to the world.[3] Opinion can free itself from the narrowness of the limited life-world horizons without ceasing to be opinion, that is, without relinquishing its place to, or being replaced by, ἐπιστήμη.

Such a mutation of opinion is made possible when the many not only naively *have* their many opinions but rather become aware of the fact that there is an all-encompassing sphere of opinion as such; here all opinions compete with one another and assert themselves against one another. This dawning of the self-consciousness of δόξα *as* δόξα does not change the fact that every particular opinion remains bound to the life-world horizon of those having an opinion. But it does signify an openness, because all those who have an opinion must form their opinions by submitting their δοκεῖ μοι to a test; they must ask this question: how can I formulate my opinion in such a way that it can be taken seriously in the competition of opinions? In the formation of my δοκεῖ μοι I must take up the perspectives of others in order to give my opinion the chance to be heard by others. Long after Greek philosophy, Kant would describe this reflective character of forming an opinion as the operation of refletive judgment.[4]

Aristotle could claim such an opening of δόξα itself because the self-consciousness of opinion just sketched had institutionalized itself in the Greek-speaking world as the form of communal life. With the introduction of democracy the Greek πόλις became an open place for the competition of opinions, which are released from the limitedness of their particular life-world horizons. In transcending this limitedness the πόλις became a special type of whole which converges with the philosophical tendency toward the whole as such. The sense of this whole consists precisely in making the transcendence of limitedness possible. On the one hand, the openness of an opinion is secured by its referring to the institutional whole of the πόλις, and on the other hand, the πόλις is constituted by that openness of opinions for the whole.

The δόξα, which is released from its limitedness by its relation to the πόλις and is in this sense a political δόξα, is characterized by Aristotle as φρόνησις, "prudence." The order of a πόλις depends on prudence. The constitution of a πόλις, which best fulfills the claims of prudence, is called by Aristotle πολιτεία, "polity." Later Cicero recognized the traits of polity in the Roman *res publica*. In its historically realized form as "republic," the polity then became the paradigm for Machiavelli. Just as polity is the correlate of the Greek φρόνησις, republic is the correlate of the Latin *prudentia*—in Machiavelli's early Italian, *prudenzia* or *prudenza*.

The politically prudent citizen and his milieu, the republic, became the decisive paradigms of ancient political philosophy between Aristotle and Cicero. For the first time in philosophy this double paradigm clears the path for the many to become open to the whole as such, the world, as the theme of philosophy. Therefore the origin of classical premodern political thought, whose complex of ideas is focused on this twin paradigm, is not peripheral to philosophy. The δόξα which is open for the republican πόλις is still δόξα, that is, bound to the pregiven horizons of the life-world. Thus it still lies within the grasp of the many, and yet it prepares them as citizens capable of judgment in democracy—the political form of the many—to open themselves to the whole as such; in terms of their everyday existence, humans receive a foretaste of the world as world—they become citizens.

The paradigm of the polemical critic of δόξα, which guides the original self-understanding of the philosopher, is now concretized in the correlation of φρόνηεσις with πολιτεία and has taken on a revised form: the correlate of the δόξα-critical attitude was the whole of the world. The correlate of the political δόξα is likewise a whole: the political communal life as the place for the exchange of opinions; and this whole is the forerunner of the all-encompassing whole, the world as world.

That the political whole is in fact a world which comes to the fore *as* world can be seen in its public character. All citizens support the republic with their political δόξα. What concerns everyone must therefore be decided by everyone. This presupposes that we can freely exchange opinions about our common concerns. As objects of such a general dialogue the common concerns must not remain secret and hidden; they must be visible for the many, that is, they must be exposed so that the many can judge openly in the exchange of opinions. Visibility understood in this way gives the political communal space the character of publicness, and therefore the character of world.[5] It was Hannah Arendt who discovered this fundamental context.

That Aristotle already glimpsed the world-character of the political communal space can be seen in his well-known distinction between πόλις and οἶκος, the house as the communal space of the family. In this space, life unfolds from generation to generation. This life is the habitual life bound to its narrow horizons, which are not yet opened to the world-horizon of philosophy. Life remains restricted to the particular, to the ἴδιον, of the particular segment of the life-world; it is robbed of the openness to the common whole, to the κοινόν. Let us recall that "robbed" is in Latin *privatus*: because the small world of private persons is closed with respect to the whole, it does not belong to the light of public space. Instead, it has the character of hiddenness.

Since the public political world constitutes itself in the freedom of opinions, its concrete formation depends fully upon free contingent decisions. Greek philosophy, however, conceives every formation as the process of taking on the shape of a determinateness, an εἶδος. The determination, or the τέλος of all becoming, as well as action based on decision making, is prefigured by the εἶδος. Accordingly, for Aristotle there is also an εἶδος of the πόλις and an εἶδος of humanity which form their essence. With respect to their essence, human beings are determined for communal life in the πόλις: a human being is a ζῷον φύσει πολίτικον, and its political prudence is not a completely free exercise of judgment; prudence is only the ability to find a way to goals that are determined eidetically in advance in the face of ever new practical situations.

On this interpretation prudent judgment becomes a second-class possibility of knowledge. It is merely the application of insights, gained through the εἶδος, to the mastery of contingent situations. The first-class mode of knowledge is insight into the εἶδος itself, the ἐπιστήμη as θεωρία. Just as the εἴδη are unchangeable and eternal, so correspondingly is theoretical knowledge enduring.

By virtue of them we are open to the whole as such, to the world, which is immutable and stable in contrast to the mutable horizons of the life-world. In comparison to theoretical knowledge the changeable situational knowledge of prudence cannot open the world.

On the one hand, with the paradigm of the prudent judging citizen Aristotle begins to do justice to δόξα as itself having the ability to become open to the world. But on the other hand, the εἶδος, on which Greek philosophy as θεωρία is focused, takes away the impact from the paradigm of the republic correlative to civic prudence. It actually prevents one from being able to conceive the institutionalized place of opinion, the public space of the many, as world.

II

In the history of philosophy this was made possible only when the εἶδος was radically disempowered and freedom triumphed. This occurred during that crisis of medieval theology that we label voluntarism. It is the watershed dividing the premoderns and the moderns in philosophy. Following in the line of Neoplatonism, the εἴδη were transformed into thoughts in the Spirit of God, which were then understood in voluntarism as freely posited by God's omnipotent will. From the *potestas Dei ordinata*, the power of God bound to the eidetic order, emerged a *potestas absoluta*, a power freed from this order. Because humankind was still understood as bearing God's image, even at the close of the Middle Ages this change in the theological paradigm had the effect of freeing the power of decision making of the human will from any tie to eidetic orders.

The will, and thereby the political will, appeared as absolutely disassociated from eidetic rules or, put politically, laws prescribed for it by Divine Reason. Political absolutism and its philosophical justification became possible. The establishment of a *potenza assoluta*, of an "absolute power," as Machiavelli would say, is one of the possible responses to the radical loss of order and security that human reason would first suffer through voluntarism.

The Renaissance may be described as a period of transition in which all of these responses were originally put forth in such a way that they appear as simple revivals of the paradigms of antiquity. In political philosophy this occurs in its most radical form in the thought of Machiavelli.[6] The twin paradigm of civic prudence and the republic reappears, but it is pressed into service in a voluntaristic context. It was certainly to Machiavelli's advantage that he served for fourteen years as secretary of state for the Republic of Florence. He can present, in full clarity for the first time, the republic as political *world*, for he interpreted it voluntaristically as a product whose origin and continuation rest exclusively on the free power of decision making of the human will. The opening upon the πόλις no longer appears for Machiavelli as the realization of the εἶδος of humanity but rather only as a contingent historical possibility.

Because of its unrestricted contingency, the political world is entirely artificial. It is produced through the power of the will to make a decision. Such a power is originally found only in individuals. A society possesses this power only by virtue of the individuals who give it this power. The ancient Romans had already observed this in their republican tradition: the political world is dependent upon the power of decision making, that is, upon the force of the individual's will. This was known in Latin as *virtus*, from *vir*, meaning "man." The will's power to act on the basis of its decisions was embodied for the Romans in a man who had earned this characterization. Thus *virtus* is understood from the perspective of the will, of the *voluntas*. The *virtus* understood in this sense reappears in Machiavelli as *virtù*.

The *uomo virtuoso*, the man possessing outstanding *virtù* presupposed by the existence of the political world, formed the central, new voluntaristic paradigm for Machiavelli. What is both new and foundational, what instituted a new sense, to put it concretely, is the way he combined the paradigm of the *uomo virtuoso* with the ancient paradigm of the prudent republican citizen. The plurality of these citizens is the set of the many which, according to the foundation of political philosophy in antiquity, supports the political world with its δόξα. That is why in politics Machiavelli sets the *virtù* of great individual personalities in contrast to the opinions, the *opinioni*, of the *vulgo*, the great multitude of average humanity. With regard to its character of plurality, he expressly calls this multitude "the many," as had Heraclitus and Plato in the early days of philosophy.[7]

In the interplay of opinions public space is constituted as the region of what is manifest for all. What is manifest in general and what is discussed under different interpretations stands in the light by virtue of which things seem to be thus and so. Indeed, the Greek word δόξα was not only the substantive of δοκεῖ μοι, of the "it appears thus to me" expressive of an opinion, but it also referred to what appears publicly as having a good reputation. Insofar as the public exchange of opinions concerns the *virtù* of individuals, the *uomo virtuoso* acquires a good reputation, honor, and fame. In his book on the republic the republican Cicero already emphasized the philosophical meaning of this connection.[8] Publicly appearing in the light, the shining forth of fame, first allows *virtù* to come forth fully in its true character. Machiavelli does use the concept *virtù* as a general label for all the praiseworthy traits of a person. But in certain decisive texts it is clear that there is a *virtù* in a strict and narrower sense, a power of decision making that yields, to the one who possesses it, broad recognition among the people.[9]

The political world is constituted in the correspondence between the *virtù* of the great leaders' personalities and the political δόξα of the people. The common life, politically understood, is a world; it is the living-space which presents itself publicly in the interplay of the opinions of the many. Appearing, or self-presenting, is not a quality that could be added to the pure existence of the political dimension. It is essential to the political that it manifests itself as a public spectacle. The political has the character of phenomenon, of appearance in the strong sense; it is an appearance which brings to appearing its own appearing.[10]

The production of its own appearing can be recognized in everyday life from phenomena such as manifesting a character in performance. The splendor of public self-presentation was familiar to the Middle Ages through the phenomenon of the self-presentation of the classes, especially the ruling class in public space. The Latin label for the public position of a person in the hierarchy of classes is *status* (in Italian, *stato*). Machiavelli borrowed this concept from the medieval Italian political tradition and used it as a term for the political world, with its character of appearance. The English expression "in state," implying an exhibition of pomp and showiness, as does the German expression "mit etwas Staat machen," echoes this original meaning of *stato*.

The *virtù* of the *uomo virtuoso* is power of the will. Power must exert itself, like energy radiating outwardly. The "outside" to which *virtù* radiates can only be the dimension in which it makes its appearance, that is, the δόξα of the many. Power exerts itself in the conquest of opposition. Politically seen, the power of the *uomo virtuoso* encounters its opposition in the people. As a result, a kind of force field arises between the two. It is based in the recognition by the masses of the full effectual power of the *uomo virtuoso*. When this recognition takes on a certain permanent quality, it is called political power. We can define Machiavelli's *stato* as this very political power which comes to appear in public δόξα.

Because *stato*, as the appearing force field of political power, is bipolar, its basic character depends upon where the balance of power lies. Is it held by a ruler with absolute power or by the people, with their δόξα? In the first case we have the constitution of a principality, that is, the reign of a sole sovereign, a *principe*, or prince, about which Machiavelli's work of the same title was written. In the second case we have a republic. The balance of power lies with the people, and government operates within the boundaries of the laws and institutions established by the citizens. This is the subject of Machiavelli's other major work, *Discorsi*, or *Discourse Upon Livy*.

Due to the wholly contingent and artificial nature of the political living-space, two basic problems arise. First, as something entirely new, how can it be brought into existence at all, that is, how is it to be grounded? And second, how is its existence to be maintained?

The people, after all, cannot implement the ground of the *stato*. That requires the innovative power of the *uomo virtuoso*, ruling as a *principe*, or prince. According to the ancient distinction of republican political philosophy between the hidden sphere of private life and the unconcealed public life, Machiavelli distinguishes between the private life, *vivere privato*, and the *vivere politico*, a career and life in the public light. Only an individual with outstanding power of will is capable of ascending from the everyday, narrow life-world horizons of the private individual, *privato*, to the *vivere politico*.[11] Machiavelli celebrates the achievement of the will in such mythical political heroes as Romulus, Kyros, and Theseus. Their feat lies in sparking the initial opening up of the pregiven horizons, and thereby the constitution of the political world. These great founders established a way for the many to open up the political world.[12]

With the political living-space established, the second question concerning its preservation comes into focus. Due to its total artificiality, the *stato* cannot rely upon any natural advantage—its very existence is, in principle, constantly threatened. By its nature, the very preservation of *stato* carries with it an inherent difficulty, *difficoltà*, in Italian. It is telling that this word, together with the expression *mantenere lo stato*, or "preservation of *stato*," ranks among Machiavelli's most frequently used terms.[13] Basically, *stato* is never out of danger.

It is characteristic of real dangers that they are not recognized at first as dangers. They have the unique characteristic of keeping their threat concealed with their initial emergence.[14] Thus the situation under which such dangers come to be is one of essential ambivalence. Whether or not they pose a threat is unclear. The preservation of *stato* hinges on the art of recognizing danger at this early stage, that is, of bringing to light its hidden appearance. This demands resoluteness and, with it, willpower, *virtù*. Here we discover the basis of *virtù*, namely, that focused intellectual insight which wrenches the initial appearance of danger from its concealment. This insight unveils approaching danger and is, therefore, a glimpse into the future, is *pro-videntia*. As Cicero correctly observed, *prudentia* in Latin is etymologically rooted in the term *pro-videntia*.[15]

With his concept of *prudenzia* or *prudenza* Machiavelli interprets the civic prudence introduced by Aristotle as *pro-videntia* and with this as a decisiveness of the will. As such, it can serve as the foundation for power of will in general, for *virtù* in its totality, analogous to the way in which prudence formed the foundation of all ἀρετή, of all virtue, in Aristotle's concept of φρόνησις.

For the preservation of *stato*, prudence is required on both sides, on the part of those holding power and of the people alike. But what matters above all else for the founding *stato* is the prudence of the prince. His prudence therefore is the main subject of the work bearing this title. In Machiavelli's view this founding situation involves the total loss of order, itself the result of political voluntarism. With this depiction he anticipates the early modern Hobbesian theory of the state of nature of being in complete disarray. Prior to the social contract unhemmed will rules totally and strives to possess all. It has the character of unlimited, insatiable avarice—what Machiavelli termed *ambizione*.[16] The self-destructive struggle of all against all, arising out of *ambizione*, can be terminated only by the *virtù* of the prince.[17]

Since these voluntaristic premises require us to assume that *ambizione* destroys the people, the people cannot be an equal partner with the prince in the founding moment. As political innovator, the prince needs to consider the δόξα of the people only insofar as it is absolutely necessary for the grounding of the *stato*. Δόξα is constitutive of *stato* as the very dimension of its appearing. For this appearing, however, mere semblance would suffice. In relation to the people, the prince need only defend his semblance. He must act in such a way as to create the semblance which will secure him the requisite level of public support needed to maintain power.[18]

In the realm of semblance, anything goes. In particular, the moral justification of the means used to uphold power is irrelevant. It is sufficient, should the public judgment of the prince be of any concern, that his actions *appear* moral. Moral qualifications play no role in determining the *being* of his actions.[19] Their being lies solely in their function as means to securing political power. Prudence, as that reason which guides the prince's actions, becomes a mere calculation of the risk of using a particular means to reach its predetermined end. With his paradigm of civic prudence Aristotle tied that reason constitutive of the political space to reflective judgment. But here reason in the form of prudence is degraded to something purely instrumental, that is, in the broadcast sense, to technical reason.

Because the prince is bound only to the appearance of moral norms, the people become mere pawns in his strategic calculations. Here we can already see prefigured the later attempt at a philosophical justification of absolutism. Machiavelli had distinguished the *ordine assoluto*,[20] or absolute order of the *stato*, from the civic political order in which the people are not a mass to be manipulated but rather shareholders through their own political δόξα. The prince's unscrupulous calculation in the *ordine assoluto* seems to be the harbinger of all the fateful developments of modernity in which the people—the vast majority of citizens—are robbed of their rights and potential. As a result, Machiavelli earned the reputation of being a demonic apologist of political amorality, as being the Old Nick, the devil. And, in fact, he does pay a high price for the clarity of this new paradigm of *virtù* in that, with a view toward self-preservation, he privileges the extramoral technical reasoning of the *potenza assoluta*,[21] of absolute political power.

Still, the traditional picture of Machiavelli is one-sided. His revival of the paradigm of prudence is ambivalent. There is not only the instrumentally perverted prudence of the prince but also room in his thought for trust in a genuine prudence arising from the δόξα of the populace. The republic, based on this genuine prudence, is a political world constituted in the interplay of the multiplicity of opinions. It is on this that Machiavelli, the impassioned Florentine republican, depends. It is only because his prudence is indispensable to the creation or renewal of the republic that the prince is allowed the unscrupulous use of strategic calculation.[22] The absolutist relationship to the people is but the initial phase of his political innovation. Were it a permanent condition, it would ruin the space in which the political lives.

But how is it that Machiavelli trusts the prudent δόξα of the people? What protects the mass of the many from purely instrumental calculation in the service of its own *ambizione*? Where does the unrestricted willing and taking, the avarice which must be taken for granted after the voluntaristic loss of order among the people, find its limits? Is it conceivable under these circumstances that something could bind the will of the prince or the people in spite of its infinite freedom? That is, is an ethos still even possible in modernity?

In various contexts Machiavelli hints that the finitude of time is what binds the infinitude of the will of the *uomo virtuoso*. It is already entailed by the fact that Machiavelli envisioned only a determinate moment of time for the unscrupulous exercise of power in the *ordine assoluto* during the founding or refounding phase of the republic. It is not possible to do just anything at any time. We need opportunities which come at the right time. The right time is that moment the Greeks called καιρός. Already included in Aristotle's paradigm of the prudent citizen is the idea that prudence must seize the καιρός. This καιρός is what Machiavelli calls *occasione*, opportunity, that is, opportunity for an act of *virtù*.

It is for the resolute judgment of prudence to decide whether a situation really is an opportunity. While prudence does disclose an opportunity, it does not, however, create it. Opportunity must present itself out of itself; thus all human will remains finite. The power of will can express itself only with respect to a resistance, that is, to a force directed against it. In order to prove itself as will, *virtù* requires opportunities from without.[23] That which gives opportunities to *virtù* is called *fortuna*, fortune, by Machiavelli.[24] *Fortuna*, then, is like a *force* in competition with free will, for it is incalculable. The Romans had already recognized the uncalculable Fortuna as a divine power. To the voluntaristic loss of order in the Renaissance, the incalculability of fate as determining power was rediscovered.

Most opportunities that *fortuna* offers political action are fleeting situations that the *uomo virtuoso* must instantaneously recognize and then seize. There are, however, also situations that remain longer and are more difficult to survey. These comprise the great constellations of political culture, which provide the setting for the emergence of the many evanescent opportunities. Machiavelli terms them *qualità de' tempi*, a quality of the times.[25] The success of the *uomo virtuoso* is first of all dependent upon his prudent mastery of the καιρός, in an encompassing and enduring historical situation. Missing the καιρός in this sense is tantamount to political downfall. The acts of the *uomo virtuoso* then no longer suit the time, all too evident to the people. His power collapses.

If *fortuna* destines one to failure in a certain *qualità de' tempi*, escape is precluded. The *uomo virtuoso* can only do justice to the enduring quality of the times in which he acts by forming habits of action that suit the basic characteristics of his time. Prudent action demands a congruence between the lasting nature of the καιρός and that of basic habits. However, it is precisely this lasting quality of habit which necessarily prevents the *uomo virtuoso* from adapting to further shifts in the *qualità de' tempi*.[26] When *fortuna* so decrees, the blinding of great politicians, who had always succeeded by virtue of their basic habits, is inevitable. In the end Machiavelli's paradigm of *virtù* displays a tragic view of politics. His resignation to the inevitable failure and the finitude of the political world kept him from the metaphysical belief in historical progress prominent in later political philosophies of modernity. And this indicates what we can learn from Machiavelli for philosophy "after Modernity."

III

It is time that binds and renders the infinite will finite again. As we have just seen, time enfolds its binding force for action through habit. Machiavelli described this only in connection with the prudent action of the prince. But it must also hold for the people and their political δόξα. Regarding the actions of those who are politically responsible, the many expect honesty, not simply "show";

they expect the politically responsible to live authentically, since the lasting character of the *stato* depends upon the reliability of those in power. Reliability, however, rests on good habits. Thus the people's standards of virtue are rooted in good habit, in ἦθος.

Yet the question remains: must not the infinite avarice of *ambizione* set loose by voluntarism also destroys the good habits of the people and, with this, its so-called standards of virtue? Machiavelli assumes that this is unavoidable. Due to this unavoidability every republic must at some time fall into ruin; only a radical cure by a prince can help; the unscrupulous exercise of absolute power permits the prince to manipulate the people in every way. If it is successful the radical cure, however, leads to a new obedience by the people to the laws. According to Machiavelli the laws and the institutions founded in them protect the people from unbounded *ambizione*.[27] But the people's readiness to follow the laws can only be grounded in good habits.[28] Thus Machiavelli presupposes that in the political phase of innovation a renewal of good habits is also possible. Machiavelli does not give reasons for this confidence. But we can reconstruct them by considering the binding power of time.

Habits arise when forms of action solidify in the course of time. This process restricts the infinite power of the will, which is driven to its extreme in voluntarism. This is the case because habitualization is not triggered by the resolve of the free will; rather, it runs counter to the activity of the will and is formed passively by the power of time. We can never get to the bottom of this "power of time." It harbors something unnameable, inaccessible, which withdraws from our will's power. One could characterize it, following Heidegger, as withdrawal. We recognize the withdrawal in the attitude of awe.

The civic spirit of the republic is based in the recognition of the inviolability of each person who makes up the many. Persons are distinguished from other persons as uniquely who they are through their habits. These habits are gifts, as it were, from the withdrawal. The recognition of the inviolability of each person is the appropriate response to this gift and accordingly is rooted in the attitude of awe in the face of the withdrawal. Through the reciprocal attitude of awe, habits, which we call good habits, emerge in common life. The will's infinite power driven to its extreme in voluntarism endangers awe in the face of the inaccessibility of the withdrawal. But it cannot fully eliminate the possibility of such an awe; for the mysterious power of time, which is in play in habits, holds the will's power in check. Thus it was also possible in the modern period, after the voluntaristic turn, for good habits to restrict *ambizione*.

Concretely understood, the restrictions generated by good habits are limits. The limit which demarcates our field of vision we call, in Greek, ὅρισμα. Prudent citizens form opinions in the horizons of the life-world. It is revealing to note that Aristotle occasionally characterized prudence as a capacity possessed by the prudent person. Although that sounds tautological, he means that the particular horizons of judgment of the individual prudent citizen form the basis of his prudence. These horizons are correlated to his habits; they accrue to the citizen together with habits through habitualization. Awe in the face of the withdrawal—through which habits and horizons of judgment are habitualized—founds the respect with which we accept the limitedness of each opinion in the republic, and therefore the insuperable plurality of opinions.

To say that the power of time keeps the possibility of awe alive is to say that there is always a chance for reflective judgment, for this is the manner of thought by which we take up the perspectives of others. These perspectives are possibilities of judgment which are limited by habitual horizons. And we feel ourselves bound to this manner of thought only when we respect this limitedness in the form of awe.

For Kant reflective judgment is that type of cognitive faculty which, in contrast to determining judgment, finds the universal in the given particular. In the context of the political common space, the given particulars are the commonly experienced situations of our political actions. Reflective judgment allows us to find general rules of actions for these situations. Situations are given to us as opportunities, *occasioni*, for action. In several idioms of European languages it is possible to say "time gives or grants opportunities." Such expressions are not merely metaphorical. We always experience the presentation of opportunities as "coming at the right time." This coming has in each case a surprising character, for time had the power to withhold the present opportunity from us. Whether or not time makes an exception for that withholding does not depend on the power of our will. The fact that opportunities basically depend on time is another kind of experiencing of the withdrawal.

Thus reflective judgment presupposes the withdrawal which is at play in the power of time in a twofold manner. First, without the withdrawal there would be no opportunities for action; and second, with regard to others there would be no habitual horizons of judgment which we respect in awe. Because the will, which is driven to its extreme in voluntarism, reaches its limits with this double withdrawal and remains finite, reflective judgment and likewise the prudent δόξα of the many remains possible. And the correlate of this δόξα, the republican communal space as a political world, can be further constituted.

With Machiavelli's *virtù* paradigm it finally becomes clear that the constitution of that world is based in the power of the will. It is what enables human beings to transcend the character of habit unique to prepolitical and prephilosophical δόξα. The act of breaking out of the narrow confines and limited horizons of this δόξα, which had made possible the original task of early Greek philosophy, has shown up since the Renaissance as the intervention of the will in habit.

The voluntaristic turn allows the world to come into relief clearly as world for the first time, namely as the willfully constituted world. That is especially clear in the political world, which is recognized for the first time in its phenomenality by Machiavelli's concepts of *prudenza* and *virtù*. But the cost of this openness of human beings to the world as world is that the world loses its character of horizon, which it had as the life-world of the prepolitical and prephilosophical δόξα. Thus the connectedness to the habitual horizons is lost with Machiavelli's amoral unscrupulous exercise of power in the founding situation. And the withdrawal, which is in play in the horizons, is lost in forgetfulness. Since the one holding power disdains any type of awe, the many, who by virtue of their many opinions constitute the public sphere and therefore the world character of *stato*, become the manipulable mass whose opinions no longer count.

What was seen with the example of Machiavelli in the field of political philosophy could be witnessed in other areas: the original task of philosophy, effecting the openness to the world as world, becomes fulfilled by the voluntaristic turn. But the fulfillment is at the same time a failure; for in arriving at the world as world, the world is closed again: without its horizon-character the world is no longer world. It *does* have the character of horizon in the prepolitical and the prephilosophical life-world. The world as world, which becomes the correlate of the philosophical transcendence of δόξα, can be no other than this life-world. One could characterize the modern epoch as a forgetfulness of the life-world, following Husserl, or as a forgetfulness of the withdrawal, following Heidegger. The question is: do we even have a chance of finding a way out of this forgetfulness, and if we do, what are the opportunities? This is the temporally critical question of phenomenology—"phenomenology" understood not as a school of thought but as the sort of philosophy that, on the one hand, explicitly poses the task of preserving the oldest idea of philosophy, the opening to the world as world, and simultaneously, on the other hand, of rehabilitating δόξα, that is, "appearance," in the form of the horizonally bound δοκεῖ μοι.

In my view, reflection on the political δόξα is one of the paths that phenomenology must follow, because this δόξα has two faces. On the one hand it is the preparation for the most radical transcendence of the δόξα; it prepares the philosophical openness to the world as world, which reaches its apex in the modern period as the forgetfulness of the life-world and as the infinity of the will. But complementing this movement, on the other hand it secures the reference of this transcendence back to the horizons of the prephilosophical δόξα made possible by the withdrawal. It is still possible for these horizons to give judgment and action a normative binding character through the transformation of δόξα into republican civic prudence. In this sense the ancient paradigm of the prudent citizen still holds good in its adaptation to the will of the modern *uomo virtuoso*. It maintains its force through the modern period, the period of unbridled *ambizione*, and remains a viable possibility for the future.

Translated by Anthony Steinbock, revised by the Editor

NOTES

1. On the first page of the dialogue "Dell'arte della guerra," Machiavelli places his own peculiar conviction in the mouth of Colonna, the leader of the dialogue: "Io non mi partirò mai, con lo esemplo di qualunque cosa, da' miei Romani."

2. I have extensively developed this self-understanding in Klaus Held, *Heraklit, Parmenides und der Anfang von Philosophie und Wissenschaft. Eine phänomenologische Besinnung* (Berlin, 1980).

3. I have developed this connection more fully in Klaus Held, "Die Zweideutigkeit der Doxa und die Verwirklichung des modernen Rechsstaats," in J. Schwartländer and D. Willoweit, eds., *Meinungsfreiheit. Grundgedanken und Geschichte in Europa und USA* (Kehl, 1986), p. 9 ff.

4. Hannah Arendt discovered the fundamental significance of Kant's analysis of reflective judgment for political philosophy. Only because her phenomenology of the political *world* pointed out the way for me have I been able, in the present essay and in other works, to attempt to reconstruct the inner relation between the original Greek foundings of the sense of philosophy in general and political philosophy.

5. On the world-character of the political, see Klaus Held, "Eigentliche Existenz und politische Welt" in K. Held and J. Hennigfeld, eds., *Kategorien der Existenz. Festschrift für Wolfgang Janke* (Würzburg, 1993).

6. Within the limits of an essay it is impossible to engage the burgeoning secondary literature on Machiavelli in anything like a comprehensive manner. Therefore we will make do with a general reference to the selected bibilography in the very good and judicious introduction to Machiavelli by Wolfgang Kersting, *Niccolò Machiavelli*, (Munich, 1988).

7. Machiavelli sketches the relation of *i molti, opionioni,* and *vulgo* at the end of ch. 18 of *Principe*. How high an opinion the republican Machiavelli had of free opinion is evident in *Discorsi*, Book 1, ch. 10, the remark on the "golden age" of good in a people, "where everyone can have and defend whatever opinion he wants" (dove ciascuno può tenere e difendere quella opinione che vuole). On the philosophical scope and significance of the concept of "the many," see the study cited in n. 2, p. 127 ff.

8. See Cicero, *De re publica,* Book 3, 40 (28): "Vult paene virtus honorem, nec est virtutis ulla alia merces."

9. See *Principe*, ch. 8: "Non si può ancora chiamare virtù ammazzare e' sua cittadini, tradire gli amici, essere sanza fede, sanza pietà, sanza religione; li quali modi possono fare acquistare imperio, ma non gloria." It is especially evident in ch. 34 in the third book of *Discorsi* how important for Machiavelli is the problematic of good reputation (*guona riputazione*) among the people, one's standing based on public opinion (*publica fama*).

10. Inspired by Arendt and working through the constitution of the political by means of reflective judgment, Ernst Vollrath has worked out these as well as other fundamental features of the political. See Vollrath, *Grundlegung einer philosophischen Theorie des Politischen* (Würzburg, 1987), p. 185 ff., on the phenomenality of the political.

11. For example, see *Principe*, chs. 9 and 14. Ch. 28 in Book 3 of *Discorsi* is one of many places that show especially clearly how important the basic distinction between public and private is for Machiavelli.

12. See *Discorsi*, Book 1, ch. 9, and *Principe*, ch. 6.

13. The short ch. 3 of *Principe* likewise contains the verb *mantenere* three times and already in the first sentence of ch. 4 the catchword *difficoltà* appears. Thus Machiavelli speaks already in the *Proemio* of the first book of *Discorsi* of "mantenere li stati."

14. In *Discorsi*, Book 1, ch. 33, when, for example, it is a matter of the harbingers of the demise of the Roman republic, it "is difficult to recognize such misfortunes as they arise—a difficulty that is caused by the illusion that things in the beginning summon up in one" (è difficile conoscere questi mali quando ei surgano, causata questa difficultà da uno inganno che ti fanno le cose in principio).

15. Cicero, *De re publica*, Book 6, 1.

16. On the essence of *ambizione*, see the beginning of ch. 37 in Book 1 of *Discorsi* and the summary of ideas near the end of *Proemio* of Book 2.

17. In particular, see *Discorsi*, Book 1, chs. 18 and 55.

18. See *Principe*, ch. 19.

19. See *Principe*, ch. 18. On the meaning of "seeming" (*quel che pare*) to the people, see also ch. 25 in Book 1 of *Discorsi*.

20. See *Principe*, ch. 9.
21. See *Discorsi*, Book 1, ch. 55.
22. Ibid.
23. See *Principe*, ch. 6.
24. See *Principe*, chs. 6 and 25. On the relation of *fortuna, virtù,* and *occasione*, see *Discorsi*, Book 2, ch. 30.
25. See *Principe*, ch. 25.
26. Ibid. On the great importance of the power of time in Machiavelli, see *Discorsi*, Book 3, chs. 8 and 9.
27. See, for example, *Discorsi*, Book 1, chs. 4, 58.
28. Habit—*abito*—is also mentioned by Machiavelli in *Discorsi*, Book 1, ch. 17.

EIGHT

Is the Present Crisis a Specifically Modern Phenomenon?

Paul Ricoeur

Perhaps the notion of crisis was chosen as central to the theme of this Hannah Arendt Memorial Symposium because we want to know whether today we are experiencing an unprecedented crisis, one that for the first time in history is not transitory but rather permanent and definitive.

If we put the question this way, it requires us to raise the question of the meaning we attribute to modernity. Is it too an unprecedented phenomenon, one that excludes any looking back toward, or any help from, the past? Must it leave us with no hope for the future? To put it another way, is modernity one cause of the broad crisis we all seem to sense, which I referred to in opening, or is what we are experiencing, in fact, the crisis of modernity itself?

If these few brief remarks capture the sense of the issue that brings us together, if they point to what is really at stake, we might then begin by first asking whether such an immense question is really answerable at all. And indeed we must do so for at least three reasons.

First, the very notion of crisis seems to involve a number of equivocations. What is there in common between a personal crisis, a governmental one, and a crisis in values or of civilization? Is not such a ragbag concept which can include all these things really a pseudo-concept? To deal with this apparent conceptual confusion, it seems to me that it might be helpful to include in our initial reflections a brief review of some of the less contestable uses of the term *crisis*, or to put it differently, that we might find it helpful to begin with some essentially "regional" forms of the notion of a crisis. If we are able to identify some of the anchorage points in our narrower uses of the notion of crisis, we may then be in a better position to consider whether there is anything more than a vague family resemblance between these regional concepts and thus whether this kinship tells us anything at all about our broader sense of crisis today.

A second difficulty in considering the present sense of crisis is that the alleged crisis seems to mark the passage from what I just called regional concepts of crisis to a global concept that has to do with what the French sociologist

Marcel Mauss called the "total social phenomenon." But this total social phenomenon can be reached only by way of the representations society has of itself. How then, we must ask, do we in practice reach such a level? Are there perhaps some indications of it in our regional models of how to do so, and if so, what are they? But we shall also have to consider the counterclaim that such representations are the very ideology operative in our society, and this being the case, we may find ourselves forced to concede that it is not clear that any consensus is reachable in contemporary society concerning the identification, and even more, the evaluation, of the leading ideas or values or ideologies that serve as the bearers of these representations, which are our only means of access to the total social phenomenon.

Third, the phenomenon of modernity referred to in my initial question does not designate just one social phenomenon among others, but our age or our epoch. Maybe it is the very meaning of the present that is at issue. But the present by nature is confused, since the conflicts that are occurring are by definition unresolved. This is why we, as the protagonists of such a crisis, may be tempted to overestimate the originality of the age in which we live, and to believe—which is almost a tautology—that it is unprecedented. This conceptual handicap will be especially crippling to any examination of the issue before us, inasmuch as all the regional concepts of crisis I shall refer to have at least one feature in common: they designate a transitory phenomenon. In one way or another, be it one crisis or many, there is to be an outcome. So how are we to know whether our contemporary crisis in the broad sense just referred to is for the first time a crisis that is not transitory, since by definition we are in the midst of it and we do not know what judgment future historians will make about us?

All these questions indicate that our topic is not an easy one. To proceed, let us provisionally set aside my second and third sources of perplexity and begin by concentrating on the first one, linked to the extreme polysemy of the term *crisis.*

Some Regional Concepts of Crisis

Let us begin by looking for a few basic meanings attested to by some typical uses of the term *crisis.* In this way I think we can discern four or five focal points or anchorage points—*Einsatzpunkte*—of the notion of a crisis, which may have broader applicability.

The first focal point comes from the medical use of the notion. A crisis is the moment when an illness is characterized by a sudden change, when the hidden pathology reveals itself and the outcome of the illness is decided for better or worse. I see four traits here that we may retain for use later, when I shall attempt to generalize the inquiry toward a more global notion of crisis: a pathological context whose principal symptom is suffering or things not going well; a break in the temporal rhythm of the illness itself, which we often characterize either as a breakthrough or a sudden attack; the intervention of some clinical examination that interprets the symptoms and proposes a diagnosis; and the prognosis of the outcome that takes the form of an alternative, either improvement or aggravation. This last trait is particularly important, since by adding a decisive aspect to the revelatory aspect of a crisis, it points to a time after the crisis, an escape from the crisis, through some salvific or fatal outcome. In the case of a happy outcome, the crisis may even retrospectively be clothed with not just a medical but also a medicinal value, in the sense that we speak of purgative herbs. So in this sense, there is room for hope for, if not certainty about, the future.

A second cluster of meanings can be discerned on the psychological-physiological plane of development. Here *crisis* refers to a state of profound unrest, which is both corporeal and mental, linked to the passage from one age in life to another. Rather than the transition taking place in a continuous manner, the fact that we speak of it as a crisis indicates a discontinuity between a prior state of equilibrium that is breaking apart and the subsequent state of equilibrium that is emerging. For example, in this sense, we speak of a crisis of adolescence. Erik Erikson, as is well known, has even extended this notion to every critical age in life and counted seven such critical phases between birth and death. Such an alternation between states of equilibrium and phases of disequilibrium is characteristic of this second model, which we might call the developmental one. The kinship between my first example and this one is not broken, in that the critical phase is again felt as painful. And once again it is relatively brief in comparison with the longer phases of continuous development. Also, at each critical phase, the symptoms are revelatory of a profound disequilibrium, and in each case an alternative is opened between improvement or possible aggravation. For Erikson, for example, each phase is characterized by a specific alternative: trust versus mistrust, autonomy versus shame and doubt, initiative versus guilt, industry versus inferiority, identity versus a confusion about identity, intimacy versus self-absorption, generativity versus stagnation, integrity versus despair. "Crisis is used here," he comments, "in a developmental sense to connote not a threat of catastrophe, but a turning point, a crucial period of increased vulnerability and heightened potential, and therefore, the ontogenetic source of generational strength and maladjustment."[1] Taken in this sense, every crisis is an identity crisis on the pathway of life's stages, which, taken together, constitute the life cycle.

A third, regional model, close to the preceding one, can be called the cosmopolitan model, in the sense Kant gave this term in his writings on the philosophy of history, for example, in his "Idea for a Universal History with a Cosmopolitan Intent" (1784).[2] Once again we find the previous developmental schema but this time applied to humanity as a whole. It is at the level of the "species" that the philosopher deciphers the manifestations of the complete development of every individual's "natural capacities directed toward the use of his reason."[3] So in this third model, it is the succession of generations that becomes the bearer of the whole process. The crisis consists in the fact that it is only under the prodding of what Kant calls "men's unsocial sociability"[4] that humanity develops its capacity for civil society and the rule of law. In this way, he observes, we may "transform a pathologically enforced agreement into a society and, finally, into a moral whole."[5] This idea of a pathologically enforced agreement is certainly a prefiguration of the Hegelian theme of the cunning of

Reason, which marks the apotheosis of the idea of crisis on the level of the philosophy of history. But it is also significant that Kant sees such crises as contributing to the growth of society as a whole.

We need also to take note of the resemblances and differences between our second and third models of crisis. In the first place, only the ascending phase of the process of development is retained. The model thus becomes that of the passage from the state of minority to that of majority, from immaturity to maturity. Second, the accent that was put on the internal dynamism governing the maturation of an organism in the developmental model is here put on the phenomenon of external domination, therefore upon our relation to and dependence upon others in the minority or immature stage. The crisis is the passage from the one stage to the other. As we read in Kant's essay "An Answer to the Question: What is Enlightenment?" (also from 1784), "Enlightenment is man's release from his self-incurred tutelage. Tutelage is man's inability to make use of his understanding without guidance from another. This tutelage is self-incurred when its cause lies not in lack of understanding, but in lack of resolve and courage to use it without guidance from another. *Sapere aude!* 'Have the courage to use your own understanding!'—that is the motto of enlightenment."[6]

This shift in accent from the idea of childhood to that of minority or immaturity entails a profound transformation in the role of the public educator, whom we might see as a representative of society and its ideology. Such a person does not so much accompany an immanent organic development as assist in the development of a critique of the situation of domination held to be responsible for the lag in the development of humanity as a whole. Any resulting crisis will consequently be a result of criticism in the sense of "critique," to the extent that critical philosophy puts itself in the position of the educator of the human species as a whole. Such an extension does not take place, however, without several important mutations that get expressed in the relation between the notions of critique and crisis. As Reinhart Koselleck has shown in his work that bears this title—*Critique and Crisis*—the accent was initially placed by prerevolutionary thinkers on the moral criticism of institutions of domination, and it was only under the pressure of events that this moral criticism of the system of institutions became a political crisis, that is, a state of revolution and civil war.[7] So long as criticism remained confined to the moral sphere and did not lead to a political decision, the century of criticism, Koselleck shows, could get along without the concept of crisis. This issue was even concealed by the representation of progress, which, in this sense, blinded the critique to part of itself. The passage from criticism to crisis occurred when the optimistic idea of endless progress ran up against the question of political decisions, overlooked until then. Rousseau is one of the witnesses to, as well as one of the agents of, this transition. In *Emile*, he writes: "You trust in the present order of society without imagining that this order is subject to inevitable revolutions, and that it is impossible for you to predict or to prevent those that will affect your children." Also: "We are approaching the state of crisis and the century of revolutions."[8] The term *crisis* here means more than just revolution, which in the eighteenth century had nothing in common with civil war but instead denoted an upsetting of one of the realms of life and a return to some other already known form. (Diderot declared: "Revolutions are necessary, there have always been revolutions and there always will be revolutions.") In other words, the term *revolution* had not yet broken away from cosmology, from which it drew its necessity and its relative innocuousness.[9] In penetrating the political sphere, crisis dramatizes criticism. It also brings along its medical connotation, particularly its revelatory power concerning some underlying illness, and above all its ability to state a decision regarding improvement or aggravation. ("We are approaching a crisis that will lead either to slavery or freedom," Diderot stated).[10] This either/or belongs to the moment of prognostication which follows that of the diagnosis: the moment of the reading of the symptoms. It is the alternative of despotism or freedom that allowed integration of the perspective of civil war, with its terrifying hazards, into that of revolution, which was still reassuring. To be sure, the acceptance of such a huge threat was further made possible by the transference of the eschatological category of the last judgment to the philosophy of history, which was itself confused with political philosophy. The threat of civil war was thus clothed with the aspect of a punitive action carried out by critical reason, set up as a tribunal to judge tyrants, and the utopian element inherent in the idea of progress was changed into an immanent aspect of justice.

It is especially noteworthy that the conjoining of *Weltgeschichte*, universal history, and *Weltgericht*, the last judgment, should have taken place in prerevolutionary thought, for this was a conjoining that set the stage for the Terror ahead of the fact. However, the most important kernel of the idea of crisis was thereby also preserved, namely, that it is not just transitory but also potentially beneficial in that it possibly points to a better future. Note, too, that the idea of a permanent crisis is still unthinkable on these terms given the decisive aspect of any crisis. For example, Koselleck cites the Abbé Reynal as saying, "The crisis will be born out of oppression . . . and the day of awakening is not far off."[11] In this way, the ideology of progress could integrate the idea of crisis within a resolutely optimistic political philosophy, but we still have not reached the stage of a general societal crisis.

A quite different model of crisis is provided by the history of science. This epistemological model is exemplified by Thomas S. Kuhn's well-known work on the structure of scientific revolutions. I shall not repeat the details of his analysis, but allow me to recall how Kuhn underscores the discontinuous aspect of scientific invention. Far from proceeding in a simply cumulative fashion, scientific progress occurs through a series of breaks that separate two coherent theoretical systems. Such breaks occur when facts, experiments, or anomalous results that cannot be integrated into the existing synthesis of scientific knowledge occur in sufficient number. A change in paradigm is then called for. What is important to note for our reflections is that we rediscover in this model a number of the features of the preceding models we have considered: temporal discontinuity, the idea of an alternation between states of equilibrium and phases of disequilibrium, and the idea of increased knowledge taking place through a series of qualitative jumps. Here also the crisis is transitory. It is only after the fact that we can recognize the new paradigmatic configuration. However, no idea of pathology, suffering, or sickness is attached to this model of a crisis, unless we attach such labels to the state of intellectual disarray that characterizes the upholders of the surpassed intellectual synthesis.

Lastly, we come to the economic concept of crisis. I did not want to begin with this usage, which is so common today and so dominant, so as not simply to take for granted the general tendency to make this model the only one shaping our ideas about crisis. Nor did I want to accept the idea that today's crisis is just economic, or that it can be strictly dated (1929) and localized (the New York Stock Exchange). To reject this twofold reduction, however, does not absolve one from having to take account of the influence of this model. For myself, I would say that the economic crisis is far from being in a relationship of infrastructure to superstructure as regards all the other crises affecting the cultural sphere. We ought, rather, to say that in a civilization like ours, which places economics at the top of its hierarchy of values, the economic form of our crisis tends to get set up as the one model for all the other forms. I shall return to this point in the second part of my remarks, which will be devoted to the total social fact and to the process, which is essential to it, of ordering values in a hierarchy. For the moment, allow me to offer a schematic description of the notion of an economic crisis, without taking into account its relations to the values and ideas that underlie society as a whole.

When we speak of an economic crisis, it is important first of all that we maintain the plural form and speak of crises in order to take into account "the diversity, the chronological succession of specific crises, each of which can be identified and each of which presents features that distinguish it from all others."[12] The advantage of this descriptive and historical point of view over a systematic and strictly economic one is that it does not limit us to the crises of the capitalist system in the nineteenth and twentieth centuries but leaves room for the older crises in preindustrial and precapitalist economic systems. What is more, this point of view has the advantage of taking into account the social effects, the sufferings inflicted on the great mass of human being without which we would not talk of a crisis. As in the medical model, it is always the felt sufferings that serve to reveal the disparities, the inequalities, the contradictions that affect the social system as a whole. And in the final analysis, it is these sufferings that cast a threat over every other form of equilibrium and even the dominant ideology; that is, over the hierarchy of values by means of which society defines itself.

The most empirical aspect here, the one that allows us to gather together—albeit provisionally—every crisis under one general concept, is that of "a loss of equilibrium, a crack, followed by a fall in productive activity, in trade, profits, wages, and stock markets, accompanied by a rise in bankruptcies, unemployment, and suicides."[13] It is in terms of this descending trajectory of forms of suffering, which express themselves as symptoms, that the conjunctural accident becomes revelatory of dysfunctions affecting structures and that worse omens come to light.

I shall not try to go into any detail about particular economic crises, lacking the expertise to do so. Instead, I would like to point to three phenomena that seem to me to underlie any theorizing about such crises and which point in the direction of a general social crisis.

First there is the increasing autonomy of economic phenomena in relation to other social phenomena: in the processes of production, especially industrial production; as regards the banking system in relation to the production and exchange of goods; and as regards cycles of speculation. It is this phenomenon of autonomization that is felt by the public as a kind of external fatality, of which Hegel gave a premonitory description in his *Philosophy of Right* when he opposed the "system of needs," conceived of as an external state of affairs, to the mutual recognition among citizens in the political constitution of a state based on law. Now it may be that it is precisely a society that puts the highest value on the economic layer of its existence that will most experience economic disorder not as some partial disorder but as total disorder. (How, for example, are we to make sense of the fact that there are too many foodstuffs in one place and not enough in another, that in one place surpluses have to be burned and in another people are dying of starvation?)

Second, there is the phenomenon of the periodicity of crises (the Kondratiev cycle, etc.). This phenomenon is perhaps the one that best specifies the economic model of crisis in relation to every other model and, at the same time, thanks to the predominance of the economic phenomenon in the hierarchy of the values in advanced industrial societies, leads to an extrapolation that tends to become a global claim. In virtue of this periodicity, "crisis is conceived of in terms of the framework of the movement that envelops it, the cycle, with a time of growth, the crisis itself, depression, and finally another take-off. It is the cycle as a whole that is a problem, with its short-term waves and apparent long-term recurrence."[14] Here again, I shall not attempt to enter into the disputes among different schools, among them, of course, the clash between Marxist and non-Marxist theses. Instead I will concentrate on certain aspects of such periodicity thrown into relief by such theories that reinforce the family resemblances among the different concepts of crisis we have considered. The fact is that the economic history of different peoples seems able to advance only by way of an alternating between accumulative processes (which augment the vulnerability of the growing system by diminishing its capacity for adaptation) and episodes of losses of equilibrium. Furthermore, it is in the phases of depression that the resources get assembled which then allow for another increase. Through these two aspects, the cycles that characterize economic crises strongly resemble the life cycles described by psychologists and psychoanalysts. Let us go even further and say that the periodicity of economic crises paradoxically leads to hope for the future. The crisis is always transitory. There is always an exiting from it.

The third phenomenon worth noting brought to light by the theory of economic crises is the worldwide scale of contemporary crises. This is relevant to our reflections in at least two ways. First, it reveals an underlying phenomenon, the worldwide nature of the marketplace. To understand this phenomenon requires us to move beyond the limited framework of economic analysis, for this phenomenon does not concern just the economy as such but also ideology taken as the representation a society gives itself of its overall functioning. Indeed, it is one ideology, that of economic liberalism, that has imposed on the Western world the representation of economic phenomena "as separate from society and constituting in themselves a distinct system to which everything else is subjected."[15] This ideology, far from being "natural," however, is an innovation of the nineteenth century. It is the ideology of the desocialization of the economy. From this comes a much more radical interpretation of the crisis of the 1930s of our own century, one that forces us to shift the idea of crisis to another level inasmuch as "the great crisis the 1930s imposed a resocialization of the economy on the world."[16]

This insight has numerous implications if we want to evaluate more fully the phenomenon of crisis being extended to a worldwide, or even a societal, scale. For we are dealing, it seems, not just with a geographical extension of a purely economic disorder but also with something that extends, as I have said, to the ideological crisis underlying autonomization and the predominance of the marketplace.

One way this works out, I think, is that insofar as the marketplace and the ideology of economic liberalism are connected to each other, the extending of the marketplace to the whole world has radically different social effects depending on the culture in question. In the Western world, where economic liberalism has become one of the components of what we call modernity, an economic crisis is for us a crisis about our modernity. We might therefore say that one thing we export, through the worldwide economic crisis and the worldwide market, is this crisis of modernity itself as defined in Western terms. However, during this same period, the rest of the world did not define itself in terms of the ideology of economic liberalism. This is why, when the expanding worldwide marketplace reached these cultures, it forced all of them to redefine themselves not just in terms of the economic crisis but also in terms of the crisis in the ideology that made the market an autonomous factor. This, it seems to me, is one of the ways in which today's crisis gets displaced from the economic plane to that of the representations of the total social phenomenon.

There is a second aspect to the worldwide scale of today's crisis that is also relevant for our investigation. By expanding geographically, the current economic crisis brings into play a properly political dimension beyond ideological cultural factors. This was especially true for the crisis of 1973–74. Whereas the crisis of 1929 struck what was still a basically autonomous economy, that of 1973–74 also affected the political policies which different states used to responded to it. If we follow Karl Polanyi's analysis in *La grande transformation*, liberal capitalism in its pure form, which was already moribund in 1939, was unceremoniously buried by fascism. It has been the resulting mixed economies—in differing forms—that have been struck by the crisis of the last ten years. The broader public has felt this less as an economic crisis strictly speaking than as an impasse in the ability of political states to respond to this crisis; in other words, public opinion has experienced it as a failure to find a political outcome to our crisis. This is why the crisis we are still in is felt to be more radical, inasmuch as politics—or, more precisely, the state—is more intimately linked to global society than is the economy per se, yet also because there is no worldwide state equal to our crisis. By becoming worldwide, the economic crisis thus reveals a number of things, particularly as regards the public's loss of confidence in its leaders and as regards the contradiction between nation-states and the international dimension of our crisis.[17] Thus, even though the economic crisis may not provide the only definition of today's crisis, it does fit in with larger-scale phenomena that force anyone analyzing it to carry the analysis to the level of the total social fact.

Criteria for a Concept of "Generalized" Crisis

In my introductory remarks I referred to the difficulties one encounters in any effort to move from regional concepts of crisis to a generalized one, the concept of which would be what we call a societal crisis. We must speak here, I said, of society as a whole, or, to use Marcel Mauss's phrase, of the total social fact. This holistic approach means that we must apprehend that configuration of ideas and values by means of which society understands itself. However, as we have seen at several points along the way, this global point of view was anticipated in the way each regional concept we considered suggested a possible generalization. The medical criterion, for example, can be generalized to the extent that we may speak of a social "body" and apply pathological terminology to it. A social crisis—if there is one—would indicate that this body as a whole is sick, that is, affected in its capacities for (synchronic) integration and (diachronic) equilibrium. Yet there are clear obstacles to such a generalization. Is the social body anything more than a metaphor? And is not this metaphor a dangerous one owing to its organicist connotations? As Max Weber said, the cells of an organism do not think! And if we speak of social pathology, what physician is competent to pronounce either a diagnosis or a prognosis?

If we turn next to our psychological model, its developmental assumption can also be generalized. The idea of development with its corollaries of minority and majority, immaturity and maturity, can be applied to a people, even to humanity as a whole, as Kant attempted to do with his cosmopolitan view of history. In this case, it is the model of an identity crisis as discussed by psychologists, psychoanalysts, and educators that is most useful for clarifying the notion of a social crisis. However, here again, the resulting pedagogical model loses some of its relevance if we retain only the idea of maturity without any reference to aging or death, as can be seen in the history of the idea of progress. The notion of a life cycle also loses much of its relevance in this way. Finally, if we emphasize the passage to maturity to the point of isolating it from everything else in life, the process ends up only referring to a teleology of growth, one that makes crisis appear as something unequivocally beneficial, thereby overlooking the possibility and the dangers of decadence.

As for the political criterion of crisis, it suggests a generalization of another order. What is in question here is the need for legitimation that stems from the political fact. By creating a difference between those who command and those who obey in the social order, political institutions—be they charismatic, traditional, or rational, to recall Weber's typology—generate an unavoidable problematic, that of power or domination (*Herrschaft*). It is this structure that has to be legitimated. Crisis, in this sense, is a crisis of legitimacy. Such a crisis does seem to constitute a crisis affecting society as a whole, to the extent that the state is the organization of a historical community so that it can make decisions—to use a definition from Eric Weil's *Philosophie politique*. It is the capacity or incapacity of global society to make decisions which will lead to an eventual crisis of legitimacy on a worldwide scale. But, at the same time, we are sent back to ethics from politics inasmuch as the legitimization of power refers to the axiological configuration in terms of which society defines itself. And there remains the question whether it is at all possible to approach directly those ideas and values by which society gives itself a representation of itself, that is, an ideology.

The epistemological model is no less rich in potential for generalization. Husserl's *Crisis of European Sciences and Transcendental Phenomenology*[18] is a good introduction to this possibility. Husserl expressly distinguishes between crises internal to a science—what in Kuhn's vocabulary we have spoken of as paradigm changes—and the crisis of foundations, which is transcendental, not epistemological, in the sense that it has to do with the ultimate justification of knowledge. The gigantomachy that sets transcendentalism against objectivism culminates, for Husserl, in the contemporary crisis arising out of our powerlessness to respond to the demand for an ultimate justification, our refusal even to raise that question. In this respect, a book such as Richard Rorty's *Philosophy and the Mirror of Nature*, which condemns every foundational enterprise, would be interpreted by Husserl both as a symptom and a confirmation of the crisis of foundations confronting us.[19] This idea of a crisis in foundations certainly has a power of generalization equal to that of the crisis of equilibrium, or that of identity, or even that of legitimation. However, this generalization also acknowledges its limits. This is the question of how the issue of ultimate justification gets integrated into the set of ideas and values underlying the total social phenomenon. To be sure, philosophy is at the center of this process to the extent that it is typically Western and therefore one agent of modernity in the West. And in this regard, we could say that it structures Europe's memory insofar as Europe is not some region of the world but an "Idea," as Husserl would have it. However, we may doubt whether philosophy has ever succeeded in establishing, even in Europe, the "transcendental society" capable of exercising the "architectonic function" Husserl assigns to it. We may also wonder whether the Eurocentrism implicit in Husserl's undertaking escapes the arrogance of one particular society. And we may ask whether a naiveté worse than arrogance does not affect the self-designation of Western philosophers as the "functionaries of mankind."[20] These unresolved questions make difficult the whole generalization of the epistemological model elevated by Husserl to the rank of a transcendental model, but they do not negate the fact that it has been so extended.

We touched upon one other holistic approach that allows us to join the concept of a societal crisis with the economic model of crisis. If we stick with a straightforwardly causal point of view, however, phenomena such as the unification, extension, and emancipation of the marketplace might be taken as the effects of other changes, especially on the level of mentalities; but marketplace phenomena can just as easily be considered the causes of those changes. Now, if we turn to a more structural viewpoint, it becomes evident that these phenomena belong to the configuration of ideas and values characteristic of modern society taken as a whole. This makes the market forces and the "mentalities" even more closely interconnected. More precisely, we can then say that the exaltation of the idea of the marketplace characterizes one important aspect of this configuration, by the very place it holds in the hierarchy of values in modern societies. Here we have, I believe, an important breakthrough in the direction of the total social phenomenon; I mean the fact that society as a whole, in the modern period, defines itself by the autonomy of the marketplace extended to the whole world. The operative ideology here is that everything is a kind of merchandise.

These remarks have been intended to show both that a holistic approach to the concept of crisis is legitimate—that we can never understand any social phenomenon except in relation to all the others, within a more structural than causal perspective—and that such an approach still remains very indirect and incomplete. Even when generalized, our regional criteria do not completely overlap. Obviously there is a need to try to find an all-encompassing model capable of ordering these imperfect sketches. We might therefore be tempted to move to the other extreme and oppose a directly holistic approach to the analytic and fragmentary one we have begun with. And we find encouragement for such a move in those existential philosophies that present the notion of crisis as a permanent structure of the human condition.

For example, in the tradition of Max Scheler—in the work of Paul Landsberg and Emmanuel Mounier—the militant conception of an engaged humanity leaves much room for conflict, breakthroughs, and risks, and, in this sense, for the notion of crisis. For Landsberg, for example, the person is depicted in dramatic terms as torn between the forces of life that pull her toward darkness and those spiritual forces that pull her toward a higher form of ecstasy. Being caught between these two extremes is our crisis, constitutive of the courage to be. Note, however, that it is not so much the person as the process of personalization, understood as the conquest of individuality and difference, that contains the seeds of all the partial figures of crisis we have already encountered. There is a crisis because human beings do not have a natural place in the universe—to allude to a well-known work by Scheler, *Man's Place in Nature*.[21] We find this place only through a hierarchizing operation that discovers, as much as it creates, an *ordo* that is not the natural universe. Since this hierarchizing activity does not take place without an accompanying evaluative judgment, spiritual homelessness is a crisis that breaks through the confusion caused by our instincts.

I perceive a situation as a crisis, I would say, on the basis of Landsberg and Mounier, when I am no longer able to know my place in the stable universe, no longer able to know what stable hierarchy of values can guide my decisions, no longer able to distinguish my friends from my enemies. Then commitment is my only way of discerning an order of values capable of making demands on me, a hierarchy of preferences that will identify me with a cause that surpasses me. So commitment is the source of the conviction—another Hegelian term—that constitutes the person as the outcome of a crisis. The decisive point about all this for the remainder of my reflections is that the heart of crisis lies in the temporal structure of the process of personalization. Commitment is an effort directed toward the formation of the human future. The crisis takes place at the crossroads where such commitment struggles against our tendency toward inertia, flight, desertion.

It is this relationship between temporality and crisis that another thinker—by the way, not so favorable to existentialism—has illuminated with his analysis of the category of personality. I mean Eric Weil in his *Logique de la philosophie.*[22] Personality is that moment of the logic of meaning in which a human being "interprets himself," constitutes himself as the center of a world that deprives this person of freedom. It is "an absolute value, the source of all values."[23] So defined, personality is indicative of the conflict that opposes the desire to be oneself and other people's values. Internalized, the conflict turns into a crisis: "Liberation through creation takes place, then, through the crisis that is an evaluation and at the same time a judgment. I (future present) look at and judge myself (past present)."[24] Hence we have to say that "personality always lies in the crisis; always—that is, at every instant. It creates itself by creating its image which is its being yet to come."[25] It is not by accident that Weil cites Goethe's *Faust* at this point: "Was du ererbt von deinen Vatern, erwirb es, um es zu besitzen." To be sure, Weil does not stop here, but instead submits this claim of the rebellious individual to "the unique and absolutely coherent discourse wherein he disappears as a personality"[26] in order to rediscover that concrete freedom of intelligible action and thereby to reach the category of "work."[27] For Weil, this category is indicative of the outcome of the crisis, just as for Landsberg, this occurred through commitment, by identifying oneself with some cause. For both thinkers, though, we may say that however transitory the process may be, going through a crisis necessarily characterizes the human itinerary, and the core of the crisis lies in the confrontation between the future and the past in the process of personalization.

Despite the help our meditation finds in this existential concept of crisis, we ought not to be entirely satisfied with such a complete generalization of the notion that it becomes applicable to anything and everything, something we have tried to avoid since the beginning of our reflections. In fact, we have reached the point in our argumentation that Plato, without irony, characterized in the *Philebus* as follows: when some too quickly make everything multiple, we are forced to reply by making everything too quickly one. Or to put it another way, following Kant this time, have we not substituted for too narrow a concept one that is too broad? By submerging the concept of crisis in a philosophical anthropology applicable to everything, have we not divested it of its discriminating value? For if everything is a crisis, then nothing is. In short, it seems as if to escape diversity we have simply given in to confusion.

What path to the mixed, what thought about a measure or mean, will allow us to cross the distance that separates our widely scattered concepts of crisis from a completely undifferentiated one? I think there is one indication in the preceding analyses that we have yet to exploit adequately, namely the link between crisis and temporality (or temporalization). Indeed, if we transpose to the level of historical consciousness what has been said on the level of the person, we encounter a structure that is both universal and determined, one that is capable of providing a concept of crisis that will preserve the universal, atemporal (or transtemporal) features of our earlier analyses, while orienting them toward a more precise characterization of modernity. This structure is the one that Reinhart Koselleck proposed in *Futures Past: On the Semantics of Historical Time.*[28] His approach is based on a semantic inquiry into historical concepts, wherein he undertakes to evaluate the successive τόποι in which historical consciousness has been incarnated, in light of the relations between two transcendental conditions of historical consciousness: our horizon of expectation and our space of experience. These are transcendentals in the sense that they provide the framework within which it is possible to evaluate the varying relations between our lived horizon of expectation and our lived space of experience. These differences are no doubt noticeable only when they have been accentuated, but this, in effect, is what happened in the Age of Enlightenment, as can be seen in terms of three themes: the newness of time (let us not forget that in German modernity is called *Neuzeit*), a sense of the shortening of the delays that still separate us from the reign of mature humanity, and the idea of the availability of history for human activity, its *Machtbarkeit.*

In the Enlightenment, the variation in the relationship between the horizon of expectation and the space of experience imposed itself upon public awareness. This *prise de conscience* was so powerful that it can serve as revelatory of the categories in terms of which this variation can be thought. There is one important corollary to note. By characterizing the τόποι or modernity as a variation in the relationship between our horizon of expectation and our space of experience, conceptual history contributes to relativizing them. So we are today in a position where we can situate them within the same space of experience as the eschatological political thought that reigned until the sixteenth century, or with the political vision governed by the relation between *virtù* and Fortune, or even in terms of the τόπος of the lessons of history, *historia magistra vitae.* In this sense, to cite one more example, the formulation of the concepts of a horizon of expectation and a space of experience gives us a means of understanding the dissolution of the τόπος of progress as one plausible variation of this very relationship. What concept of crisis, then, which is both general and determinate at the same time, results from these categories, which are not so ahistorical as those of existential philosophy, but rather transhistorical? Essentially something like the following. When the space of experience gets narrowed by a general denial of all tradition, of every heritage, and when the horizon of expectation tends to withdraw into an ever more vague and indistinct future, peopled by utopias or rather by uchronias, with no hold on the actual course of history, then the tension between the horizon of expectation and the space of experience becomes one of rupture or schism that may well be called "crisis." Here I think we have a concept that conserves something of the too broad existential concept of crisis, namely its core in human temporality, and that also draws upon the possibly accidental results of generalizing from our regional concepts of crisis, which I should like to mention one last time in reverse order: the "crisis" of economic liberalism, that of the foundations of knowledge, that of the legitimacy of power, that of the identity of our community, and that of the equilibrium and integration of the social body. I have listed them in reverse order so that it is the medical criterion that finally serves as the discriminating term for a historical structure that is also endowed with broad generality. *Today's crisis is the pathology of the process of the temporalization of history. It lies in a dysfunctioning of the normal relation between our horizon of expectation and our space of experience.*

Criteria for a Concept of our "Modern" Crisis

The third difficulty I listed in my introductory remarks is the most difficult to deal with. If we assume that we can characterize the "total social fact" of a society far from us in space and time, can we apply the criterion of global crisis we have reached to the present age? If there is no history of the present, is there a sociology? What is at stake is quite obviously what we mean by modernity, where this notion refers not just to a global fact but able to a present one. In this case, the total social fact has to be deliberately approached from the point of view of the ideas and values that structure the social bond, along with the hierarchy of these values due to which a dominant theme can encompass those adverse values that may exist on lower levels. However, we encounter such ideas and values only through ideologies, that is, through the representations of the total social fact that are formed either by dominant groups or subordinate groups, or through the insights of eminent personalities endowed with a rare ability to discern what is happening. The difficulty is obvious. A society is not transparent to itself. This opaqueness is indicated by the very term *ideology*. An ideology operates "behind the backs," or perhaps we should say "behind the heads," of the individuals in any society under consideration. So if a society partially does not really know itself, perhaps the best we can do is partially to circumvent the difficulty in one of two ways. We may try to interpret the present as the *terminus ad quem* of an evolution that goes back a long way, thereby stepping back somewhat from the present, or we can interpret it in comparison with other societies. This method was already operative in the *Persian Letters* and it is still used today in comparative anthropology. To bring into view the total social fact, it seems, we have to try to take some distance from the present.[29]

Yet we have to admit that the results thereby obtained can be misleading. Even given the double condition of a sense of history and taking a distance, we may still doubt whether there is a single hermeneutic key sufficient to interpret the present. The state of the current discussion amply confirms this. In fact, several interpretations of modernity compete with one another, so let us briefly mention a few of them to see what is at issue.

According to Louis Dumont, individualism is what distinguished modern from traditional societies, which for him are either distant societies, such as the caste system in India, or ancient ones, such as the one which Christianity undermined from within two millennia ago. By individualism, he means the ideology that sees the individual as having a higher value than the group, class, or people; in other words, the individual as superior to the social whole. Economic liberalism is one variant of this individualism. However, he tempers his evaluation by adding that this dominant ideology encompasses its contrary, the values of traditional society, as is shown by the defeat of economic liberalism in its purest and harshest form in the first half of this century, as well as by the creation of mixed economies arising out of the crisis of 1929. Dumont chooses therefore to speak of these mixed ideologies as postmodern, which leads to the curious result that modern society, arising out of the crisis of traditional society, has in its turn become the seat of a crisis leading to what may be called postmodernity. We may wonder, therefore, whether the true crisis today does not resemble a parting of three roads where our society cannot decide among traditional (recessive) society, modern (dominant) society, and (embryonic, still unborn) postmodern society.

A similar judgment was reached by the Frankfurt School in the period of Adorno and Horkheimer. If we identify modernity with the Enlightenment, then our crisis results from its unkept promises. What we have is as much the crisis of modernity itself as one generated by modernity. Essentially, it consists in the fact that modern rationality, by becoming instrumental, has exhausted its liberating potential. The only possibility that remains is for a critical theory that would develop a negative dialectic, one that would reject the perverse effects of post-Enlightenment rationality. Once again, the question can be posed as that of postmodernity, which is one possible outcome of the crisis of modernity.

An even more radical evaluation of the dominant tendency of our age comes from Nietzsche and his definition of modernity as nihilism. Nihilism is the loss of values, the "devaluation" of all our highest values, which means, essentially, those values linked to Christianity, interpreted as a Platonism for the people. This critique finds its initial handhold in Nietzsche's rational critique of tradition (for example, in *Dawn* and *The Gay Science*); then it hands rationalism itself over to the violence of his accusations. The most noteworthy offspring of rationalism—for example, democracy and socialism—are then lumped together with

Christianity and other expressions of the ethics of the "weak." One result is that Nietzsche, too, looks like an antimodern thinker, one who tosses modernity onto the same ash heap as he did his old adversary, Christianity.

But even antireligious humanism, in whatever form, must then also appear as an impotent palliative to the uprooting stemming from the decline of Christianity, because unwittingly that humanism draws its strength from the very values it contests. At least this is one way of understanding post-Nietzschean movements which associate the death of man with the death of God. To the extent that agnostic or atheistic humanism is taken as a branch of the Platonic-Christian tradition, it has to whither and die as soon as it is cut off from its roots. Thus if we identify modernity with this moribund humanism, the "modern" crisis must again be that of modernity itself. Max Weber, in his moments of Nietzschean lucidity, caught sight of this when he said that the triumph of rationality, which in other places he extolled, leads to a disenchanting of the world, which perhaps is unbearable. One important corollary of this disenchantment of the world, however, is that it lays bare the antagonistic aspects of values. Modern people, whether we call them modern or postmodern, experience both the withdrawal of God and the rending of all values. And it is a fact that we do not bear these two wounds well. On this interpretation, the present crisis lies in just this suffering.

Finally, Heidegger's proclamation of the end of metaphysics recapitulates in a quite original way the three models of modernity in crisis we have just considered. The Cartesian *Cogito*, by putting the subject in place of the *Subiectum*, understood as an underlying ground, inaugurates the modern forgetfulness of being. Having begun as an agent of the crisis, humanism has become its seat and finally its victim through its internal decomposition. As for technology—another name for instrumental reason—it is nothing more than the modern figure of the metaphysics of subjectivity, inasmuch as the emphasis on the subject has as its counterpart the reduction of nature to an object over against us, there to be dominated and exploited. Even Nietzsche's Will to Power, which he opposed to the will to truth, still belongs to the cycle of the metaphysics of the subject, and it crowns the modern forgetfulness of being. Here, once again, to understand modernity is to see it as the end of an epoch beyond which in some ways we have already moved. Only the union of poetic thinking and thinking poetry can open the way to a postmodernity whose ethical and political contours cannot be discerned, much less its social realization on the scale of society as a whole.

What seems common to these diverse interpretations of the contemporary crisis is the idea of the superimposing of two crises, that of traditional society under the pressure of modern society and that of modern society itself insofar as it appears as an aborted offspring of traditional society. Having said this, my initial doubts concerning the possibility of proceeding to a global evaluation of the present age is reinforced by a new argument.

To be brief, it seems quite clear that our age cannot be defined in terms of a single ideology. Rival definitions of modernity and, even more, the quarrel between modernity and postmodernity testify instead to what we may call the equivocity of present times, which may in fact be the case in every age for those who live through it. Furthermore, in light of the interaction between the observer and the observed in the human sciences, even the dogmatic assertion that the disenchantment of the world is the truth of our day cannot be taken as an objective (*wertfrei*) assertion. That assertion also testifies to the loss of conviction in the one who is offering the diagnosis and who thereby contributes to bringing about what it describes. Here, then, is what seems to me to be the best characterization of the crisis of our age: on the one hand, the absence of any consensus in a society divided, as I have said, between tradition, modernity, and postmodernity, and on the other, the even more serious general loss of convictions and of a capacity for commitment that follows from this loss—or, what comes down to the same thing, a general withdrawal of the sacred, whether we mean by this the vertical sacred (the religious in the broad sense) or the horizontal sacred (the political in the broad sense).

Past crises were transitory, as is also suggested by our analysis of various regional models of crisis. Is today's crisis, for the first time, an interminable one, the definitive crisis, one without any outcome? No one can say, given our inability to take temporal or spatial distance from it. My own wager and hope is that, despite the lack of consensus and strong convictions in our pluralistic society, there is still a chance for renewing the heritages we have received from the past in light of our hope for the future, a double opportunity for renewal and reinterpretation. In pursuing this opportunity, it is fitting that we recall and honor the work of Hannah Ardent, who taught us to consider the importance of the public realm in understanding the present as our time of initiative and who perhaps pointed us toward a recovery of the present as such a time of initiative.

Translated by David Pellauer

NOTES

1. Erik H. Erikson, *Identity: Youth and Crisis* (New York, 1968), p. 96.
2. Immanuel Kant, *Perpetual Peace and Other Essays on Politics, History, and Morals*, tr. Ted Humphrey (Indianapolis, 1983), pp. 29–40.
3. Ibid., Second Thesis, p. 30.
4. Ibid., pp. 31–32.
5. Ibid., p. 32.
6. Ibid., p. 41 (translation modified).
7. Reinhart Koselleck, *Critique and Crisis: Enlightenment and the Pathogenesis of Modern Society* (Cambridge, Mass., 1988).
8. Jean-Jacques Rousseau, *Emile or On Education*, tr. Allan Bloom (New York, 1979), p. 194 (translation modified).
9. Regarding these points, see Koselleck, *Critique and Crisis,* pp. 160–61, n. 6.
10. Quoted in ibid., p. 172.
11. Ibid, p. 182, n. 79.
12. *Encyclopaedia Universalis*, "Crises économiques."
13. Ibid.

14. Ibid.

15. Louis Dumont, Preface to Karl Polanyi, *La grande transformation*. Dumont defines the ideology of economic liberalism as follows: "the doctrine that, the free play of the economy being the condition for order, every interference in it by the state is fated. The central institution was the market, the market was considered as self-regulating, and society ought to submit to it whatever may happen" (p. vi).

16. Ibid.

17. The issue of worldwide debt is especially revealing as regards both this need and this lack.

18. Edmund Husserl, *The Crisis of European Sciences and Transcendental Phenomenology: An Introduction to Phenomenological Philosophy*, tr. David Carr (Evanston, 1970).

19. Richard Rorty, *Philosophy and the Mirror of Nature* (Princeton, 1979).

20. Husserl, *Crisis*, p. 17.

21. Max Scheler, *Man's Place in Nature*, tr. Hans Meyerhoff (New York, 1971).

22. Eric Weil, *Logique de la philosophie* (Paris, 1967).

23. Ibid., p. 238.

24. Ibid., p. 294.

25. Ibid., p. 304.

26. Ibid., p. 219.

27. Ibid., p. 344.

28. Reinhart Koselleck, *Futures Past: On the Semantics of Historical Time*, tr. Keith Tribe (Cambridge, Mass., 1985).

29. Both methods are combined in Louis Dumont's *Essays on Individualism: Modern Ideology in Anthropological Perspective* (Chicago, 1986).

NINE

Remarks on the History of the Concept of Crisis

Reinhart Koselleck

Anyone who opens a newspaper these days comes across the expression *crisis*. The concept indicates uncertainty, suffering, an ordeal, and refers to an unknown future whose suppositions will not permit sufficient clarification. That much is established by a French dictionary first published in 1839, and the definition of *crisis* is no different today.[1] The inflated use of the term all but encompasses the scope of our activities—domestic and international politics, culture, economics, the church and religion, every branch of the humanities and social sciences, the natural sciences, technology and industry—inasmuch as these are conceived to be component parts of our political and social systems; in short, the term is an inalienable aspect of our everyday world. If the multiple uses of the word were a sufficient index of actual crisis, we would be living in a crisis of all-encompassing proportions. This latter remark, however, better illustrates a widespread manner of speech than it provides a contribution to the diagnosis of our plight.

In what follows I intend to pare from the history of the concept *crisis* some of its structural characteristics, hopefully thereby contributing to the strengthening of my contentions and making them more precise. I begin with a broad characterization of the history of the concept. Then I sketch several semantic models of the concept to which its modern usage can be traced. Finally, I pose anew a few questions that follow from the liaison of modern conceptual speech with the Christian tradition.

An Historical Synopsis of the Concept

Κρίσις belongs among those fundamental concepts of the Greek language for which there cannot be found substitutes. The word is derived from κρίνω, "to separate, select, decide, judge; to size up (e.g., opponents for competition), clash, fight"; κρίσις tended toward "a final, irrevocable decision." The concept implied final alternatives which allowed for no further revision: success or catastrophe, justice or injustice, life or death, ultimate salvation or damnation.

For example, in battle κρίνω referred to those forces that would carry the day. With this usage Thucydides discretely inserted the great battle into the general scheme of things (as Montesquieu would do later as well), thus making it possible for the battle to quietly decide the outcome of the war with Persia.

In the Hypocratic School κρίνω referred to the critical stage of an illness in which the struggle between life and death was played out, where a verdict was pending but had not yet arrived.

In the area of politics—as given in Aristotle—it referred to both the maintenance of the law and its making, in which every citizen was called to participate; as in political decision making, each man was granted the imperative right to judgment.

Within theology, at least after the New Testament, *crisis* and *judicium*—both adopted from the language of law—acquired new and, as it were, unsurpassable significance: that of the judgment of God. Crisis was present in the life and times of the faithful whether as the crisis of the Last Judgment at the end of time or as the judgment thought to have already come with the worldly appearance of Christ and his everlasting light. Potentially, the concept comprehended each and every decisive moment in the inward and the outward lives of the individual and his community. *Crisis* dealt with definitive alternatives between which a choice or commensurate judgment had to be made; in each respective case to which *crisis* referred, the alternative outcome could always also apply.

Crisis was therefore a concept which implied a temporal dimension or, in modern terms, implicitly expressed a theory of time. Whether order was to be generated through the maintenance or the creation of law or whether it depended upon proper identification, as was the case, per Galen, in medical judgment—the precise phase of an illness had to be diagnosed in order to risk a prognosis—it was always the case that a certain point in time had to be ripe for any action to succeed. *Crisis* in theological terms also had a temporal context, but one regarding whose precise moments human actors remained ignorant. Consider the case of Saint John, who accepted God's message in order to *hic et nunc* escape damnation, although the time of the last judgment remained shrouded in ignorance.

Crisis directs itself, as it were, toward the necessity of time to make itself comprehensible as a concept. In almost every discussion of *crisis* there is the awareness of uncertainty as well as the obligation to forecast the future so as to prevent a calamity or to find deliverance. In the course of these discussions the respective point of termination becomes limited in different ways to the thematic conditions of everyday experience.

From antiquity to the early modern period both the word and the concept *crisis* sustained themselves in the Latin tongues, as *crisis* in medical parlance and as *judicium* or *judicium maximum* in theology. For example, Thomas Aquinas, in his *Compendium Theologiae* (ch. 242), distinguished three temporal phases in the judgment exercised by the Son of God: the judgment that the individual meets during his lifetime; the judgment at the hour of death; and finally, after Christ's return, the Last Judgment. During this period *crisis* evolved, so to speak, in the language of its trade, bound back upon the institution of the Church and thereby to each of the four faculties of Scholasticism.

After the adoption of the Greco-Roman word into the various European languages—that is, after the waning of the middle ages—a gradual and increasing extension of usages can be indexed. The concept came to comprehend more and more realms of experience: daily politics, warfare, psychology, a self-developing economics, and finally, a rediscovered history. One can venture the claim that the concept *crisis* even contributed to the founding of these considerations as independent branches of learning.

The medical usage of *crisis* stands above all the rest as godfather to its further application. In advancing this concept, the medical usage advanced as well the concept of the nation-state as metaphorical corpus. It served that end by diagnosing the state's sickness or health, by pronouncing upon its prospects for life or death.

By the eighteenth century, however, the concept had become self-reliant. Reference to the medical sense of *crisis* was now deliberately metaphorical, as can be seen in Rousseau. For instance, in Germany talk centered on the structural and administrative crisis within the *Reich*. In the course of these discussions the point arose that the internal laws and the form of the federal constitution were no longer sufficient for the stabilization of the empire; therefore a supplementary federation of princes was instituted, from which descended the wording of the Preamble of 1785.

Also by the eighteenth century, *crisis* had traversed a course similar to that of *revolution* and *progress*, other concepts which became temporalized and self-reliant as their spatial or natural portent evaporated with the Enlightenment; this had permitted them to gain the status of primary and historical concepts. During the Great Northern War, with the ascendancy of the Russian Empire, the first evidence of the temporalization of the crisis appears with Leibniz, who saw rising up in his mind's eye a new constellation of world powers: "Momenta temporum pretiosissima sunt in transitu rerum (The moments of the times are most precious as things shift). . . . Now Europe is in a state of flux and crisis the likes of which it hasn't seen since Charlemagne."[2] Here the concept came into a historical philosophical context; moreover, it opened this context in such a way that the course of the eighteenth century was obliged increasingly to fulfill its stipulations.

Crisis rose to become a fundamental concept for the philosophy of history, which ushered in a claim to interpret the entire course of history from a particular point in time. Since then, it has always been one's own point in time which is experienced as critical. And the reflection of one's own temporal circumstances not only arrays the entire past for judgment but also displays for prognosis the future as well.

Since the French Revolution, *crisis* has been the central interpretive factor for both political and social life. This is certainly true for the long, open-ended period of the Industrial Revolution, which was accompanied and influenced by scientifically differentiated theories of crisis and the business cycle.

Given the practice of interpreting the entire course of history from one standpoint, and in surprising contrast to the example of national economy, no explicit theory of crisis was developed during the nineteenth century. The work of Jacob Burkhardt is the only exception. Marx, who tried to connect his economic theory with a philosophy of history, came to a dead stop while elaborating a theory of crisis, as Schumpeter explicitly declaimed. Even in the twentieth century, theories of crisis confine themselves to specific areas of inquiry such as psychiatry and political science. Global theories of crisis, like those implicitly behind the efforts of the eighteenth-and nineteenth-century philosophers of history, are today quickly dismissed as not serious; they are thought to be insufficiently demonstrable empirically and thereby unworthy of defense.

Three Semantic Models

While the original medical sense of *crisis* strongly influenced the political application of the term, a great many theological usages were also fed into the basic historical concept. This was already true in the time of the English Civil War of 1640–60, as its descriptions demonstrate. It was also true regarding the historical-philosophical and reflective use of the term prevalent from the late Enlightenment. The power of God's judgment and the dynamics of the apocalypse continually echoed in the use of *crisis,* and doubts should arise regarding the theological derivation of this newly constituted formulation, although this derivation does not show itself by mere proclamation. This derivation can be seen in the fact that the historical-philosophical diagnosis of *crisis* readily functions with concrete, compulsory alternatives; these are detrimental to a differentiated diagnostic but nevertheless seem to be effective and plausible because of the prophetic *gestus* of language itself.

Of course, in putting forth three semantic models of *crisis,* I risk unduly simplifying the historically proper use of the concept. All reservations aside, however, three options can be specified. First, history can be interpreted as continual crisis. World history is world judgment; only world history passes judgment on the world. This model deals with one concept of process. Second, *crisis* can designate another, singular, accelerating type of process, in which conflicts burst open an existing system; following the crisis the system reconstitutes itself with a new set of circumstances. Here *crisis* indicates the passing of an epoch, a historical watershed, a process which, *mutatis mutandis,* can repeat itself. Although in terms of isolated cases, history always remains unique, this concept engenders the possibility that change can take place in analogous forms. Therefore I suggest that it be labeled as the concept of the iterative epoch or event. Third, *crisis* can suggest the last crisis within a prevailing historical moment; in this conception comparisons to the Last Judgment are only metaphorical. Measured against the present course of our history this model must be labeled utopian, but it cannot be ruled out. Considering the means which prevail for our total destruction, it has every opportunity for realization. Nonetheless, this conception of *crisis* is purely future-oriented and, in contrast to the other models, it points toward a final resolution of conflict.

These models actually never appear in the pure forms of my description. As encountered in the language of philosophical or theoretical history they are rather found to be mutually supporting. They overlap one another in their applications. They measure out differently in different contexts. What is common to all three models despite their impregnation with theological connotations, is the fact that they offer historically immanent patterns of explanation which dispense with, at least in theory, references to the intervention of God.

A CONTINUOUS PROCESS

"World history is world judgment" is an expression from Schiller, advanced as the motto of modernity. The passage appears by chance in a love poem where Schiller bemoans a situation come and gone, which on its face is forever irretrievable. "What one declines at the appointed hour not even eternity can return."[3] Formally speaking, the line secularizes the Last Judgment, whose temporality it retains faithfully. In this sense it carries with it a pronounced anti-Christian element, since every transgression relentlessly enters the individual's biography, enters the moral and political history of the active community, indeed, enters world history itself. The model is compatible with that fate Herodotus lets shine upon all unique examples from history, which can always be read as the action of an immanent sense of justice. But Schiller's dictum raises a larger claim. Not only is an intrinsic sense of justice demanded for the unique historical event, which seems here to possess an almost magical air of appearance; it is also expected for world history as a whole. Logically, every act of injustice, every incommensurable action, every unpunished crime, every senseless and useless act, is apodictically precluded. Consequently, the burden of proof as regards the meaning of history considered in this way increases enormously.

It is no longer the historian who, on the grounds of his superior knowledge of the past, believes himself capable *ex post* of morally judging it. Now history itself is accorded the powers of an active subject. Now history becomes the judge of history. Now history equals justice itself. It was Hegel who took it upon himself to cushion the moral discrepancies and shortcomings that Schiller's dictum yields. Hegel's world history remains world judgment because the "world spirit" or "thought of God" must part with itself in history so as to find itself as judgment. Viewed theologically, his world history deals with the last possible and last conceivable heresy for one who more or less intends to do justice to a Christian interpretation.

Schiller's dictum can be applied intact so long as history is interpreted as an immanent process. Liberals never tire of calling upon this position to deduce for their actions a moral legitimacy. Darwinian and imperialist philosophies of history can also be linked to this view, since such ends as the survival of the fittest are seen as redeeming the actions which produced them; consider Hitler's sentimental renunciation of self-pity: whoever goes to ruin has justly earned his fate.

There are semantic options whose implications may not in any way be attributed to their linguistic origins. Whosoever undertakes to trace the derivation of Hitler back to Hegel or Schiller succumbs to a claim of historical actuality, of cause and effect, which only proceeds selectively. World history as world judgment asserts before all else that every situation is stamped with the same decisive earnestness, that everyone faces the consequences of his actions.

In this sense Schiller's dictum is also adaptable theologically: as Richard Rothe stated in 1837, "The entirety of Christian history is one great continuous crisis of the race,"[4] or as Karl Barth said, stripping this enduring crisis of all teleological overtones in order to explicate it existentially: "So-called Sacred History is merely the continuously running crisis of all history, not history within or next to history."[5] Here, as a concept, *crisis* has forfeited finality, the transitional nature of its temporality; pure and simple, *crisis* becomes a structural category within a Christian conception of history; eschatology itself, so to speak, is assimilated to history.

AN INTERACTIVE PROCESS

Crisis is less exacting in terms of what I have called "the concept of the iterative epoch." This concept looks to the conditions of various possible courses of history to distinguish points of comparison and commonality as well as points of difference. This model does not raise the claim that it can interpret history in a lasting fashion or as a totality. Jacob Burckhardt understood anthropological constants in history as being available—within their respective historical articulations—as different courses of action for given crises. For example, he defined the period of the barbarian invasions during the decline of the Roman Empire as historically unique and not without significance, as a crisis that favored the rise of a church with claims to universality. In fact the only period which can be counted a lasting and open-ended crisis is the modern period in which he wrote. Behind every other example of historical crisis Burckhardt discovered more aspects of continuity than his startled colleagues had cared to admit.

The economic concept of crisis belongs under the aegis of the iterative model. Behind the example of economic crisis stands the weight of the metaphorical apparatus of the eighteenth-century understanding of equilibrium, which can never be empirically redeemed in its entirety. Roughly speaking, crisis appears when the equilibrium between supply and demand, between production and consumption, between the circulation of money and the circulation of goods, is disturbed; when this happens recession and the slide down the economic scale are said to become visible everywhere. Yet it is held as a law of experience that following a recession induced by a crisis comes a general rise in productivity. The paradox of this doctrine seems to lie in the fact that equilibrium can only be maintained, or rather regained, if productivity rises continually and does not stagnate; otherwise decline appears to be inevitable. Inasmuch as this principle is dependent upon progress for its cogency, without progress it cannot be empirically redeemed. As Molinari, a nineteenth-century theoretician of business cycles, said, "Every advance, large or small, contains its crisis."[6]

That crisis should be the engine of progress—this semantic variant appears to me to have been redeemed only in the areas of the natural sciences, economics, technology, and industry. But there is a semantic parallel to this usage in the theological discourse of the middle ages, *vitae non progredi, retrogradi est* (not to progress on the path of life is to regress), attributed to Bernard of Clairvaux (1090–1153). Put bluntly, "Whosoever does not gain, loses." This formulation hints at a possible common anthropological basis upon which the concept of iterative crisis might be founded, but it does not lead me to add theology to the list of areas in which this principle has apparently triumphed.

At any rate, I must refrain from describing this model by means of the incalculable number of quotations available out of the course of history; a single example may stand for them all: "Out of every crisis mankind rises with some greater share of knowledge, higher decency, purer purpose." These words are Franklin Delano Roosevelt's, spoken the day before his death.[7]

Regarding this option, finally, the question must be asked, is "progress" *the* lead concept for "crisis," or is rather the concept of the iterative event that guiding concept under which "progress" must be subsumed? If "crisis" as a conceptually iterative event lays claim to an enormous explicative potential, then progress, which crisis indisputably yields, can be accredited its relative claim to efficacy. Indeed, this type of progress is undoubtedly being called upon to solve our impending ecological crisis.

THE FINAL RESOLUTION OF CONFLICT

That at some time one finds oneself in a crisis that can be the last, great, one-time resolution of conflict within one's life or within the life of the times, following which, from a standpoint in the future, history itself will appear totally different—this semantic option is more frequently taken the less one believes in an absolute end to history via the Last Judgment of God. What is under consideration is the reshuffling, so to speak, of the theological grounds of belief, as demanded by the design of immanent history. There is no shortage of testimonials to this: Robespierre saw himself as wielding a moral justice which secured its ultimate success through the application of involuntary force; Thomas Paine believed, in view of the American and French revolutions and the implication of crisis which they portended, that an absolute turn of events must lie in the not-distant future; and those original partisans of the French Revolution who became the embittered adversaries of the Bonapartistic consequences of their actions can also bear witness to the character of this semantic option. For examples of German extraction one need only sound the names of Friedrich Schlegel, Fichte, and Ernst Moritz Arndt.

The absolute nadir of history guarantees the sudden turn toward deliverance: in the case of France, the birth of sociology out of the spirit of the Revolution (not just that of the Restoration) can be offered as evidence. Saint-Simon and August Comte knew they were in the "Grande Crise Finale" which by scientific planning and rising industrial production could be ridden to conquer the moment once and for all. Lorenz von Stein may also be mentioned in this context, for he perceived in the effort to arrange a compromise between capital and labor Europe's last best chance to forestall cultural recidivism and the fall into barbarism. It has been demonstrated that maintaining equilibrium meant producing progress through crisis. Although on its own terms this formula was successful only in limited areas of endeavor, it had consequences elsewhere.

Karl Marx was, so to speak, left hanging in an intermediate position: on the one hand, he expected that the last crisis of capitalism would bring an end to class differences and yield a reign of freedom from oppression; on the other, he saw that his position was incapable of presenting this reading of capitalism's great crisis, that the crisis—instead of preserving the status quo in the new order—had to be viewed as leading to the overthrow of the entire system by force. Marx worked both with a systematic, immanent concept of crisis in which the iterative structure of economic crisis was set forth and with a concept of crisis which demanded the violent overthrow of that same iterative structure. Moreover, he deduced this latter conclusion from a set of circumstances which seemed to be driving world history toward a final great crisis; the supposed final struggle between the proletariat and bourgeoisie doubtlessly took place for Marx within the framework of a theological Last Judgment, which he was never able to ground purely economically.

Crisis as a Question for the Christian Tradition

In every case in which crisis is expected to utterly change the world, the expectation is easily exposed as an illusion of perspective. It is characteristic of the finitude of all human beings to regard their own situation as more important and more serious than all the other crises that have actually taken place. But one should be careful—precisely in view of the teaching of the Last Judgment—not to dismiss the above self-fashioned, slip-on evaluation of humanity as merely another error of perspective. For when it comes to a question of securing our survival, is it not the case that a great many acts of judgment are put forth as final? Κρίσις in the Greek sense of compelling sound judgment and prompt action under the commanding presence of some urgent necessity remains an indispensable concept given the complex conditions of contemporary society. I want to illustrate this last point with an historical *Gedankenexperiment.*

It belongs to Christian teaching that God will foreshorten time before the coming of the end of the world. Behind this doctrine is the cosmological idea that God, as the lord of time, can bring about the anticipated end of the world before it is foreseen and that he will do so for the sake of the chosen people whose suffering is to be curtailed. (Mark 13: 20, Matthew 24: 22). Now this mythological language of apocalyptic expectation can be subjected to psychologization or idealization. To see faith in an immanent foreshortening of time as evidence of a wish on the part of the suffering and oppressed to exchange their misery for paradise as quickly as possible is not difficult. Yet to observe the eschatological foreshortening of time among its many historical interpretations is to stand before the astonishing realization that since the first occurrence of this idea, which itself stands over and above historical time, there has been in fact a successive acceleration of history.

From a wholly different perspective, the history of scientific discoveries received an analogous interpretation. For Bacon it was a matter of hope and expectation that discoveries occur in shorter and shorter intervals of time so that an even better mastery of nature would be made possible. Such early moderns as Leibniz inferred from their data that historically immanent progress was getting faster and faster, accelerating, so as to lead to a better world order. Now, although the acceleration of historical progress came out of the apocalyptic foreshortening of time, the contents of the interpretive model changed completely. The attainment of paradise after the end of the world and the possibility of its attainment in this world are logically mutually exclusive conditions.

The cosmic foreshortening of time which was to precede the Last Judgment never fully incorporated the sense of the concept *crisis.* Neither does the accelerating pace of modern history, the actuality of which is not to be disputed, allow itself to be properly conceived as crisis. Scientifically or not, deliberately or not, sound judgment and prompt action are obviously due regarding the matter of whether and how survival on this globe is to be possible. The cosmic foreshortening of time, which, in the prior language of myth, was to precede the Last Judgment, can today be empirically verified as the accelerating sequence of historical events. In the words of Burckhardt, "All of a sudden the progression of the world transpires with frightening speed; developments which otherwise take centuries seem, like fleeting phantoms, to pass by in months and weeks and with their passing to be resolved."[8] The common generic term for the apocalyptic foreshortening of time that is to precede the Last Judgment, as well as for the phenomena of historical acceleration, is *crisis.* Should this be considered mere coincidence, as simply two distinct usages for the same figure of speech? In the Christian as well as the non-Christian sense of the term, in every instance, *crisis* indicates an increasingly urgent set of circumstances the meaning of which mankind seems unable to escape.

In conclusion, therefore, a temporal hypothesis is called for that is not the least bit new. Consider the history of the genus Homo. This history can be represented by three exponential time-curves. Measured by the five billion years since our planet was covered with a firm crust, the one billion years of organic life represent a relatively short span. But much shorter still is the span of ten million years of the genus Homo's probable existence, the last two million years of which self-fabricated tools give evidence.

The second exponential time-curve can be plotted in the two million years since members of the species *Homo erectus* distinguished themselves with tools of their own making. The first document of genuine art is 30,000 years old, and the beginnings of agriculture and animal husbandry can be dated at about 10,000 years ago. The approximate 6,000 years of urban culture which have left traces of a written tradition are, in the context of the two million years of human productivity, a very short span indeed, and the achievement of poetic, philosophical, and historiographical reflection certainly takes place in its very latest moments.

The third exponential time-curve follows in outline the self-organization of urban culture, which began 6,000 years ago. Measured against this comparatively continuous history, modern industrial society, which is based on science and technology, unfolds over the past 300 years. The curve of the acceleration is indicated by three additional series of facts: the dissemination of information has accelerated to such a point that the identity of the event and the news corresponding to it are theoretically the same. Furthermore, the acceleration of travel has increased approximately tenfold since the replacement of natural travel aids (wind, water, animal) by the technological means of the steam engine, the electric motor, and the internal-combustion engine. The acceleration of the means of communication has enabled the world to shrink to the dimensions of a spaceship. The population explosion runs along an analogous exponential time-curve: from half a billion people in the seventeenth century, the planet's population rose, despite mass exterminations, to two and a half billion at the middle of our century, heading in the direction of eight billion people by the century's end.

Although in some respects the three exponential time-curves might be dismissed as playing with figures, they openly delineate a limit beyond which further technical or scientific progress cannot take us. For it must be remembered that the potential of autonomous humanity for self-destruction has multiplied many times over along these same lines.

Thus the question arises whether our semantic model of crisis, as a kind of final resolution of conflict, has no better chance of realization than it might have had at any time previously. If this is the case, then everything depends upon directing our energies toward preventing extinction. It should be noted that the Katechon is similarly a theological response to crisis.

The three exponential time-curves can of course, be read as an intensifying of the rate of acceleration that makes it completely impossible to risk speculative accounts of the future. Perhaps the proper response to crisis consists in being on the lookout for those stabilizing factors which can be deduced from the long duration of the history of humankind. Then again, it could be that such questions can be formulated not only historically and politically but also theologically. Whatever the case, from the historical point of view we need to accommodate the acceleration that involves the special uniqueness of our time. Even this conclusion might prove an error in perspective, or better still, an error in judgment, if we discover in time the enduring conditions for our survival.

NOTES

1. "Crise," *Dictionnaire politique* (Paris, 1839, 1868), p. 298. For all succeeding examples and further reference, see my article "Crisis" in *Geschichtlichte Grundbegriffe*, ed. Otto Brunner et al., vol. 3 (Stuttgart, 1982), pp. 617–50.

2. G.W. Leibniz, *Konzept eines Briefes an Schleiniz* (23.9.1712), in *Leibniz' Rußland betreffender Briefwechsel*, ed. Wladimir Iwanowitsch Guerrier (Petersburg/Leipzig, 1873), part 1, vol. 2, p. 227 f.; 1961, p. 39 ("Et l'Europe est maintenant dans un état de changement et dans une crise où elle n'a jamais été depuis l'Empire de Charlemagne").

3. Friedrich von Schiller, *Resignation: Eine Phantasie*, in *Collected Works*, ed. Eduard von der Hellen (Stuttgart/Berlin), vol. 1, p. 199 ("Die Weltgeschichte ist das Weltgericht," "Was man von der Minute ausgeschlagen, gibt keine Ewigkeit zurück").

4. Richard Rothe, *Die Anfänge der christlichen Kirche und ihre Verfassung* (1837); quoted in Peter Meinhold, *Geschichte der kirchlichen Historiographie* (Munich/Freiburg, 1967), vol. 2, p. 221 ("Die ganze christliche Geschichte überhaupt ist eine grosse kontinuierliche Krisis unseres Geschlechts").

5. Karl Barth, *Der Romerbrief*, 9th ed. (Zollikon-Zurich, 1954), pp. 57, 32 ("Die sogenannte 'Heilsgeschichte' ist nur die fortlaufende Krisis aller Geschichte, nicht eine Geschichte in oder neben der Geschichte").

6. Gustave de Molinari, *L'Evolution économique du XIXe siècle: théorie du progrès* (Paris, 1880), p. 102 f. ("Jeder kleine oder grosse Fortschritt besitzt seine Krise").

7. Quoted in W. Besson, *Die Politische Terminologie des Präsidenten* F. D. Roosevelt, (Tübingen, 1955), p. 20.

8. Jacob Burckhardt, *Weltgeschichtliche Betrachtungen*, ed. Rudolf Stadelmann (Pfüllingen, 1949), s. 211 ("Der Weltprozeß gerät plötzlich in furchtbare Schnelligkeit; Entwicklungen, die sonst Jahrhunderte brauchen, scheinen in Monaten und Wochen wie flüchtige Phantome vorüberzugehen und damit erledigt zu sein").

TEN

Heritage and Revolution

Cornelius Castoriadis

I

My title for this essay may sound bizarre. The term *heritage* connotes something conservative, if not something downright reactionary, perhaps some organization in the United States. Or else it brings to mind legal papers, deeds, and notaries. *Revolution,* on the other hand, is a term which has been prostituted by the contemporary publicity industry: every now and then, there is a revolution in vacuum cleaners or toilet paper. But in common parlance, between 1789, when La Rochefoucauld-Liancourt used it for the first time in its modern sense, and somewhere around 1950, it meant a radical change, a subversion of the existing, instituted order of things (not to be confused with gun firing and bloodletting). So my title needs some explanation.

I do not think the game is over. And I do not want the game to be over. I mean the political game, in the grand sense of the term *political;* I am not talking about Mr. Reagan or Mr. Mitterrand. Nor do I have in mind the management of the current affairs of government. By politics I mean a collective activity endowed with self-reflection and lucidity, aiming at the global institution of society.

The historical singularity of Western Europe and, before it, eighth- to fifth-century Greece, is that they are the only societies to have *created politics* in the sense of an activity explicitly attempting to change society and succeeding to a substantial extent. In all other societies we have court intrigues, group rivalries, machinations, open competitions, complicated games to obtain power—but these are always *within* the existing instituted framework. In Ancient Greece and in Western Europe (including, of course, the United States), we have *politics.*

Considered this way, politics is a moment and an expression of the project of autonomy; it does not accept passively and blindly what is already there, what has been instituted, but calls it into question. Now, what is called into question may be the constitution or a body of law. It can also be the prevailing collective representations about world, society, truth, or values. In the latter case, the calling into question is, of course, philosophy in the pristine sense. The creation of politics and the creation of philosophy, as expressions of the project of autonomy, go together, and together indeed they have gone in actual history.

These expressions of the project of autonomy also take on, almost immediately, the *content* of autonomy. The Greek πολῖται, or the European *bourgeois,* did not set out to change institutions simply to manifest their capacity to do so. Rather they tried to bring about the realization of social and invididual autonomy. This is the *democratic* component of their political activity and of the resulting institutions. (The same can be said, *mutatis mutandis*, about philosophy as realization of intellectual and psychical freedom, but this is not our present object.)

What this means is that *our* heritage, *our* tradition, is the democratic heritage and the revolutionary tradition in their strictest senses. So much for the coexistence of these two words in my title.

Such things can of course be seen differently, even from an opposing view. It could be argued that our heritage is just what is there, that there is nothing more to be done except to manage its legacy, to take care of this fortune, large or small. We should be clear about the consequences of this position. The central part of our heritage lies in making our institutions; we can change them, and we ought to change them if we think fit. Now the assertion that we have nothing to change, at least nothing important, that there is nothing to do beyond the day-to-day legislation and management of the Congress or Parliament, is tantamount to the statement that things are perfectly satisfactory as they are, that we have reached the highest state of society or, at any rate, the least imperfect one. It is saying, in other words, that our society is such that any attempt to change its institutions will inevitably bring about something worse. As is well known, this position has been argued explicitly for more than a decade now.

One has only to open one's eyes to dismiss this view. Regardless of whether one is "satisfied" or "dissatisfied," the existing state of affairs is untenable in the long run because it is self-destructive, and, by this I mean self-destructive *politically*. It produces a glacier of privatization and apathy; it dislocates the social imaginary significations that hold institutions together. An apathetic and cynical society cannot maintain for long even the few liberal institutions existing today. And a society of liberal institutions based upon the relentless pursuit of individual self-interest is sheer nonsense.

Another suggestion has surfaced in the last few years: that we come to live under a new form of "democratic politics," made up of the juxtaposition of various "social movements"—or rather, nonmovements—none of which would be concerned with envisaging society as a whole, but whose additive synergy would work to produce a "democratic" state of affairs. It is not difficult to see that these "movements," stripped of general concerns, take inevitably the form of lobbies, the mutually opposed pressures of which currently contribute to the stalemates of society on substantive issues. Recent developments have amply illustrated this point.

A final preliminary remark. Formulations which suggest, for example, that the ideas of the Enlightenment have not yet been fully implemented are defective in more than one way. Our heritage goes far beyond the *Aufklarung* and has not been, to say the least, exhaustively "recapitulated" by it. The Enlightenment itself, important as it is, forms only one phrase in the symphonic creation of the project of autonomy. Many important things have happened since the *Aufklarung* which are not limited to the implementation of its ideas. Above all, if and when a new period of political activity oriented toward autonomy begins, it will carry us not only far beyond the *Aufklarung* but also beyond anything else we are now able to imagine.

II

To minimize misunderstandings, I should now make clear some of my further presuppositions. Human history is creation. It is, first and foremost, wholesale self-creation, the separation of humanity from sheer animality, which is at once never complete but abyssmal. This self-creation manifests itself as unprecedented new forms of being, "models" or "causes" in the presocial world. Some such forms of being are language, tools, instituted rules, meanings, and anthropological types. Others are the particular global forms society takes on in different times and places: Tupi-Guarani or Hebrew, Greek or medieval European, Assyrian or capitalistic bureaucratic.

These elemental facts—the self-creation of humanity, the self-institution of societies—are, almost always, almost everywhere, veiled; they are concealed from society by its very institution. And almost always, almost everywhere, this institution contains the instituted representation of its own extrasocial origin. The *heteronomous* character of the institution of society consists in the fact that its social law is not posited as created by society but is seen rather as having a source beyond the reach of living human beings. This is the root of the religious character of the institution of almost all known societies—and likewise of the unbreakable link between religion and heteronomy. The institution of society has found both the guarantee of its validity and its protection against internal contestation and external relativization through the instituted representation of an extrasocial origin for itself.[1] "God has given us our laws, how could you dare change them?"

Every institution of society aims at its perpetuation. And it generally succeeds in creating appropriate means for this, since human beings can exist only insofar as they are socialized, i.e., humanized, by such an institution while the positings of institutions are conformal to it and tend to reproduce it indefinitely. To put it in another way, newborn bipeds become social individuals only through internalizing the existing social institutions.

This should have entailed that a social order, once created and barring external factors, would last forever. We know that this is not so. More precisely, we know that although this was *almost* the case for a very long time, it then ceased to be so. We know that there have been many extraordinarily different societies, and that they are all to some degree historical in the proper sense, that is, self-altering. I shall now describe briefly two important types of this self-alteration or historicity.

As far as we know, some degree of self-alteration, however small or slow, seeps through in all societies. Language offers perhaps the most striking example of this. Every day, several anonymous and untraceable changes are introduced into the English language as it is spoken, say, in the United States, in the guise of new slang words, semantic shifts, etc. A similar process has been going on with a slower tempo for thousands of years in "primitive" or "savage" societies as well as in "traditional" peasant societies such as those under "Asiatic despotism" or those in Eastern Europe.

This minute but continual self-alteration will persist as long as there are human beings and societies, for it has to do with the nature of human beings as well as that of social institutions. If institutions were made of iron, they would still be subject to alteration, but not *self*-alteration; rather, like iron, they would rust. If they were made of rational ideas, they would last forever. But institutions are actually made of sanctioned social meanings and the corollary procedures for giving meaning. These meanings are at heart imaginary—not "rational," not "functional," not "reflections of reality"—they are *social imaginary significations.* They can be effective, and effectively alive, only as long as they are invested ("cathected") and lived by human beings. The same is true of the procedures for the sanction of these meanings.

Human beings are essentially defined not by being "reasonable" but by being possessed with a radical imagination. It is this imagination which has to be tamed and brought under control through social fabrication, but such taming never fully succeeds, as witnessed by the existence of *transgression* in all known societies. Thus the activities of innumerable human beings always introduce infinitesimal alterations in the ways of doing things, as well as in the manner of effectively living, or "interpretating," the instituted social imaginary significations. As a result, a slow—and, of course, unconscious—self-alteration is always in process in actual social life. This self-alteration is usually the object of an occultation on the part of the existing institutions of society in the same way and for the same "reasons" that the creative dimension of self-institution is such an object. The occultations of self-institution (of the self-creation of society) and of self-alteration (of the historicity of society) are two faces of society's heteronomy.

The second type of self-alteration, leaving aside the extremely important class of "intermediate" cases consisting in relatively swift but fully blind social change, concerns the periods of rapid and important societal self-alteration in which an intense collective activity, endowed with a minimal degree of lucidity, is successfully aimed at changing institutions. Such periods manifest another mode of being of the social-historical, the explicit calling into question of its laws of existence and the corresponding work toward their lucid transformation. These periods I would call revolutionary. In this sense I speak of a revolutionary period in the Greek world from the eighth to the fifth centuries B.C., and in Western Europe from, say, the thirteenth century onward. During these two periods the project of social and individual autonomy was created, thanks to which creation we can today think and speak as we do.

III

I come now to the idea of revolution as an explicit political project—or, rather, as a dense period of time within which a radical political project takes hold upon social reality.

What does *radical* mean in this context? Of course, the idea of a total revolution, of the creation of a social *tabula rasa*, is absurd. In the most radical revolution imaginable, the elements of social life that would remain unaltered—language, building, tools, ways of behaving—are immensely more numerous than are those which might be changed; they are also the most important, heaviest parts of the socio-psychical structure of human beings. This can be seen as a great *fact* which, made explicit, sounds like a truism. But it can and must also be seen as a crucial problem for political action.

This problem, as far as we know, was raised explicitly for the first time by Plato. Given what humans are—which means, for Plato, given that human beings are utterly and hopelessly corrupt—how is it possible to make changes, and who is going to bring them about? Plato's answer in the *Republic* is well known: philosophers ought to become kings, or kings philosophers. Plato himself considers both eventualities unlikely.

Plato's position is unacceptable to us, or at least to me. Certainly, to call Plato a totalitarian is to misuse and abuse terms—it is even silly. It is also wrong to call him a conservative: what he intended was not at all the conservation of an existing state of affairs or the return to some previous one. Any decent Athenian conservative would recoil with horror at Plato's proposals regarding property and women and children. Rather, Plato aimed to arrest the movement of history (this can be more clearly seen in the *Laws*), and the hidden, certainly not fully conscious, presupposition behind his political attitude and his bitter hatred of democracy was the understanding that history is the work of the human collectivity. Once you give free rein to the will of the many and to its expression, then γένεσις—change and becoming, the negation of true Being—and its concomitant decay set in.

Nevertheless the diagnosis of the problem was correct, and its formulation remained, by and large, the same during the subsequent millennia. How can you change society if both the actors and the instruments of change are living individuals, that is, the embodiment of that which is to be changed? Accordingly Rousseau could write in the second half of the eighteenth century, "Celui qui ose entreprendre d'instituer un peuple doit se sentir en état de changer, pour ainsi dire, la nature humaine (The one who dares to endeavor to institute a people must feel himself capable of changing, so to speak, human nature)."[2] It is true that in this passage Rousseau deals explicitly with the question of "first" institution; but the whole of his political writing shows that he is in the grip of Plato's problem. To give institutions to a people, one has to change, first of all, the *mores*, the *Sitten*, the ways of being of the people. Without such a change, the new institutions are useless and cannot even function. But it is precisely in order to bring about change in these ways of being that new institutions are required.[3] Rousseau, like Plato, like Machiavelli, like Montesquieu, like all great political thinkers (and in contradistinction to recent political theorists) was very lucid on this point. There cannot be a "political" institution which is not, from top to bottom, from its most superficial to its deepest level, linked to the *mores*, the *Sitten*, the whole anthropological, socio-psychical structure of the people living in that society.

Let us dwell a bit longer on Rousseau's formulation. "The one who dares to endeavor to institute a people, to give institutions to a people . . ." Behind this statement one sees the image, the figure, and the story of *the* legislator, the canonical list of whom includes Machiavelli, Moses, Theseus, Lycurgus, Numa. . . . Now Rousseau is a deep thinker, and, in a sense, a democrat. Why then does he think only of *celui qui . . .*, "*the one who . . .*," as a subject of action and of the people, *le peuple*, as a *passive object* of this action, an object which has to be *formed* (*formed* is the precise term in the first version of the *Contrat*: "celui qui se croit capable de former un peuple . . .", formed by the active legislator not only in terms of a narrowly conceived political constitution but also in respect of its *mores*, its ways of feeling, thinking, doing, and being? That Plato could speak in these terms is understandable. Regardless of any contradiction that this view might have with his ideas about the human being or the soul, he firmly believes that the people are rabble and says so repeatedly. But Rousseau?

One could argue that Rousseau is very pessimistic, indeed gloomy, about the people of his time and about human nature in general. Contrary to the widespread, popular misunderstanding, this was indeed the truth of the matter—and, as we know, events rapidly proved him wrong (the *Contrat Social* was published in 1762; Rousseau died in 1778). What is more important and deeper is the fact that the common ground on which Plato and Rousseau stand is the philosophical equivalent of the imaginary of heteronomy. Both Plato and Rousseau would recognize that people have been active in bringing about the given state of political affairs. But they would also be quick to point out that it is a bad, corrupted state of affairs—and necessarily so. Framed in these terms, the aporia has no solution; indeed, that is what Rousseau says in the first paragraph of chapter VII, Book II, of the *Contrat*: "il faudroit des Dieux pour donner des loix aux hommes (Gods would be required to give laws to humans)," an echo of Plato's "God is the measure of all things."

People, and history, can bring forward something "new"—but only in the sense of *destruction*, of *decay*, of a *less good* state of affairs. By virtue of the Platonic conflation of Being and Good, *less good* means also *less being*, ἧττον ὄ. Such a "new" thus is new by virtue of a deficit or negation and therefore not truly new.

In the view of the heteronomously instituted society, the laws are not created by men. According to Plato and most other philosophers, the laws are humanly made, and that is precisely why they are so bad. They ought to be the reflection (or translation, or whatever) of a superhuman order, mediated by an "exceptional" being (for Rousseau, see the whole of chapter VII of Book II of the *Contrat*), and protected against human attempts at their alteration by a "noble lie," the fable of their divine origin (*Republic*, 414 b-c).

But the trails of Rousseau and Plato, because they are radical thinkers, lead to the heart of the matter. Let us reformulate the idea in question: "one who wants to institute a people has to change the *mores* of the people." Who in actuality changes the *mores* of people? The answer is obvious: the people themselves. Thus we have at least a formal answer to our question. If there is to be a true change in institutions, it must be accompanied by a deeply consonant change in *mores*. Changes in *mores* are brought about by the people. So the only assurance for this consonance is that the people be as active in bringing about the political (formal institutional) change as they are in changing their *mores* (though, of course, in a different way).

We may recall that Marx confronts this same question in the third of his *Theses on Feuerbach*: "The materialist theory of the change in circumstances and of education forgets that circumstances are changed by man and that the educator must be himself educated. . . . The coincidence of the change in circumstances and of human activity can be rationally considered and understood only as revolutionary praxis." The problem as posed by Marx is that human beings are conditioned by their own times and that such times cannot be changed except by their actions. But why should human beings want to change their times, if they are conditioned by them to function in conformity with them? Marx's apparently facile answer, "revolutionary praxis," means that people change by changing the circumstances in which they find themselves.

Things will become clearer, I hope, if we use the ideas I introduced before, for it is through the same historical process that people change "anthropologically," that is, change their *mores* and socio-psychical organization, and change also the (formal) institution of society. It appears that all of the elements required for the solution of our problem presuppose each other, and that we find ourselves caught in a vicious circle. It *is* a circle, but it is not "vicious," for it is the circle of historical creation. Did the Greek πολῖται create the πόλις or the πόλις the πολῖται? This is a meaningless question precisely because the πόλις could only have been created by the action of human beings who were simultaneously transforming themselves into πολῖται.

Why and how, one may ask, do people start changing themselves and their institutions? And why is it that they do not do so all the time?

We have, in a sense, already answered this question. Human history is creation. We can elucidate this creation in its general character, or in its concrete contents, after it has happened. But we can neither "explain" nor "predict" it, because it is not determined; it, rather, is determinant. Likewise, its tempo and its rhythm are themselves part of the creation. It is only in an external, descriptive sense that historical processes take place in measurable, homogeneous calendar time. Intrinsically, in its concrete content and texture, the time of a historical epoch is an integral part of it and congruent with its deepest imaginary significations. That Greek time, or Western European time, differs deeply from Trobriand or Pharaonic Egyptian time hardly needs stressing; but it does require thinking.

It is useful to revert for a moment to Marx, for he has been till now the most explicit thinker of revolution. I cannot enter here into the ambiguities and antinomies of Marx's thought, which I have discussed elsewhere.[4] Despite the third *Thesis on Feuerbach*, quoted above, and similar formulations, when it comes to the socialist revolution, Marx is unable to maintain the irreducibility of praxis; to put it more sharply, he proves unable to see its creative character, looking instead for solid causes, that is, guarantees, of and for the revolution. The direct result is that he pays scant attention to the problems of political action and organization proper. Instead he looks for economic "laws" which would somehow engineer the collapse of capitalism. Such laws, even if true, would of course be irrelevant and useless; there is nothing to ensure that a collapse of capitalism would be followed by socialism rather than fascism, the *Iron Heel*, *1984*, or even cannibalism.

More to the point are Marx's attempts to find in capitalist circumstances the conditions for the creation of a "revolutionary class," not just a class striving to overthrow the system but a class capable, after this overthrow, of establishing a new society with a fully "positive" character, capable, in Marx's terminology, of the "inferior," then the "superior" phase of communism. This class is the proletariat, or the working class. But why should this be so?

There are three kinds of answer to this question in Marx:

- The proletariat is subject, under capitalism, to total alienation or absolute deprivation; it is a pure negation, which therefore can only produce the absolutely positive. This Hegelio-Christian position has to be dismissed straightaway as factually erroneous, logically nonsensical, politically inconsistent and philosophically arbitrary.
- "Laws of history" demand that capitalism be fulfilled by an "end of history" or, rather, an end of "prehistory." This is communism. The proletariat will thereafter be "historically compelled, in conformity with its being," to do whatever is necessary to bring about the new society (*The Holy Family*). This arbitrary eschatology does not need to be discussed either.
- Capitalist circumstances, especially work in the factory and life in working-class neighborhoods, *positively instill* into the proletariat a new mentality consisting of solidarity, practicality, soberness of mind, depth of understanding, "humanity," etc., which is intrinsically homogeneous with the new society to be established. In other words, capitalist circumstances produce not only a working class but also, in the person of this class, a new anthropological type and a new socio-psychical structure, which are the necessary conditions for the production of a new society. Capitalist circumstances change human beings in such a way that they will in turn change circumstances in the wished-for direction.

For a series of reasons, the most compelling of which is the huge quantitative decline of the proletariat in its Marxian sense, this discussion might appear to have only historical interest. In fact it brings us back to the center of our theoretical and political preoccupations.

Marx was correct, to a considerable degree, in diagnosing a change in the socio-psychical structure of the working class. In the main capitalist countries, the working class in the nineteenth and first half of the twentieth centuries behaved and acted in a way no other exploited and dominated class had ever behaved and acted before. This was not the "product" of "circumstances" but truly the self-creation of the working class as a class and as an active factor in capitalist society. The passage from a proletariat "in itself" to a proletariat "for itself" was not (and is not) "necessary," nor was it *determined* by the objective conditions of life and work under capitalism. It was the British, the French, the German, and then the American workers who struggled to free themselves from illiteracy, to acquire, shape, and spread political ideas, to organize, to formulate, and finally to impose demands aimed at altering their "circumstances."[5] *Some,* but not *all,* working classes in other capitalist countries showed similar performances.

Now the difference between, say, English workers of the early nineteenth century and Brazilian workers until 1964 (or, for that matter, today's English workers) is certainly not a reflection of genetic disparities. Part of the difference may just be "there," and unexplainable. But part may be accounted for by dissimilarities in *historical* endowment, in the total "circumstances" of the countries involved, including their political traditions, *beyond* the establishment of capitalism per se. The fact is that the first, most important, inaugural and instituting steps in the worker's movement took place in countries where a tradition of struggle against oppressive authority in favor of popular political regimes, or in favor of freedom of thought and inquiry, was part of the historical sediment. Once started in these countries, the movement could and did spread elsewhere—though not, emphatically not, everywhere—with these characteristics, despite "capitalist circumstances."

The worker's movement in the "European" (*lato sensu*) countries created itself; but it was able to do this on the basis of the heritage, the tradition, of the democratic movement it found in the history of these countries, the tradition which was, with reference to the social-historical project of autonomy, born within the "European" world. It is therefore also fully comprehensible that before its bureaucratic degeneracy (whether social-democratic or Bolshevik), the worker's movement created institutions of a deeply democratic character, some of which go beyond the forms of the bourgeois democratic movement and resurrect long-forgotten principles embedded in ancient Greek institutions, such as can be seen in the rotation of people in posts of responsibility within the British trade unions of the first period, the importance of sovereign general assemblies, and the permanent revocability of delegates instaurated by the Paris Commune and revived or rediscovered every time workers formed autonomous organs like Councils (as they did in Hungary in 1956). The radical demands of the worker's movement concerning the ownership of the means of production belong to the same sphere of signification. Democracy entails the equal sharing of power and equal possibilities of participation in the process of political decision making. This is, of course, impossible when individuals, groups, or managerial bureaucracies control centers of economic power, which, especially under modern conditions, immediately translates into political power.

IV

Our heritage, our tradition, includes many contradictory elements. Our history has created democracy—but it is also the only history to have created totalitarianism. The Athenians are accountable both for *Antigone* and for the dreadful massacre of the Melians.

But our tradition has also created another sense of freedom: the possibilities and the responsibility of *choosing*. Choosing is a political act at the basis even of philosophy, properly speaking. To enter philosophical activity one has to choose for thinking and against revelation, for unlimited interrogation and against blind acceptance of what has been inherited.

Our heritage contains antinomic elements. And it contains the possibility of and the responsibility for choice. This entails freedom in a sense much deeper than the "constitutional" one. When reading Thucydides, one never sees the Athenians complaining that their plights are brought by god's wrath; they recognize in them the results of their own decisions and actions. Neither, I hope, would people within today's democratic tradition seek extrasocial causes for their collective predicaments.

In this heritage, we choose the project of individual and collective autonomy for an endless series of reasons, but ultimately because *we will it*, and all that goes with it. "All that goes with it," that is the best in our culture, as we know it.

Will is not "voluntarism." Will is the conscious dimension of what we are as beings defined by radical imagination, that is, defined as potentially creative beings. To will autonomy entails willing some types of institution of society and opposing others. But it entails also willing a type of historical existence, a type of relation to the past and to the future. Both of them, relation to the past and relation to the future, must be progressively recreated.

Today the relation to the past is either through cheap touristic archaeology or by erudition and study of museums of various sorts. We must oppose pseudo-modernity and pseudo-subversion—the *tabula rasa* ideology—as well as eclecticism ("postmodernism") and servile adoration of the past. A new relation to the past means that we revive the past as our own *and* as independent of us; it entails being able to discourse with it as well as to let ourselves be questioned by it. Here again perhaps the relation of fifth-century Athenians to their past offers itself, *not* as a model but as a germ, as an index of actualized possibilities. Tragedy does not "repeat" the myths; it reelaborates and transforms them so that they, originating in a past immemorial, can vest themselves in the language and the forms of the most vivid present, thereby addressing human beings in all possible futures. This uncanny "dialogue" with the past, two one-way runs apparently disjointed and yet actually not so at all, is one of the most precious possibilities our history has created for us. In the same way that we ought to recognize in individuals, in groups, in ethnic or other units their true alterity, and organize our coexistence with them on the basis of this recognition, we must recognize in our own past an inexhaustible source of proximate alterity, a surface of rebound for our endeavors and a line of resistance to our always imminent folly.

And we have to establish a new relation to the future, so that we stop seeing it as an indefinite "progress" giving us ever more of the same, or as the locus of undefined explosions. Neither should we bracket our relation to the future with the disingenuous term *utopia*. Beyond the so-called possibilities of the present, fascination with which can only generate repetition, we must, without abandoning judgment, dare to will a future—not *any* future, not a blueprint, but this ever unforeseeable, ever creative unfolding, in the shaping of which we can participate, working and struggling, for and against.

NOTES

1. See Cornelius Castoriadis, "Institution de la société et religion" (1982), *Domaines de l'homme. Les carrefours du labyrinthe II* (Paris, 1986), pp. 364–84.

2. Jean-Jacques Rousseau, *Du contrat social*, Book 2, ch. 7, in *Oeuvres complètes* (Editions de la Pléiade), vol. 3, p. 381. A similar formulation may be found in the first version of the *Contrat*, Book 2, ch. 2, p. 313.

3. See Montesquieu, *Considérations sur les causes de la grandeur des Romains,* ch. 1.

4. In particular, see Cornelius Castoriadis, *Imaginary Institution of Society*, tr. Kathleen Blamey (Cambridge, Mass., 1987). See also François Furet, *Marx et la Révolution française* (Paris, 1986). A work on Marx's concrete analyses or other historical transitions, in the light of the problematic formulated here, would be very helpful. His ambiguities concerning the French Revolution receive an excellent analysis from Furet.

5. I argued this point at length in "La question de l'histoire du mouvement ouvier," *L'expérience du mouvement ouvrier*, vol. I. (Paris, 1973), pp. 11–120. (A very poor English translation has been published in *Telos*, Nr. 30, Winter 1976–77.) The text is included in my *Social and Political Writings*, University of Minnesota Press (Minneapolis, 1993).

ELEVEN

Jacob Burckhardt and Max Weber: Two Conceptions of the Origin of the Modern World

Wolfgang Hardtwig

I

At the beginning of the revision of traditional German historical studies after World War II, Friedrich Meinecke indicated that Jacbo Burckhardt had illuminated the dark side of history more profoundly than Ranke or any of his contemporaries. Yet today we still know nothing more specific about what this dark side consists of or wherein the potential for rationality—and explanation of such an illumination—might lie. This essay therefore attempts to rethink questions developed in Burckhardt's historical writings that have not been adequately pursued.

Burckhardt, more implicitly than explicitly, develops a new conception of culture that, although influenced by historicism, leaves historicism behind on quite substantial points. My general thesis, provocatively formulated, is that with his conception of culture, Burckhardt turns our understanding of human beings on its head but that he does this differently from Marx. He assumes a motivational structure, an orientation and operation for human action and production, that also differs from the anthropological premises of the German historians Humboldt, Ranke, and Droysen.

The distinguishing characteristics of the structure of modernity as presented by Burckhardt—the depth and differentiation of subjectivity, the trend toward rationalism, the problem of the profaning of life and the cultivation of modern individuality—are reminiscent of Max Weber. Although this perspective appears initially to ignore a number of incompatibilities, in my opinion an extensive agreement between Burckhardt and Weber leads them to take similar approaches to the structural analysis of the modern world. That this similarity has remained largely unnoticed is due in part to differences in choice of subject (for Burckhardt, the Renaissance and the culture of Catholic Italy; for Weber, the Protestant ethic), in part to differences in descriptive style (narrative and depictive for Burckhardt, discursive and analytical for Weber), and in part to their belonging to different disciplines (Burckhardt to history and Weber to national economics and sociology). Their different operational impact, the ways both have been received, and the different expectations tied to their names were also important.

In my reflections I will first take up Burckhardt's *Civilization of the Renaissance in Italy*, elaborating the new ideas that the work brings to the concept of culture. The results of this analysis will be confronted with Weber's theses on the construction and emergence of the modern world. For this latter task I must limit myself to *The Protestant Ethic*, a deficiency that will, however, not prove an obstacle for the question at hand.

II

The topic of *The Civilization of the Renaissance* was considered by its contemporary and later readers to be the development of a new kind of individualism in Italy during the sixteenth century. That Burckhardt should not begin with the depiction of this new character trait but instead with the state—under the noteworthy title "The State as a Work of Art"—deserves special attention.

In the initial part of "The State as a Work of Art" Burckhardt describes the tyranny of small and medium-sized states in the fourteenth and fifteenth centuries. He then pursues in detail the exercise of sovereignty and the fates of such new dynasties as the Visconti, Sforza, Gonzaga, and Este, discussing also the opponents of tyranny, their conspiracies, murderous deeds, and ideological justifications. This is followed by a description of state constitutions, administrative practices, governmental maxims, and the self-perceptions of the republics of Florence and Venice. A chapter follows about foreign politics, that is, the forms of warfare between the Italian states and then, in closing, a chapter about the church-state, which describes the condition of the papacy—its financial affairs, nepotism, buying and selling of offices—and its implication for the dynastic politics of the Italian princes. Burckhardt elaborates on the longevity of these changes, the corollary instability and lack of guarantee for the prevailing status quo. Such illegitimacy, and the uncertainty of the authority stipulated by it, engendered "fear" as a formative and reformative life-governing power. All ways and means of the state came ultimately to serve only one purpose: to secure the person of the ruler. Lawlessness within the state was converted into unhindered eternal power struggles in the form of merciless trade competition between cities; these, however, in no way bestowed more lawfulness or security on their victors. The "evil which was forever troubling the peace of the city was its rule over once-powerful and war-conquered rivals."[1] One cannot overemphasize Burckhardt's depiction of the unlimited lawlessness and instability of these states, their claim to omnipotence, and the rude behavior of their rulers. Burckhardt sets the tone for the entire book in his first chapter when he describes an unhappy existence in which the dark side always stands in the foreground, for what the Italian states accomplished, in his view, was the unleashing of an extraordinary amorality.

Burckhardt's picture of state life is shaped by a predominance of violence and crime, of cruelty and despotism, of lawlessness and instability. As a yardstick of action, only serviceability of authority—and the rational calculation of its appropriation and preservation—held its own, moved only in exceptional cases by such customary norms or motives as awareness of responsibility, need for welfare, or Christian ethics. In terms of the objective work of sovereignty, the state was primarily the victim of exploitation by ruling princes or parties. The dark feature of the epoch gets its sharpest emphasis from this. Burckhardt clearly shows that egocentrism, exorbitance, and moral degeneracy found no limits.

This unrestrained incarnation of evil impulses did not remain confined to the politically powerful. It seized the spirits of educated people, particularly the humanists. Burckhardt describes the new "development of the individual" by means of two attitudes that come into focus in contrast to medieval society: passion for glory and pleasure in derision. His words here are as unequivocal as in his depiction of tyranny: "we see with frightful evidence a boundless ambition and thirst after greatness regardless of all means and consequences."[2] Burckhardt's thinking in terms of "thirst" makes clear what was elementary in the drive; it asserted itself as indifferent to social tolerability, indifferent, as well, to the humane value of sought-for recognition, and morally indifferent with an additional tendency to absolutize itself.

Wit and derision correspond to the passion for glory. They document a highly developed demand for limitation and isolation, the wish to demonstrate personal superiority and to triumph over others. Burckhardt considers their forms of expression to be among the "most brutal and malicious"[3] things that humans can do to one another. Out of a personal passion for glory sprang a "spirit of denial" toward the other. A new inclination to negate values came to prevail. Burckhardt infers that the lifestyle and the work of the humanists also came to be ruled by the aspiration for naked power. The achievements of the poet-philologists, who gave the new individualistic culture its stamp, were the products of the "poisonous blood of impotent wits"[4] who wrote to overcome their infirmities.

The epoch can be summarized as an unleashing of this instinctual triad: the urge to possess, hunger for power, and sensuality—according to Burckhardt, the usual "earthly aims." Ruler, educated class, and, in a sense, "common people" shared this new disposition. Even Burckhardt's final chapter on customs and religion, which describes the forms of piety of these classes that escaped the tight constraints of an antiquated education, concerns itself largely with bad habits and areligiosity, robbery, murder, and vendetta. The priority that Burckhardt awards the thirteenth- to sixteenth-century Italians in the development of European culture is, first of all, the priority of moral depravity: "If therefore egotism, in its wider as well as narrower sense, is the root and fountain of all evil, the more highly developed Italian was for this reason more inclined to wickedness than the member of other nations of that time."[5] Obviously, a strict moral value is always present in Burckhardt's repeated references to evil. One may want to disregard that stance and ask: objectively, what constituted this evil? It sprang from the lack of any restraint and inhibition in living out universal human impulses such as the urge for possession, the urge for power, and sensuality, and it was the elemental weight with which these impulses pressed upon and controlled the lifestyle of an entire society. At the same time these impulses and the power of their appearances were, according to Burckhardt, the basis for all the unusual civilizing achievements with which the modern world began.

Burckhardt does not attribute this new valance of evil moralizingly to single persons, although he in no way eliminates the judgmental category of "blame." On the whole, he represents unfettered individuality and morally questionable instincts as a "world-historical arrangement," which goes beyond the will of the individual, imprinting upon all from the outside the characteristics of their historical fate. This arrangement and its assumptions are, for Burckhardt, historically reconstructible.

Illegitimate sovereignty, and with it the lawlessness and uncertainty of life, were the result of the battle between "Imperium" and "Sacerdotium"—Emperor and Pope—and of the consequent internal decay of both authorities. This battle led to the forfeiture of real power and esteem by the Emperor of Italy. Neither the tyrants nor their subjects, according to Burckhardt, continued to recognize his sovereignty. In this vacuum of authority and legitimacy, access to all posts and positions of power became conceivable for every man.

The singular disintegration of traditional sovereignty from the thirteenth to the sixteenth century created a further condition for the development of the modern individual: the suspension of class restrictions. Under both tyranny and democracy, all are equal. The illegitimate sovereign who acquired his position on the grounds of his personal claim and his capability surrounded himself with *Condottiere*, encoders, officials, writers, and companions who owed him their talent and supported themselves solely on their "inner resources." The frequent change of sovereigns in the tyrannies corresponds to the frequent change of parties in the republics, especially in Florence. Both impelled scholars and office holders to emigrate, but also held out the possibility of returning to their previous positions or to a similar one won within an altered political constellation.

To summarize, the modern individual developed out of a crisis in religious and secular institutions, a crisis driven by a striving for power that so infiltrated the old authorities as to rob them of their traditional socializing power. That this hunger for power could in fact be liberated was the result of an historical constellation in existence at the end of the Middle Ages. The developmental process that it set in motion was, for Burckhardt, irreversible.

III

Tyranny and lawlessness, chaotic norms, the sacrifice of a firm reference to the certainty of other-worldly salvation—all of these resulted in an unfettering of the "evil" in human nature never witnessed before. On this gloomy background, the cultural blossom of the epoch unfolded, exhibiting two distinguishing features: individualization and rationalization.

Burckhardt sees the core of the new individuality, first of all, in a different valuation of emotional life. From this point of view, the source of Renaissance culture lay in a deepening of subjectivity, an increase in the violence and variety of psychic events. The deepening of emotional life, with its heightened claim to individuality, and the rationalization of relations to the world are, for Burckhardt, two sides of one and the same event. Burckhardt described this event comprehensively in the introduction to his chapter "Development of the Individual": "In the Middle Ages both sides of human consciousness—that which was turned within as well as that which was turned without—lay dreaming or half awake beneath a common veil. The veil was woven of faith, illusion, and childish prepossession, through which the world and history were seen clad in strange garb. Man was conscious of himself only as a member of a race, people, party, family, or corporation—that is, he was conscious of himself only through some general category. This veil evaporated into thin air first in Italy; there an objective treatment and consideration of the State and of all things of the world became possible. The subjective side at the same time asserted itself with corresponding emphasis; man became a spiritual individual and recognized himself as such."[6]

The distinguishing features of Renaissance culture are thus the repression of unconscious attitudes and an increase in independent reflection. Everything became the object of a thought which no longer took into consideration tradition, dogma, and the prohibitions of the church and state. The individual acquired the right to personal perception, judgment and comment and subjected himself and his surroundings to the grasp of his reason. He opened himself to an independent and critical approach to what had long been unquestioningly accepted, tabooed, disregarded, or marginalized. The individual accomplished this in regard to the structure of civil authority and the societal distribution of power, in regard to his relation to himself—the exploration of the movements of his soul and his passions—and in regard to his relation to nature and to the culture in which he found himself.

This new power of subjectivity persevered not simply by itself, in thoughtless feeling and living; it also urged its intellectual assimilation. A new balance hung between the deepening and differentiating of feeling and the controlled, conscious attitude founded upon it. The balance of a deepening subjectivity and an increased rationality, together with the disclosure of the causal relations operative in all areas of nature and culture, find Burckhardt's express appreciation throughout. As sarcastically and unequivocally as he branded amorality and the instability of life in the world of the Italian state, he affirms with equal thoroughness the new rational condition of the world as a form of independence from inconceivable powers and as a step toward the possibility of a freer form of life.

IV

To designate the forms of this new, conscious conduct of life Burckhardt selects the concept *work of art*. This innovative turn of phrase points to a rule appropriated by components of the conscious attitude, that is, by rationality. The idea of the state as a work of art is based on an objective analysis of the laws of acquisition and preservation of power; foreign relations and the nature of war are thus seen to be based on "rational treatment." The households of the educated class were constructed "as a conscious product . . . as a work of art."[7] The appearance of the individual as well as the increased sociability of the upper class is conceived of as a free, conscious work of art.

This formation of life founded upon rational knowledge, with its nonallegiance to any sensibly established authority and its self-conscious, objectified access to the world, developed out of motivating forces of action that are anything but rational: the instinctual triad of urge for power, hunger for possession, and sensuality. Tearing open this tension and deriving culture from these forces constitute the uniqueness of Burckhardt's conception.

In neither *The Civilization of the Renaissance* nor the earlier *Constantine* does Burckhardt start, like Humboldt, from "ideas"; nor does he take such a concept further, like Ranke, Droysen, and their students. For Burckhardt it is not the "truly spiritual" that sets historical events and cultural development in motion. Neither is it "freedom" or the demand for its actualization, as Droysen believed; rather, it is a matter of "need" or, more clearly, of "instinct." Burckhardt anchors even education and art this way, writing, for example, of the "need for education" and the "need for representation and education in all subjects." The source of history, its movement and its driving force, is "instinct." It was not only the tyrants' hunger for power and the humanists' passion for valuation that were motivating forces; the church, in its aspiration for "omnipotence," also reserved for itself "all means of power." According to Burckhardt, "actual religiosity" is based on an "inborn instinct," just as achievements in literature and science, sociability and education, painting, sculpture, and architecture originate in a "cultural instinct" and an "artistic instinct."[8]

Now let us turn to the question of the extent to which Burckhardt's concept of the origin of the modern world can be compared to Max Weber's. Burckhardt and Weber consider the Reformation a central event that influenced the position of human beings in all areas: politics, economics, and culture. Both direct attention to one aspect of this transformative process, namely, the "influence of those psychological sanctions which, originating in religious belief and the practice of religion, gave a direction to practical conduct and held the individual to it."[9] Despite different historical perspectives—Burckhardt's the Catholic Middle Ages and the decay of authority of the medieval papacy, Weber's Protestantism and its forms of belief—they proceed from an identical historical assumption: the once-predominant character of the idea of a life to come. Finally, they find the question of free will the Archimedean point at which the specifically modern position of human beings in the world is disclosed. In both their views there is a possibility that the individual freely decides to exist in harmony with God's will, independent of generally valid, religiously sanctioned moral norms; there is also the understanding that such generally established norms either do not exist or cannot command a compelling value from individuals.

The question of free will ultimately unites with the problem of the place of "evil" in the world. Weber expresses this indirectly in a citation from the "Westminster Confession" of 1647: "As for those wicked and ungodly men, whom God as a righteous judge for former sins doth blind and harden, from them He not only withholdeth His grace" but even "exposeth them to such objects as their corruption and makes occasion of sin: and withal, gives them over their own lusts the temptations of the world, and the power of Satan."[10]

The Calvinist doctrine of predestination and the profane doctrines of the Renaissance located the place of evil in the world in different ways. In the former it remained within the dogmatic structure of belief, while in the latter it resulted form the very disintegration of dogma and/or its power of valuation. Strong parallels appear, however, in the definition of *evil,* namely, worldly interest and the removal of inhibitions from instinctual impulses, which for both brought about "satanical" effects.

As the fundamental religio-historical movement in which the spirit of modernity was released, Burckhardt and Weber point—for their divergent spheres of secularized Catholicism and Calvinist Protestantism—to the rationalization of the human relation to the world. The great religio-historical change produced by the Renaissance was the overcoming of magical forms of belief. In fact, it succeeded only in the educated class, and even there not fully. It heralded a new understanding of man's place in the world, overcoming dependency on the church—with its right to decide right and wrong, good and bad—as the means to grace and leading to an independence from the effects of blind external pressures. In Burckhardt's interpretation, the Renaissance takes the path to the "elimination of magic from the world which . . . had repudiated all magical means to salvation or superstition and sin";[11] this is the path that Weber sees concluded with Puritanism.

For both Burckhardt and Weber, overcoming the authority of superstition is stipulated in the development of a new type of "individualism." Among puritanical people, according to Weber, this overcoming "forms one of the roots of that disillusioned and pessimistically inclined individualism,"[12] while for Burckhardt's Italian Catholics it had an optimistic feature. In both cases, however, it constituted the modern world. Burckhardt determines that the Renaissance man owed everything to his own will, his energy and his achievement, and not to any powers outside of himself. It was this same absolutizing of the individual that arose as an unintended consequence of the doctrine of predestination in the puritanical search for salvation. The "phenomenon of the religious sense of grace,"[13] in both cases, was misplaced. The individual found the yardstick of his action exclusively within himself, and this led to efforts to discipline his affective desires in new ways and to sublimate them in extraordinary cultural achievements—here in the sphere of economic production, there in the realms of knowledge, philosophy, art, and refined forms of sociability. Both cultural spheres, here world-enjoying subjectivity, there ascetic Protestantism, exacerbated the same physical consequences of individualism, the "extraordinary loneliness of the single individual." The individual is "forced to follow his path alone to meet a destiny which had been decreed for him from eternity"[14] and, in the Renaissance, by the choice of fortune. That the sacraments ceased to be recognized as the means for obtaining God's grace yielded religious abandonment in both cases.

During the Renaissance the decay of authority of the institution of the church made possible an influx of ancient philosophies that finally attacked even the church itself. None of these philosophies was strong enough to earn general esteem and compel allegiance; rather, a variety of doctrines stood side by side, some mixing with Catholic dogma, others becoming synchronistically amalgamated. The individual could choose freely between traditional doctrines and their modern adaptations. No one had the authority to establish as generally binding either the truth of Christian belief or the veracity of ancient doctrine and to alleviate thereby the solitude within the commonality of conviction.

In both cases, the consequence of a new type of personal claim to greatness followed from increased individualism. The wish for public recognition, the wish to be seen as special, was characteristic of the new significance of the individual and of the claims connected with it. Although Weber does not explicate this aspect as clearly as Burckhardt, it is nevertheless important for his interpretation of the process of individualization. He describes the origin of a "spiritual aristocracy," "saints in the world predestined from eternity through God." While Calvinists originally derived their selectedness and sanctity from foreordination "out of eternity," in the course of its development Calvinism added something positive to this, "the idea of the necessity of proving one's faith in worldly activity."[15] Its legitimation and the claim to uniqueness thus shifted in their grounding from providence to worldly capability, with the result that the latter had to be visible to the world.

For Burckhardt the claim to uniqueness also has its roots in spiritual concerns. He states empathetically that the profane ideal of historical greatness took the place of "holiness" as a guiding image. Burckhardt explicates the manner in which an intellectual, no longer religious "aristocracy" shook off consciousness of acting in the name of an otherworldly power. This aristocracy gave up its ethical bond to otherworldly guidance more swiftly and visibly than did the "spiritual aristocracy" of the predestined ascetics, establishing itself and its claim as openly absolute.

In its effect, the spiritual, inner-worldly destiny of the Calvinists is hardly distinguishable from the earthly intellectuality of Renaissance men. Both established their position in the world upon proven truth; both increasingly isolated themselves within society and constructed new limits in relation to their fellows. The "sympathetic understanding based on consciousness of one's own weakness," a deeply spiritual motive, receded. The Calvinist developed an attitude of "hatred and contempt" toward his fellow man as to an "enemy of God."[16] The Renaissance man sought to annihilate his fellow man with derision and scorn for the benefit of his own glory. In both cases the individual in society stood out in contrast to the other and claimed a unique status.

That Burckhardt and Weber respectively speak of the educated class and the spiritual aristocracy as the bearers of religious cultural development requires an explanation. Both diagnose the freeing of inner-worldly claims to greatness as a mass phenomenon, although the reasons for this are not readily apparent. Within Calvinism, being chosen was possible in principle for everyone; therefore everyone was to "attain self-confidence" by "intense worldly activity" because "it and it alone disperses religious doubts and gives a certainty of grace."[17] The motivating hope of being called in a particular way and of demonstrating this calling by achievement therefore expressly encompasses broader social groups. Likewise, the entire educated class of the Renaissance was seized by a mentality centered on the new concept of honor and its demands. The democratic and massive quality of the novel claim to uniqueness appears thus as a structural feature of the modern world.

For modern societies it was important above all that the claim to destiny relate to the need to exercise power. Burckhardt indicates this explicitly. This aspect is also present in Weber, although it remains concealed. When Weber speaks of the "consciousness of divine grace of the elect and holy (Gottesgnadentum der Erwahlten und deshalb Heiligen),"[18] he brings a concept into play that is—in the historical thought of the nineteenth century—tied to the singular right to exercise sovereignty. That concept cannot be separated from *Gottesgnadentum*, or royal authority legitimized by God. The democratization of the spiritual grace of God—in terms of the massively effective religious doctrine of destiny—included the democratization of a political claim to sovereignty that was originally limited to one person: the prince. A right that in premodern societies came to one on the basis of traditional legitimacy and authority and always included an abundance of power became in principle accessible to everyone in modern society. Sociopolitical life in the modern world thereby gained a wholly new dynamic; Burckhardt expressly voices this point of view in his chapters on the state and tyranny and in those about the individual. Weber applies this view but does not explain it.

Reference should be made to a substantial commonality in Burckhardt and Weber regarding the understanding of culture, particularly modern European culture. Like Burckhardt, Weber proceeds anthropologically from an understanding of the instinctual nature of man without developing his fundamental premise: such things as the effective mechanisms of elementary needs and psychic processes are identified but not described in detail. Burckhardt places the scope of action obtaining for these instincts under the structural stipulations of the Renaissance—society and authority—prominently in the foreground, but pursues instead the results of their assimilation of rational attitudes. Likewise, for Weber the roots of rational access to the world lie in the sphere of the preconscious, the feelings. The human being "had developed a systematic method of rational conduct with the purpose of overcoming the *status naturae* to free man from the power of irrational instincts . . . to subject man to the supremacy of a purposeful will" and to "bring his actions under constant control with a careful consideration of their ethical consequences."[19] Unlike Burckhardt, Weber places the source of this specifically modern motivation by affectivity, with its act-steered reason, in occidental monasticism; this, however, does not change the fact that both Burckhardt and Weber comprehend modern culture as a singular form of the sublimation of powerful instincts.

Burckhardt and Weber—and this, too, should not be overlooked—are in accord regarding the valuation of the process of civilization. After their attention to the psychical toll exacted from the isolated modern individual who stands only on his achievements, their concern is finally with the advance by which man comes always closer to realizing fully his possibilities. Indeed, this celebration of progress—even for the seemingly backward-glancing Burckhardt—has the character of an achievement and a conscious decision. It is wrested out of mourning over the loss of universal certainty of meaning, out of suffering the consequences of rationalism, and, for Burckhardt, out of fear for the sociopolitical consequences, or the unchaining and democratizing claims to greatness. Mourning, suffering, and fear form a dark foil to the joy, discovered by both Burckhardt and Weber, "to be able to lead an alert, intelligent life."[20]

V

In summary, understanding that Burckhardt derives power from the instinctual nature of human beings makes clear why his allusion to the conscious formation of life holds such a worthy place. This is because conscious action and production no longer appear as the obvious and the initial, rather as something later and derivative, a peculiarity and an achievement.

The unshackling of instinctual desires creates precisely the conditions for increased cultural achievement. The extent and the intensity of creative fantasy are dependent upon the energy of the original instinct. If one pursues this line of thought, not fully formulated by Burckhardt but nonetheless the basis of his developmental model of the Middle Ages and Renaissance, one sees that the volume of instinctual energy should be the same for every period. But through the decline of norms and authority in the late Middle Ages, the urge for power, instinct for valuation, and sensuality received a previously unknown breadth in the psychomoral makeup of human beings. The limits set by authority and moral discipline fell away because religious and civil regulations forfeited their powers of persuasion and thereby of accomplishment. The loss of a conscious awareness of sin and repentance, and of an otherworldly orientation in general, engendered opportunities for admitting and living out instinctual desires which had previously been kept within narrow boundaries through teaching, custom, and the threat of punishments, such as the loss of grace. In his moral view, Burckhardt characterizes the unleashing and freeing of these instincts as unmistakable and literally "evil." Yet simultaneously this unfettering of instincts created the decisive conditions for a historically incomparable increase of being in the world within a highly differentiated and fully formed culture that opened wholly new possibilities for human beings.

Weber goes less far in uncovering the instinctual impulses beneath observed changes in attitudes. But, like Burckhardt, he was convinced that in human affairs reason plays a comparatively small part, while man's struggle for power greatly affects the course of events. In *The Protestant Ethic* Weber describes a decisive step in the history of this struggle for power. He says that the new conduct of life was a response to religious anxiety induced by the doctrine of predestination. He shows that the belief in divine selection that thereby developed may have tended to express itself as a belief that individuals were also chosen for the execution of political power.

Both Burckhardt and Weber indicate that declines in traditional authority and legitimacy were the basis of modern religious and political life. Both show that the disintegration of traditional legitimacy released the possibilities for an individually determined conduct of life. Authority was transferred from the institutions "state" and "church" to the single individual, and church and state had to adapt themselves to its new claim. This was possible only by rationalizing both the determining values of life and the personal justification of individuals. As a consequence, state and church had to develop rational ways to justify their authority.

Both Burckhardt and Weber make clear that this process, whether initiated by the transformation of authority in the Italian Renaissance or in puritanical England, has not yet come to an end. With the decline of traditional authority and the process of secularization, the elementary individual claim for power has been released. It enters—more or less delayed and hesitant, but successfully—the field of politics and finds new patterns of justification. Eventually state constitutions must accept this claim for power from the community of single, self-confident individuals and legitimize the demands for authority that are based upon it.

NOTES

1. Jacob Burckhardt, *The Civilization of the Renaissance in Italy*, tr. S. G. C. Middlemore (New York, 1954), p. 67.
2. Ibid., p. 114.
3. Ibid., p. 117.
4. Ibid., p. 121.
5. Ibid., p. 340.
6. Ibid., p. 100.
7. Ibid., p. 278.
8. Ibid., p. 411.
9. Max Weber, *The Protestant Ethic and the Spirit of Capitalism*, tr. Talcott Parsons (New York, 1958), p. 97.
10. Ibid., p. 101.
11. Ibid., p. 105.
12. Ibid., p. 105.
13. Ibid., p. 101.
14. Ibid., p. 104.
15. Ibid., p. 121.
16. Ibid., p. 122.
17. Ibid., p. 112.
18. Ibid., p. 122.
19. Ibid., pp. 118–19.
20. Ibid., p. 119.

PART II.

Contemporary Τόποι: *Nihilism and Subjectivity*

TWELVE

Nothing and Nothing Else

Jean-Luc Marion

N'est-ce rien que ce rien qui vous délivre
de tout?
—Paul Claudel, *Soulier de Satin*, 1, 3

I

How could it be possible to utter anything about nothingness? Nothingness is something—the only thing—we have nothing to add to. It seems trifling to discuss such a trivial issue. Therefore all the positive sciences rest upon a basic statement: they all plainly acknowledge that they have nothing to say concerning nothingness; far from being a shortcoming, this declaration is supposed to liberate the sciences from nothingness and open them to positive facts. Science appears where and only where nothingness disappears.

However, as soon as we test it, this obvious conclusion proves self-defeating. Heidegger emphasized this with extreme acuteness: the very statement which denies nothingness compels one to admit nothingness as a given and stubborn fact; for when any positive science claims to know nothing but facts and know nothing about nothingness—in a word, when it claims to deal with facts and nothing else (*und sonst nichts*)—it focuses our attention directly on this "nothing else."[1] If the alleged obviousness of mere facts still appeals to the argument of "nothing else" to resist the alleged obscurity of nothingness, then the more positive science denies nothingness, the more stress it lays on it.

Is such a paradox mere sophistry, introducing the appearance of something where there is absolutely nothing? But again, if there is nothing here, we are compelled to acknowledge that there is nothing, that is, nothingness. This paradox—to deny nothingness means to recognize nothingness—ought not to be dismissed. We ought to face it. Here is the point; nothingness is nothing and at the same time something, that is to say, nothingness itself. This essential ambiguity is termed by Heidegger its *zwiespaltiges Wesen.*[2]

To be fair, let us dwell on this paradox for a while. Nothingness looks like a strange counterpart of God: both take advantage of an ontological argument. God is supposed to exist merely in consequence of the perfection of his essence, and nothingness claims to be thanks to the absolute imperfection of its essence.

In both cases we are compelled to admit an item as given simply because we think of it. Let us repeat one more time the non-ontological argument which introduces nothingness into thought. Either nothingness is not, then it is nothing; according to the principle of identity, A = A, nothingness is equal to itself, therefore it is itself—in short, it is. Or, if we try to avoid this trap, we shall say that nothingness is not even nothing, is less than nothing—as we say in French, *moins que rien, rien de rien*; but the phrase "less than nothing" reinforces the paradox: it makes it clear that a *nihil negativum* is now behind the *nihil privativum.*[3] Exactly as God, to achieve existence, only needs to be possible, nothingness only needs to be impossible (as it is) to claim a quasi-existence. Two unconditional facts thus stand at the two extremes of the field of metaphysical being. May we admit both as unquestionable phenomena? In particular, may we concede to nothingness the dignity of a full-fledged phenomenon? And if we refuse to, how shall we justify our denial of an obvious fact? We have to bear in mind that, when Bergson and Carnap made every endeavor to ride out nothingness, they only managed to emphasize the irreducible fact of negation without being able either to dismiss it or to explain its "so-called power."[4] Therefore, if we cannot deny nothingness, we must face it.

II

To face nothingness means to admit its paradox as a genuine philosophical issue. This issue could be characterized as follows: is the logical inconsistency of any definition of nothingness a sufficient ground to deny its possibility of being given as a phenomenon? This question proves twofold. First, is negation the origin of nothingness, or is nothingness the ground on which every negation rests? Heidegger made a choice, without explaining it at the time: "Wir behaupten: das Nichts ist ursprünglicher als das Nicht und die Verneinung."[5] This statement is founded on the possibility that nothingness could appear and be given as a phenomenon. Hence the second point: will this appearance ever come about? According to Husserl's "principle of all principles," this means that nothingness has to be given to and by some intuition, whatever it may be. And Heidegger fully agrees with that principle: "Wenn das Nichts, wie immer, befragt werden soll—es selbst—, dann muß es zuvor gegeben sein. Wir müssen ihm begegnen können (As always, if nothingness itself is to be interrogated, then it must first be given. We must be able to encounter it)."[6] This is the challenge: to encounter nothingness as such in an original intuitive givenness.

In the field of classical phenomenology, no phenomenon can ever appear except within a horizon. But as Heidegger denies that either negation or logic can provide us with the horizon within which nothingness could appear, his charge is to open another horizon. And in fact he does so, but without any straight and direct statement, as if he were hesitant; nevertheless, some texts indirectly point out this horizon, first as beings (*Seiende*)—"Das Nichts ist die vollständige Verneinung der Allheit des Seienden (Nothingness is the complete negation of the allness of beings),"[7] then as being itself: "Im Sein des Seienden geschieht das Nichten des Nichts (The nihilation of nothingness occurs in the being of beings)."[8] Those two denominations of the horizon do not contradict each other insofar as the entity in question remains directly connected with being, solely within which it unfolds itself: ". . . zur Wahrheit des Seins gehört, daß das Sein nie west ohne das Seiende, daß niemals ein Seiendes ist ohne das Sein (. . . it belongs to the truth of being that being never comes to be without beings, that a being never is without being)."[9] This connection would soon be celebrated as the ontological difference. The ontological difference sketches being as the unique horizon for nothingness, beings, and other related phenomena.

Let us now consider this result. If nothingness appears as a phenomenon within the horizon of being, are we not compelled to admit that nothingness is . . . ? No matter what it is, provided it just has to *be* . . . : in this case, Heidegger seems to be caught in the snare which we have already met—to speak of nothingness as if it could be something else than nothing? But, far from being ridiculous (as Carnap thought), Heidegger's tautology that "das Nichts selbst nichtet"[10] forms the first statement concerning nothingness which does not contradict itself. However, Heidegger seems unfair when he puts aside this empty but correct analytical tautology for the sake of a synthetical but arbitrary statement: "Das Sein nichtet—als das Sein (Being nihilates—as being)." In the same page of the *Brief über den Humanismus*, nothingness seems reduced by force to being: "das Nichten west im Sein."[11] The greatest difficulty lies less in discovering nothingness as such, as Carnap and Bergson believed, than in interpreting it as something other than nothing itself. Heidegger himself was tempted to turn away from nothingness as soon as possible, as if he had been afraid of facing it too long. However, if we proceed here according to phenomenology, that is, according to the "principle of all principles," we must take things as they appear. The question must be asked: does nothingness appear—if it appears at all—within the horizon of being, that is, as something other than nothing?

III

Before answering this question, we shall try to understand how, according to Heidegger, nothingness becomes a genuine phenomenon, that is, how we can experience it really as a given fact.

The main features of the famous analysis are well known. Let us only emphasize one point. Dasein is anxious, and, in conformity with anxiety, it deals with beings, but in a very paradoxical way: Dasein has no fear of any of them; its anxiety lies precisely in the absence of any actual threat from any being whatsoever. Beings arouse anxiety because none of them clearly threaten Dasein. All around Dasein, there is no specific being to be afraid of, and therefore its anxiety arises only because of this lack. In anxiety, everything seems to shrink away from Dasein; and it is this disappearance of beings which makes Dasein anxious. Anxiety arises from nothingness. More exactly, nothingness introduces itself into Dasein by way of anxiety. Heidegger sums up this situation as "*abweisend Verweisung*," a reference (to nothingness) by expelling (beings as a whole).[12] We can immediately notice two questionable points. First, if nothingness appears only in the way anxiety expels beings and thereby remains bound to the horizon of being, does nothingness appear as such, or only as a mere absence—an empty box—of beings? Second, the concept of reference (*Verweisung*) that leads to nothingness was previously defined by Heidegger. In *Sein und Zeit*, §7, *Verweisung* does not pertain to the genuine and complete phenomenon (named *Phänomen)*, but to mere appearance, *Erscheinung*, " . . . meint einen seienden Verweisungsbezug im Seienden selbst, so zwar, daß das Verweisende (Meldende) seiner möglichen Funktion nur genügen kann, wenn es sich an ihm selbst zeigt, 'Phänomen' ist" which "means a reference-relation which *is* in beings themselves such that what refers (or announces) can fulfill its possible function only if it shows itself in itself and is thus a 'phenomenon')."[13] In fact, appearance does not appear directly as such, but only by referring to another full-fledged phenomenon; this reference (*Verweisung*), not unlike the *Anzeige* of Husserl's opening pages of *The Logical Investigations*, does not show what it means: reference contradicts phenomenality. Therefore, if nothingness appears only as and through the reference performed by anxiety, it does not appear at all. At least Heidegger was bound to concede such an indirect and second-order phenomenon still had to be interpreted from the point of view of another direct and full-fledged phenomenon.

There is no doubt that Heidegger implicitly admitted this, for he made many attempts, in different works and at different points in time, to reduce the alleged phenomenon of nothingness to another, more obvious one. Let me give a few examples. In *Sein und Zeit*, nothingness refers to *in-der-Welt-sein:* "Wenn sich demnach als das Wovor der Angst das Nichts, das heißt die Welt as solche herausstellt, dann besagt das: *wovor die Angst sich ängstet, ist das In-der-Welt-sein* (So if nothingness, which means the world as such, exhibits itself as that before which one is anxious, this means that *being-in-the-world itself is that in the face of which anxiety is anxious*)."[14] How can we explain that two years later the same analysis of the same anxiety reaches another phenomenon: nothingness as such? In fact, even *Was ist Metaphysik?* seems at odds with the identity of nothingness and being. Only two sentences mark it, and neither does so convincingly. The first says, "Im Sein des Seienden geschieht das Nichten des Nichts (The nihilation of nothingness occurs in the being of beings),"[15] however, this is not a demonstration but a mere assertion; and far from asserting the identity of anxiety, nothingness, and being, it only states one more time that being opens the horizon for nothingness. The second passage—"Sein und Nichts gehören zusammen (Being and nothingness belong together)"[16]—sounds like a mere repetition of the Hegelian motto, although (or because) it denies it; in any case, no phenomenological description backs it up. One must wait until 1943 to read in the *Nachwort* added to *Was ist Metaphysik?* the definitive identification of nothingness to being: "Dies schlechthin Andere zu allem Seienden ist das Nicht-Seinde. Aber dieses Nichts west als das Sein (That which is simply other than all beings is the null-being)." But to justify this "*west als* (comes to be)," Heidegger puts in play a new phenomenological issue, the "voice of being," which "den Menschen in seinem Wesen in den Anspruch nimmt, damit er das Sein im Nichts erfahren lerne (lays claim to man in his essence such that he could learn to experience being in nothingness)."[17] Do these different attempts demonstrate the reference of nothingness to being and the relevance of being as the ultimate horizon of nothingness? We can doubt it, for at least three reasons. First, as anxiety and nothing are linked with many different phenomena, we can suppose that Heidegger himself hesitated to decide which was the right one. Second, the last identification of nothingness—to being—depends on a new mediation, that of the call of being. But why did Heidegger need it if there was no difficulty at all to identify nothingness and being? Third, are we definitely committed to applying the structure of reference (*Verweisung*) to nothingness? Why should we deny it the dignity of a full-fledged, sufficient, and self-referential phenomenon?

IV

Far from paying attention to those questions, Heidegger, when he commented in 1949 on his essay of 1929, endeavored at all cost to fill the gap to which his own phenomenological analysis led. Thus to explain the key definition of anxiety and nothingness as *abweisende Verweisung*, expelling reference, he did not hesitate, twenty years later, to insist as follows: "ab-weisen: das Seiende fur sich; ver-weisen: in das Sein des Seienden (ex-pelling: beings as such; re-ferring: to the being of beings)."[18] Moreover, on the same page, the essence of nothingness, which in 1929 had made possible the openness of beings in general ("Ermöglichung der Offenbarkeit von Seiendem überhaupt"), that is, which did *not* reach being, came, by the violent interpretation of 1949, to place beings "eigens vor Sein des Seienden, vor den Unterschied (before the being of beings, before the difference)." On the following page, the original phrase "in das Nichts hineinhalten (to extend into nothingness)" is misunderstood by the addition of "d.h. Nichts und Sein das Selbe (that is, nothingness and being the same)."[19] But the issue is precisely that they do *not* appear as the same and that Heidegger has not at all demonstrated but only asserted their alleged identity.

Of course, Heidegger was aware of this difficulty. To deal with it, he alluded to a new item—the call of being, whose voice calls man (or Dasein) to being itself through the silence of nothingness. The texts, quoted from the *Nachwort* added in 1949, are well known: ". . . den Anspruch, damit er [der Mensch] das Sein im Nichts erfahren lerne (the claim by virtue of which man could learn to experience being in nothingness)"; "Dieses Denken antwortet dem Anspruch des Seins (such a thinking answers the call of being)"; "Das Opfer ist heimisch im Wesen des Ereignisses, als welches das Sein den Menschen für die Wahrheit des Seins in den Anspruch nimmt (The offering is at home in the essence of the event in which being lays claim to man for the truth of being)."[20] We may sum up Heidegger's last argument in these few words: nothingness does not, as such, reveal being because it reveals nothing other than nothingness itself; but in the silent desert the call of being, which claims man for itself, can be heard.

Let us cross-examine this claim to a claim of being by asking two questions: can such a claim, if any, be heard? If heard, could it be answered? First, Heidegger himself admits that the call of being remains soundless, *lautlose;*[21] it may seem a bit difficult to hear a soundless call; nevertheless, we have all had the experience of such a silent call, for instance in a close relationship, private language, or deep emotional intercourse; silence does stimulate our attention, captures our will, and, to this extent, calls us, but we are not involved in such rich emotional contexts here because we are supposed to stand in the desert of nothingness; here there is no soul nor thing at all which could mean some call by its silent presence or by a visible glance. But let us not forget this: be it granted that in the desert of nothingness we are capable of hearing some call, how could we know that it definitely comes from being? How could we recognize it as being? The difficulty of identifying nothingness and being remains as insoluble with the hypothesis of a claim or a call as without it. And second, even if such a call can be heard as the call of being, can it be answered? Of course we could, but we *may not.* For Heidegger himself alluded to the possibility that man would not answer the call claiming him (*Anspruch*): *Was ist Metaphysik?* said in 1929 that within anxiety, everything and we too fall into an indifference ("Alle Dinge und wir selbst versinken in eine Gleichgültigkeit"); this indifference, added a footnote of 1949, makes us become indifferent to every being, for beings literally say nothing to us: "das Seiende spricht nicht mehr an (beings no longer make a claim)."[22] Indifference means that as soon as anxiety rules us, beings sink into indetermination, so that we too become indifferent to beings, to their being and their nonbeing. But if nothingness means absolute indifference, even to the being of beings, why could it not bring about indifference to being itself? Heidegger reinforced this hypothesis when, just before his discussion of anxiety, he described another *Stimmung*, called *tiefe Langweile*, "deep boredom."[23] If beings may also make us feel bored, why should being be unable to do the same? At least it seems possible to admit that we could resist, through boredom and indifference, the claim raised by the call of being. In this hypothesis, the silence of man would answer the silence of nothingness without any hint to being.

Nothingness, we said, says nothing other than nothing. Nothingness does not mean anything; nor does it refer to anything, nor show anything—and being less than anything else. Nothingness opens no way to being, but proves a dead end or—which amounts to the same thing—refers to itself only.

V

So nothingness says nothing but itself. Its nature is neither a first name nor a prolegomenon to being. "Est enim nihil nihil aliud quam nihil," Nicholas of Cusa said.[24] But to acknowledge this rule is not enough to fulfill it. The mere equivalence, nothingness = nothingness, falls short of an object upon which to think. To reach such an object, we must find a concept of nothingness that is without any reference—even negative—to beings and being, but still intelligible.

Is this possible? Not at all, as long as we follow the metaphysical track to nothingness, which only leads to the lack of beings. Nevertheless, the history of philosophy (and of theology) bears witness to a completely different concept of nothingness, which appears no longer within, but beyond, beings and being. Following the daring sentences of Plato, that the Good stands "beyond the essence (ἐπέκοινα τῆς οὐσίας)" and of Plotinus, that the One stands "beyond being (ἐπέκεινα ὄντος)," and Proclus, that it stands "beyond all the beings (ἐπέκεινα τῶν ὄντων),"[25] the so-called Pseudo-Dionysius did not hesitate to suggest an illuminating paradox: "As the cause required by all for their being, [God] himself [is] nothingness, standing beyond any essence αἴτιον μὲν τοῦ εἶναι πᾶσιν, αὐτὸ δὲ μὴ ὄν, ὡς πάσης οὐσίας ἐπε κεινα"[26] According to authorized commentators, there remains no doubt concerning the interpretation of this sentence. John of Scythopolis emphasized it: "το οὐδὲν εἶναι τον φεὸν οὕτω νοητέον, ὡς τῶν ὄντων μηδὲν ὄντα ὀπὲρ γὰρ τὰ ὄντα ὀ αἴτιος των ὄντων (The non-being of God is to be understood as follows: He is not one of the beings; for the cause of beings [is] beyond beings)."[27] In his commentary on Dionysius's work, Thomas Aquinas, though he tried elsewhere to establish the *esse* as the first name of God, nevertheless recognized that God remains far beyond the being of beings: ". . . Deus, cum sit 'omnius existentium causa,' ipse 'nihil' est existentium, non quasi deficians ab assendo, sed supereminenter 'separatus ab omnibus' (God, as the 'cause of all existences,' is Himself 'nothing,' not because He would lack being, but because He is 'separated from everything' by overeminence)."[28] Far from indicating a deficiency, as if the most perfect thing could be the only one lacking being, this "nothing" marks the bare result of the exceptional situation of God toward beings, existence, and being. He does not belong to them because He causes them all. By the way, "nothing" pertains to God not as one result of the fact that every name may be applied to Him, but as what is most proper to His original and overwhelming goodness: "καὶ δία τοῦτο, τὸ μὴ εἶναι μαλλον, δία τὸ ὑπερεϊναι ὡς οἰκειότερον ἐπ' αὑτου λεγόμενον προσιέμενος (It is rather the 'not being' that fits Him, for the sake of the 'beyond being')," says Maximus. Scotus Erigena confirmed this approach: "Dum ergo incomprehensibilis intelligitur, per excellentiam nihilum non immerito vocitatur (Because he is thought of as incomprehensible, we may justly call Him 'nothing' by excellence)." Nicholas of Cusa repeated the paradox: "Et propterea magnus Dionysius dicit intellectum Dei magis accedere ad nihil quam ad aliquid (Therefore, the great Dionysius says that understanding God means coming to nothing rather than anything whatsoever)."[29] This is a fact which we have to cope with: several traditional (and orthodox) theologians gave up the common characterization of God by beings and being, which runs from Aristotle to Heidegger, and understood God as far beyond Being and beings—as nothing.

From this fact, two consequences follow, one positive, one puzzling. The positive consequence is obvious: if God claims nothing as His most fitting name, nothing could mean no more than the mere lack of being, that is, the relative nothing reached in the absence of entity, as Heidegger admitted in the first step of his analysis: "die vollständige Verneinung der Allheit des Seienden (the complete negation of the allness of beings)."[30] What we face with *this* particular nothing can be reduced neither to the lack of beings (because it means the overwhelming excess of beings) nor to being itself (because even Heidegger did not succeed, as we have demonstrated, in referring nothingness to the phenomenon of being). An objection can of course be raised against such a non-ontological, that is, theological, nothingness: we cannot understand it. But this objection seems quite irrelevant for two reasons. First, philosophical nothingness, as equivalent to being, remains unintelligible too, because, according to Heidegger, being itself escapes the grasp of concepts and because, notwithstanding Heidegger, nothingness cannot be reduced by phenomenology to being. Second, the impossibility of understanding a nothingness appropriated to God does not contradict but plainly confirms its relevance, because God, if there is any, remains unintelligible—more, cannot be understood; to understand God means to understand why and how much we cannot understand Him. So the unintelligibility of nothingness proves to be an objection against its ontological interpretation (that is, against Heidegger's), and a confirmation of its theological interpretation.

The second consequence seems more puzzling. If we agree with the non-ontological reference of nothingness to God, we seem to be compelled to reduce its significance to the extreme, and to give up the possibility of defining it. What is even more puzzling is that the theological interpretation leads us to contradict the epigram of our lecture: now, nothingness does not amount to nothing and nothing else, but means something else—God himself. How can we face this contradiction?

VI

The self-contradiction in our interpretation of nothingness lies in the single fact that it reduces too quickly the non-ontological feature of nothingness to God; but the possibility still remains that God may appear only as the first item of such a non-ontological nothingness, and not as the only one. To interpret nothingness without referring it to being might not mean to refer it directly to God. Our challenge, in this case, can be summed up in a few words: is it possible to apply nothingness to other items than God in a non-ontological horizon?

Let us go back to our starting point: Dionysius. When he defines God as "beyond beings" and as "nothing," he also calls Him Goodness; and he insists on the fact that the transcendence of Goodness toward being and beings allows even things which are not to desire it and, in the process, to pray to it as the absolute cause: "ἧ ἵνα συλλαβῶν εἴπω, πάντα τὰ ὄντα ἐκ τοῦ καλοῦ καὶ ἀγαθοῦ καὶ πάντα τὰ οὐκ ὄντα ὑπερουσίως ἐν τῷ καλῷ καὶ ἀγαθῷ. (To sum it up, all beings [come] from the Beauty and the Good; but all the nonbeings [the nothings] remain too, in a way far beyond essence, in the beauty and the Good)." More precisely: "ἡ τἀγαθοῦ θεωνυμία (. . .) καὶ εἰς τὰ ὄντα, καὶ εἰς τὰ οὐκ ὄντα ἐκτεῖναι (the divine name of Goodness . . . reaches out to beings which are, but also to that which is not)."[31] Therefore, nothingness here pertains both to God and to the extreme opposite of God—up to things which are not. What does that paradox reveal? That the propriety of God—to remain quite indifferent to the difference between being and nonbeing, because, as nothingness, He remains far beyond being and beings—reaches other things; things which are not and remain far behind the poorest being receive, despite their lack of being, the influence of Beauty and Goodness, which they, being not, can nevertheless celebrate as theirs. So things which are not seem as indifferent as God to the difference between being and nonbeing, that is to say, indifferent to the ontological difference between beings and being. To be or not to be—that is no longer the question for things that are not, as well as for God.

Nothingness in this non-ontological interpretation does not deal only with God but also with every thing (even things which are not), provided that it remains in a very particular relation to God. Nothingness reveals the ontological indifference as a non-ontological horizon. However, one could object: how could finite things, which *are* (just as common, standard beings are), appear within such a non-ontological horizon? In their case, could we speak of a non-ontological horizon? To outline an answer, let us point out three features of such a non-ontological nothingness.

In this essay I have used the word *nothingness.* But this plain word may give us an indication, provided we notice that *nothingness* does not refer to "beings" (as the French *neant* does), but to "thing," (not unlike the French *rien* from the Latin *res*); it means the absence or negation of anything, of every thing; the German word *Nichts* too comes from an old negation of *etwas.*[32] This simple fact leads to a meaningful consequence: nothingness can be explained according to "thing" and nothing else. However, "thing" differs from "beings" in at least one respect: when dealing with things, we are not supposed to know with certainty what, or even if, they are. In colloquial language, we use "things" when we don't exactly know what or if some event happened; we often say "thing," rather than more precise words, to mean dangerous, ominous, threatening, disgusting, irrational, mysterious issues; in horror movies, is not the invisible and unknown agent of the growing terror invading the house often called the thing? The opposite of a being, a thing can deeply affect us, although we don't know if it is or is not; therefore, a thing can play its part in complete indifference to the ontological difference; as for nothing, for a thing in this proper sense, it means nothing to be or not to be.

Hence the second feature. When, in daily language, we use the word *nothing,* it mainly occurs in a very simple context: we have supposed that "something is just happening," no matter what or whether this "thing" is; but after a while, the expected event did not take place at all or proved meaningless; then we conclude, "it was nothing." But, of course, it *was* something: the content was real, the plot was actually performed, and, at the very moment when we made our statement, the characters and things involved in the expected event were still real. What does it mean to say that nothing happened? Obviously "nothing" here does not refer to nonexistent beings—therefore they actually *are*—but to the fact that our expectation of a particular and significant event was unfulfilled; "nothing" does not mean beings which are not, but beings which are different from what we expected, that is, beings toward which we remain indifferent. The sentence "It is nothing," does not describe the actual absence of some things, but our indifference to the difference between their being and their not being. Nothingness, in this non-ontological interpretation, does not deny, destroy, or eliminate any being; it makes beings indifferent—either to their own being or to us. In *this* nothingness, everything remains in its own place, without any change or disappearance, but everything is as if it was not: the cloud of ontological indifference uncovers the gap between being and not being; to be or not to be—that means "nothing," that is, makes no difference at all.

The third feature has been alluded to before; it is the fact that non-ontological nothingness implies a certain relation—according to Dionysius, a relation to God. In fact, the relation itself is more important here than the identity of its pole. For neither could an entity which actually is appear *as* nothing, nor could a nonbeing appear as something, if they were not both viewed from an absolute, transcendent pole of reference from which the difference between beings and nonbeings may appear empty according to another deeper difference. This situation is expressed by a widespread formula: "Todas las cosas de la tierra y del cielo, comparandas con dios, nada son" (or "Omnia Deo comparata nihil sunt, et tamen simpliciter non nihil sunt").[33] This comparison points out that things reduced to nothingness might remain actually real beings ("simpliciter non nihil sunt"); yet, those two opposite states (beings and nothingness) do not contradict each other because each one appears within a different horizon: "simpliciter non nihil" refers to the horizon of being, "Deo comparata nihil" refers to a non-ontological horizon. The pole to which the comparison refers defines more precisely the identity of this non-ontological horizon. We must notice that the mere mention of God is not sufficient to define it, because of the equivocity of God's names. If it remains the task of theology to study the names of God, it belongs to phenomenology to distinguish between the different horizons. Therefore, if the non-ontological approach to nothingness was referred by Dionysius to the divine names of Goodness (as distinct from being), phenomenology seems compelled to examine how far Goodness (or other connected or disconnected issues) can explain the horizon within which nothingness appears.

VII

My intention was to free nothingness from its ontological interpretation. I first tried to cross-examine and criticize Heidegger's attempt to reduce nothingness to nonbeings and/or to being. I discovered another quite different concept of nothingness, one which referred to the original indifference of things to the ontological difference. Eventually, I could only ask the question of the identity of the non-ontological horizon of nothingness and suggest the issue of Goodness. But all the stages of my inquiry deal with a well-known and plain, though less explained and less understood, statement: "Das Nichts selbst nichtet" (Heidegger), "Est enim nihil non aliud quam nihil" (Nicholas of Cusa); that is to say, nothingness and nothing else.

NOTES

1. M. Heidegger, *Wegmarken*, in *Gesamtausagabe*, vol. 9 (Frankfurt, 1976), p. 105.
2. Ibid., p. 106
3. I. Kant, *Kritik der reinen Vernunft*, A 290/B 347 sq.
4. R. Carnap, "Überwindung der Metaphysik durch logische Analyse der Sprache," *Erkenntnis*, vol. 2 (Vienna, 1932). As a clear refutation of what, for Heidegger, makes up the whole problem, Carnap's critique provides an especially good means for striking a telling blow: does logical negation by itself suffice to eliminate nothing? On the contrary, does it not derive from it and thus attest to it? The guileless confidence of one who objects reinforces precisely the issue he denies. H. Bergson, "L'idée de néant," *Revue Philosophique* (1906), republished in *L'évolution créatrice* (Paris, 1907), cited according to *Oeuvres. Edition du Centenaire*, ed. H Gouhier and A. Robinet (Paris, 1963). Here, respectively pp. 730, 734, 745, and 731. These themes reappear in "Le possible et réel" (comments at Oxford in September 1920, reprinted in *La pensée et le mouvant* [Paris, 1934], cited according to *Oeuvres*). The strange concensus that brought Bergson and Carnap together is also ascribed to by J.-P. Sartre: "Without doubt Heidegger rightfully insisted on the fact that negation draws its foundation from nothing. But if nothingness provides a ground for negation, it is because nothingness envelops the *not* within itself as its essential structure. In other words, it is not as undifferentiated nothingness or as a disguised otherness that founds negation. . . . It founds negation as act because it is negation as being"; *Being and Nothingness*, tr. Hazel Barnes (New York, 1968), p. 18. Still more surprising appears the critique of E. Tugendhat: *nicht* does not lead to *Nichtsein*, but only to *Nichts* as "the universal *condition* of the understanding of being and not being [*Nichtsein*]"; indeed, "To be able to hold onto nothing [*an nichts halten*] is one of the genuine possibilities of experience; to be able to hold onto Nothing [*an das Nichts halten*] is, on the contrary, hardly possible"; it is necessary to renounce Nothing and to come back to logic; "Das Sein und das Nichts," in *Durchblicke. Martin Heidegger zum 80. Geburtstag* (Frankfurt, 1970), pp. 159 and 160.
5. Heidegger, *Wegmarken*, p. 108.
6. Ibid.
7. Ibid., p. 109; see also p. 113.
8. Ibid., p. 115.
9. Ibid., p. 306.
10. Ibid., p. 114.
11. M. Heidegger, *Brief über den "Humanismus," Wegmarken*, p. 360.
12. Heidegger, *Wegmarken*, p. 120.
13. M. Heidegger, *Sein und Zeit*, § 7, p. 31.
14. Ibid., § 40, p. 187.
15. Heidegger, *Wegmarken*, p. 115.
16. Ibid., p. 115.
17. Ibid., pp. 306, 307.
18. Heidegger, *Gesamtausgabe*, vol. 9, p. 114, n. a.
19. Heidegger, *Wegmarken*, p. 114, nn. a and d; p. 115, n. c. For a more accurate analysis of these notes, see Jean-Luc Marion, *Réduction et donation* (Paris, 1989), c. II, § 7 and c. VI, § 3.
20. Heidegger, *Wegmarken*, pp. 307, 309, 311. The lecture *Was ist Metaphysik?* never uses the formula *Anspruch des Seins*; the word *Anspruch* appears once, to the benefit of

science: ". . . nimmt sie in Anspruch" (p. 106). The sentence "Das Seiende spricht nicht mehr an" was introduced in 1949; *Gesamtasugabe*, vol. 9, p. 111.

21. Heidegger, *Wegmarken*, p. 310.

22. Ibid., p. 111.

23. Ibid., p. 140.

24. Nicholas of Cusa, *De Venatione Sapientiae*, XIV, in *Philosophisch–theologische Schriften*, ed. L. Gabriel, (Vienna, 1967), vol. 1, p. 166.

25. Plato, *Republic*, VII, 509b; Plotinus, *Enneades*, V, 5, 6; Proclus, *The Elements of Theology*, § 8, ed. E. R. Dodds (Oxford, 1933, 1963), p. 8.

26. Denys l'Aréopagite (so-called Pseudo-), *De Divinis Nominibus*, I, 1 (see 1, 5), in *Opera omnia*, ed. B. Corderius, P.G. 3, *Des Noms Divins*, I, 1, col. 588d and I, 5, col. 593d, respectively. I take the liberty of referring to my commentary on these texts in Jean-Luc Marion, *L'idole et la distance* (Paris, 1977, 1989), § § 13–14. Denys's decision here renders null and void Heidegger's critical remark that for the dogmatic Christian, "Das Nichts wird jetzt der Gegenbegriff zum eigentlich Seienden, zum *summum ens*, zu Gott als *ens increatum* (Nothing now becomes the counterconcept of genuine beings, to the *summum ens*, to God as the *ens increatum*)," *Wegmarken*, p. 119. It is true that Heidegger is blissfully ignorant of Denys and all the speculative theology of the church fathers.

27. John of Scythopolis (the attribution of Maxime the Confessor, which still supports P.G. 4, has been rectified, in particular by H. U. Balthasar, "Das Schlienwerk des Johannes von Scythopolis," *Scholastik*, 15, 1940), *Scholia in Lib. De Divinis Nominibus*, P.G. 4, col. 204d.

28. Thomas Aquinas, *In De Divinis Nominibus*, III, (concerning I, 5, col. 593c), in *Opuscula omnia*, ed. P. Mandonnet (Paris, 1927), vol. 2, p. 259. Also see I (concerning I, 1, col. 588b), p. 233 and *In Sententiarum Lib.*, I, d. 8, q.l, a.1, *ad* 4 (citing Denys about *De Fide Orthodoxa*, I, 14).

29. John of Scythopolis, *Mystagogia, Praefatio*, P.G. 91, col. 664; *De Divisione Naturae*, III, 19, P.L. 122, col. 681a; *De Docta Ignoratia*, I, 17, vol. 1, p. 252. Among the numerous tenants of this position we cite, almost by chance, Meister Eckhart: "End enist er noch güete noch wesen noch wârheit noch ein, waz ist er denn? Er ist nihtes niht, er enist weder diz noch daz. Gedenkest dû noch ihtes, daz er sî, des enist er niht" (*Predigt 23,* in *Die deutschen Werke*, ed. J. Quint, vol. 1, Stuttgart, 1958 sq., p. 402; see *Predigt 1* and *83*, vol 1, p. 14 and vol. 3, p. 442 respectively); or again, Charles de Bovelles: ". . . theologia [. . .] in nichilum usque pertransit ipsiusque nichili nomen Deo interdum ascribit, veraciter praedicans ac in mysterio pronuncians nichil esse Deum, quem quod sit finire est impossibile, cujusve ratio et conceptio nulla est" (*De Nihilo*, XI, f. 73 v., Paris, 1510. reedited F. Fromann Verlant, Stuttgart, 1970; ed. O. Magnard, Paris, Vrin, 1983, p. 126); or Jacob Boehme: "Wenn ich betrachte, was Gott ist, so sage ich: Er ist das Eine gegen der Kreatur, als ein ewiges Nichts" (*Mysterium Magnum*, I, 2, in *Sämmtliche Werke*, ed., R. W. Schiebler, Leibzig, 1843, vol. 1, p. 7); and again Angelus Silesius: "Gott ist ein lauter Nichts/ ihn rührt kein Nun noch Hier:/ Je mehr du nach ihm greifft, / je mehr entwird er dir" (*Cherubinischer Wandersmann*, in *Sämmtliche poetische Werke*, ed. G. Ellinger, Berlin, 1924, vol. 1, p. 25).

30. Heidegger, *Wegmarken*, p. 109.

31. Denys, *De Divinis Nominibus*, IV, 10, and V, 1, in P.G. 3, col. 706d–708a and 816b (see also IV, 9, col. 697a).

32. "Rien, ren, *n.f.* (. . . *lat.* rem, *acc de* res, *chose*). 1. "*Chose*" (A. J. Greimas, *Dictionnaire de L'ancien français jusqu'au milieu du XIVème siècle, s.v.,* Paris, 1969, p. 566). And in the same sense: "1. Le sens étymologique et propre de *rien* est chose. 2. Avec la négation *ne, rien* niant toute chose, équivaut au latin *nihil*" (E. Littré, *Dictionnaire de la Langue française, s.v.,* Paris, ed. 1875, vol. 4, p. 1728). However, *nihil* refers, with a negation, to a "thing," that is the *hilum* (French *hile*, defined as follows by Littré: "Terme de botanique. Le point d'attache par où la graine adhère au funicule et en

recoit les sucs nourriciers: (*op. cit. s.v.,* t. 2, p. 2025). German does the same: *Nichts* as a name, comes from *nie etwas*, which, of course, refers to the "thing," neither to "beings," nor to being (see H. Paul, *Deutsches Wörterbuch*, Halle, 1921(3), p. 536, et F. Kluge, *Etymologisches Wörterbuch der deutschen Sprache*, ed. W. Mitzka, Berlin, 1967(20), p. 510). In English, "nothing" comes from "not any thing" (see C. T. Onions, *The Oxford Dictionary of English Etymology*, Oxford, 1966, p. 615. But, contrarily, Italian coins *niente* on the basis of the Latin *nec entem* in the same way that French does *néant* (G. Battisti, G. Alessio, *Dizionario Etimologico Italiano*, Firenze, 1954, vol. 4, p. 2585).

33. Saint John of the Cross, *Subida del Monte Carmelo*, 4, § 3, then I, 4, § 4, in *Vida y obras de San Juan de la Cruz*, ed. Crisogono de Jesus, Matias del Niño Jesu, and Lucianio Ruano (Madrid, 1978), p. 462. See also, among many other texts, *Cantico espiritual*, XXVIII, 1, *op. cit.*, p. 778; *Llama de amor viva*, I, 32, *op. cit.*, p. 907sq. Among other testimonies of an uninterrupted tradition, see Saint Augustine: "Ita enim ille est, ut in ejus comparatione ea quae facta sunt, non sint. Illo non comparata sunt, quia ab ipso sunt; illi autem comparata non sunt, quia verum esse, incommutabile esse est, quod ille solus est: (*Ennarationes in Ps. CXXXIV*, 4, PL 37, col. 1741); Saint Anselm: "Si enim diligenter intendatur, ille solus [Deus] videbitur simpliciter et perfecte et absolute esse, alia vero omnia fere non esse et vix esse. Secundum hanc igitur rationem solus ille creator spiritus est, et omnia creata non sunt" (*Monologion*, XXVIII)—where he will emphasize, in view of the quasi-nullity of creatures, God himself, strictly speaking, is not, since "sic [. . .] extra sicut est supra omnem substratiam" (*ibid.* XXVI); Saint Thomas Aquinas: ". . . omnia Deo comparata nihil sunt, et tamen simpliciter non nihil sunt" (*De Veritate*, q. 2, a. 2, to 8)—a text which thus comes to distinguish, in the *nihil*, the Nothing (*Rien*) from nothingness (*néant*); M. Eckhart: "Wan alliu dinc sint in gote und von im, wan Ozwendic im und âne in enist niht in der wârheit: wan alle créatûren sint ein snoede dinc und ein blôz niht gegen gote (*Predigt 77,* in *Die deutschen Werke, op. cit.,* vol. 3, p. 339, etc.); Ch. de Bovelles: "Homo ad Deum velut nullus et nichil. Materia ad Deum nichil et non ens, omnisve creatura ad Deum ut nichil, ut id quod non est et ut non ens" (*De Nihilo*, V, f. 68, r., *op. cit.,* p. 80; Benoît de Canfeld: ". . . vivant continuellement avec toute constance en cet abîme de L'Etre de Dieu, et en la nihilaité (*sic*) de toutes choses" (*La Règle de Perfection*, III, 13, Paris, 1610[3], ed. J. Orcival, Paris, 1982, p. 410); Bérulle: "Et comme Dieu a voulu employer sa puissance à tirer l'âme du néant par création, il veut aussi employer sa puissance suprême à un autre néant, afin qu'elle ne soit plus qu'une capacité de Dieu (. . .)" (*Opuscule 150,* in *Oeuvres Complètes,* ed. J. P. Migne, Paris, 1856, column 1194); Pascal: "Le fini s'anéantit en présence de l'infini et devient un pur néant (*Pensées*, ed. Lafuma, § 418). See, on this point as on many others, the work of G. Kahl-Furthmann that is still indispensible today, *Das Problem des Nicht. Kritisch-Historische und Systematische Untersuchungen*, Munich, 1934, Meisenheim, a./G., 1968[2]. On the disqualification that strikes the very pride of being, see our analyses in *Dieu sans l'être*, Paris, 1982, ch. II–IV and *Réduction et donation,* Paris, 1989, ch. VI, §§ 4–7, whose general line of reasoning, moreover, we follow here.

THIRTEEN

Nothingness and the Professional Thinker: Arendt versus Heidegger

Jacques Taminiaux

Nothingness was a major issue very early in the history of philosophy.[1] As soon as Parmenides discovered that thinking is related to being, he confronted nothingness as an unthinkable counterpart of being. And ever since then it looks as though the more a philosopher was speculative, the more he was concerned with nothingness. In the modern world, Leibniz, Hegel, and Heidegger are good examples of this tendency. In Kant's language, speculative thinkers are those whose predominant interests are the unconditioned, the totality, the ultimate ground. Their field of investigation is metaphysics. Insofar as they dedicate most of their time to this issue they become "professional thinkers." The phrase is used by Kant near the end of the *Critique of Pure Reason* (B 871), and it is quoted by Hannah Arendt at the beginning of the introduction to *The Life of the Mind*. Right at the outset of her investigation into the activity of thinking she stresses the paradoxical character of the fact that she has decided to deal with such an awesome topic, for, as she says, "I have neither claim nor ambition to be a 'philosopher' or to be numbered among what Kant, not without irony, called *Denker von Gewerbe* (professional thinkers)."[2] In other words she felt that she had to justify herself for handling a subject which traditionally had been left to professional thinkers. But while reading her justification, one realizes that this first paradox is not the only one at stake in her investigation.

Her well-known justification was twofold. First, while attending the trial of Eichmann in Jerusalem, she had been struck by the discovery that this criminal never gave evidence that he was in the least involved in the activity of thinking. He was thoroughly thoughtless. This awakened the question: "Could the activity of thinking as such . . . be among the conditions that make men abstain from evil-doing?"[3] Her second justification was a self-criticism. In *The Human Condition* she had, to a large extent, taken for granted that thinking is a process which attains its accomplishment in a quiet condition of contemplation. She was thereby taking for granted the old distinction between *vita activa* and *vita contemplativa*. To some extent, however, she had some doubts about the identification between thinking and contemplation, and this is why she ended her study of active life with a curious sentence ascribed to Cato: "never is a man more active than when he does nothing, never is he less alone that when he is by himself."[4]

At this juncture we encounter a second paradox, which has less to do with the intellectual situation of the author than with the nature of her topic and the possible approaches to it. Her first topic in *The Life of the Mind* was thinking, considered as a specific activity. Granted that thinking is an activity, it should be obvious for people like you and me that it is not the only activity but one activity alongside other activities of the mind such as willing and judging, and also alongside the activities through which people are linked to life, or to a human world, or to their fellow human beings. Moreover, even nonspecialists are involved in thinking now and then. Now the trouble is that the specialists in the activity of thinking, precisely because they are professionals dedicating most of their time to thought, have a professional bias regarding the matter. It is a *déformation professionnelle* among them to conceive of the activity of thinking as ruling all other activities, or even as absorbing them. To Arendt this extraordinary privilege given to thinking by many professional thinkers is a professional prejudice, a "metaphysical fallacy," as she puts it. She considered that an inquiry about thinking requires a dismantling of all metaphysical fallacies. Since she did not claim to be a professional thinker, it is obvious that such dismantling was to be carried out on the basis of the attention that she had always paid to the world of appearances, which we share most of the time with our fellowmen in our active life. But it is precisely from that realm of appearances or phenomena that the activity of thinking has to withdraw in order to take place. As a result of such withdrawal the activity of thinking runs the risk of erasing the realm of appearances without which thinking could not even begin. Consequently dismantling metaphysics implies a deconstruction of the fallacies that metaphysics displays concerning the realm of appearances to which everyone belongs, including the metaphysician. The metaphysical paradox consists, in the first place, in covering up the belonging of the thinker to the realm of appearances. That paradox increases when the metaphysician produces fallacies not only about the belonging of everyone, including the metaphysician, to the common realm of phenomena but also about the very activity of thinking. As a matter of fact Arendt herself had been a victim of just such a fallacy in *The Human Condition*. Indeed, because she trusted professional philosophers from Plato on, she then believed to be right in claiming that thinking is in the final analysis a state of quiet contemplation, whereas in fact it is an endless activity of searching for meaning. Thus the basic paradox of metaphysics consists in this: it transforms thinking, which is an activity requiring some withdrawal from appearances, into the calm beholding of appearances which are of a higher rank than the common ones.

Nevertheless, in spite of this basic metaphysical paradox, of which there are several variations and offspring, metaphysics is the only record we have about the activity of thinking. As Arendt says, "the metaphysical fallacies contain the only clues we have to what thinking means to those who engage in it."[5] In other words, to the metaphysical paradox there corresponds a methodological paradox inherent in the project of dismantling metaphysics. To some extent the very dismantling of metaphysics needs the help of metaphysics.

There was no doubt in Arendt's mind that those two paradoxes are ultimately rooted in an anthropological paradox, by which I mean "the paradoxical condition of a living being that, though itself a part of the world of appearances, is in possession of a faculty, the ability to think, that permits the mind to withdraw from the world without ever being able to leave it or transcend it."[6] Consequently all the semblances that Arendt calls metaphysical fallacies consist in the final analysis in the covering up of the unavoidable tension inherent in the paradoxical condition of a being which belongs to a common world of appearances while having to withdraw from it in order to raise again and again questions of meaning that are necessary for the world to be human but lead us astray if such withdrawal does not give way to a return to the common world. Such a return requires responsible judgment about human affairs in the midst of human plurality.

Among the professional thinkers whose writings testify to these metaphysical fallacies, two names emerge: Plato, the first metaphysician of our tradition, and Heidegger, the one who first claimed to bring that tradition to its fulfillment, before subsequently contending that his task was to mediate upon its overcoming. If I put these two names together in an essay on Arendt and Heidegger I do not do so in an arbitrary fashion. There are at least two reasons for evoking Heidegger and Plato together. First, when Arendt alludes to Heidegger in *The Life of the Mind*, she does so most of the time in relation to Plato and in an attempt to show that in many respects Heidegger's writings bear witness to the recurrence of metaphysical fallacies that can be traced to Plato. Second, at the time when she was a student and an intimate friend of Heidegger in Marburg she attended his celebrated lecture course in which she discovered with fascination Heidegger's way of reappropriating Greek philosophy. The lecture course offered in 1924 dealt with Plato's *Sophist*. The first third of the course was an interpretation of the *Nicomachean Ethics* in terms of an introduction to Plato. Taken as a whole the course was a presentation of Heidegger's own philosophical project of a science of the meaning of being. The course had a tremendous impact on Arendt, and it is perhaps not an exaggeration to claim that her own theoretical writings—above all *The Human Condition* and *The Life of the Mind*—bear many traces of her reaction to and disagreement with Heidegger's teachings in this course. This is what I would like to suggest by discussing a specific topic: Heidegger and Nothingness. In order to limit the scope of my exposition I shall focus on fundamental ontology.

Fundamental ontology is the heading of Heidegger's early philosophical project. Whereas regional ontologies in Husserl's sense of the term aim at defining the constitutive properties of particular regions within the totality of beings, fundamental ontology addresses a more primordial question: what does it mean to be? Heidegger has claimed several times that the foundational question of the meaning of being intensely preoccupied him from the moment he read, in 1907, Brentano's thesis *On the Manifold Meaning of Being in Aristotle.*

Brentano's dissertation shows that in Aristotle being is predicated in four ways. Heidegger's early question became: if it is the case that there are several meanings of being, is there a unity to that manifold, and where is it to be found? It took him several years to articulate the question in the form of a specific field of inquiry. The articulation became possible when he realized that the being that we are is the basis upon which a unified understanding of the meaning of being can be attained. Human Dasein is a being which understands being. Such understanding is even the basic characteristic of human Dasein. Therefore Dasein has to be the ontical basis of ontology as the science of being, and the first step of fundamental ontology must be an ontological analysis of Dasein. *Being and Time* is the book in which that first step was made. The book demonstrated that the finite time of Dasein is the focus for a unified understanding of the meaning of being.

It is not without reason that *Being and Time* starts with a quotation of Plato's dialogue the *Sophist*. As a matter of fact the lecture course on the *Sophist*, offered by Heidegger three years before the publication of *Being and Time*, is the document in which the articulation of the question of the meaning of being into a specific field of investigation is intimated for the first time with some detail. That lecture course of which Arendt was a fascinated auditor is not yet published, but I had the good fortune to obtain a reliable transcript of it made by Simon Moser. Allow me on the basis of the transcript to outline the main points of the connection between fundamental ontology and a few basic concepts of Greek philosophy as they are interpreted by Heidegger in these lectures.

Right at the beginning of the course Heidegger insists that philosophy in its primordial form, which is metaphysics, is not a doctrine but a form of existence and even the highest one. In the *Sophist*, he said, "Plato considers human existence in one of its most extreme possibilities, namely philosophical existence."[7] In other words the philosophical discovery of being is a matter of existence. However, says Heidegger, Plato does not elucidate in a direct manner philosophy as the highest form of existence. Instead Plato proceeds in an indirect way by objecting to a way of existing from which philosophical existence has to demarcate itself. That way of existence is sophistry, the way of being of the sophist. The one who lives as a sophist never goes beyond δόξα. Δόξα is a seeing narrowly attached to what proximally appears and shows itself. Plato teaches that it is by proceeding through and beyond what proximally appears within δόξα that philosophical existence has to disclose (*erschliessen*) its proper affair, its *Sache*, that is, "*das Sein des Seienden*." To what proximally appears in δόξα Plato opposes truth, ἀλήθεια. The negative and privative structure of this word is significant. It means, Heidegger says, "that the Greeks understood that the 'uncoveredness' of the world has to be conquered. The world is not proximally available; it is not proximally disclosed. And what is disclosed in natural life is precisely what is at the same time covered over again, and covered by δόξα. Moreover, opinions become fixed in statements that are repeated without any genuine (*ursprünglich*) view."[8] This is why, says Heidegger, the life work of Socrates, Plato, and Aristotle was "a struggle against sophistry and rhetoric."[9]

The struggle is the conquest of a way of existing dedicated to the ultimate possibility of disclosing (*erschliessen*). At this juncture in the course, in view of clarifying disclosing in terms of existence, Heidegger refers to an Aristotelian treatise which, he claims, focuses upon a detailed description of the possibilities of disclosing which characterize human Dasein. This treatise is the *Nicomachean Ethics*. For that reason the *Nicomachean Ethics* is taken by him to be the best possible introduction to a study of Plato's struggle against sophistry. I quote: "Truth is a character of beings while they confront us, but in its ownmost (*eigentlichsten*) sense it is however a definition of the being of human Dasein itself."[10] This is what emerges to expression when Aristotle says, ἀληθεύει ἡ ψυχὴ (1139b 15). In as much as the ψυχή constitutes the proper being of man, "being-in-truth is a determination of Dasein."[11] Because Aristotle carefully explores the various ways of being-in-truth available to man while granting the highest status to a philosophical existence entirely devoted to σοφία, that is, the "authentic understanding" (*eigentliche Verstehen*)[12] of the being of beings, for that reason the *Nicomachean Ethics* is considered by Heidegger as an ontology of Dasein whose study retrospectively sheds light on the Platonic conquest of philosophical existence.

Allow me to recall briefly the main points in Heidegger's analysis of what he takes to be Aristotle's ontology of Dasein. I would like to suggest that those main points indicate the very structure of Heidegger's own analytic of Dasein, which is the first stage of his fundamental ontology. By the same token I would like to suggest that those main points were decisive and burning topics in the very fabric of Arendt's own interpretation of the active life and the life of the mind. In other words, a conflict between two different readings of Aristotle is at stake here, a conflict which is much more than a matter of philology or even of the hermeneutics of ancient texts. Heidegger's reading leads to an understanding of the world in terms of nothingness. By contrast, Arendt's reading leads to what she called *amor mundi*.

What Heidegger discovered in the description by Aristotle of the human possibilities of disclosing is a hierarchy of ways of being. According to Heidegger the Aristotelian ethics is an investigation of the human possibilities of disclosing (ἀληθεύειν) which correspond to two levels of comportment. On the lower level there is a comportment which is deliberative and active, whereas on the upper level there is a comportment which is contemplative and theoretical. Let me consider first Heidegger's analysis of deliberative comportment.

The deliberative comportment is itself divided into two types of activity which are not of the same rank. They are the activity of producing or working, which is called ποίησις, and, on a higher level, the activity of action, which is called πρᾶξις. To those two comportments there correspond two modalities of disclosing, or of being-in-truth. The way of disclosing corresponding to the productive comportment is τέχνη. In the activity of work ruled by τέχνη the principle of the being which is to be produced lies within the productive agent, the producer. It is an εἶδος, a pattern or model of the product. But that principle is in no way in the product, for the product does not emerge on its own, or naturally. Conversely the end or goal or τέλος of the pair τέχνη-ποίησις is in the product in which the activity of work reaches its fulfillment, namely, in the completion that Aristotle calls ἐνέργεια or ἐντελέχεια. However, strictly speaking, the product of working is a τέλος only as long as the productivity continues. Once the product is finished it acquires an independent status, an existence separated from the producer. In other words, the τέλος is not in the producer. Moreover as a result, the product, as soon as it is there, is instrumental for various goals and for the needs of various individuals. It falls within an endless cycle of means and ends. For all of these reasons, the ontological dignity of the pair τέχνη-ποίησις, or "know-how"—production—is, according to Heidegger, marked by a deficiency. It is easy to recognize in this reading of Aristotle an anticipation of the analysis of everydayness in *Being and Time*. To be sure, Heidegger was always very discrete in relation to his sources of inspiration. In this case, however, the Aristotelian inspiration is suggested by at least three factors: first, by the care Heidegger takes in ontologically depreciating τέχνη and ποίησις; second, by his terminology (for instance, he translates τέχνη by *sich auskennen in einer Hantierung*;[13] now, *Hantierung* in German is almost a synonym for what *Being and Time* was soon to call *Besorgnis*, concern); third, by the early descriptions by Heidegger of everydayness (for example, in the *Prolegomena to the History of the Concept of Time*), which multiply the use of terms such as *Werk* and *Herstellung* and abound in the interpretation of τέχνη-ποίησις in the course of 1924.

On a higher level than the pair τέχνη-ποίησις, there is the pair φρόνησις-πρᾶξις. Φρόνησις is the way of disclosing specific to action (*Handlung*). Heidegger claims that φρόνησις overcomes the ontological deficiency that I just mentioned concerning τέχνη. Indeed the goal of φρόνησις is nothing outside the acting individual, nothing indifferent to it. The τέλος of φρόνησις is nothing παρά, or outside of, the agent; rather it is the very being of the agent. The goal is "of the same ontological character as φρόνησις."[14] It is εὐπραξία, that is, human Dasein itself considered in the "how" (*wie*) of its action. But the goal is the principle (ἀρχή) as well: "In φρόνησις," says Heidegger, "Dasein's own being is itself the topic and herewith both the principle and the end of deliberation are apprehended in one stroke";[15] in other words, "πρᾶξις is for φρόνησις at once ἀρχή and τέλος."[16] The most striking feature of this reading is its transformation of what in Aristotle is ethical into a strictly ontological issue. What is at stake in φρόνησις is for Heidegger only "the proper being of Dasein."[17] To this extent it is not exaggerated to acknowledge in Heidegger's analysis of φρόνησις an anticipation of the analysis of care and authentic existence in *Being and Time*. Two remarks suffice to indicate this anticipation. First, Heidegger insists that φρόνησις is required because primordially "Dasein conceals itself before itself and forgets itself."[18] Second, the constellation of German notions by means of which he brings to light the structure of the relation φρόνησις-πρᾶξις imposes a parallelism with the later analysis of care and the specific seeing adjusted to the ownmost being of Dasein. The anticipation appears with a still stronger clarity in the very question with which Heidegger introduces his analysis of what, in Aristotle, is above φρόνησις and beyond ἐπιστήμη the highest possibility of disclosing. This highest possibility is σοφία, translated by Heidegger as authentic understanding. Heidegger states that both ἐπιστήμη and σοφία are forms of πρᾶξις, or of existence, aiming at conquering the unconcealment of being. Then he insists that σοφία is for Aristotle of a higher rank than φρόνησις and that it features the highest meaning of human existence for a Greek, "namely, the βίος θεωρητικός."[19] And here is his question: Why, since φρόνησις is oriented toward Dasein itself, is there still room for σοφία taken to be of a still higher rank than φρόνησις? Or, in other words, why is there not in Aristotle an "identification between σοφία and φρόνησις?"[20] And again, the same question put in ontological terms: "What is the meaning of being on the basis of which Aristotle grants to σοφία a higher rank than φρόνησις?"[21]

The answer to this question, as you no doubt realize, is a matter of being as well as a matter of time. It is a matter of being because to the Greeks Dasein is not the highest being and consequently the being of Dasein is ontologically deficient. It is a matter of time as well because for the Greeks the highest being is a being which is forever, whereas Dasein is mortal. Therefore the Greeks believed that human Dasein attains its highest possibility of disclosing and of being not by being oriented toward Dasein itself but "when it stays as long as possible in the pure consideration, or in the pure presence, of what is forever."[22] Σοφία is that consideration by which the Greek philosopher, who lives the βίος θεωρητικός, immortalizes himself or reaches εὐδαιμονία, a word that Heidegger translates as *Eigentlichkeit*, authenticity.

Thus the meaning of being on the basis of which Aristotle grants the highest rank to σοφία is time, but a peculiar time which is understood in terms of a constant presence. In Heidegger's view this raises the following questions: How does the present get such a privilege? Why cannot the past and the future claim such a right as well? Should not being be understood from temporality taken as a whole?

The questions, you may realize, were decisive for fundamental ontology, which was to show a little bit later that the time in which past and future count as much as the present is indeed the finite temporality of Dasein. As a result of this shift of focus, Aristotle's ontology of Dasein had to undergo a complete metamorphosis in Heidegger's appropriation of it. In this reappropriation Heidegger still agrees with Aristotle and Plato to the extent that he also claims that the βίος θεωρητικός is the highest possibility of Dasein. Yet he disagrees with them entirely when he changes the orientation of θεωρία. Instead of considering the perpetual being of φύσις, Heidegger's θεωρία reflects the mortal being of Dasein. Consequently instead of being separated from φρόνησις, σοφία turns out to be intimately associated with it. Moreover, the only task of σοφία henceforth consists in duplicating φρόνησις, provided that φρόνησις be understood in purely ontological terms as the preontological uncovering of the being of Dasein. In other words the metamorphosis essentially consists in projecting σοφία and θεωρία upon the axis of φρόνησις and πρᾶξις. This very projection includes a deconstruction of the Greek privilege of οὐσία, or the presence of the present. As a matter of fact the deconstruction was carried out by Heidegger with the help of a peculiar reappropriation of Aristotle's theory of ποίησις. In the framework of this reappropriation, ποίησις is described by Heidegger as the comportment we have primordially and most of the time in everydayness. In such a comportment Dasein is supposed to be in a condition of falling away from its ownmost possibility of being. Within the condition of falling Dasein pays attention to οὐσία, that is, *Vorhandenheit* or presence-at-hand, instead of paying attention to existence. In other words, it pays attention to the being of nature instead of paying attention to its own being. And the reason for this is that being in the sense of a perpetual presence is what is taken for granted and ever again presupposed by the activity of production.

All this, I hope, suffices to outline the framework in which the question of nothingness is treated by Heidegger. But I hope by the same token that the outline I have sketched so far allows one to realize the tremendous impact that the lecture course on the *Sophist* had on Hannah Arendt. As a matter of fact most of the main topics of *The Human Condition* as well as several topics she discusses in *The Life of the Mind* are at the very core of the lecture course, though her two books give to the topics in question a meaning which is no longer Heideggerian at all. It is obvious, for example, that distinctions like work and action or the public and the private, which are extensively dealt with in *The Human Condition*, were already treated by Heidegger in the lecture course on the *Sophist*. But of course the point is to realize the extreme contrast in the two treatments of these subject matters. I would like to show how strong and sharp the contrast is by focusing on the question of nothingness, which is a crucial one in Heidegger's fundamental ontology. It is precisely Heidegger's emphasis on nothingness that is, in the final analysis, entirely discarded by Arendt in *The Human Condition* and *The Life of the Mind*.

Let me try to explain this. In 1946, several years before the publication of *The Human Condition*, Arendt expressed the basic tenor of her work in a *Partisan Review* article in which she stressed her total disagreement with the emphasis that *Being and Time* puts on nothingness. The article was entitled "What Is Existenz Philosophy?" Taking sides with Jaspers against Heidegger, she concluded the article in the following way:

> Existence is never essentially isolated; it exists only in communication and in the knowledge of the existence of others. One's fellow men are not, as in Heidegger, an element which, though structurally necessary, nevertheless destroys existence, but on the contrary, existence can develop only in the togetherness of men in the common given world. In [Jasper's] concept of communication there lies embedded, though not fully developed, a new concept of humanity as the condition for man's existence. In any case, men move together within this surrounding being; and they hunt neither the phantom of the self nor do they live in the arrogant illusion that they can be being generally. . . .

These sentences announce the basic topics of Arendt's later analysis of active life. They mean that it is not the self in Heidegger's sense of the word that is in the world. Instead of being the most intimate correlate of a single self, the world here is common to a plurality of people; they share it in common and dwell in it. These sentences on Jaspers conclude a survey of the philosophy of existence, which is treated by Arendt under the following heading: "The Self as All and Nothing: Heidegger."[23] This highly significant heading sums up her criticism of Heidegger in the article. In *Being and Time* the self is all, since it is in it that the answer to the meaning of being is to be found. Moreover it is all by virtue of the fact that its essence is to exist. The Self, Arendt says, now occupies the place of God in traditional metaphysics, and therefore it becomes the "master of being." But the self is nothing as well. The reason for this is that the authentic way of being for which Dasein cares in its ownmost potentiality for being ultimately implies the nothingness of all beings, of the others, and even of itself since it is in the anticipation of its own death that Dasein becomes a self. For Arendt, Heidegger's notion of resoluteness—"the arrogant passion to be a self"—is contradictory. Only an entire withdrawal from the world could make it successful. But such a withdrawal is impossible. Therefore the self is doomed to a constant "falling" and its resoluteness to be a self amounts to an acknowledgment of an insurmountable guilt. This notion of the self, in addition to being contradictory, is, she says, "contrary to man."[24]

> the most essential characteristic of this self is its absolute egoism, its radical separation from all its fellows. The anticipation of death as existential is introduced to achieve this; for in death man realizes the absolute *principium individuationis.* Death alone tears him from the context of his fellows within which he becomes a public person and is hindered from being a self. . . . Hence the self is the concept of man according to which he can exist independently of humanity and need represent no one but himself—his own nothingness.[25]

When reading this early criticism while remembering Arendt's later work—above all *The Human Condition* and *The Life of the Mind*—one is inclined—with a good deal of justification, I believe—to see the article of 1946 as the matrix of the books. As far as *The Human Condition* is concerned, her criticism clearly anticipates a non-Heideggerian treatment of at least three topics—the world, the principle of individuation, the public—a treatment in which nothingness is no longer the focus as it is in Heidegger. As far as *The Life of the Mind* is concerned, the article of 1946 already broaches a topic which much later on was going to be at the foundation of her deconstruction of Heidegger as a Platonic metaphysician. This topic is the withdrawal of the philosophical self from the world. This deconstruction amounts to a deconstruction of Heidegger's notion of nothingness. In these two books, I have no doubt, the course on the *Sophist* had a continuing impact: it remained for Arendt a foil over against which she developed her own thought.

Allow me a few remarks about *The Human Condition* and the three topics in it that testify to a basic disagreement with Heidegger. In fundamental ontology there is a sharp distinction between what in everydayness we take to be the world and what the world is in its properly ontological sense. The world of everydayness is an *Umwelt*, that is, a functional contexture in which instruments appear as means to several ends. This surrounding world is the intentional correlate of a comportment whose basic characteristic is production. In productive comportment we are concerned by goals to be attained and by means instrumental to them. Production and concern go together. This comportment is enlightened by a specific modality of being-in-truth, which is practical circumspection and prospection. All of this well-known description is the result of Heidegger's appropriation of Aristotle's analysis of ποίησις and τέχνη. What is not Aristotelian, however, in the reappropriation—though it is certainly inspired by Plato's doctrine of truth—is the interpretation of ποίησις and τέχνη in terms of an ontological falling. The everyday world is taken to be inauthentic or improper to the extent that in production and concern we deal with beings whose way of being is not our own. In contrast to this, world in the proper sense has the way of being of Dasein itself. The authentic sense of the world is intimated when the stability and security of the surrounding world is shaken and vanishes into nothingness, as for example when tools no longer work. This points toward the true experience of the world. The true experience of the world is the experience of nothingness that we are supposed to have in the basic attunement of anxiety. In this fundamental mood the surrounding world, which was shared with fellows in everydayness, is reduced to nothing. This experience of nothingness reveals that the world in its authentic sense is not at all a habitat, a home in which we dwell in common. The authentic world is the *Worumwillen* (for the sake of which) of a self which is strictly for its own sake and in relation with itself alone. Again this analysis is the result of a very peculiar reappropriation of an Aristotelian topic handled by the course on the *Sophist*, namely, the analysis of πρᾶξις as an activity which is οὗ ἕνεκα, for the sake of itself. But what is not at all Aristotelian in this is the fundamental solipsism involved in Heidegger's notion of πρᾶξις as being-in-the-world.

It is against this demarcation between an inauthentic common world and an authentic, solipsist one, that the whole description of the world in *The Human Condition* is directed. Instead of having the negative connotation of a fall, the activity of work (ποίησις) is described by Arendt as an activity making possible a properly human habitat beyond the biological environment in which the activity of labor is trapped. The activity of working by producing useful objects beyond consumer goods is what gives "the world the stability and solidity without which it could not be relied upon to house the unstable and mortal creature that is man."[26] A detailed analysis of Arendt's description of the activity of fabrication would probably show that she reappropriated many insights of Aristotle about ποίησις. To this extent her indebtedness to the *Sophist* lecture course is real, but there is no trace in her own reappropriation of Aristotle of the Heideggerian move toward the homelessness of the Dasein. On the contrary, if the mentality of *homo faber* is considered by her to have a basic flaw, the reason for this is not at all because craftsmen are attached to the world as a home but because their utilitarianism is inclined to transform all ends into means for further ends, thereby jeopardizing the stability of any dwelling place. Moreover in Arendt, if action is necessarily a higher activity than work, this distinction is not at all, as in Heidegger, intended to demarcate it from the dwelling place built by the worker, which is to say it is not predicated of an ontological homelessness. On the contrary, action is necessary for safeguarding a common world; it is called for by an *amor mundi*, which has no place in Heidegger's fundamental ontology.

This invites me to turn to the second topic: the principle of individuation. In Heidegger's treatment of the principle of individuation, nothingness again is a central issue. Let me quote from *Being and Time*: "In [anxiety] Dasein finds itself face to face with the 'nothing' of the possible impossibility of its existence. . . . Anticipation [Being-toward-death] utterly individualizes Dasein, and allows it, in this individualization of itself, to become certain of the totality of its potentiality-for-being."[27] One gets individualized by coming face to face with nothingness, which means that all business with things as well as all interactions with fellow people must vanish in order for Dasein to become an individual. Moreover, even all communication and expression must vanish. At the end of the analysis of conscience, considered as the call of care allowing someone to resolutely become a self, Heidegger writes: "Dasein is authentically itself in the primordial individualization of the silent resoluteness which exacts anxiety of itself."[28] In other words, the question "Who is Dasein?" is answered by Heidegger in terms of an ontological nihilation of all sharing of words and deeds. This nihilation is what is ultimate in Heidegger's peculiar reappropriation of Aristotle's teaching concerning the οὗ ἕνεκα of πρᾶξις.

Arendt's concept of individuation is by all accounts a reaction against these views. To be sure she raises the question "Who are you?" Moreover in apparent agreement with Heidegger she also argues that individuation is not truly possible in the activity of work but rather needs action in order to emerge. However, her definition of individuation is no longer Heideggerian at all. Whereas Heidegger focuses upon being-toward-death, she insists on what she calls natality. Whereas Heidegger, because of his emphasis on death, divorces individuation from any link whatsoever with human interaction, she situates individuation within human plurality. Whereas Heidegger separates authentic πρᾶξις from any communication, she insists, in a quite opposite direction, on an essential link between πρᾶξις and λέξις: "When I insert myself into the world, it is a world where others are already present. Action and speech are so closely related because the primordial and specifically human act must always also answer the question asked of every newcomer: 'Who are You?' The disclosure of who somebody is is implicit in the fact that speechless action somehow does not exist, or if it exists, it is irrelevant."[29] I cannot conceive of a more forceful way of saying how far she is removed from Heidegger. One last feature confirms this divergence. At the beginning of the introduction to the ontology of Dasein Heidegger insists, in full agreement with Plato in the *Sophist*, that the first philosophical step consists in not μῦθόν τινα διηγεῖσθαι, in not telling a story.[30] On the contrary, in a move that is a sort of revival of Aristotle's *Poetics* against both

Plato and Heidegger, Arendt insists that "it is precisely in stories that the actual meaning of a human life finally reveals itself."[31] No less obvious is their disagreement concerning the public realm. Every reader of *Being and Time* is familiar with Heidegger's assessment of the public realm in terms of inauthenticity. In everydayness everyone is no one, a fragment of the "they." Since the everyday comportment is work, this amounts to a claim that the public realm is the intentional correlate of the activity of ποίησις. By contrast, when Heidegger retrieves, in his own way, Aristotle's concept of πρᾶξις and transforms it into authentic existence, it turns out that πρᾶξις for him is essentially private and appears to the self alone. Consequently a public πρᾶξις would be a contradiction in terms. This of course is a very unusual reading of Aristotle, who celebrates Pericles in his analysis of πρᾶξις.

Arendt reverses Heidegger's view of the matter. For her, not ποίησις, of which only the product appears, but πρᾶξις is really public because it is essentially conditioned by human plurality, by a sharing of words and deeds in a common world of appearances. This reversal is at the very foundation of her political thought. At this juncture I am compelled to touch upon the burning issue of the link between fundamental ontology and Heidegger's commitment to National Socialism in 1933. Many careful readers of Heidegger claim that *Being and Time* is apolitical. Consequently, they say, there is no direct inference between fundamental ontology and Heidegger's Nazism. However, they also agree that the language of fundamental ontology, though transposed to the Dasein of the German people, permeates Heidegger's Nazi speeches and proclamations as well as several declarations of support of the regime in the lecture courses of 1934–35. In all these writings the resolute facing of nothingness is once again a central issue. On the basis of this observation one might be inclined to believe that the very fact of the transposition I just mentioned testifies to a tremendous shift which is in no way anticipated by *Being and Time.* I do not deny that there was a shift. I would even grant that *c'est l'occasion qui fit le larron.* However, I am not so sure that fundamental ontology in its first phase was entirely apolitical. There is indeed one passage in the lecture course on the *Sophist* which is worth meditating upon: "As far as the task of bringing Dasein to its best is concerned, φρόνησις is the way. Supposing that φρόνησις were the most serious and decisive knowledge, then the science which develops in the field of φρόνησις would be the highest science. As far as man is a ζῷον πολιτικόν, as far as its Dasein is with others, then the πολιτική, political knowledge, would be the authentic σοφία. Accordingly the philosopher would be the politician. Here you can see offhand Plato's view shine through."[32] This is assessed by Heidegger in 1929 in a commentary on the *Nicomachean Ethics*, taken by him to be the best introduction to Plato. To be sure, Heidegger's comment is ambiguous. He was quite aware that for Aristotle φρόνησις is not the most serious and decisive knowledge for the simple reason that the mortals are not for him the highest beings. But if, he says, it turned out that Dasein were the highest being, then the philosopher would be the right politician, which means that Plato's concept of the philosopher-king should be revived. This proves, to say the least, that Heidegger paid no attention to the many signs of Aristotle's resistance to Plato's concept of politics. It also proves that as early as 1924, in the framework of a very peculiar reappropriation of Aristotle, Heidegger's attempt to project σοφία and θεωρία upon the axis φρόνησις-πρᾶξις included the conviction that the fundamental ontologist is the ideal ruler. This Platonic conviction, all things considered, was the basis of "The Rectoral Address" of 1933, which after all was a National Socialist reappropriation of Plato's *Republic.*

Let me conclude by returning to what I was suggesting at the beginning. Arendt's ironic attitude toward professional thinkers had very deep roots in her intellectual development. There is no doubt, in my view, that she came to understand what occurred to Heidegger in 1933 as a distant consequence of the Platonic bias of the course of 1924. I have no doubt either that her critical meditation on her notes is still in the background of what she wrote in her tribute to Heidegger for his eightieth birthday: "We who wish to honor the thinkers, even if our own residence lies in the midst of the world, can hardly help finding it striking and perhaps exasperating that Plato and Heidegger, when they entered into human affairs, turned to tyrants and Führers. This should be imputed not just to the circumstances of the times and even less to preformed character, but rather to what the French call a *déformation professionnelle.*"[33] Indeed because of their very dedication to ultimate questions, professional thinkers overlook the specific articulation of the active life from which they withdraw. By the same token, since the βίος θεωρητικός is for them the only real activity, they take common activities and ways of thinking to be entirely superficial, trapped in the Cave (Plato), or in natural consciousness (Hegel), or in inauthentic comportment (Heidegger). Thus they believe that common φρόνησις, immersed in human plurality, is part of an inauthentic policy. As far as Heidegger is concerned, his early tendency to substitute an ontological φρόνησις (authentic resoluteness) for the common one amounted to a substitution of σοφία for common judgment, thereby putting the philosopher in the position of substituting an ontological policy for the supposedly inauthentic one. In this ontological policy, facing nothingness turned out again to be the only issue. *The Human Condition* is a book that should be read as a deconstructive reaction against these metaphysical fallacies. But professional thinkers display metaphysical fallacies not just concerning active life; they do so as well concerning the very activity to which they dedicate their life, thinking. This is what Arendt discovered little by little after she wrote *The Human Condition*, a book in which thought is still taken to be essentially contemplative. On this point only, the book was still under the spell of the 1924 course in which, in deed as well as in fundamental ontology as a whole, thinking is a matter of knowing and knowing a matter of seeing. As a matter of fact, fundamental ontology is entirely articulated around the hierarchy of three levels of seeing. On the lowest level there is the consideration of the present. This seeing proves to be abstracted and derived from a higher seeing, which is practical circumspection. But this seeing again proves to be derived from a still higher one, namely, the moment of vision in which the Dasein ontologically sees its own potentiality-for-being. All of this is anticipated in the lecture course on the *Sophist*, in which Heidegger insists that in the final analysis νοῦς is ἄνευ λόγου, without speech. Arendt gradually discovered that this concept of the mind as a seeing ἄνευ λόγου is the most fundamental fallacy of metaphysics. And this is what she expresses and discusses extensively in *The Life of the Mind*. Her point is this. The one who claims, like Plato or Heidegger, to have achieved the status of an ultimate seer ἄνευ λόγου cannot but fallaciously nihilate the world of common appearances that human beings share in common with their fellows. Such a person cannot but sustain some version of the two-world theory, cannot but overlook or even despise human plurality and the faculty of judging. In other words, this person cannot but substitute some form of Manichaeism for the anthropological paradox I mentioned at the beginning of this essay. This is not to say that Heidegger is meaningless. Quite the contrary, he was a thinker; his work is an endless food for thought; his withdrawal from common appearances was entirely motivated by the activity of thinking as a search for meaning, and a constant questioning. Yet the comic aspect of such a withdrawal emerges when the thinker, instead of questioning, claims to be the only true spectator. Taking the part of the Thracian girl whom Aristotle talks about in the *Nicomachean Ethics*, Arendt was right in laughing at that pretension. But there is a tragic element also in all of this, for Heidegger, while fallaciously transforming thinking into knowing, somehow put himself in a position which is quite symmetrical to the one occupied by the thoughtless man of the Jerusalem trial: Eichmann was incapable of telling right from wrong by reason of thoughtlessness; Heidegger came perhaps to have the same incapability because his pretension had put him far beyond good and evil.

NOTES

1. Since this essay was written, Heidegger's lecture course *Platon: Sophistes* has been published in Martin Heidegger, *Gesamtausgabe*, vol. 19, ed. Ingeborg Schüssler. This edition is an attempt to restore the substance of the 1924–25 lecture course with the help of notes which were preserved by members of the Marburg audience. Since my quotations are based on a single transcript, i.e., the one made by S. Moser, they do not always match *expressio verbis* the published version. But as far as the meaning is concerned, the pages of the volume that I refer to correspond to the quotations I make.
2. Hannah Arendt, *The Life of the Mind* (New York, 1978), p. 3.
3. Ibid., p. 51.
4. Ibid., pp. 7–8.
5. Ibid., p. 12.
6. Ibid., p. 45.
7. Heidegger, *Gesamtausgabe*, vol. 19: *Platon: Sophistes* (Frankfurt, 1992), p. 12.
8. Ibid., p. 16.
9. Ibid.
10. Ibid., p. 23.
11. Ibid.
12. Ibid., p. 22.
13. Ibid.

14. Ibid., p. 49.
15. Ibid., p. 50.
16. Ibid., p. 51.
17. Ibid.
18. Ibid., p. 52.
19. Ibid., p. 61.
20. Ibid., p. 136.
21. Ibid., p. 164.
22. Ibid., p. 172.
23. Hannah Arendt, "What Is *Existenz* Philosophy?" *Partisan Review*, 12 (1946), p. 46.
24. Ibid., p. 51.
25. Ibid.
26. Hannah Arendt, "Labor, Work, Action," in *Amor Mundi: Explorations in the Faith and Thought of Hannah Arendt*, ed. James W. Bernauer, S.J. (Boston, 1987), p. 34.
27. Martin Heidegger, *Being and Time*, tr. J. Macquarrie and E. Robinson (New York, 1978), p. 310, H266.
28. Ibid., p. 369, H322.
29. Arendt, in *Amor Mundi*, pp. 39–40.
30. Heidegger, *Being and Time*, p. 26, H6.
31. Arendt, in *Amor Mundi*, pp. 40–41.
32. Heidegger, *Platon: Sophistes*, p. 44.
33. Hannah Arendt, "Martin Heidegger at Eighty," *New York Review of Books*, October 21, 1971, p. 55.

FOURTEEN

The Passion of Facticity: Heidegger and the Problem of Love

Giorgio Agamben

I. The Absent *Stimmung*

It has often been observed that the problem of love is absent from Martin Heidegger's work. While *Being and Time* contains a vast treatment of fear, of anxiety, and of the *Stimmungen* (moods) in general, nevertheless love is mentioned only once, in a note that gives two quotations, one from Pascal and one from Augustine. As a result, W. Koepps[1] in 1929 and Ludwig Binswager[2] in 1942 criticized Heidegger for not having made any place for love in his analytic of Dasein, which he founded exclusively on *Sorge*; and in an undoubtedly hostile *Notiz*, Karl Jaspers wrote that Heidegger's philosophy is "ohne Liebe, daher auch im Stil unliebenswürdig."[3]

This sort of critique, as Karl Löwith has observed,[4] will remain idle as long as it is not able to replace the Heideggerian analytic with an analytic based on love. Heidegger's silence—or apparent silence—on love remains nonetheless problematic. We know, in fact, that between 1923 and 1926, while completing his major work, Heidegger had a passionate relationship with Hannah Arendt, who at the time was his student at Marburg. Although the letters and poems that attest to this relationship, which are currently held in the Deutsches Literaturarchiv in Marburg, are not yet accessible, we know by way of Arendt's own claim[5] that twenty years after the end of their relationship, Heidegger affirmed that this love had been "the passion of is life (dies nun einmal die Passion seines Lebens gewesen sei)," and that the writing of *Being and Time* had thus taken place under the sign of love.

How do we then explain the absence of love in the analytic of Dasein—especially since, on Arendt's part, the relationship had produced a book on love? I am referring to her doctoral dissertation (published in 1929 but never reprinted), *Der Liebesbegriff bei Augustin*, in which it is not difficult to discern Heidegger's influence. Why, then, does *Being and Time* remain so obstinately silent on the subject of love?

Let us examine more closely the note on love in *Being and Time*. It is found in §29, which is dedicated to an analysis of *Befindlichkeit* (state-of-mind) and *Stimmungen*. The note contains not one word of Heidegger's but only the two quotations, from Pascal ("And hence it comes about that in the case where we are speaking of human things, it is said to be necessary to know them before we love them, and this has become a proverb; but the saints, on the contrary, when they speak of divine things, say that we must love them before we know them, and that we enter into truth only by charity; they have made of this one of their most useful maxims") and Augustine ("non intratur in veritatem, nisi per charitatem [one does not enter into truth except through charity]"). The two quotes thus reaffirm a sort of ontological primacy for love in being the access to truth. Thanks to the publication of the last Marburg seminars of the 1928 summer semester, we know that the reference to this fundamental role of love originates from conversations with Max Scheler on the problem of intentionality. "Scheler," Heidegger writes, "particularly in the *Liebe und Erkenntnis* essay, was the first to show that intentional behaviors are of a different nature, and that, for example, love and hate found knowledge (*Liebe und Haß das Erkennen fundieren*). Scheler here takes motifs that are present in Pascal and in Augustine."[6] In the essay cited by Heidegger as well as in a contemporary text posthumously published as *Ordo amoris*, Scheler on several occasions insists on the preeminent role of love. "Der Mensch," one reads in *Ordo amoris*, "ist, ehe er ein *ens cognitans* ist oder ein *ens volens*, ein *ens amans*." Heidegger was thus perfectly conscious of the foundational importance of love, foundational in the sense that it conditions the very possibility of knowledge and the access to truth.

On the other hand, in the 1928 summer semester seminars, the reference to love takes place within the context of a discussion on the problem of intentionality, wherein Heidegger criticizes the current conception of intentionality as being the cognitive relation between a subject and an object. This text is invaluable, for by means of a critique that does not spare his teacher Edmund Husserl, Heidegger shows how he achieves the overcoming of the notion of intentionality in a movement toward a structure of transcendence, which in *Being and Time* is called *In-der-Welt-Sein* (being-in-the-world).

In the conception of intentionality as a relation between a subject and an object, that which for Heidegger remains unexplained is exactly that which is to be explained, that is to say, the relation itself:

> This lack of explaining impinges on the indeterminacy of that which is there in the relation. . . . There have been attempts recently to conceive this relation as a relation of being [*Seinsbeziehung*]. . . . With this category one does not clarify anything, as long as one does not indicate what kind of being is here in question and as long as the kind of being [Seinsart] of the beings, among which the relation must play, remains obscure. . . . Being is here thought, both in Hartmann and in Scheler, as *Vorhandensein*. Now, this relation is nothing, but it is nonetheless not Being in the sense of a *Vorhandenes*. . . . One of the initial fundamental tasks of *Being and Time* is to bring this relation to light in its original essence.[7]

Even more original than the subject-object relation there is, for Heidegger, the autotranscendance of *In-der-Welt-Sein*, wherein Dasein opens itself to the world on this side of all knowledge and all subjectivity. Before something like a subject or an object can form itself, Dasein—and this is one of the central theses in *Being and Time*—is already open to the world: "das Erkennen selbst gründet in einem Schon-Sein-bei-der-Welt."[8] And it is only by starting from this original transcendence that something such as an intentionality can be understood in its own way of being.

If, then, Heidegger, in recognizing the fundamental role of love, does not treat this problem thematically, it is precisely because the way of being of the most original opening of all knowledge (that which, according to Augustine and Scheler, takes place in love) is, in a certain sense, the central problem of *Being and Time*. On the other hand, love, if it is to be understood in terms of this opening, can no longer be conceived according to the current representation as a relation between a subject and an object or as a relation between two subjects. It should rather find its place and its own articulation in *Schon-Sein-bei-der-Welt*, which characterizes the transcendence of Dasein.

Now, what is the mode of being of this *Schon-Sein-bei-der-Welt*? In what sense is Dasein always already close to the world and the things that surround it even before knowing them? How is it possible for Dasein to open itself to something without making it the objective correlate of a knowing subject? And how is it possible that the intentional relation itself is brought to light as far as its mode of being is concerned and in its primacy in relation to the subject and the object? It is in this context that Heidegger introduces the notion of faciticity (*Faktizität*).

II. Facticity and Dasein

The important new element contributed by the publication of the courses of the early 1920s has a central position and must henceforth be acknowledged: the notion of facticity and factical life in the development of Heidegger's thought. The abandonment of the notion of intentionality (and that of the subject, which was correlative to it) was made possible by the establishing of this category; the path was thus: intentionality–facticity–Dasein. In the years to come, one of the tasks of Heideggerian philology will certainly be that of clarifying the meaning of this path and of reconstructing its genealogy (as well as explaining the progressive eclipsing of the concept of facticity in the later Heidegger). The considerations that follow are but an initial contribution in this direction.

First of all one must say that Heidegger's earliest students and friends have already emphasized the importance of the concept of facticity in the shaping of the master's thought. As early as 1927, the mathematician and philosopher Oskar Becker, in a publication that makes up the second half of the *Jahrbuch für Philosophie und phänomenologische Forschung*, where the first edition of *Being and Time* also appeared, was able to affirm that "Heidegger designates as ontology the hermeneutics of facticity, that is to say, the interpretation of the human Dasein."[9] Becker is here referring to the title of the course for the 1928 summer semester at Freiburg: "Ontologie oder Hermeneutik der Faktizität."[10] What does this title mean? In what sense is ontology, the doctrine of being, a doctrine of facticity?

Heidegger's usage of the term *facticity* is clearly different from the usages of Husserl and Sartre. Heidegger distinguishes the *Faktizität* of Dasein from *Tatsächlichkeit*, the simple factuality of worldly beings. It is at the beginning of *Ideen* that Husserl defines the *Tatsächlichkeit* of the objects of experience. These objects, he writes, present themselves as something that is found in a determined point of space and time and which possesses certain contents of reality but which, given its essence, could also very well be elsewhere and otherwise. Husserl thus insists on contingency (*Zufälligkeit*) as being an essential character of factuality. On the other hand, facticity's very own character is not, for Heidegger, *Zufälligkeit* but *Verfallenheit*. With Heidegger everything is complicated by the fact that Dasein is not simply, as in Sartre, thrown in the *there* of a given contingency; rather, it is and has to be its *there*; it is itself the *Da* (there) of being. Once again, the difference between the modes of being is decisive here.

The origin of the Heideggerian definition of the term is not likely to be found in Husserl but rather in Augustine, who writes that "*facticia est anima*,"[11] the human soul is factical in the sense that it was "made" by God. In Latin, *facticius* is the opposite of *nativus*, and it means *qui non sponte fit*, that which is not natural, which did not come into being itself ("which is made by hand and not by nature," as Calepin says). The crudeness of the term must be understood, for it is the same adjective that Augustine employs to designate the pagan idols, in a definition which seems to correspond perfectly to our term *fetish*: *genus facticiorum deorum*, a genre of factical gods.

We must not forget this origin of the word, which leads us back to the semantic sphere of the nonoriginal and of shaping, if we are to understand the development of this concept in Heidegger's thought. What is important here is that the experience of a facticity, thus of a constitutive nonoriginarity is precisely, for Heidegger, the original experience of philosophy, the sole point of legitimate departure for thought.

One the earliest attestations of this definition of the term *faktisch* appears (as far as one can tell by the current state of the *Gesamtausgabe*) in the 1921 summer semester course on Augustine and Neoplatonism, about which we are informed by the testimony of O. Pöggeler and Oskar Becker.[12] Heidegger wants to show here that primitive Christian faith (unlike Neoplatonic metaphysics, which thought of being as something *stets Vorhandenes* and, consequently, *fruitio dei*,[13] as the enjoyment of an eternal presence) was an experience of life in its facticity and in its essential restlessness (*Unruhe*). As an example of this *faktische Lebenserfahrung*, Heidegger analyzes a passage from chapter 23 of book 10 of the *Confessions*, where Augustine questions man's relation to truth:

> I have known men that would willingly deceive, but none that would be willingly deceived . . . they love truth when it shows itself to them, they hate it when it shows them to themselves. And the tax that truth inflicts upon them is this: they do not want to be revealed by it, but it reveals them nonetheless, and yet remains hidden to them. This is the essence of the human heart: blind and lazy, indignant and dishonest, it wishes to remain hidden, but does not want that something remain hidden to it. But what happens instead is that it does not remain hidden from truth, while truth remains hidden to it.

What interests Heidegger here as a mark of factical experience is this dialectic of latency with nonlatency, this double movement by which the one who wants to know by remaining hidden in knowledge is known by a knowledge that remains hidden to them. Facticity is the condition of that which remains hidden in its opening, of that which is exposed by its own withdrawal. From the outset, facticity is in this way characterized by this very co-belonging of latency and nonlatency which marks, for Heidegger, the experience of truth and of being.

It is this very movement, this restlessness of facticity, which is at the center of the Freiburg seminars of the 1921–22 winter semester, whose title is *Phänomenologische Interpretation zu Aristoteles*, but which are for the greater part dedicated to the analysis of that which Heidegger now calls *das faktische Leben* and which will later become Dasein. Heidegger begins here by affirming the original and irreducible character of facticity for thought:

> [The determinations of the factical life] . . . are indifferent qualities that could be ascertained in a trivial manner, as when I say: this thing is red. They are alive in facticity, that is to say, they contain the factical possibilities from which they could never free themselves—never, thanks be to God [*Gott sei Dank nie*]; as a result, a philosophical interpretation which aims for that which is most important [*die Hauptsache*] in philosophy—facticity—is in its being authentic, factical, and this in such a way in its being philosophico-factical, it radically gives itself the possibilities of decision and, by this, it gives itself. But this it can do only if it exists—according to the mode of its Dasein [*wenn sie da ist—in der Weise ihres Daseins*].[14]

Far from signifying (as in Sartre or in Husserl) the immobility of a factual situation, facticity designates the "character of Being" (*Seinscharakter*) and the very "emotion" (*Bewegtheit*) of life. The analysis which Heidegger here outlines constitutes a sort of prehistory of the analytic of Dasein[15] and the autotranscendance of *In-der-Welt-sein*, where one finds again, under other names, all of the fundamental determinations. For the factical life is never in the world as a simple object: "e-motion [of factical life] is such that, as a movement, it gives itself to itself in itself; it is the e-motion of the factical life which constitutes this life, so much so that factical life, in its living in the world, does not itself produce its own movement, but it lives the world as the in-what [*worin*], the of-what [*worauf*] and the for-what [*wofür*] of life."[16]

The *Grundbewegung* of the factical life is called *Ruinanz* (from the Latin *ruina*, "a collapsing," "a fall") by Heidegger: it is the first appearance of that which will become *die Verfallenheit* in *Being and Time*. *Ruinanz* presents the same entanglement of proper and improper, of *spontaneous* and of *facticius*, as that which characterizes the *Geworfenheit* of Dasein: "a movement which builds itself up and which nevertheless doesn't do this itself, rather the void does within which it moves: its absence is its possibility of movement."[17] And, in its expressing the fundamental structure of life, facticity is connected by Heidegger to Aristotle's concept of *kinesis*.[18]

That which his vocabulary was still searching for in the seminars of the early 1920s finds, with *Being and Time*, the theoretical device which has become familiar to us. Now, beginning with §12, in the moment of defining the *Grundverfassung* of Dasein, Heidegger introduces the concept of facticity. In order to correctly situate this concept, we must first place it in the context of a distinction of modes of being. *In-der-Welt-sein*, Heidegger says, does not signify the property of a being-present-at-hand (*Vorhandenes*), for example, a corporal thing (*Körperding*), which would be in another being of the same mode, as water is in a glass or an outfit in the closet. *In-sein* expresses instead the very structure of Dasein: it is a matter of an *Existential* and not a *Kategorial*. For two worldless beings (*Weltlos*) could very well be one beside the other (in the way that one says that the chair is close to the wall), one could also say that the one touches the other. But in order to be able to speak of a touching in the proper sense of the word, in order for the chair to be truly close to the wall (in the meaning of *Sein-bei-der-Welt*), the chair first of all must be able to encounter the wall.

What happens to the Dasein which, itself, is not *weltlos*? We need to understand the conceptual difficulty which is here in question. Certainly, if Dasein were a simple intraworldly being, it could never encounter the being which it is or other beings; but, on the other hand, if it is lacking a factual dimension, how could it encounter anything? In order to be close to beings, in order to have a world, Dasein must, so to speak, be a *faktum* without being factual (*Vorhandene*); it must at once be a *Faktum* and have a world. It is here that the notion of facticity comes into play:

> [Dasein] can with some right and within certain limits be taken as merely present-at-hand. To do this, one must completely disregard or just not see the existential state of being-in. But the fact that Dasein can be taken as something which is present-at-hand and just present-at-hand, is not to be confused with a certain way of "presence-at-hand" which is Dasein's own. The latter kind of presence-at-hand becomes accessible not by disregarding Dasein's specific structures but only by understanding them in advance. Dasein understands its ownmost being in the sense of a certain "factual being-present-at-hand." And yet the "factuality" of the fact [*Tatsache*] of one's own Dasein is at bottom quite different ontologically from the factual occurrence of some kind of mineral, for example. Whenever Dasein is, it is a fact; and the factuality of such a Fact is what we shall call Dasein's "facticity." This is a definite way of being [*Seinsbestimmtheit*], and it has a complicated structure which cannot even be grasped as a problem until Dasein's basic existential states have been worked out. The concept of "facticity" implies that an entity "within-the-world" has being-in-

> the-world in such a way that it can understand itself as bound up in its "destiny" with the being of those entities which it encounters within its own world.[19]

From a formal point of view, facticity confronts us with the paradox of an *Existenzial* which is also *Kategorial* and of a *Faktum* which is not factual. Neither *vorhanden* nor *zuhanden*, neither pure presence nor object of use, facticity is a specific mode of being whose conceptualization marks in an essential way the Heideggerian reformulation of the question of being. This is above all—we must not forget—a new articulation of the modes of being.

The clearest explanation of the characteristics of facticity is found in § 29 which is dedicated to the analysis of *Befindlichkeit* and of *Stimmung*. In *Stimmung* there takes place an opening up which, as we know, precedes any knowledge and any *Erlebnis*: it is *die primäre Entdeckung der Welt*, the original disclosure of the world. But that which characterizes this disclosure is not the pure light of origins but precisely an irreducible facticity and opacity. Dasein is brought before other beings by *Stimmungen* and, from the very beginning, before the being which it itself is; but since it did not by itself bring itself in its own *Da*, it is irremediably delivered to that which henceforth confronts it and which regards its *Da* as an inexorable enigma.

> In having a mood, Dasein is always disclosed moodwise as that entity to which it has been delivered over in its being; and in this way it has been delivered over to the being which, in existing, it has to be. "To be disclosed" does not mean "to be known as this sort of thing". . . . The pure "that it is" shows itself, but the "whence" and the "whither" remain in darkness. . . . This characteristic of Dasein's being—this "that it is"—is veiled in its "whence" and "whither," yet disclosed in itself all the more unveiledly; we call it the "thrownness" of this entity into its "there"; indeed, it is thrown in such a way that, as being-in-the-world, it is the "there." The expression "thrownness" is meant to suggest the facticity of its being delivered over. . . . *Facticity is not the factuality of the* factum brutum *of something present-at-hand, but a characteristic of Dasein's being—one which has been taken up into existence, even if proximally it has been thrust aside.*[20]

Let us deal for a moment with the traits of this facticity, this factical thrownness (we have seen that Heidegger brings *Geworfenheit* back to facticity) which, in being a category which conditions the analytic of Dasein, has often remained uninterrogated as far as its provenance and own structure are concerned.

The first trait of facticity is *die ausweichende Abkehr*, evasive turning-away. The opening up of Dasein delivers it to something from which it cannot escape but which nevertheless eludes it and which remains inaccessible in its constant diversion: "Ontologically, we thus obtain as the first essential characteristic of states-of-mind that they disclose Dasein in its thrownness, and—proximally and for the most part—in the manner of an evasive turning-away."[21]

To this characteristic of Dasein's being there thus belongs from the outset a sort of original turning away: *abgedrängte*, the adjective Heidegger uses, designates something that has been displaced, turned away, but which has not completely receded, and which rests, so to speak, present under the guise of its withdrawal, as in the Freudian *Verdrängung*.22

But the most essential trait of facticity, from which all the other traits ensue, is expressed by Heidegger in the form that has numerous variations but which remains constant as far as its conceptual core is concerned: "Dasein is delivered to the being it is and has to be," "Dasein is and has to be its own *Da*," "Dasein is each time its own possibility," "for Dasein in its being has to do with this very being." As expressions of facticity, what do these formulations mean?

The Marburg seminars of the 1928 summer semester (which often contain invaluable commentaries on certain major passages in *Being and Time*) explain them without any possible equivocation: "[Dasein] bezeichnet das Seiende, dem seine eigene Weise zu sein in einem bestimmten Sinne ungleichgültig ist ([Dasein] designates the being for which its own proper mode of being in a definite sense is not indifferent)."[23]

Dasein is and has to be its way of being; its manner, its "way" could be translated with a word which etymologically and semantically corresponds to the German *Weise*.[24] We need to reflect on this paradoxical formulation, which marks for Heidegger the original experience of being and moreover without which the repetition of the *Seinsfrage* or the relation between essence and existence as outlined in § 9 remains quite unintelligible. The two determinations of classical ontology, *existentia* and *essentia*, the *quod est* and the *quid est*, the *Daß-sein* and *Wassein*, are contracted the one into the other in a constellation which is charged with tension. For Dasein (as much as it is and has to be its own *Da*) there is the same indissociability of ὄν and of ποῖον, of being and of being-such, of existence and of essence with Plato, in the *Seventh Letter*, claims belong to the soul.[25]

"*Das Wesen des Daseins liegt in seiner Existenz.* Die an diesem Seienden herausstellbaren Charaktere sind daher nicht vorhandene 'Eigenschaften' eines so und so 'ausehenden' vorhandenen Seienden, sondern je ihm möglische Weisen zu sein und nur das. Alles Sosein dieses Seienden ist primär Sein."

"All the being-such that this being possesses is first of all being"[28]: rather than the definition of the ontological status of God (*Deus est suum esse*),[27] we need here perhaps to think of Schelling's positive philosophy and of his concept of *Seyende-Sein*, being the being, where the verb *to be* is to be equally understood in its transitive sense: Dasein is to be its own being-such; it is to exist its essence and essencify its existence.[28]

As for *Seinscharackter*, facticity thus expresses the original ontological characteristic of Dasein. If Heidegger could, by way of one and the same gesture, pose again the question of the meaning of being and distance himself with respect to ontology, the being that is at stake in *Being and Time* has from the outset the characteristic of facticity. For this reason all qualities, all *Sosein*, are never for Dasein a "property" but solely a "*mögliche Weise*" *zu sein*, a formula that must be understood according to the same ontological contraction as the one expressed in Nicholas of Cusa's *posset*. The original opening up is produced in this factical movement where Dasein has to be its *Weise*, its way of being, and where being and its guise are at once discernible and one. We need here to understand the term *façon* (way, manner) both in its etymological meaning (of *factio, facere*) and in the meaning which the word has in Old French: *face, visage*. Dasein is factical, for it has to be its own guise, its way, its manner, and, at the same time, that which shows it and exposes it, that into which it is irremediably thrown.

It is here that we must look at the root of *ausweichende Abkehr*, the evasive turning away, and of the constitutive impropriety of Dasein. It is because it has to be its guise that Dasein remains there disguised: buried in that which opens it, hidden in what exposes it, obscured by its own light. Such is the factical dimension of this *Lichtung* whose appellation is truly something like a *lucus a non lucendo*.[29]

The formulation according to which Heideggerian ontology will be a hermeneutics of facticity achieves here its full meaning. Facticity is not added afterward to Dasein, but it is inscribed in its structure of being. We are here in the presence of something that could be defined with an oxymoron, as an "original facticity," or *Urfaktizität*. It is exactly such an "original facticity" that in the seminars of the 1928 summer semester are called *transcendentale Zerstreung* (transcendental distraction or dissemination) or *ursprüngliche Streuung* (original dispersion). I do not want to dwell on these passages, which have already been analyzed by Jacques Derrida;[30] let it suffice to recall that Heidegger here sketches out the figure of an original facticity that constitutes "die innere Möglichkeit für die faktische Zerstreuung in die Leiblichkeit und damit in die Geschlechtlichkeit (the intrinsic possibility for being factically dispersed in bodiliness and thus into sexuality)."[31]

III. Facticity and Fetishism

How must we understand this original facticity? Is *Weise* something like a mask which Dasein must assume? Is it not rather there that a Heideggerian ethic can find its proper place?

Here the terms *factical* and *facticity* show all of their pertinence. The German adjective *faktisch*, like the French *factice*, appeared relatively late in the European lexicon: in the second half of the eighteenth century for German, and a little earlier for French. But in both cases it was a learned formation, coined on the basis of the Latin, which is grafted onto a much older history of linguistics. From the Latin *facticius*, French had in the thirteenth century derived, in accordance with its phonetic laws, the adjective *faitis* (or *faitiche, fetiz*) as well as the noun *faitisseté (faiticheté)*. The German had formed, at the same time, possibly borrowing from the French, the adjective *feit*. Now *faitis*, like its German counterpart *feit*, simply meant "beautiful, pretty." "Faitisse estoit et avenante / je ne sais femme plus plaisante," we read in the *Roman de la rose*; and again, in other authors: "votre gens corps votre beauté faictisse" (Baudes), "voiz comme elles se chaucent bien et faitissment" (Jean de Meun), "ils ont doubz regard et beaulté / et jeunesse et faitischeté" (Gaces). But it is in a text of Villon's that one can best understand the proper meaning of the word *faities*: "Hanches charnues, / eslevées, propres, faictisses / à tenir amoureuses lisses." In conformity with its genealogy, *faitis* here designates that which in a human body seems to be intentionally made, fashioned with art, made for . . . , and for this it attracts desire and love. It is as if the being-such of a being, its guise or its manner, were to detach itself from it as beauty in a sort of a paradoxical autotranscendence. It is in the context of this semantic history that we are to locate the appearance of the term *fétische* (German *Fetisch*). The dictionaries tell us that in the eighteenth century this word entered into the European languages through the Portuguese *feitiço*. But the word is in reality morphologically identical to the adjective *faitis* ("factical") which, by borrowing from Portuguese, was to thus enjoy a sort of resurrection.

An analysis of the meaning of the term in Freudian and Marxian usage is, from this point of view, particularly instructive. Let us recall that, for Marx, the characteristic of fetish (or of goods), that which made its characteristic elusive, does not solely consist in its artificial character but rather in the fact that the product of human labor is at once endowed with a value of use and a value of exchange. Similarly, for Freud, a fetish is not a postiche object: it is at once the presence of something and the sign of its absence; it is and it is not an object. And this is so because it irresistibly attracts desire without ever being able to satisfy it.

One could say in this sense that the structure of Dasein is marked by a sort of original fetishism, of an *Urfetischismus*[32] or *Urfaktizität*, that makes it such that it could never appropriate the being to which it is nevertheless irremediably delivered. Neither *Vorhandenes* nor *Zuhandenes*, neither value of exchange nor value of consumption, being, which is to be its ways of being, exists factically. But, by way of this, its *Weisen* are not enactments which it could, in being a free subject, take on or not take on; they belong from the outset to its existence and they originally constitute its *ethos*.[33]

IV. The Proper and the Improper

It is from this perspective that we must read this unresolved dialectic of *eigentlich* and *uneigentlich*, of the proper and the improper, to which Heidegger dedicates some of the best pages of *Being and Time*. We know that Heidegger always made a point of specifying that the words *eigentlich* and *uneigentlich* are to be understood in their etymological meaning of "proper" and "improper." By virtue of its facticity, the opening up of Dasein is marked by an original impropriety; it is constitutively divided into *Eigentlichkeit* and *Uneigentlichkeit*. Heidegger several times underlines that the dimension of the impropriety and of the everydayness of *das Man* is not something derivative, into which Dasein will fall, so to speak, accidentally; it is, on the contrary, as original as propriety. Dasein is co-originarily in truth and in nontruth, in the proper and in the improper. The original characteristic of this co-belonging is obstinately reaffirmed by Heidegger: "Dasein, as *verfallen*, is, by its constitution of being, in nontruth"; "Open in its *Da*, Dasein equiprimordially holds itself in truth and in nontruth."[34]

Heidegger often seems to draw back before the radicalness of this thesis and to fight against himself in order to maintain the primacy of the proper and of the true. But a more attentive analysis shows that not only is the equiprimordial never denied, but that several passages instead would leave us to infer a primacy of the improper. Each time, in *Being and Time*, we have to understand the experience of the proper (as for example in being-toward-death), it is always and solely by means of an analysis of impropriety (for example, being-toward-factical-death) that the path is open. The factical link between these two dimensions of Dasein is so intimate and original that Heidegger is able to write: "die eigentliche Existenz ist nichts, was über der verfallenden Alltäglichkeit schwebt, sondern existenzial nur ein modifiziertes Ergreifen dieser";[35] and, on the subject of the decision itself: "[das Dasein] eignet sich die Unwahrheit eigentlich."[36]

Authentic existence has no other content but inauthentic existence; the proper is nothing but the seizing of the improper. We must reflect on the characteristic of the noncircumventability of the improper which is implied by these formulations. Both in being-toward-death and in the decision, Dasein seizes only its impropriety; it becomes master only of alienation; it pays attention only to distraction. Such is the originary constitution of facticity. But what can seizing an impropriety mean? How can one properly appropriate nontruth? If we do not reflect on these questions, if we continue to attribute to Heidegger simply the primacy of the proper, not only will we not understand the most profound intention of the analytic of Dasein in *Being and Time*, but we deny ourselves access to the thought of *Ereignis*, which constitutes the key term of Heidegger's later thought and which here has, in the dialectic of *eigentlich* and *uneigentlich*, its *Urgeschichte* in the Benjaminian sense of the term.

V. A Theory of Passions

Let us now return, after this long digression, to the problem of love which was our point of departure. A more attentive analysis shows that the affirmation according to which Heidegger's thought will be *Ohne Liebe* is not simply imprecise from a philosophical point of view; it is also so at the philological level. Several texts could here be invoked; I would like to focus solely on the two texts which seem to me to be the most important.

About ten years after the end of his relationship with Hannah Arendt, in the 1936 course on Nietzsche (*The Will to Power as Art*), Heidegger treats love thematically in a few very dense pages where he sketches out an altogether singular theory of passions. He begins by subtracting affects and passions from the sphere of psychology, by defining them as "the fundamental ways [*Grundweisen*]. . . in which humans test their *Da*, the opening and withdrawal of the being in which it finds itself."[37] But, soon after, he clearly distinguishes love and hate from the other feelings by presenting them as passions (*Leidenschaften*) opposite to simple affects (*Affekte*). While affects, such as anger and joy, are born and die in us spontaneously, love and hate, in being passions, are always present in us and lurk in our being from its origins. This is why we can say "nourish hate" but cannot say "nourish anger" (*ein Zorn wird genährt*).[38] We must at least quote the decisive passage on passion:

> Because hate lurks much more deeply in the origins of our being it has a cohesive power; like love, hate brings an original cohesion and perdurance to our essential being. . . . But the permanent cohesion that comes to human existence through hate does not close it off and blind it. Rather, it grants vision and premeditation. The angry man loses the power of reflection. He who hates intensifies reflection and rumination to the pont of "hardboiled" malice. Hate is never blind; it is perspicuous. Only anger is blind. Love is never blind; it is perspicuous. Only infatuation is blind, fickle, and susceptible—an affect, not a passion. To passion belongs a reaching out and opening up of oneself. Such reaching out occurs even in hate, since the hated one is pursued everywhere relentlessly. But such reaching out in passion does not simply lift us up and away beyond ourselves. It gathers our essential being to its proper ground; it exposes our ground for the first time in so gathering, so that the passion is that through which and in which we take hold of ourselves and achieve lucid mastery over the beings around us and within us.[39]

Hate and love are thus the *Grundweisen*, the two fundamental guises or ways in which Dasein tests its *Da*, that is to say the opening up and withdrawal of the being which it is and will be. Contrary to affects, which are blind to the same thing which they reveal to us and which, like the *Stimmungen*, reveal only in diversion, in love and in hate humans take a more profound footing in that in which they have been thrown; they appropriate their own facticity and thus they gather and work their own foundation. It is thus not by chance if hate, with its "original cohesion" here holds a primordial position beside love, like evil in the course on Schelling and furor (*das Grimmige*) in the "Letter on Humanism": the dimension which is here in question is precisely the original opening up of Dasein, wherein "from being itself there can come the assigning [*Zuweisung*] of these orders [*Weisungen*] which will become for humans norms and laws."[40]

VI. Potentia Passiva

This original status of love (to be more exact, of passion) is reaffirmed in a passage from the "Letter on Humanism," where the importance for the problem we are dealing with could hardly be overvalued. Here "to love" (*liebe*) is connected to *mögen* (which means both "to want" and "to be able to") and the latter is identified with being, from a perspective where the category of power-possibility is thought of in an entirely new way:

> To embrace a "thing" or a "person" in its essence means to love it, to favour it. Thought in a more original way such favouring [*mögen*] means to bestow essence as a gift. Such favouring is the proper essence of enabling [*Vermögen*], which not only can achieve this or that but also let something essentially unfold in its provenance,

that is, let it be. It is on the "strength" of such enabling by favouring that something is properly able to be. This enabling is what is properly "possible" [*das Mögliche*], that whose essence resides in favouring. From this favouring being enables thinking. The former makes the latter possible. Being is the enabling-favouring, the "may be" [*das Mögliche*]. As the element, being is the "quiet power" of the favouring-enabling, that is, of the possible. Of course, our words *möglich* [possible] and *Möglichkeit* [possibility], under the dominance of "logic" and "metaphysics," are thought solely in contrast to "actuality"; that is, they are thought on the basis of a definite—the metaphysical—interpretation of being as *actus* and *potentia*, a distinction identified with the one between *existentia* and *essentia*. When I speak of the "quite power of the possible" I do not mean the *possible* of a merely represented *possibilitas*, nor *potentia* as the *essentia* of an *actus* of *existentia*; rather, I mean being itself.[41]

In order to understand the thematic unity which is here evoked, we must connect it to the problem of freedom as it is presented in the last pages of "Vom Wesen des Grundes." Again, the dimension of facticity (or better, of the original or transcendental facticity) is here essential: "To exist always means: in the middle of beings, to be in relation with beings—with that which is not in the mode of Dasein, with its self and with what is similar to it—and this in such a way that, in its emotively placed relation, there where it goes is the potentiality-for-being [*Seinkönnen*] of Dasein itself. In the plan of the world, an excess of the possible is given [to Dasein] in relation to—and in being invested and traversed by the real being which pushes it from all sides—comes forth the 'why.'"[42]

Freedom thus places Dasein in its essence as "potentiality-for-being in possibilities, which open themselves wide before its final choice, that is to say, in its destiny."[43] Dasein, in that it factically exists (that is to say, in that it has to be its ways of being), is always in the mode of the possible: in excess of the possibilities with regard to beings and, at the same time, lacking, for its possibilities revert to radical powerlessness before the beings to which it is always delivered.

It is this co-belonging of power and of powerlessness that is analyzed in a passage from the seminars of the 1928 summer semester, which anticipates the themes of "Vom Wesen des Grundes" and affirms the superiority of the category of the possible with regard to the real:

Insofar as freedom (taken transcendentally) constitutes the essence of Dasein, Dasein, as existing, is always, in essence, necessarily "further" than any given factical being. On the basis of this upswing, Dasein is, in each case, beyond beings, as we say, but it is beyond in such a way that it, first of all, experiences beings in their resistance, against which transcending Dasein is powerless. The powerlessness is metaphysical, i.e., to be understood as essential; it cannot be removed by reference to the conquest of nature, to technology, which rages about in the "world" today like an unshackled beast; for this domination of nature is the real proof for the metaphysical powerlessness of Dasein, which can only attain freedom in its history. . . .

Only because, in our factical intentional comportment toward beings of every sort, we, outstripping in advance, return to and arrive at beings from possibilities, only for this reason can we let beings themselves be what and how they are. And the converse is true. Because, as factically existing, transcendence and world-entry, the

> powerlessness, understood metaphysically, is manifest, for this reason Dasein, which can be powerless (metaphysically) only as free, must hold itself to the condition of the possibility of its powerlessness, to the freedom to ground. And it is for this reason that we essentially place very being, as being, into question regarding its ground. We inquire into the why in our comportment toward beings of every sort, because in ourselves possibility is higher than actuality, because with Dasein itself this being-higher becomes existent.[44]

The passage on the *mögen* (and its connection with love) in the "Letter on Humanism" must be read in close relation with the primacy of possibility. *Potentia* which is here in question is in fact essentially *potentia passiva*, the δύναμις τοῦ πάσχειν to which Heidegger, during the 1931 summer semester course on Aristotle's *Metaphysics*, underlines its secret solidarity with active power (δύναμις τοῦ ποιεῖν). All power (δύναμις), Heidegger here writes in interpreting Aristotle, is powerless (αδυναμία) and all power/capacity (δύνασθαι) is essentially passivity (δέχεσθαι).[45] But in this powerlessness there takes place an original event (*Urgeschehen*) which determines the being of Dasein and which opens the abyss of its freedom: "That Dasein be, according to its possibility, an itself and that it be each time factically in conformity with its freedom, that transcendence temporalizes itself as an original event, all of this is not due to the power of this freedom itself. But such a powerlessness (being thrown) is not the result of the encroachment of beings over Dasein; instead, it determines the being of Dasein as such."[46]

Passion, the *potentia passiva*, is thus the most radical experience of possibility (*mögen*) which is at stake in Dasein: a power with not only power/force (the ways of being which are in fact possible) but also and above all else *powerlessness*. It is for this reason that the experience of freedom coincides for Dasein with the experience of its powerlessness: it locates itself at the level of the original facticity or "original dispersion" (*ursprüngliche Streuung*) which, according to the 1928 summer course, constitutes the "intrinsic possibility" of the factical dispersion of Dasein.

Passion, in being passive power and *Mögen*, has a capacity for its own powerlessness; it allows not only the possible but also the impossible to be and in this way it gathers Dasein on its ground to open it and eventually to make it master of beings in and around it. The "immobile force of the possible" is, in this sense, essentially passion, passive power; *mögen* (to be able to) means *lieben* (to love).

But how could such a mastery, which does not appropriate a thing but powerlessness and impropriety, come to pass? How is it possible to be capable not of a possibility and power but of an impossibility and powerlessness? What is freedom which is above all else passion?

VII. The Passion of Facticity

Here we see, then, that the closeness of the theme of love, as passion, with that of *Ereignis* constitutes the central motif of Heidegger's reflections beginning in the 1940s. It could be precisely love, as passion of facticity, which allows us to shed some light on this concept. We know that Heidegger explains the word

Ereignis and the term *eigen* and understands it as "appropriation," as he implicitly places it at the heart of the dialectic of *eigentlich* and *uneigentlich* in *Being and Time.* But we are dealing with an appropriation where that which is appropriated is only something foreign, other, which must become proper or must come from the shadows to light. That which is here appropriated and brought not to light but to *Lichtung* is singularly an expropriation, an eclipsing as such. "Das Ereignis ist in ihm selbst Enteignis, in welches Wort die frühgriechische λήθη im Sinne des Verbergens ereignishaft aufgenommen ist (*Ereignis* is in itself expropriation, a word which recovers the ancient Greek λήθη in the sense of withdrawal)."[47] In this way the thought of *Ereignis* "is not the effacement of the forgetting of being, but a 'setting in' it and a 'self-keeping' in it. Awakening [*erwachen*] from the forgetting of being, this forgetting itself, is to de-awaken [*entwachen*] in *Ereignis*."[48] Now that which comes to pass is "die Verbergung sich nicht verbirgt, ihr gilt vielmehr das Aufmerken des Denkens (the withdrawal no longer hides, all of the attention of thought goes to it)."[49]

What do these enigmatic phrases mean? Just as what humans must here appropriate is not a hidden thing but the very fact of being hidden, the very impropriety and facticity of Dasein, consequently, "to appropriate oneself of it" can only mean: to be *properly improper*, to abandon oneself to the inappropriable. The withdrawal, the λήθη, must here come to thought as such, facticity must show itself in its closure and in its opacity.

The thought of *Ereignis*, as the end of the history of being, is then somehow also a reprise and a realization of the thought of facticity which, in the early Heidegger, marked the reformulation of the *Seinsfrage*. It is not just a question of the multiple ways (*Weisen*) of the factical existence of Dasein but of this original facticity (or transcendental dispersion) which constitutes its *innere Möglichkeit*. The *Mögen* of this *Möglichkeit* is neither power nor act, neither essence nor existence, but a powerlessness whose passion freely opens the ground of Dasein. In *Ereignis*, original facticity no longer escapes in the evasive diversion or in an historic destiny but is appropriated in its own evasiveness, held in its λήθη.

The dialectic of the proper and the improper thus reaches its end. Dasein no longer has to be its *Da*, no longer has to be its *Weisen*; from now on it definitively inhabits them in the mode of this *Wohnen* and of this *Gewohnheit*, which, in § 12 of *Being and Time*, characterized the *In-sein* of Dasein.

In the word *Ereignis* we should then understand the Latin *assuescere*—on the condition we think the *suus* of this term, the *se* that constitutes its core. And if we remember that the origin of the destinal characteristic of Dasein was (according to the note on page 42 of *Being and Time*) its having-to-be, we also understand why *Ereignis* is without destiny, *geschicklos*. Being (the possible) has here truly exhausted its historical possibilities, and Dasein, which has the capacity for its powerlessness, reaches its extreme mode: the *immobile* force of the possible.

This does not mean all facticity be abolished, all e-motion effaced. "The absence of the destiny of *Ereignis*," Heidegger states, "does not mean that all e-motion (*Bewegtheit*) is lacking in it. Rather, it means that the most proper mode of movement to *Ereignis*, the *Zuwendung in Entzug*, shows itself for the first time to thought as that which is to be thought."[50] It is here we find the meaning of this *Gelassenheit*, of this "abandonment," which a late text defines as *die Offenheit für das Geheimnis*,[51] being open for the mystery: *Gelassenheit* is the e-motion of *Ereignis*, the opening up, never nonepochal, for the "*Uralte* which is hidden in the name Ἀ-λήθεια."[52]

We can now perhaps achieve a less provisional definition of love. That which humans introduce into the world, their "own," is not simply the light and opening up of knowledge but above all else and for the first time the opening up to a closure and to an opacity. Αλήθεια, truth, is the custodian of λήθη, of nontruth; memory, the custodian of forgetting; light, the safeguard of obscurity. It is only in the insistence of this abandonment, in this forgetful safeguard of everything, that something like knowledge and attention eventually becomes possible.

It is all that which love suffers (in the etymological sense of the word *passion*: *pati*, πάσχειν). Love is the *passion of facticity*, wherein humans hold this nonbelonging and this opacity, and it appropriates (*adsuefacit*) them by keeping them as such. It is not thus, according to the dialectic of desire, an affirmation of the self in the negation of the loved object, but passion and exposition of the facticity itself and of the irreducible impropriety of beings. *In love, the loved one arrives, at the same time as the lover, to the light of his/her veiled being, in an eternal facticity and beyond being.* (This is perhaps what Hannah Arendt means when, in a text from 1930 written with her first husband, she says, with Rilke's words, that love "is the possibility of one veiling their destiny to the other.")

As in *Ereignis* the appropriation of the improper means all at once the end of the history of being and that of its epochal dispatchings, so in love, the dialectic of the proper and of the improper reaches its end. It is because, in a definitive sense, there is no sense in distinguishing authentic love from inauthentic love, celestial love from mundane love, love of God from love of self. Lovers support to the extreme the impropriety of love as long as the proper can come forth as an appropriation of this free powerlessness which passion brought to its extreme. Lovers go to the limit of the improper, in a senseless and demonic promiscuity; they establish themselves, in sensual delight and in lover's discourse, in regions which are always new with impropriety and facticity, to the point of exhibiting its essential abyss. In fact, humans do not originally remain in the proper, but they no longer inhabit (according to the all-too-facile suggestion of contemporary nihilism) the improper and the unfounded; *it is rather he/she who is properly impassioned with the improper, he/she who, among those who are living, has a capacity for their powerlessness.*

It is so because if it is true that, according to Jean-Luc Nancy's beautiful expression, love is where we are not masters,[53] that to which we never have access but which always comes to pass for us, it is also true that humans can appropriate this powerlessness and that, according to the words addressed by Hölderlin to Böhlendorf, "der freie Gebrauch des Eigenes das Schwerste ist (the free use of the proper is the heaviest task)."

Translated by Paul Colilli

NOTES

The volumes of Martin Heidegger's *Gesamtausgabe* are cited under the abbreviation *GA*, followed by the volume number. Heidegger's other works are abbreviated as follows: *SuZ* = *Sein und Zeit* (Tübingen 1972); *WM* = *Wegmarken* (Frankfurt, 1967); *N* = *Nietzsche* (Pfüllingen, 1961); *SD* = *Zur Sache des Denkens* (Tübingen, 1969).

1. W. Koepps, *Merimna und Agape* (1929).

2. L. Binswanger, *Grundformen und Erkenntnis menschlichen Daseins* (Zurich, 1942).

3. K. Jaspers, *Notizen zu Heidegger* (Munich, 1978), p. 34.

4. K. Löwith, *Phänomenologische Ontologie und protestantische Theologie*, in O. Pöggeler, *Heidegger. Perspektiven zur Deutung seines Werks.* (Königstein, 1984), p. 76.

5. Elizabeth Young-Bruehl, *Hannah Arendt: For the Love of the World* (New Haven, 1984), p. 247.

6. *GA*, vol. 26, p. 169.

7. Ibid., pp. 163–64.

8. *SuZ*, p. 61, "Knowing is grounded before hand in a Being-already-alongside-the-world."

9. O. Becker, *Mathemathische Existenz. Untersuchung zur Logik und Ontologie mathematischer Phänomene, Jahr. für Phil. und phän. Forschung*, vol. VIII (Halle, 1927), p. 621.

10. In the *GA* the title of the work (in vol. 62) is "Ontologie. Phänomenologische Hermeneutik der Faktizität." According to the note on p. 72 in *SuZ*, Heidegger had been dealing with the "Hermeneutik der Faktizität" since the courses of the 1919–20 winter semester.

11. See the article on *facticius* in the *Thesaurus linguae latinae* and the article on *facio* in Ernout-Meillet's etymological dictionary.

12. O. Pöggeler, *Der Denkweg M. Heideggers* (Pfüllingen, 1963), pp. 36–45. See also O. Becker, *Dasein und Dawesen* (Pfüllingen, 1963), and K. Lehmann, "Christliche Geschichtserfahrung und ontologische Frage beim jungen Heidegger," in Pöggeler, *Heidegger. Perspektiven*, pp. 140–68.

13. The Augustinian opposition between *uti* (making use of something in view of other ends) and *frui* (to enjoy something for its own sake) is important for the prehistory of the distinction between *Vorhandenheit* and *Zuhandenheit* in *SuZ*. As we will see at a later point, the facticity of Dasein is in opposition to *Vorhandenheit* as it is to *Zuhandenheit* and thus could not properly be the object of either a *frui* or of an *uti*.

14. *GA*, vol. 61, p. 99.

15. See, with the same meaning, the considerations of H. Tietjen, "Philosophie und Faktizität, *Heidegger Studies*, vol. 2 (1986).

16. Ibid., p. 130.

17. Ibid., p. 131.

18. "Problem der Faktizität, kinesis—Problem," ibid., p. 117. If we recall the fundamental role which, according to Heidegger, κίνησις plays in Aristotle's thought (again in the Thor seminars, he presented κίνησις as the fundamental experience in Heidegger's thought), one could also evaluate the central position which the concept of facticity occupies in the thought of the early Heidegger.

19. Martin Heidegger, *Being and Time*, tr. J. Macquarrie and E. Robinson (New York, 1962), p. 82.

20. Ibid., pp. 173–74.

21. Ibid., p. 175.

22. The analogy is of course purely formal. But that Heideggerian ontology assumes the traits of a psychology is not indifferent for its place in the history of the *Seinsfrage*.

23. *GA*, vol. 26, p. 171.

24. The word *Weise* (from the same root as the German *wissen* and Latin *videre*) must

be considered as a *terminus technicus* of Heidegger's thought. In the seminars of the 1921–22 winter semester, Heidegger plays on the possible meanings of the verb *weisen* and its derivations: "Leben bekommt jeweils eine Grundweisung und es wächst in eine solche hinein. . . . Bezugssinn je in einer Weise ist in sich ein Weisen und hat in sich eine Weisung, die das Leben sich gibt, die es erfährt: Unterweisung" (*GA*, vol. 61, p. 98).

25. Plato, *Seventh Letter*, 343 b–c.

26. *SuZ*, p. 42.

27. In the "Letter on Humanism," Heidegger explicitly denies this interpretation of the *existentia/essentia* relation: "But it would be the ultimate error if one wished to explain the sentence about man's ek-sistent essence as if it were the secularized transference to human beings of a thought that Christian theology expresses about God (*Deus est suum esse* [God is His Being]); for ek-sistence is not the realization of an essence, nor does ek-sistence itself even effect and posit what is essential." See "Letter on Humanism" in Martin Heidegger, *Basic Writings*, ed. D. F. Krell (San Francisco, 1977), p. 207. Another passage from the same letter shows that the existence/essence relation remains fundamental in Heidegger's thought, even after *Being and Time*: "in *Being and Time* no statement about the relation of *essentia* and *existentia* can yet be expressed since there it is still a question of preparing something precursory," p. 209.

28. A genealogy of the *essentia* and *existentia* contraction offered by Heidegger shows that this relation has often been thought of, in the history of philosophy, in a more complex way than as a simple opposition. Without speaking about Plato (who explicitly asserts the indiscernibility of ὄν and of ποῖον in the *Seventh Letter*), the Aristotelian τί ἦν εἶναι could itself be understood in the same perspective. As far as Stoic substance is concerned, the notion of ἴδιος ποῖον implies the very paradox of a "Being-such" (ποῖον) which is its own. In a similar way, V. Goldschmidt showed that "the manners of Being" (πος ἔχειν) do not constitute an extrinsic determination of substance but reveal it and exercise it (they "do their gymnastics," according to Epictetus's beautiful image). What remains to be interrogated is the relation between Spinoza's *causa sui (cuius essentia involvit existentiam)* and the Heideggerian determination of Dasein (*das Wesen des Daseins liegt in seiner Existenz*).

29. The observation is L. Amoroso's in "La Lichtung," *Il pensiero debole* (Milan, 1983), pp. 137–63.

30. J. Derrida, "Geschlecht," *Cahiers de l'Herne:* M. Heidegger (Paris, 1983).

31. *GA*, vol. 26, p. 173. In the same text, Heidegger puts the facticity of Dasein into relation with its spatiality (*Räumlichkeit*). If one considers that the word *Streuung* comes from the same root as the Latin *sternere (stratum)*, which refers to extension and to horizontality, one can then see in this *ursprüngliche Streuung* one of the reasons for the irreducibility and for the spatiality of Dasein to the temporality which is affirmed at the end of *Zeit und Sein*.

32. This word is evidently to be understood in an ontological sense and not a psychological one. It is because facticity originally belongs to Dasein, that it could mean something like a fetish in the narrow sense of the term. On the status of the fetish in § 13 of *Being and Time*, see W. Hamacher's important considerations, "Peut-être la question," *Les fins de l'homme* (Paris, 1981), pp. 353–54.

33. "Das Dasein existiert faktisch. Gefragt wird nach der ontologischen Einheit von Existentialität, bzw. der wesenhaften Zugehörigkeit dieser zu jener" (*SuZ*, p. 181).

34. *SuZ*, p. 22.

35. Ibid., p. 179.

36. Ibid., p. 299.

37. *N.*, l, p. 55.

38. Ibid., p. 58.

39. M. Heidegger, *The Will to Power as Art*, tr. D. F. Krell (San Francisco, 1979), pp. 47–48.

40. *WM*, p. 191.

41. "Letter on Humanism," p. 196.
42. *WM* p. 64.
43. *Ibid.,* p. 70.
44. *GA*, vol. 26, pp. 279–80.
45. Ibid., vol. 33, p. 114.
46. *WM*, p. 70.
47. *SD*, p. 44.
48. Ibid., p. 32. The thought that is here expressed is so disconcerting that the French translators (followed by the Italian translator) did not want to admit that which is nonetheless evident: that the word *entwachen* cannot in this context mean the same thing as *erwachen*. Heidegger here establishes a perfectly symmetrical opposition to the existing one between *Enteignis* and *Ereignis.*
49. Ibid., p. 44.
50. Ibid.
51. M. Heidegger, *Gelassenheit* (Pfüllingen, 1959), p. 24.
52. *SD*, p. 25.
53. J-L. Nancy, "L'amour en éclats," *Alea*, 7 (1986).

FIFTEEN

A Medieval Model of Subjectivity: Toward a Rediscovery of Fleshliness

Rémi Brague

Introduction

My topic is difficult, for many reasons. Making a detailed survey of so long a period as the Middle Ages and taking a synoptic view of a thousand years of thought in Greek, Latin, Arabic, and Hebrew is a feat of scholarship to which I am utterly unequal. Even if we suppose that a birds-eye view of the field should become possible, does it make sense to elicit something like a unified model of subjectivity from texts by so many different writers? Therefore I must first claim some indulgence.

But at the same time, I must defend my choice. Why did I choose such a topic? A first answer would be that it belongs to my field. I happen to be a medievalist, or a would-be medievalist, or an apprentice in the field of medieval studies.[1] But how is it there are medievalists? The relevance of medieval studies should not be taken for granted.

A case on their behalf might receive some support from the so-called "post-modern" movement. Should we admit, as a hypothesis, that we are after modernity, we could gain new freedom in our practice of the history of philosophy. We would dismiss the very idea of a teleology, of an orientation toward more and more "modern" ideas. Therefore premodern, especially medieval, thought would not be more antiquated or obsolete than any other kind of thought. On the other hand, we would not have to preach, as many medievalists did, for a return to the Middle Ages, for a *zurück zu*. The main reason is that the very idea of a return, of a going backward, itself supposes that there is a teleology in history. To go against history's grain, history first must have a grain—the very assumption that postmodernity calls into question.[2]

As for the question I am trying to ask, if this hypothesis could be confirmed, some elements of premodern thought could possibly be retrieved, not only ancient thought but that of the Middle Ages as well. The idea of subjectivity may be the core of the modern project. Does a premodern period in the history of philosophy, especially the very period that modernity wanted to do away with, i.e., the Middle Ages, have something to tell us on this matter? Can we spot in the medieval frame of mind some elements we could make use of in a postmodern synthesis? In particular, could these elements help us toward a more adequate model of subjectivity? Such a question must remain more of a program for research in progress than a bundle of ready-made answers.

A Research Program: Heidegger on Subjectivity and Modernity

We should take our bearings by gaining a clearer understanding of the concept of subjectivity and of the relationship that obtains between this concept and the nature of modernity. The existence of such a link between modernity and subjectivity is not an exceptional claim. Nor is it a new one. It occurs in Hegel, but with some qualifications, since subjectivity is present already within Judaism and in the Roman world with the emergence of Christianity, though it becomes conscious of itself—as freedom—only in modern times. The strongest plea for a quasi-identification of modernity with the domination of subjectivity and its thoroughgoing analysis may be gathered from a cluster of texts by Heidegger. All of them were written in the late thirties, when Heidegger, just recovering from his Nazi hangover and working on his *Contributions to Philosophy*, sketched a first draft of an analysis of the modern world: the lecture courses "The Question of the Thing" (winter 1935–36), and "European Nihilism" (on Nietzsche) (second trimester 1940, now in *Nietzsche*, vol. 2), as well as the essay "The Age of the Word Picture" (June 1938).

Heidegger calls into question the common interpretation that presupposes that man is a subject, the famous "*(Wir) Menschen als Subjekte*" of Husserl.[3] The question to be asked is: how is it that man became a subject?[4] Or, conversely, how is it that the place of the subject, which had been the decisive place since the outset with Aristotle's ὑποκείμενον, came to be occupied by man? More generally, how is it that the role of "subjectity" came to be played by subjectivity?[5]

Man is a subject because it necessarily accompanies every representation along with the object that is its content of representation,[6] i.e., because the subject is the first object of certainty: "The representing I is far more essentially and more necessarily co-represented in every 'I represent,' i.e., as the one toward which and back to which and before which all that is re-presented *(Vor-gestellte)* is presented *(hingestellt)*."[7] In my own words: the subject itself is first and foremost an object, i.e., the object of certainty (not of the "I"). The I must ascertain itself of its own being before it can become the "subject." The subject is the I, but only once it is determined with certainty. The subject reigns, but it does so only insofar as it is submitted to certainty.

In the more elaborate essay "The Age of the World Picture," we get a momentous statement: man becomes a subject in the same measure as the world becomes an image.[8] This gives us an important clue: what already is, or is not yet, a subject has something to do with the world. The world, on the other hand, can be either an image or not yet an image. There must be some presubjective mode of being of the "ego." And this way of being that the ego has before it becomes a subject corresponds to a mode of being of the world that is not yet an image. We can ask: What was the world when man was not yet a subject? What was man when the world was not yet an image?

Heidegger's account of modern subjectivity is far from being exhaustive. For instance, it has been objected that he hardly does justice to the "ego" of British empiricism, or to Kant.[9] He devotes a lengthy and careful analysis to the Greek "ego," exemplified by the sophist Protagoras. Furthermore, large parts of the *Introduction to Metaphysics* can be read as the study of the Greek ego he promises elsewhere.[10] On the other hand, however, Heidegger gives short shrift to the way in which the ego was experienced between the Greek era and the Cartesian revolution. Neither does he explain how the world was. Medieval thought hardly does more than furnish him with a backdrop against which modern thought becomes visible. It does not receive any definite content: for instance, Heidegger often alludes to the Christian certainty of salvation, but only as a remote forerunner of the modern certainty of subjectivity.[11] The emphasis on the certainty of salvation, on the other hand, is less medieval than Protestant, namely, premodern. Be that as it may, in spite of his early background as a medievalist, the Heidegger of the thirties, unlike the Heidegger of the formative years, does not deal with the Christian experience of the I as such, let alone with its medieval version.

Flesh as an Anthropological Criterion: Man and Angels

Thus our task should be to give a descriptive account of the medieval experience of the I and of the world. It goes without saying that the field that lies before our eyes is boundless. In order not to get lost, I will have to follow a definite theme. Of course, I could have chosen other themes. Some may even be more relevant. But this one, I hope, was not chosen totally at random. My Ariadne's thread through this maze will be flesh, fleshliness, our fleshly nature.

In the present essay, I will first study three aspects of the medieval experience of the flesh: its relevance for a definition of man, its link with the medieval theory of knowledge and self-knowledge, and finally its moral reflection in humility. Then I will sketch some possible points of contact between this experience and some trends in contemporary thought.

Let me begin with an historical remark: man's carnal dimension became relevant to anthropology thanks to early Christian and patristic writers, who made a powerful case against Platonic dualism.[12] Still, since the scope of this essay is limited to medieval thought, I shall skip this historical theme.

For medieval thought, man is defined in various ways. According to the classical and most authoritative definition, bequeathed by Greek thought, man is an *animal rationale mortale*. The formula belongs to the hoard of stock definitions common to all medieval thinkers and dates earlier than the rediscovery of its source in Aristotle's *Politics*[13] during the Aristotelian renaissance of the thirteenth century.[14] To be sure, we find a more Neoplatonic formula in Augustine and in the Augustinian tradition: man is a rational soul making use of a mortal and earthly body.[15] But, unlike the Neoplatonists, Augustine insists on the fact that the link between the soul and the body is not unnatural.[16]

Now, for medieval thought, there are other living and intelligent beings, i.e., rational animals, namely angels. Medieval thought admits their existence from two sources, the streams of which intermingled in many ways: revealed religions and Neoplatonic philosophy. The former unanimously recognize beings intermediate between man and God; the latter says that man is located at the frontier of two worlds, between the angels and the animals. The idea of man as a μεθόριον, as an amphibious being, is older than the Middle Ages. We find it in many places in late Antiquity.[17] What is new is that the beings that tower above man are angels, not celestial bodies.[18]

As for angels, their existence is required by the logical necessity that underlies the definition of man. Let us quote a passage by Augustine: "homo medium quiddam est, sed inter pecora et angelos; ut, quia pecus est animal irrationale et mortale, angelus autem rationale et immortale, medius homo esset, inferior angelis, superior pecoribus, habens cum pecoribus mortalitatem, rationem cum angelis, animal rationale mortale."[19] In almost the same way, al-Farabi is said to have deduced a more complete scheme of created living beings—the jinns are added—from the various combinations of the two basic properties of rationality and mortality: the angels are rational and nonmortal; men are rational and mortal; the animals are nonrational and mortal; the jinns are nonrational and non-mortal.[20]

The ontological status of angels remained a moot point throughout the Middle Ages. They were agreed to be immortal. But it was a matter of controversy whether they were bodily or purely spiritual in nature. The second theory is the main trend among writers who were influenced by philosophy, especially by Neoplatonic speculation about pure intelligences as forms without matter. This is the case of Dionysius Areopagita, who drew heavily on Proclus.[21] On this matter, Muslim philosophers too were in the wake of Neoplatonism.[22] The Jews took up the same doctrine.[23] No wonder, then, that many Christians followed suit.[24]

For medieval man, the angels were not necessarily easy to experience, but they played a part in the intellectual scheme of being and had to be accounted for. Now, man is located between animals, which have bodies, and angels, which are either completely bodiless or whose bodies—celestial bodies—are incorruptible. If the superior beings are bodiless, the difference is the possession or non-possession of a body. If, on the other hand, they possess purer bodies than ours, the difference is the fleshly nature of our own body. This gave fleshliness a great relevance. One could not define man, hence locate him on the scale of beings, without taking into account his fleshly nature. Among created living beings, man had to distinguish himself on both sides: it was not enough to stress that his share in rationality differentiates him from brute beasts. One had to distinguish him from the angelic beings, too. And one could do that because of his fleshliness, a characteristic he alone among all rational beings possessed. Man is unique because he is flesh.

Flesh does not mean "body," although the body is fleshly. The word *flesh (caro)* stresses the weakness and flimsiness of the human body, when the latter is *in via*. This is clearly expressed by Augustine: "corpus enim sine corruptione, non proprie dicitur caro et sanguis, sed corpus. Si enim caro est, corruptibilis atque mortalis est; si autem jam non moritur, jam non corruptibilis; et ideo sine corruptione manente specie, non jam caro, sed corpus dicitur,"[25] i.e., sensitive and mortal. On the other hand, whereas our body makes of us a singular being, our flesh is a principle of continuity. It links us up to what we are not, but becomes us or helps us become ourselves. Flesh is made of the food we borrow from nature. And it is handed over to us by other members of the same species or by us to them—our parents, siblings, and children. And even after our resurrection it links us up to our previous bodies, inherited from the whole fabric of mankind. Such is the background of the theory of the "radical flesh" (*caro radicalis*) we keep as risen bodies.[26]

This idea of a fragility of the flesh does not mean that flesh should be conceived of as bad. On the contrary, there exists a positive outlook on the flesh in medieval thought. I will leave aside the early Christian forerunners of this idea in order to concentrate on the way in which the positive conception of fleshliness was once again brought to the fore during the high Middle Ages. This happened in the twelfth century.

Let me show this with the example of Bernard of Clairvaux. The context of the quotation I will cite is important: Bernard has to interrupt the continuity of his commentary on the Canticle because of the death of his brother, whose funeral homily makes up the twenty-sixth "Sermon on the Canticle." It is interesting to note that the speech he gave on this occasion was retained as an integral part of what Bernard wanted to say about the Canticle. Furthermore, Bernard once again had to interrupt his sermon to give vent to his grief in a gush of tears. After resuming his speech, he says that he was attached to his brother not only by carnal relation (*carnis necessitudo*) but also by a deeper unity. Therefore his death severed bonds that obtained between two parts of a same body. In view of such a bereavement, Bernard's flesh is not brazen (*nec caro mea aenea est*). Should anybody call his emotion (*affectus*) carnal, he would not haggle about it and confess he is human, for he is a man. He even risks a further step: "Sic nec hoc sufficit, nec carnalem negaverim. Nam et ego carnalis sum, venundatus sub peccato, addictus morti, poenis et aerumnis obnoxius. Non sum, fateor, insensibilis ad poenas, mortem horreo meam et meorum."[27] He therefore introduces or reintroduces in medieval thought a positive outlook on the flesh.[28]

As a further reflection on this text, we should draw attention to the subtle way in which many dimensions of fleshliness are intertwined. First, Bernard feels the sentiment of a loss in continuity in the fleshly web of human relationships. A brother is more akin than any neighbor because he comes from the same flesh. Second, he expresses his consciousness of his own finitude and mortality. Flesh is there to be torn asunder. Third, the break in continuity reveals this kind of affection, i.e., self-affection, as essential to man. The angels cannot suffer in this way, not only because they exceed our mortality but also because they do not share in a common species. They cannot experience, as we do, the rending of the web that links us to our fellows.

This conception of the flesh explains one of the main theses of Bernard's theory of love, the well-known idea according to which love must begin with carnal love. Carnal love is a positive first step on the path that leads love to its full bloom in charity toward oneself because of one's love for God.[29] Therefore it is remarkable to see that the fleshly nature of man can appear, in many passages, as something positive as such, not only as far as it is tempered by human dignity. It is present in the heavens themselves: even in Paradise, we were originally made of earth. But this clay was "clay of Paradise" (*limus paradisi*).[30]

The question as to which creature, man or angel, is the better remained open throughout the Middle Ages. Furthermore, the answer commonly received was not the same in every religious tradition. Among Jewish thinkers, a majority decided in favor of the angels.[31] In the Muslim world, the Qur'an spoke most decisively in favor of man.[32] In the Christian world, on the other hand, a discordant albeit discrete note was struck. The accent is laid more decisively on man's historicity. The latter is a consequence of his fleshliness. Human love must ripen to charity, which involves time. The angel decides in no time and remains eternally what it once chose to be. Man can fall and be redeemed. From this point of view, man is to some extent more worthy than angels. Angels can learn something from man, for what happened in human history is inaccessible to angelic minds.[33] This is one of the reasons that induce some medieval authors to speak of a certain superiority of man over angels.[34]

Flesh and Consciousness: The Sense of Touch

Fleshliness is behind the commonly accepted medieval theory of knowledge, i.e., the theory according to which every knowledge must take its bearings from sensory experience. This holds true even where knowledge is supposed to grasp the immaterial.[35] Such a theory may be read even before the invasion of Hellenic knowledge through the Arabic channel in the twelfth century. We find it under the pen of Saint Bernard, who died in 1153, in his commentary on the Canticle—to be precise, in the fifth sermon, probably pronounced in 1135. The context is a comparison between four kinds of spirits: God, the angels, man, and the animals. The doctrine may come from Dionysius Areopagita, although we cannot ascertain precisely through which channels. Man is bodily. He must have a body in order to grasp the material world.[36] But he must as well go through the body in order to reach higher, spiritual realities (*ad spiritualia et intelligibilia proficiendo pertingere*). Man is a spirit wrapped up in flesh and an inhabitant of earth (*involutus carne ac terrae incola spiritus*). Therefore, he must begin with the consideration of sensible things (*ex consideratione sensibilium proficiens*), in order gradually and slowly (*gradatim quodammodo paulatimque*) to arrive where the angels arrive without effort.[37]

Can we be more specific about this sensory perception? It is often the case that a cultural world is characterized through the central part played in it by a definite organ of sensation. For instance, the Greeks are supposed to have been men of the eye,[38] whereas ancient Hebrews allegedly were men of the ear. I do not believe very much in the worth of such sweeping statements, but they may have a heuristic value. If we try to find which sensation helps us characterize the medieval world, I suggest we choose touch.

In what follows, I will try to show how touch has the closest relationship with flesh. I will do that through a sketch of Aristotle's doctrine of touch and of the flesh. I can to some extent legitimate my choice of this theme. First, it is a matter of common knowledge that medieval philosophy is grounded on Aristotle. This is especially true where the Western world is concerned, be it Latin-speaking or Arabicized, for in Byzantium and in eastern, Avicennian, Islam, a powerful Neoplatonic trend somewhat curbed Aristotelianism. On the matter of psychology, however, as a part of physics, even the Neoplatonists remained by and large in the wake of Aristotle. Second, in the Western world, although Aristotle's influence on the Church Fathers was minimal, Christian thought as such, even before it confronted the texts of Aristotle, was already in keeping with the latter's anthropology. For its doctrine of resurrection adduced it in stress the unity of the human person—body and soul indissolubly welded together.[39]

This primacy of touch exists in the philosophical realm, too. For Aristotle, knowledge is grounded on sensory perception, since intellectual knowledge proceeds through abstraction and cannot take place without some reference to an image (φάντασμα).[40] Furthermore, sensory perception is basically touch. There is no perception without some sort of touch;[41] every perception occurs through touch.[42] What is touch? Aristotle explains that every sensation occurs through a medium. This seems obvious for sight, hearing, and smelling, for we perceive colors, sounds, and smells from a distance. In the same way as scents are wafted to us through air, light is the act of the diaphanous (διαφανές) that separates the eye from the colors that are its limits on the bodies. However, we perceive tangible qualities as soon as, and only when, we come in contact with them. Nevertheless, Aristotle shows that there is a medium of touch. This medium is flesh.[43] Flesh is made of earth; the latter is not pure, for then it could not perceive anything; rather, it is mingled with air and water. Touch is basically earthly.[44] It is the most bodily of all sensations.[45]

The doctrine according to which flesh is the medium of touch was hailed by Averroes as one of the most extraordinary speculative feats of Aristotle.[46] We will have to agree. But we will first have to mention the difficulties this doctrine had to cope with. To begin with, every sensation takes place through a medium, but it must affect an organ. What is the organ of touch? Aristotle's "official" doctrine is that the organ of touch is the heart,[47] which is the ultimate organ of every sensation as well.[48] But there is another fascinating passage in which flesh is explicitly said to be the organ (αἰσθητήριον) of touch, either the first organ, in the same way as the pupil in vision, or the medium taken with the organ (τὸ δι' οὗ συνειλημμένον), as if the transparent in its entirety were taken together with the pupil.[49] Elsewhere, we read again that in touch and consequently in taste, the organ is either the body or some part of the body of the animals.[50]

Later commentators were at a loss how to understand that.[51] Areios Didymos contended that the sense of touch requires an outer medium. This may be a distortion arising from the use of some indirect source, most probably in a textbook.[52] But Alexander, who had a direct access to the texts, did not recoil from calling into doubt the very status Aristotle gave to flesh. According to him, flesh is not the medium but the very organ of sensation.[53] Avicenna tried to remain faithful to the First Teacher by steering a middle course: flesh is the organ of touch, but it acquires the capability of receiving tangible impressions from the nerves that transmit those impressions to the authentic organ, the heart.[54] For Averroes, flesh is the organ of touch.[55] Touch does not even require any medium to perceive.[56] A medium is needed, either when the sensibles are not in contact with the organ or in order that it be lifted from a material to a spiritual mode of being[57]—which is hardly faithful to Aristotle. There is an external medium, too, which we do not perceive,[58] and which may be the thin layer of air that separates our skin and the external bodies.[59] On this matter, Aquinas follows the "Commentator" implicitly.[60] However, he does speak of the *organum et medium tactus*.[61]

We need not expatiate further on doxographic data. All that matters is that the commentators' perplexities point to a lack of clarity in Aristotle's account. In my opinion, this is grounded in the paradoxical character of the phenomenon itself. We are at a loss how to distinguish the medium and the organ. The part that flesh plays in touch is a peculiar one. In other kinds of perception, the medium is outside. In touch, it is inside. Writes Themistius: "in the case of the other sensations, what undergoes an alteration is not the medium itself, but the sensory organ through the medium. . . . In the case of touch, the organ and the medium are affected together (ἅμα πάσχει): flesh itself becomes colder and warmer."[62] "The animal does not perceive through flesh, but together with flesh (ἅμα τῇ σαρκί)."[63]

In touch, the medium is said to be inside, connatural, or, if I may venture an overly fastidious translation, "added through a process of natural growth (προσπέφυκος)."[64] At first sight, this distinguishes touch from other senses: as a rule, the medium is outside. In touch, it is inside. However, once we have acknowledged the peculiarity of touch, we can see that it is no real exception. There is something like an inner medium for other perceptions: sight takes place through the transparent (διαφανές) as medium. But there is some of the transparent in the very organ of sight, some water in the eye.[65] In the same way, there is some air in the ear.[66] The distinction between inner and outer refers again to fleshliness: "in us" means surrounded with flesh. Flesh is in contact with itself before it can perceive.

The medium is inside. Inside or outside of what? We do not get any answer from Aristotle. He does not tell us exactly to what flesh, as the medium of touch, is connatural or "naturally added." Shall we understand "to the body as the organ of perception"? But what is the sensing body apart from flesh? For even if the organ of touch is the heart, the heart is fleshly, hence connatural to the medium. The bones? They exist for the sake of touch,[67] but they cannot perceive, because they are made of earth exclusively. Flesh is, so to speak, added to itself. Flesh is its own addition: an inner distance that cannot be measured from some external point. Flesh is something like a dimensionality without dimension.

Knowledge is basically sensory perception, and sensory perception is basically touch. We can even go further and say that knowledge is basically thought of on the model of perception through touch. For Aristotle, knowledge is the encounter of a knower (subject) and of something known (object). Both reach their climax, nay, become what they are, through this encounter. Knowledge is the common act of the knower and the known.[68] Therefore the knower knows itself in the very act of knowing something else. This is the case because the knower is produced as such through nothing else than the act of knowing. Hence the act of knowing furnishes every attempt at knowing the knower with its very object. In touch we perceive what we touch and, at the same time, what makes us touch.[69] We do not see our eye, hear our eardrums, or smell our nostrils: we feel our flesh. We perceive not only the fact but also what makes it possible at the same time. Therefore touch is a transcendental perception of sorts. In it the I knows itself. But it does not take hold of itself in the same way as the modern subject does, at least if we are to trust Heidegger's analysis. It does not make sure of itself prior to its knowing things.

On the contrary, its knowledge of itself is a side issue of perception or the intellectual grasp of other things.[70] If knowledge and self-knowledge are grounded on the sense of touch, we cannot grasp ourselves without the body. In my opinion, what is at stake here is not so much an implicit thesis on the "mind-body problem" as it is a phenomenological datum of our experience of the body. Such an experience may be expressed, too, in the ancient and medieval idea that our body is made of earth. This is more than a statement on the chemical composition of our organism—a statement, by the way, to which modern biology has given the lie. This is basically a statement on the relationship we have to our body. According to Husserl's well-known text against Copernicus, our relationship to earth is analogous with our relationship to our body.[71] Earth is what we must presuppose, what we cannot create, the ground on which we build, the basis on which we walk. It is analogous to the absolute immobility of the First Mover.[72] In the same way, we wake to conscious life and discover ourselves already in a body that we have not created.

Modernity began with the Cartesian ego. But in the Middle Ages we can find an interesting point of comparison in Avicenna's so-called "argument of the flying man." This argument has drawn the attention of many philosophers and scholars. As is well known, some historians thought of tracing back Descartes's *cogito* to it.[73] I will examine only one aspect of it. I will quote its first formulation in the so-called Book of Healing (*shifâ*):

> Everyone among us should imagine that he was created all of a sudden, and created in his perfect state. But his sight is veiled from the perception of external things. He

> was created falling in the air or in the void, so that the existence of air does not affect him in any way that he should sense it. There is a separation between his limbs, so that they do not cling to one another nor are in contact with each other. Then, it is inquired upon whether he would affirm the existence of his essence. There is no doubt that he would affirm that his essence is extant, although he will not affirm an extremity of his limbs or an inner part of his bowels, no heart, no brains, nothing external whatsoever. But he will affirm his own essence. He will not affirm any length, breadth or depth.[74]

This thought experiment is not very fair. We really cannot know how we would feel in such a state. Even if we leave this issue aside, however, it helps us better to understand what is at stake with the sense of touch. For what is excluded with so much care is first and foremost the sense of touch. Self-consciousness is supposed to remain when physical continuity with oneself is removed. The modern, or at least premodern, ring of this text lies in the exclusion of the body, more precisely in the reason that leads to its exclusion: the body is not discarded in a Platonic or Augustinian style, i.e., because of his material nature, but because it symbolizes what consciousness has to receive from outside and cannot construe.

Humility as Consciousness of Fleshliness

The virtue through which we are conscious of our fleshliness and its consequences is humility.[75] Are we allowed to link up humility to fleshliness? In Latin-speaking circles, such as the medieval clerics in Western Europe, the word *humilitas* was felt to stem from *humus*, "earth." *Humilis* is "prone to the earth," *humo clinis*.[76] In the same way, the word for "man," *homo*, was felt—as it is by modern philologists—to derive from *humus*.[77] We find the same etymology in other languages, Hebrew, for example: *adam* is related to *adamah*, the earth. The earth, as what we call a planet, is not only the abode of man. It is at the same time, as an element, the stuff on which our bodies are made. Bernard writes: "est tibi altera quaedam terra propinquior," and this earth is *caro*, flesh.[78] Elsewhere, we read "Hanc terram corpus nostrum intelligo"[79] or "caro, quae quasi terra in homine est."[80] We can show the link between flesh and humility in greater detail on three levels. I will call them anthropology, theory of knowledge, ethics.

From the point of view of anthropology, humility means our being conscious that we are not angels but earthly beings made of flesh and blood. We are first of all denizens of the earth, the lowest point in the universe, which receives all kinds of influences from above and becomes a sort of a cosmic dustbin.[81] Furthermore, our body is made of earth, a coarse and impure material that muddles the alacrity of thought.[82] Our fleshliness is vividly expressed by the ever-recurrent image of the "vessel of clay" (ὀστρακίνον σκεῦος). The comparison is Pauline.[83] It is echoed in many texts.[84] For instance, virgins are said to carry a priceless treasure in an earthen vessel and to know that it is extremely difficult to live the life of an angel among men, to dwell on earth in the same way as the heavenly beings, to lead a life of chastity in the flesh.[85]

Humility is not so much an affect as a kind of knowledge.[86] It is first of all self-knowledge: "humility is the virtue through which man becomes vile to his own eyes by means of a self-knowledge that reaches the peak of truth (humilitas est virtus, qua homo verissima sui cognitione sibi ipse vilescit)."[87] Now, the structure of knowledge that is involved in self-knowledge, such as humility enacts it, is the same as the structure we have witnessed in the case of touch. For the theory of knowledge, the primacy of touch means that we know ourselves because we know other things. We would not become conscious of ourselves if we were not previously affected, touched by outer things. In the same way, humility is mediated self-knowledge, a knowledge of the self that recognizes that the self does not receive its own selfhood from itself. This kind of knowledge is thematicized and receives the name of *consideratio*. In *consideratio*, the subject ensures its own continuity and purifies itself in order better to know.[88] But, unlike modern subjectivity as Heidegger describes it, this does not involve an attempt at taking hold of oneself.

Some Contemporary Issues and the Medieval Model of Subjectivity

Thus far I have tried to describe some dimensions of medieval subjectivity through the concept of flesh, together with some concepts that, in my opinion, are related to it. Now I will reflect briefly on the possible relevance of these ideas for our own philosophical scene.

ANTHROPOLOGY

We could, perhaps not without a modicum of pedagogical exaggeration, characterize modernity as the time without angels. It would be a fascinating task to tell in some detail how the angels disappeared from human consciousness, to write the history of the waning of the angels. Schopenhauer's quip against Kant's enlarging moral law to every rational being whatsoever may be its last page.[89] The consequence of the disappearance of the angels is either that man is alone or that man and God face one another in their common possession of reason. Modernity can be defined as the period during which we are or (supposing we are not modern any more, but "post-modern") were the only living beings that were supposed to partake of rationality. Now, it is not indifferent whether the only, or the most heavily stressed, specific difference that defines man is rationality or some dimension of affectivity. Stressing the former can lead us to exclude irrational human beings from mankind properly speaking. We can find traces of such an attitude in medieval thought,[90] but modern philosophy furnishes it with a complete rationale.

The rediscovery of the flesh may be an important philosophical task of our epoch. Some steps toward a phenomenology of fleshliness were made by Merleau-Ponty in his later work. For him, *chair* is a translation of the German word *Leib*; the French equivalent would be *corps propre*. But since French, like English but unlike German and Italian, distinguishes flesh and meat, Merleau-Ponty's reflections on *chair* take an original turn that more often than not drives him toward formulae that strongly remind one of Aristotle.[91] This reflection can be pursued.[92] This is a medieval enterprise. For medieval man, the importance of fleshliness was a consequence of the existence of a nonfleshly rationality in the angelic nature. Can we recover the sentiment of this importance? Of course, we have no angels, but we have computers. The computer may give us a chance to recover some sense of the fact that rationality is not the only specific difference of humanity. Computers may or may not have something like reason, but they undoubtedly have enough *ratio* to be able to reckon. They are material, but even what is "soft" in them is not flesh.

HERMENEUTICS

As a rule, historians of the hermeneutic problem skip the Middle Ages, sometimes even with some contempt, in order to jump directly from Augustine's *De doctrina Christiana* to Luther.[93] It would be worthwhile to show that this problem was extant in the medieval period. The possibility of communicating was not naively taken for granted.[94] Ancient and medieval thinkers tried to secure the possibility of communication because they felt it had to be ensured. This is the case in Antiquity.[95] But the problem was not forgotten in the Middle Ages. Aquinas deals with it explicitly in *De unitate intellectus*. The basic fact that we have to take into account is *hic homo singularis intellegit*.[96] The bold answer of Aquinas is that, in the same way the other functions of the soul, intellect is the form of the body and of a physical body,[97] of an individual body. Understanding is individual. By so doing, Aquinas is a forerunner of the Romantic idea of hermeneutics: *individuum est ineffabile* If any act of understanding is not the same act as the one of my neighbor, let alone as the act of some impersonal principle common to mankind, we have to make a special effort to grasp what we want to know and to assimilate it, an effort that everyone makes in his special way.

Furthermore, the hermeneutical problem as medieval thinkers see it is linked to the problem of fleshliness. Man speaks because he is fleshly. Angels do not speak.[98] This may be a merely negative fact: the coarseness of our flesh prevents us from a direct access to the other's thought. But it points to something more positive as well. We express ourselves through what we say to our neighbor. Knowledge is mediated through a social flesh. Self-knowledge is possible only through the mediation of the friend.[99] An analogy obtains between the individual and society. The city plays the same part as flesh. Social realities are fleshly in nature.

Now, Aquinas echoes Aristotle when he reflects on what is menaced by his opponents, i.e., what he calls *conversatio civilis*.[100] The phrase is interesting, especially from the point of view of modern hermeneutics, from Schleiermacher's *Dialectics*, for which conversation is the model of linguistic communication. Conversation must go on. And this conversation is *civilis*, political, in nature.

We can then point to a political dimension of medieval hermeneutics beyond the explicit political theories, such as were expressed in various commentaries on the newly rediscovered *Politics* of Aristotle. Ultimately, the city is possible and necessary because we can communicate solely insofar as we are individuals who, because we cannot share in the same truth by insight, must attain it by exchanging our thoughts.

SUBJECT AS DASEIN

Humility supposes an implicit doctrine of the ego. The Cartesian ego, if not the modern ego in general, is a thing, a thinking thing, a *res cogitans*. For medieval thought, the ego is not a thing; it is even nothing. In a few words this doctrine holds: I am nothing. We can read this formula several times under the pen of Bernard.[101] I quote an especially relevant passage: "Woe to the man who strives exclusively toward what is exterior (*ea quae foris sunt*), ignores what is interior to him (*ignarus interiorum suorum*), and deems he is something while he is nothing (*putans aliquid se esse, cum nihil sit*), for by so doing he leaves the right path."[102]

I present this sentence divested of its context—an exhortation not to look at the external behavior of the monk and to pay attention to his heart—and I take it literally, for in my opinion it furnishes us with a clear, albeit unconscious, formulation of the ontological status of the "I" that Bernard's doctrine of humility presupposes. To believe one is something amounts to ignoring what is inside and to spilling into external things. We easily recognize the Augustinian contradistinction of the inside (*intus*) and the outside (*foris*); according to Augustine, the self is tempted to mistake itself for a body and, when it yields, it gets alienated from its own true ontological status.[103] However, although the conceptual furniture is borrowed from Augustine, Bernard gives it a highly remarkable twist. The parallel on which the passage is grounded implies a paradoxical turning of the tables. We are prepared to hear that interiority plays the part of true reality, whereas external things turn out to possess only a sham existence. Now, to the contrary, things "are" well and truly (*quae foris sunt*), whereas, the *interiora* are left without the verb "to be." Hence it is because we assimilate ourselves, through our desire, to what is outside that we mistake ourselves for something. Conversely, it is insofar as we become conscious of ourselves that we consider our inner selves, authentically, as nothing.

We could go further in this interpretation by Bernard of his own doctrine of humility. To be nothing means not to be any thing (*rem*) whatsoever. To be nothing, for the "I", means that it is none of the realities that are present in the world. This idea is akin to a whole series of theses on the nature of subjectivity that we formulated along the course of the history of philosophy. I will give four examples quoted in their chronological order. For Aristotle, passive intellect, "before it intellects, is actually none of the beings (οὐδέν ἐστιν ἐνερνείᾳ τῶν ὄντων πρὶν νοεῖν)."[104] The same can be said of intelligence (*Intelligenz*) according to Fichte, even if the reason is exactly the contrary: "No being (*Seyn*) properly speaking, no subsistance (*Bestehen*) comes to" intelligence because it is pure activity, a Doing without any Doer.[105] According to Wittgenstein, "the subject does not belong to the world, but is a limit (*Grenze*) of the world."[106] Finally, something like this can be formulated in the phenomenological vocabulary of both the early and the mature Heidegger, who, to mention this *en passant*, was a reader of Bernard, too.[107] For him, Dasein is not one of the realities "at hand" (*vorhanden*) in the world. To some extent, we can say it is "nothing."[108]

ETHICS

Humility is viewed by the Middle Ages as the ground of all virtues. It is not a single virtue, but the virtue of the virtues. It is "the guardian of all the virtues,"[109] "the salt of virtues,"[110] their ground and basis.[111] We find analogous expressions in the Jewish world.[112] Humility is the virtue of virtues because it is the mode of presence of the moral subject as such. The recovery of humility could help us toward something like an immanent ethics of Dasein, an ethics of being-in-the-world.

Humility reduces man to his own mere humanity and drives him toward a resolute sanctification of what in man is purely human. Here again, fleshliness is present. The key text may be: "in the same way, the treasure of chastity shines brighter (*illustrior*) in a vessel of clay, and virtue is better proven (*probabilior*) in a brittle flesh."[113] Bernard of Clairvaux says in a sermon on Saint Martin that his merits were all the greater that he was "plainly a human being, that did not possess anything divine in nature (*homo purus, nihil de natura divinitatis habens*)." So radically human, as a matter of fact, that Bernard feels impelled to take up the classical definition of man and to apply it to him: "a rational animal, nay mortal, earth-born (*rationale animal, etiam et mortale, terrigena*)."[114] Bernard does not set *homo purus* over against Christ, for the latter's human nature, according to orthodox theology, is not diminished by the admixture of the divine nature he also possesses. *Homo purus* is thought of in contradistinction to the patriarchs and prophets. We can feel here something like a muffled prefiguration of what will be formulated much later; it looks as if Bernard was dimly conscious of something like a disenchantment of the world (Max Weber's *Entzauberung der Welt*). We are no longer in an epoch in which the divine was more immediately accessible to us.[115] This may be a first step toward an ethics of postsecularization.

I have given a sketch of a possible approach of subjectivity in medieval thought through the concept of flesh. I have emphasized some possible points of contact with some contemporary issues that could make it relevant to us. By so doing, I do not pretend to enlist the history of philosophy in the service of any of our fads. Nevertheless, I do believe that contemporary thinkers should not suppose they can carry on dialogues with only modern or ancient thinkers and that medieval thinkers ought to be considered as worthy dialogical partners.

NOTES

1. See Rémi Brague, "Das Studium der mittelalterlichen Philosophie als Teil einer Besinnung auf die europäische Kultur," in A. Speer, ed., *Philosophie und geistiges Erbe des Mittelalters* (Cologne, 1994), pp. 53–65.

2. The phrase about history's grain is Walter Benjamin's, in *Thesen zur Philosophie der Geschichte*, § 7, in *Schriften* (Frankfurt, 1955), vol. 1, p. 498.

3. *Die Krisis der europäischen Wissenschaften und die transzendentale Phänomenologie*, in *Husserliana*, vol. 6 (The Hague, 1962), § 2, p. 4.

4. *Nietzsche* (Pfüllingen, 1961), vol. 2, p. 141.

5. Ibid., pp. 167, 182.

6. *Holzwege* (Frankfurt, 1963, 4th ed.), p. 100.

7. *Nietzsche*, vol. 2, p. 154 f.

8. *Holzwege*, pp. 85, 88.

9. See A. Renaut, *L'ère de l'individu. Contribution à une histoire de la subjectivité* (Paris, 1989), p. 40 ff.

10. Heidegger may have felt that the promise was not yet fulfilled, however, when he took part in the seminar at Le Thor (1966). See *Questions IV* (Paris, 1976), p. 222.

11. *Holzwege*, p. 103; *Die Frage nach dem Ding* (Tübingen, 1962), p. 77; *Nietzsche*, vol. 2, pp. 133, 146.

12. See G. G. Stroumsa, "*Caro salutis cardo:* Shaping the Person in Early Christian Thought,: *History of Religions*, 30, no. 1 (August 1990), pp. 25–50.

13. Aristotle, *Politics*, I, 2, 1253 a 9 f.; VII, 13, 1332 b 5. On the context, see Rémi Brague, *Aristote et la question du monde. Essai sur le contexte cosmologique et anthropologique de l'ontologie* (Paris, 1988), p. 261 ff.

14. See Augustine, *On Trinity*, VII, 4, 7 (Bibliothèque Augustinienne, vol. 15, p. 528); Scotus Erigena, *De Divisione Naturae*, IV, 7 (Patrologia Latina (= PL) 122, 768 bc); Bernard of Clairvaux, *In dedicatione ecclesiae*, V, 7 (PL 183, 533 c); S. Bernard, *Opera*, ed. J. Leclercq et al. (Rome, 1957 ff.) (= Opp.) V, 393; *De consideratione* IV, 7 (PL 182, 746 b; Opp. III, 415).

15. *De Moribus Ecclesiae catholicae*, I, 27, 52; *In Joannem*, XIX, 15 (Corpus Christianorum, Series Latina, XXXVI), p. 199.

16. See E. Gilson, *Introduction à l'étude de saint Augustin* (Paris, 1969), 4th ed., p. 58.

17. See Plotinus, IV, 8 [6], 4, 32 (*amphibios*) ; III, 2 [47], 8, 9; Hierocles, *Commentary on the Golden Verses*, XX, 462 b, ed. Mullach.

18. For an instance of the latter idea, see Hierocles, XXIII, p. 468 b.

19. Augustine, *City of God*, IX, 13, 3.

20. Farabi, *Answers to Questions People Had Asked Him*, no. 4, in *Two Philosophical Treatises*, ed. J. al-Yasin (Beirut, 1987), p. 80 f.

21. See *De Divinis Nominibus*, IV, 1 (Patrologia Graeca 3, 693 c); VI, 2 (856 c); *Caelestis Hierarchia*, I, 3 (121 c); II, 4 (144 b); *Ecclesiastica Hierarchia*, I, 2 (373 a).

22. On Muslim angelology as a whole, see F. Jadaane, "La place des anges dans la théologie musulmane," *Studia Islamica*, 41 (1975), pp. 23–61. On the philosophers, see pp. 33–42. See Farabi, *Opinions of the Citizens of the Virtuous City*, ch. 10, p. 47 (ar.) / 37 (fr.); *as-Siyāsa al-madaniyya*, p. 32, ed. Najjar; Avicenna, *Healing, Metaphysics*, IX, 4, p. 404 (ar.) / 2, 139 (fr.).

23. See Maimonides, *Guide of the Perplexed*, I, 49 beginning, etc.

24. See Aquinas, *De substantiis separatis;* Dante, *Convivio*, II, 5.

25. Augustine, *Sermon* 362, xv, 17 (PL 39, 1622).

26. See C. W. Bynum, "Material Continuity, Personal Survival and the Resurrection of the Body: A Scholastic Discussion in Its Medieval and Modern Contexts," *History of Religions*, 30, no. 1 (August 1990), pp. 51–85 quotation on p. 70.

27. *In Canticum canticorum*, 26, vi, 9 (PL 183, 909 cd; Opp. I, 177).

28. The importance of this text for a new conception of fleshliness was seen by C. Morris, *The Discovery of the Individual: 1050–1200* (London, 1972), p. 67.

29. *De diligendo Deo*, VIII, 23 ff. Same idea in William of Saint-Thierry, *Commentary on the Song of Songs*, § 20, p. 50, ed. Davy.

30. *In vigilia nativitatis*, IV, 7 (PL 183, 103 b; Opp. IV, 225). A. Maiorino Tuozzi, *La "Conoscenza di sè" nella scuola cisterciense* (Naples, 1976), p. 29, clearly saw what this image implies.

31. See the references to the controversy on whether man or angels (mainly understood as the minds of the celestial bodies) is the ultimate goal of creation (Saadia Gaon, Abraham Ibn Ezra, etc.) in the extremely rich note of H. Malter, *Saadia Gaon: His Life and Works* (Philadelphia, 1921), p. 212 s., n. 485.

32. Qur'an, II, 31 ff.

33. *Ephesians* 3: 10.

34. See William of Saint-Thierry, *De natura corporis et animae*, II (PL 180, 721 d); Aquinas, *Summa theologica*, I, q. 93, a 3; Dante, *Convivio*, IV, 19, 6.

35. See Aquinas, *Contra gentiles*, I, 12, p. 10 b.

36. *In Cant.*, 5, I, 1 (PL 183, 799 ab; Opp., I, 21).

37. *In Cant.*, 5, I, 3–4 (PL 183, 800 ab = Opp., I, 23).

38. U. von Wilamowitz-Moellendorff, *Der Glaube der Hellenen*, I, 45.

39. See Stroumsa, p. 42.

40. *On the Soul*, III, 7, 431 a 16 f.

41. Ibid., II, 3, 415 a 3; III, 13, 435 a 12 f, b 2; *On Sleep and Wakefulness*, 2, 455 a 23.

42. *On the Soul*, III, 13, 435 a 18.

43. Ibid., II, 11, 423 b 26 s.

44. *De sensu*, 2, 438 b 30.

45. *Parts of Animals*, II, 1, 647 a 20; 8, 653 b 29.

46. Quoted by Simon ben Zemach Duran, *Magen Aboth*, III, 4; reprint of the Livorno edition (1785) by Makor (Jerusalem, n.d.), p. 50 a.

47. *De sensu*, 2, 439 a 1 f.

48. Bonitz, *Index Aristotelicus*, 365 b 34–48.

49. *Parts of Animals*, II, 8, 653 b 24–26.

50. *Generation of Animals*, II, 6, 743 b 37 f.

51. See D. Kaufmann, *Die Sinne: Ein Beitrag zur Geschichte der Physiologie und Psychologie im Mittelalter aus hebräischen und arabischen Quellen*, (Budapest, 1884), pp. 172–91, a treasure-trove which I have very much drawn upon.

52. Fgt. 17 Diels. See P. Moraux, *Geschichte des Aristotelismus bei den Griechen von Andronikos bis Alexander von Aphrodisias*, vol. 1 (New York, 1973), pp. 303 ff.

53. Alexander, *In De anima*, 56, 14–59, 20. Criticized by Themistius, *In De anima*, 76, 17–24, and Averroes, *In De anima*, II, 109, 12–19, p. 299, and 116, 56–57, p. 311 f.

54. *On the Soul*, II, 3, p. 72 s., ed. Bakos.

55. *Epitome of the De Anima*, IV, 5, § 66, p. 64, ed. Gomes Nogalez.

56. *Talhîs kitâb al-hiss wa-l-mahsûs*, in A. Badawi, *Aristotelis de anima* (Kuwait, 1980, 2d ed.), p. 193, 7 f.

57. *Epitome of the De Anima*, IV, 5, § 72, p. 67.

58. *Long Commentary in De Anima*, § 113 f., p. 304 ff., ed. Crawford.

59. See Falqera, *Sefer ha–Nefesh*, in *Kitvey R. Shem Tov Falqera*, vol. 2, (Jerusalem, 1970), ch. 11, p. 16.

60. *Commentary on the De Anima*, II, xxiii, 542, p. 185 a.

61. Ibid., 548, p. 186 b.

62. Themistius, *In De anima*, IV, p. 75, 12 15, ed. Heinze.

63. Ibid., 76, 24 f.

64. *On the Soul*, II, 11, 423 a 15 s.

65. *Generation of Animals*, II, 6, 744 a 19 ff.

66. *On the Soul*, II, 8, 420 a 4 ff.

67. *Parts of Animals*, II, 8, 653 b 31.

68. *On the Soul*, III, 2, 425 b 26 f., 426 a 15 f.

69. See Brague, *Aristote et la question du monde*, p. 372.

70. *Metaphysics*, Λ, 9, 1974 b 36; *On the Soul*, III, 4, 429 b 9.

71. E. Husserl, "Grundlegende Untersuchungen zum phänomenologischen Ursprung der Räumlichkeit der Natur," in M. Farber ed., *Philosophical Essays in Memory of E. Husserl*, (1940), pp. 307–25, esp. 323.

72. *Motion of Animals*, 3, 699 a 25.

73. See S. Pines, "La conception de la conscience de soi chez Avicenne et chez Abu'l Barakat al-Baghdâdî," *The Collected Works of Shlomo Pines*, vol. 1 (Jerusalem, 1979), pp. 181–258 (on Avicenna, pp. 181–216). The first to put Avicenna in connection with

Descartes was probably G. Furlani, "Avicenna e il cogito ergo sum di Cartesio," *Islamica* (1927), pp. 53–72.

74. *Psychologie d'Avicenne*, I, 1, p. 18, 9–15, ed. Bakos; *Avicenna Latinus*, p. 36. An analogous parable occurs in V, 7, p. 252; *Avicenna Latinus*, p. 162, which refers back to the present passage. See too, the *Ishârât*, p. 303 f., tr. Goichon.

75. See Rémi Brague, "L'anthropologie de l'humilité," in R. Brague, ed., *Saint Bernard et la philosophie* (Paris, 1993), pp. 129–52.

76. Isidore of Seville, *Etymologies*, X, 116 (PL 82, 379 B); Papias, *Vocabulista*, p. 148 a.

77. Quoted by Quintilian, I, vi, 34, who does not approve of it. See Isidore of Seville, *Etymologies*, VII, vi, 4, s.v. Adam (PL 82, 275 a): "*humus hominis faciendi materia fuit*"; Papias, p. 147 a.

78. *Dominica in kalendis novembris*, II, 2 (PL 183, 347 a; Opp., V, 307).

79. *In festivitate omnium sanctorum*, I, 9 (PL 183, 457 c; Opp., V, 334).

80. Arnold of Bonneval, *De operibus sex dierum* (PL 189, 1529 E).

81. See Rémi Brague, "Le géocentrisme comme humiliation de l'homme," in R. Brague and J.-F. Courtine, eds., *Herméneutique et ontologie* (Paris, 1990), pp. 203–23, esp. 218–20.

82. See Job, 14: 4; Mishnah, *Pirqey Aboth*, III, 1 ("vile drop"—of semen); al-Muhâsibi in J. van Ess, *Die Gedankenwelt des Hârit al-Muhâsibi* (Bonn, 1961), p. 156; al-Ghazâli, *Ihyâ ùlûm ad-dîn*, III, 9 ("On the reprobation of pride and vanity"), (Istanbul, 1985), vol. 3, p. 330. One can note the sarcastic question "how can one be proud who passed twice through the channel of urine?" (al-Ghazâli, p. 329; Bahya ibn Paquda, *Duties of the Hearts*, VI, 5, p. 265, 18 s., ed. Yahuda).

83. 2 Corinthians 4, 7.

84. See Bernard of Clairvaux, *In Psalmum Qui habitat*, VII, 14 (PL 183, 208b; *Opera* IV, 423); XVII, 3 (PL 183, 251 d; Opp. IV, 488); *In nativitate Beatae Virginis Mariae*, 17 (PL 183, 447 a ; Opp. V, 287); *De diversis*, 18, 5 (PL 183, 589 b; Opera VI–1, 160).

85. *Super missus est*, III, 9 (PL 183, 75 d; Opp. IV, 42).

86. Isaac of Nineveh, *Mystic Treatises*, tr. A. J. Wensinck (Amsterdam, 1923), vol. 55, p. 298.

87. *De gradibus*, I, 2 (PL 182, 942 b; Opp. III, 17).

88. See B. Michel, "La considération et l'"unitas spiritus'," in R. Brague, ed, *Saint Bernard*, pp. 109–27.

89. *Grundlage der Moral*, § 6, p. 658.

90. See Rémi Brague, "Le déni d'humanité," *Lignes*, 12 (December 1990), pp. 217–32.

91. Maurice Merleau-Ponty, *Le visible et l'invisible* (Paris, 1964). On *chair* = *Leib*, p. 309. On the alleged radical newness of the concept, pp. 183, 193.

92. See D. Franck, *Chair et corps* (Paris, 1986).

93. See J. Grondin, *Einführung in die philosophische Hermeneutik* (Darmstadt, 1991), p. 51 f.

94. See the third part of Gorgias's *On Nonbeing*, fragment DK 82 B 3, in Sextus Empiricus, *Adv. Math.*, VII, § 65 ανερμηνευτον τωι πελας and 83–86 ; Plato, *Gorgias*, 481 c 5–d 1.

95. See Plato, *Parmenides*, 135 c 2; Aristotle, *Metaphysics*, Γ, 4, 1006 b 8; Themistius, *In On the Soul*, ch. 6, p. 104, 2 f., ed. Heinze.

96. *De unitate intellectus*, ch. 4, § 239, p. 83 a.

97. Ibid., ch. 1, § 180, p. 65 b.

98. Aquinas (who admits a *locutio*, but directly and without sound), *Summa Theologica*, Ia, q. 107, a 1, ad 1m; Dante, *De vulgari eloquentia*, I, iii, 1, p. 18, ed. Marigo. On Dante, see K. O. Apel, *Die Sprache in der Tradition des Humanismus von Dante bis Vico* (Bonn, 1975, 2d ed.).

99. See Aristotle, *Nicomachean Ethics*, IX, 9, 1169 b 33 f, and Aquinas, IX, x, § 1896, p. 496 a.

100. *De unitate*, ch. 3, § 216, p. 76 b. See Plotinus, *Enneads*, IV, 3 [27], 3, 25 ff.

101. See *De adventu domini*, IV, 4 (PL 183, 48 d; Opp. IV, 184); *De Grad.*, IV, 15 (PL

182, 950 b; Opp. III, 28); *De adventu domini*, IV, 4 (PL 183, 48 d; Opp. IV, 184); *In Psalm. Qui habitat*, XI, 5 (PL 183, 227 c; Opp., IV, 451).

102. *In capite jejunii*, II, 2 (PL 183, 172 c; Opp. IV, 360 s.).

103. See *On Trinity, X*, vii, 9, and context.

104. *On the Soul*, III, 4, 429 a 24.

105. *First Introduction to the Doctrine of Science*, § 7, SW I, p. 440.

106. *Tractatus Logico-Philosophicus*, 5. 632.

107. There exists a summary of a sermon by Saint Bernard made by Heidegger, probably when he was preparing a lecture course on the philosophical foundations of mysticism.

108. I quote the texts in Rémi Brague, "La phénoménologie comme voie d'accès au monde grec," in J.-L. Marion and G. Planty-Bonjour, eds., *Phénoménologie et métaphysique* (Paris, 1984), pp. 247–73, esp. 257 ff.

109. Cf. Jerome, *Epistola*, 148, 20; Augustine, *Sermon*, 69, I, 2 (PL 38, 441 [a]).

110. Isaac of Nineveh, vol. 72, p. 335 [499].

111. Anselm, *Miscellanea*, 17, in *Memorials*, ed. R. W. Southern; Bernard, *De consideratione*, V, xiv, 32 (PL 182, 806 d; Opp. III, 493); *De Moribus et officiis episcoporum*, V, 17 (PL 182, 821 a; Opp. VII, 113).

112. See Bahya, *Duties of the Heart*, VI, 8, p. 278, 8 ss. Yahuda; Maimonides, *Letter to R. Hisdai*, in *Qobets Teshuboth ha-Rambam ve-igerothaw* (Leipzig), vol. 2, p. 24 a; Nachmanides, *Iggereth Musar*, beginning, p. 374, ed. Chavel.

113. *In labore messis*, 3, 7 (PL 183, 642 d f.; Opp. V, 226).

114. *In festo s. Martini episcopi*, 9 (PL 183, 494 bc ; Opp. V, 405).

115. An analogous idea is to be found in Saint John of the Cross. See Rémi Brague, "L'impuissance du verbe. Le dieu qui a *tout* dit," *Eranos*, 1993.

SIXTEEN

"The First Times" in Rousseau's *Essay on the Origin of Languages*

Victor Gourevitch

Rousseau had begun the *Discourse on the Origin of Inequality* with the conjecture or abstraction of isolated, self-sufficient beings—one hesitates to call them men—and gone on to show how difficult, indeed how impossible it is to conceive why or how such beings would establish any contacts, let alone languages and communities. He had thus created the impression that language, together with all of man's other most distinctive attributes, may be altogether accidental. Nothing in the *Essay on the Origin of Languages* so much as suggests that possibility.[1] On the contrary. It begins on a most emphatically traditional note: "Speech differentiates man from the other animals . . ." (1[1], p. 240).[2]

His point of departure in the *Essay* is not isolated, self- sufficient individuals but community and communication: "As soon as one man was recognized by another as a sentient, thinking being, similar to himself, the desire and the need to communicate to him his sentiments and his thoughts made him seek the means to do so." 1[2], p. 240).Only someone looking for it would find in this statement the suggestion of a possible earlier time when men might not have recognized one another. At the end of the paragraph Rousseau does add that men had initially lived "dispersed." But he does not, in the opening chapters of the *Essay*, say anything about how we are to understand this "dispersion." Rather, he devotes these opening chapters to reflections about "the different means of communicating our thoughts." Indeed, on one level the entire work can be seen as one sustained inquiry into what is distinctive about speech and song in contrast to other modes of communication. He initially states this contrast in terms of speech and gesture; by and by he develops it in terms of speech and writing; then in terms of the vocal arts—song and, more generally, music and poetry—and the visual arts—drawing and painting; and all the while he attends to the underlying, more general and fundamental contrast between seeing and hearing. He turns to the thematic discussion of men's initial "dispersion" and of the "first" or earliest times in the second and central section of the *Essay*, chapters 8-12.

He begins this account of the beginnings with the remark that whenever he speaks of "the first times," he is speaking of the period of men's dispersion, "regardless of the age one chooses to assign to mankind at this stage" (9[1]*,

p. 260; 1[2], p. 240).[3] On one occasion he invites the reader to imagine men "dispersed" in an early paradise of "perpetual spring" and plenty (9[22], 266),[4] only to dismiss the fancy: they would never have become sociable in such a setting: "He who willed man to be sociable inclined the globe's axis at an angle to the axis of the universe" (9[23], p. 266).

Indeed, a few pages after saying that the earliest times are the times of dispersion, he notes that according to the Bible ten generations separate these earliest times from the times of the patriarchs (9[13], p. 264), and by this count his earliest times are the times of Noah's children, the times of the Flood and of the period immediately following it.[5] The Bible itself speaks of those times as the times of dispersion: the survivors were to disperse to the four corners of the earth and to repopulate it. That is the strong meaning of "dispersion." Now, the Flood can be, and often it has been understood as a new beginning.[6] On that view, the period immediately following it would, quite strictly speaking, be the first or earliest times of the new era.

> Adam spoke; Noah spoke; granted. Adam had been taught by God himself. When they separated, the children of Noah gave up agriculture, and the common language perished together with the first society. This would have happened even if there had never been a tower of Babel. Solitaries living on desert islands have been known to forget their own language. After several generations away from their country men rarely preserve their original language even when they work together and live in society with one another.
>
> Scattered throughout this vast desert of a world, men relapsed into the dull barbarism they would have been in if they had been born of the earth. By following [the thread of] these entirely natural ideas the authority of Scripture can easily be reconciled with ancient records and there is no need to treat as fables traditions that are as old as are the peoples that have handed them down to us. (9[14], [15], p. 264; cf. 9[8], p. 262 f.)

God enjoined Noah and his sons to "replenish the earth,"[7] that is to say, to disperse, and they did so. But as so often in Genesis, we are given two versions of what happened. According to the better-known and more dramatic story, Noah's sons refused to heed the divine injunction, built the tower of Babel in an effort to defy it, and had to be dispersed by direct divine intervention: "And the whole earth was of one language and of one speech. . . . And they said, Go to, let us build us a city and a tower . . . lest we be scattered abroad upon the face of the whole earth. . . . And the Lord said . . . Go to, let us go down and there confound their language, that they may not understand one another's speech. So the Lord scattered them abroad from thence upon the face of all the earth. . . ."[8] However, according to the first but less dramatic account, the sons of Noah did heed the divine injunction to replenish the earth by each taking his family and going his own way: "By these were the isles of the Gentiles divided in their lands: every one after his tongue, after their families, in their nations."[9]

It is to this earlier biblical account that Rousseau's "entirely natural ideas" regarding men's dispersion or "the first times" closely conforms. He consistently reads the biblical account in the light of such "entirely natural ideas," searching it for clues and confirmation of his own understanding not only of the earliest beginnings, but also of the successive stages in the rise and growth of societies.[10] Quite aside from prudential considerations, he would clearly like to find as much agreement as possible between this account and what can be learned from consulting the unaided human reason or the philosophical tradition—especially Plato's *Laws* and Lucretius's poem—on the one hand, and the historical record on the other.

In the *Essay*, Rousseau brackets both the biblical story of the ten generations preceding the Flood, and his own conjectures regarding the "pure" state of nature—the state of men devoid of, or prior to all artifice and convention, and in particular of family and of language—which takes up so much of Part I of the *Discourse on Inequality*. In the Exordium to the *Discourse* he had pointed out that

> if the Writings of Moses are granted the credence owed them by every Christian Philosopher, it has to be denied that, even before the Flood, Men were ever in the pure state of Nature, unless they relapsed into it by some extraordinary Occurrence: a Paradox it would be most embarrassing to defend, and altogether impossible to prove.[11]

According to the writings of Moses, men did not find themselves in that state before the Flood because the first man had "received some lights and Precepts immediately from God"; they presumably did not find themselves in the pure state of nature after the Flood because of God's convenant with them;[12] and it would certainly be a paradox embarrassing to uphold and impossible to prove that they *re*lapsed into a state in which they had presumably never found themselves in the first place. Some scholars have maintained that although Rousseau barely alludes to this embarrassing paradox in the *Essay* ("I call first the times of men's dispersion, regardless of the age one chooses to assign to mankind at that period," 9[1]*, p. 260), he does in effect uphold it in that work; some have even pointed out that he goes out of his way to call his readers' attention to the fact that it follows from the writings of Moses himself that after the Flood men did lapse into the state they would have been in if they had been born of the earth.[13] His only concession to the writings of Moses in the *Essay* is his conspicuous omission of the expressions "state of nature" and "pure state of nature"; or, more precisely, of the expression "state of nature." For the so-called "pure state of nature" has no place in the *Essay*. Even if Noah and his sons should by and by have "relapsed" into the condition they would have been in if they had been earth-born (9[15], p. 264, 9[22], p. 266) because they by and by forgot what men had been and known before the Flood, and so by and by came to be without all natural and supernatural knowledge, traditions, and skills, Rousseau depicts them as from the first living in "families" (9[1], p. 260; 9[4], pp. 261 f.),[14] and as from the first in possession of at least rudimentary, "domestic" languages (9[1]**, p. 260; 9[36], p. 274).[15] He thus incidentally confirms the hypothetical or conjectural character of the *Second Discourse's* "pure" state of nature.[16] The primitive family of the first or earliest times is, of course, not our family. Rousseau appears to have thought of it as varying in size from a small band or household to a clan, without fixed dwelling (9[8], pp. 262 f.), loose-knit but self-contained, and not exogamous: "Each family was self-sufficient and propagated itself from its own stock alone" (9[36], p. 272).[17] The decisive break in the *Essay,* corresponding to what in the *Discourse on Inequality* Rousseau calls "a first revolution,"[18] is, then, not the break separating a conjectural "pure" state of nature on the one hand and the establishment of the family on the other, but the entirely traditional and, indeed, historical break between life prior to "fixed dwellings" and life subsequent to them, or between nomadic and sedentary life, and the attendant institution of formal relations among families that marks the transition from families to "peoples."[19]

This is one reason why in the paragraph of the *Essay* which he devotes to pity (9[2], p. 261), Rousseau does not speak about what in the *Discourse* he refers to as "the goodness suited to the pure state of nature" or "the natural pity"[20] corresponding to it. At times his remarks about pity in the *Essay* have given rise to misunderstandings for want of close attention to the distinction which he draws in the *Discourse* between the "principle" of pity and its diverse manifestations at different stages in the development of the soul and of society. The "principle" of pity is the primary rule of natural right: to injure no one. It characteristically manifests itself as a "repugnance" to do hurt, or even to witness it.[21] It is true that in introducing his account of pity, he charges that Hobbes cannot account for men's assisting one another when they are not specifically obligated to do so. He implies that his teaching regarding pity can do so, and some of his examples certainly suggest an inclination to come "without reflection to the assistance of those we see suffer"[22]—mothers running risks to protect their young, Mandeville's evocation of the spontaneous inclination to help a mother and child in distress, the rabble and the market women trying to break up fights. Still, it is worth noting that all of them act in order to prevent hurt rather than in order actively to do good. Rousseau will argue that all the social virtues are forms of pity or derived from it, on the grounds that to do good is nothing but to avoid or to prevent harm. The three examples which he goes on to give in his own name—the philosopher who convinces himself that he need not come to the assistance of the man being murdered beneath his window, the populace that breaks up riots and street fights, and the sturdy savage who refrains from robbing the helpless when he can get enough elsewhere—range from the overly civilized to the noncivilized. The populace, which comes closest to exhibiting an active and possibly beneficent pity, occupies a middle position, though clearly one that is nearer to the savage than to the philosopher. Indeed, it is given in illustration of the claim that the savage always impetuously yields to the first sentiment of humanity. However, the pity of the "sturdy savage" proper—whom Rousseau is clearly contrasting with the savage Hobbes describes as a child "grown strong and sturdy"[23]—manifests itself in omission or avoidance as emphatically as does the philosopher's lack of pity. Neither the philosopher nor the savage extends help. The difference between them is, rather, that the one avoids assisting and the other avoids hurting. The example of the sturdy savage further illustrates particularly clearly that although the impulsion to pity may be as natural, as primitive, and as spontaneous as is the impulsion to self-preservation, and although it may under certain circumstances moderate it,[24] it does not override it. With the example of the sturdy savage, Rousseau tacitly rejects the possibility that even in his most austere state of nature men might find it possible to do their own good without ever hurting others. Pity is entirely compatible with violence, even with high levels of violence.

In "the first times" enmity reigned among men (9[6], p. 262). They were not engaged in constant and open fights with one another, nor were they in a "state of war" strictly and properly so-called. For they lived dispersed, and the basic physical or material needs which mainly moved them tended to keep them dispersed. They may thus perhaps be said to have been "solitary," even though they in fact lived in families or bands. They would have met seldom. But when they did meet, they were likely to fight.

> They were not bound by any idea of common brotherhood, and since they had no other judge than force, they believed themselves to be one another's enemies. It was to their weakness and ignorance that they owed this opinion. Since they knew nothing, they feared everything; they attacked in self-defence. A man abandoned alone on the face of the earth at the mercy of mankind had to be a ferocious animal. He was ready to inflict on others all the harm he feared from them. Fear and weakness are the sources of cruelty. (9[1], pp. 260 f.)[25]

Their first name for "stranger" is "giant" (3[3], p. 246).[26] By and by they recognize that these giants are no different from themselves, that they are their *semblables*, beings like themselves, though perhaps not properly speaking "fellow human beings." Although they are fierce, even ferocious and cruel, they are no more wicked or vindictive than a dog biting the stone that hit it is so.[27] They are not wicked or vindictive for the same reason that they are not properly speaking or magnanimous: they lack a developed sense of self, of their own as well as of others'. That is, of course, precisely why Rousseau is for the most part reluctant to speak of their condition as a state of war. His "first men," unlike Hobbes's men in the state of nature, are not bent on besting anyone, let alone everyone. Still, they had "no laws other than those of nature," that is to say, "no arbiter other than force" (9[1], p. 260). In his usage, "law(s) of nature," in contrast to "natural law(s)," consistently refers to the laws of material or physical nature, and in particular to the natural, "physical" inclinations and "impulsions" that move living beings to act as they do: self- preservation, the quest for subsistence, and, at least in the case of men, the aversion to inflicting pain unnecessarily. Action from impulsion may, of course, happen to correspond to what is right, or may at least not be at odds with it; action by the law of nature may happen to be in accordance with the natural law, or may at least not be in violation of it. That is the state of affairs to which Rousseau refers as "goodness."[28] However, "the most inviolable law of nature" is the law of the strongest: big fish eat little fish.[29]

Rousseau's remark that the first men do not attend to or wonder at anything or anyone (9[3][4], p. 261 f.), calls the reader's attention to the fact that neither in the *Essay*'s account of the first times, for all of its biblical references and allusions, nor in the corresponding sections of the *Second Discourse* does he so much as suggest that the first men held any religious beliefs or engaged in any religious practices. He goes so far as to speak of them as "abandoned alone on the face of the earth" (9[1]. p. 261).[30] They are afraid of everything that is unfamiliar ([1], p. 261). They take everything that is familiar for granted.[31] They cherish their own.

The most primitive social form in which the twin principles of caring for oneself and reluctance unnecessarily to hurt others manifest themselves is in the distinction between friends and enemies. Like good dogs, Plato's guardians, and philosophers, Rousseau's "first men," and even his "fathers of nations," love what and whom they know, and hate what and whom they do not know (9[4],[5], p. 261 f.). "The words for strangers and for enemies were long synonymous among most ancient peoples."[32]

It would seem that language of some kind is coeval with humanity.[33] Prepolitical, domestic societies—primitive families, households, or hordes—have "domestic languages"; larger, more developed and structured societies—peoples, nations, or political societies—alone have "genuine" or "popular" languages, what Rousseau regards as languages strictly and properly so called (9[1]**. p. 260, 9[36], p. 272). Languages strictly and properly so called develop as societies strictly and properly so called, namely civil societies, develop. Since the genuine or popular languages are the first human institutions (1[1], p. 240), the causes for their different "forms" must be "natural"; and these "natural" causes of the "forms" of language must at the same time be the natural causes of the forms of societies. Now, in tracing the dispersion of the first families from the warm climate of the Near and Middle East where mankind was born (8[1], [2], p. 259 f.) to the four corners of the earth, Rousseau's guiding premise is that initially men become what their ways—their *moeurs*—make them be, and that their ways are the ways which the climate, the terrain, and available resources force them to adopt in order to secure their subsistence (9[20], p. 266).[34] It is a corollary of this premise that men's needs will initially have tended to separate rather than to unite them (2[2], p. 245, 9[6], p. 262). Nature provides; but it does so unevenly (9[24], p. 267). When there is not enough to go around, some will set off and seek their subsistence elsewhere rather than stay and fight. The first men lead a nomadic existence. They are hunter-gatherers, or they are herdsmen. They are not farmers. Farming appears late. It presupposes a developed intelligence, developed skills, and above all secure and stable political structures. Initially the choice between a life of hunting and gathering, and a pastoral life, must at least in some measure have been influenced by temperament: the more active and aggressive become hunters and gatherers (9[16], p. 264 f.), the more placid and peaceable become pastoralists (9[17], p. 265). The more active are always on the move—"the land of the hunters does not long remain that of the hunt" (9[18], p. 265); the more placid stop pressing forward at the first opportunity. Rousseau suggests that the more peaceable pastoralists will have settled the more southerly climes. Everywhere, in the South as well as in the North, men will also have been dispersed by the various natural disasters—floods, earthquakes, fires—which, to judge by the numerous ancient traditions about them, appear to have been so much more frequent and devastating in the distant past than in more recent, historical times (9[27], p. 268). As they disperse further, they have to adjust to different climates, different terrains, and the cycle of the seasons which brings relief and renewal in the arctic and the tropical zones and which, by thus making more of the earth's surface inhabitable, makes possible a more far-flung dispersion. Still, the farther North men move, the harsher the conditions they encounter, until at last they find themselves in "those dreadful climates where everything is dead nine months out of the year" (10[3], p. 273).

The North must have been peopled by the hard race of the hunters. They may initially have chosen a hard life because of their temperament; their descendants acquired a hard temperament because of their way of life. For nature allows only the fittest to survive (10[2], p. 273). Broadly speaking, then, the distinction which Rousseau draws between the people of the North and those of the South stands for the distinction between the more active and aggressive and the more placid and peaceable.

The same natural pressures of climate and terrain which will initially have dispersed men over the face of the earth (2[2], p. 245, 9[24], p. 267), will eventually have "forced" them to unite (9[27], p. 268) into peoples with "popular" or "genuine" languages. After great natural disasters they will have come together in order to restore common losses in common; and while the cycle of the seasons makes more of the earth inhabitable for at least part of the year, it also makes for the harsh winters of the far North and the dry summers of the arid South, which "force" men to form associations (9[28], p. 268), that is to say, nations or political societies properly so-called, in contrast to families, households, troops, or tribes. It is inconceivable that they would form political societies if they lived dispersed in a state of comparative plenty and "perpetual spring." Men do not spontaneously form political associations. They are not by nature, or, more precisely, they are not by their own nature, sociable or political. They become so only in response to the pressure of circumstances: "He who willed man to be sociable inclined the globe's axis at an angle to the axis of the universe by a touch of the fingers" (9[23], p. 266).[35]

What is more, men thrive better in a demanding setting than they do in conditions of ease and plenty. North and South, harsh lands make for tougher as well as for larger populations. The excess spills out and spreads across the richer, easier lands and soon overwhelms their gentler inhabitants (8[2], p. 260, 9[25], [26], p. 267).[36] The invasions by these more savage hordes as they migrate from the more extreme to the milder climates are not due to precisely the same causes as was the initial dispersion, but they are certainly as natural, as inevitable, and hence as "providential" as that initial dispersion was.

Rousseau sketches two scenarios of how associations might first have arisen, one for the far North, the other for the arid South. The men of the North, forced during the short clement season to put in provisions for the long winters, will need one another's help and come to depend on it. Once ice and snow keep them from roaming freely, boredom unites them as much as had need. Families meet by the fire, enjoy its warmth and glow, and cook their meats over it. These gatherings become feasts, they dance, and "the sweet bonds of familiarity imperceptibly draw man to his kind, and on this rustic hearth burns the sacred flame that introduces the first sentiments of humanity into men's hearts" (9[29], p. 269). Once the snow and ice melt, they again go their separate ways.

The men of the arid South have to dig and maintain wells or at least to agree about their use. They are thus gradually drawn into a few simple cooperative ventures and a few simple conventions. Young men and women come to these common wells to water their families' flocks and linger to enjoy one another's company. By and by they hold festivals, dance, and when gesture is no longer adequate to express the feelings that well up within them, they give them voice. In these efforts to make themselves understood they gradually fashion a common "popular" tongue: "Here finally was the true cradle of peoples and from the pure crystal of the fountains sprang the first fires of love" (9[35], p. 271).

Although formally, in structure and detail, the two stories are remarkably similar, the tone and manner in which Rousseau tells them and the feelings which they evoke in the reader are very different. Only after he has told them does he bring out the differences which he most wants to emphasize: he had at first said that the men of the South had to come together in order to dig their wells and watering ditches (9[30], p. 269, 9[34], p. 270 f.), but after describing the festivals at these wells his emphasis shifts, and he now has them do their work without so much as taking notice of one another (9[36], p. 372). He from the first had the men of the North needing one another's help to lay in provisions for winter, but they appeared to have worked together silently. However, after saying that in the South it was passion that untied tongues, he now adds that in the North it was need that untied them, that in "those frightful climates where everything is dead nine months out of the year" (10[3], p. 273), men had to voice their needs because they live in constant danger and could therefore not trust gesture to convey their urgency. So that if in the South the first words were *aimez moi,* "love me," the first words in the North were *aidez moi,* "help me" (10[3], p. 274). These were, of course, not their first words. North and South, men had been speaking "domestic" languages all their lives. But, once again, by an elision characteristic of the *Essay*, Rousseau lets a single letter or sound stand for what he regards as the most basic difference in ways of life and forms of language. In the South, peoples and popular languages are formed in an atmosphere of leisure and love; in the North they are formed in an atmosphere of need and work: "Idleness, which feeds the passions, yielded to labor, which represses them" (10[3], p. 273).

Rousseau's northern scenario fully conforms to his guiding premise, that the earliest morals or ways are a function of how men are forced to provide for their subsistence: what brings and holds the men of the North together may be either the need for another's help or the lack of anything else to do; but what first causes them to speak is emphatically need for another's help. The Southern scenario conforms to this premise more loosely: what brings the men of the South together is also need, though it is not need for one another's help (cf. 12[1], p. 276) but need for water. However, what holds them together and what first causes them to speak—in the strong sense of speaking a popular or genuine language—is love and the passionate effort of members of different families who until then had spoken different domestic languages to make themselves intelligible to one another. The attachments they form around their wells are thus the "true cradles of peoples" (9[35],[36], pp. 271 f.). Civil society is from the first discontinuous with domestic society; it represents a break with the family, not its expansion. Rousseau does not deny that the feasts around the northern fires also bring together members of different families and so are also "cradles of peoples." But neither does he assert it. The fact that he does not is striking if only because it is the only feature of the southern story without a counterpart in the northern story. It would seem that he really does not think that the Northerners' feasts are cradles of peoples, at least not until a much later age; he has the Northerners each again going his own way just as soon as the weather permits (9[28], p. 268). He may have wished to suggest that in the South several families have to share the few, often widely scattered wells, whereas, by contrast, in the North each family can have its own fire or even fires. He certainly did believe that nations, or at least large nations, tend to be formed by people who follow either the pastoral or the agricultural life, rather than by people who are primarily hunters (9[18]*, p. 265); and, as we saw, he evidently did believe that pastoralists at first settled in the South, and hunters in the North; and the plain historical fact is that political societies were established in the South long before they were established in the North. Egypt and Persia, Athens, Sparta, and Rome, were empires at a time when Gauls, Britons, and Germans still lived in tribes.[37]

With the formation of peoples, the sphere of "pity" expands and its character changes: the distinction between friend and enemy that used to divide one family from another gets displaced and comes to divide one troop, tribe, or people from another.

One's superficial impression throughout this discussion of the natural causes of the formation of peoples and of the forms of popular languages, and indeed throughout the entire *Essay on the Origin of Languages*, is that Rousseau favors the South and rejects the North. He creates this impression in part by calling "South" whatever is not the Far North, and he clearly does this at least in part in order to compensate for our tendency to take our own—Northerners'—experience as the norm and to think of life as always and everywhere threatened by scarcity and danger. To do so is to commit the very same fallacy which he charges Hobbes with committing when he attributes to men in the state of nature the passions of men in civil society. It is, of course, not only a Northerners' fallacy; in support of his thesis that the natural order does not suit man, Lucretius asserts that fully two thirds of the earth—the tropical and the arctic zones—is uninhabitable.[38] Rousseau would grant the conclusion but not the premise: in a clear allusion to Lucretius's remark he asserts that, on the contrary, fully two thirds of the earth—the tropical and the temperate zones—

knows no winter to speak of (8[1], p. 259), and so certainly is inhabitable.[39] He sometimes makes it appear as if he believed that this two thirds of the earth enjoys what, like Montesquieu, he calls "happy climates" (9[25], p. 267, 9[34], p. 271; cf. 9[21], p. 266, 9[30], p. 269), where life is uniformly a life of plenty and ease, by contrast to the remaining third which, again like Montesquieu, he calls those "dreadful climates" (10[2], p. 273),[40] where life is a constant hardship. But men living unconstrained in such "happy climates" or in what, echoing Ovid, he on another occasion calls "perpetual spring," would never have had any reason or occasion to form stable, lasting associations, let alone civil societies (9[22], p. 266).[41] It may be that a North of nearly perpetual winter and a South of perpetual spring did, for some time, prevail in some places. But they cannot have prevailed widely or for long. A North of perpetual winter and a South of perpetual spring represent extremes, between which Rousseau's exemplary "South," the South of wells, but also of droughts, deserts, and dangers, occupies a middle ground.

Nor are the traits that characterize the men of the South clearly and unqualifiedly preferable to those that characterize the men of the North. The superficial impression is that Rousseau depicts the men of the North as quick to anger and indignation and the men of the South as inclined to cooperation and friendliness. But he has all men, North and South, being friendly toward those they know and hostile toward all others. The respective pull or weight of friendliness and hostility in the North differs from their respective pull or weight in the South, and so, once again, by an ellipsis characteristic of the *Essay*, he lets "North" and "South" stand for a dominant element in the balance between them. On reflection it appears that both North and South represent valuable traits, that neither by itself makes for a full human being, but that both together may. The task would, then, be to combine them. The flux and reflux of population, and especially the earliest migrations from North to South, would appear to force precisely such combinations or blendings. Their outcome is, of course, not always good. A mere chance blend—or balance—of diverse and more or less savage ways will be so only half the time; and when savage ways overwhelm the civilized, the outcome is invariably calamitous (19[4], p. 291).[42] As Montesquieu reminds us, barbarian hordes lay completely waste the lands which they invade, and their victims never recover.[43] Rousseau would not deny it. But he does not call attention to it either. When Montesquieu or Hume, who is largely Montesquieu's disciple in these matters, contrasts North and South, they do so in terms of physical as well as "moral" and "political" causes. By contrast, Rousseau concentrates on an inquiry into "physical" causes to the almost complete exclusion of moral and political causes throughout these middle chapters of the *Essay*. Art or wisdom may take over later. Rousseau's model of a language that represents a successful blend or balance of physical causes or chance and successfully serves a sound way of life is Greek. As he points out, Greece, with the possible exception of Attica, was peopled by Doric invaders from the North (9[26], p. 267), and the language was marked by this invasion. In comparison with Persia or Arabia, Greece occupies a middle ground.[44]

What might be called Rousseau's geography of the earliest times—the sharp contrast between North and South, men's dispersion, their uniting into peoples, their migrations—forms the foreground of his account of the beginnings. What might be called his history of the earliest times forms its background. It is less detailed and less in evidence, but it is no less important. He had introduced the geography by warning that we must not think that the weather is everywhere as unfriendly and the soil everywhere as unyielding as they are in the small corner of the earth which we happen to know best; the earth is not as inhospitable as it may appear to us (8[1], p. 259 f.). He introduces the history by warning that we must not think the earth has always been as orderly and stable as we now find it to be (9[31], p. 269). The earth has not always been as hospitable as it appears to us. It appears to be so to us because men have dispersed to its four corners, settled it, and introduced a measure of order among its products (9[32], p. 269 f.; cf. 2[2], p. 245). It was not always so.

The poets fancied that at first chaos reigned among the elements. It may have seemed that it did, even if it in fact did not (9[31], [32], p. 269 f.).[45] Chaos did, however, reign among the beings, especially among "the earth's products." Each kind struggled to find and to seize its niche and to choke out all others. None ever succeeded. For as it was about to do so, everything would again get jumbled. Natural accidents and frequent upheavals or revolutions restored the earlier struggle (9[31], p. 269).[46] It may at first appear that Rousseau here thinks of nature as not just devoid of order or reason but as wantonly destructive, as if upsetting every painfully achieved stability. But evidently he thinks, rather, that if the struggle among the species went unchecked, the stronger and larger would soon simply overwhelm the weaker and smaller, and that by and by only the larger trees and the ferocious animals would remain. Eventually there would not be any life left at all (9[32], p. 270). Such is the law of nature. Buffon had argued that if predation ceased, if big fish ceased eating little fish, the little fish would multiply so rapidly that they would soon lack food, and so destroy one another or perish, as, therefore, also would their natural predators. He accordingly concludes that man's being a carnivore, and hence animal slaughter, is essential to the balance and economy of nature. In a clear and rather pointed allusion to the argument of Rousseau's *Second Discourse*, Buffon adds that this is so even though such slaughter might appear to violate our natural inclination to pity.[47] Rousseau accepts Buffon's premise and therefore rejects his conclusion. In conformity with his bracketing of the antediluvian age in the *Essay*, he brackets the speculations regarding man's initial vegetarianism that dot the *Second Discourse*.[48] The first men of the *Essay* are from the first frankly carnivorous; they live off the hunt or off their herds (9[9], p. 263, [10], [17]–[19], p. 259 f.).[49] Now, on Buffon's premise it follows that the biggest and strongest will, by and by, devour all the rest. Yet Buffon evidently concludes that the animal system remains in balance. He must assume that predators, as they decimate their natural prey, create a shortage of food, which in turn causes their own number to decrease, and that as their own number decreases, their prey once again grows abundant, thus completing a cycle which, other things remaining equal, would repeat itself endlessly (9[32]*,

p. 270). Rousseau rejects this cyclical hypothesis because he does not see how or why the predators would allow their decimated prey to recover and increase in number. The stronger will simply continue to overwhelm the weaker until they alone are left, and as a result they too perish. The great cataclysms break and reverse this trend by destroying a proportionately larger number of these stronger, now dominant species. Seen in this perspective, the cataclysms appear not as wanton natural destructiveness but as a natural restoration of order and balance. They help preserve the species, if only provisionally and precariously, by returning them to their life and death struggle. The initial state is chaos, the final state destruction (9[32], p. 270). The balance between these extremes, in other words, the balance of nature, is the war of all against all, maintained or restored by periodic and, so to speak, providential cataclysms.

Eventually men come to play the role which cataclysms originally played in maintaining or restoring the balance of nature. At first, cataclysms had contributed to men's dispersion. Later they contributed to their coming together in order to repair common losses in common (9[27], p. 267 f.). They "forced" them to combine forces (9[27], [28], p. 268).[50] Labor, indeed collective labor, is clearly coeval with humanity. It is found even among animals (1[13], p. 244). Contrary to the impression created by some particularly dramatic passages in the *Second Discourse*, Rousseau does not hold that labor, even collective labor, is first introduced with agriculture. Nor does he think that it is confined to the North. It is not even particularly distinctive of it. North and South, men can survive and thrive only by taking an active hand in their circumstances. Indeed, only as and when they do, do all the other kinds survive and thrive.

> The relation between man's needs and the products of the earth is such that, as long as it is populated, everything subsists; but before men united had, by their common labors, introduced a balance among its productions, they could all subsist only if nature alone attended to the equilibrium which the hand of man preserves today. (9[32], p. 270)

Although Rousseau couches the thesis in terms of the production of "the earth" or vegetation, he indicates in the immediate sequel that man's role is equally decisive in all other realms of the earth's natural economy. The part which man plays in the natural economy does not violate the general principle of survival of the fittest. For, as he notes, the stability which man introduces and maintains is but a by-product of his attending to his needs. Initially, these may have been the bare, basic bodily needs which caused men to disperse; by and by they are more numerous and more developed material needs, as well as what Rousseau in the *Essay* calls the "moral needs," or the passions (2[3], p. 245). His reflections on man's role in the economy of nature, and in particular on how the survival of the fittest may be compatible with the survival of all and may even contribute to it, are, once again, reminiscent of Lucretius: lions survive because they are strong, foxes because they are cunning, deer because they are swift; but goats, sheep, and cows would perish if man did not protect them for his own purposes.[51]

In time, men's collective endeavors grow into lasting associations, peoples, or what the *Second Discourse* calls "nascent societies."[52] Men in society increasingly order nature to their own needs and ends; they irrigate deserts and drain swamps, domesticate some animals and hunt others.[53] As they become the masters and possessors of nature, their works and wars come to take the place of the war of nature. Formerly lightning caused vast forest fires. Now thousands of men labor for decades to clear great tracts of land. Formerly earthquakes and floods destroyed encampments, villages, and towns, together with all their inhabitants. Now men wage wars and put great cities to the torch. Massive deforestation and wars may appear to play the same role which cataclysms formerly played in checking the increase of the larger species in the two animate realms. The cataclysms and men's undertakings may delay the decline of the earth and everything on it—"without them it would proceed faster and the earth might perhaps already be under water" (9[33], p. 270)—but nothing can reverse the decline or prevent the cracking of the walls of the world. Rousseau barely alludes to the world's eventual decrepitude; he dwells on its youth, and reminds us how successful men have been in slowing its decline. Still, in the long run, men do not maintain a stable balance among the beings. Rather, they upset it "by their inconstancy" (9[32], p. 269).[54] Buffon evidently failed to see that precisely because of their active role in the economy of nature, men only accelerate the unchecked dominance by the larger species and the ferocious animals. We are reminded that the only ferocious animal Rousseau had specifically identified as such is man (9[1], [18], [35], pp. 261, 265 f., 271; cf. 9[5], p. 262).[55] Yet once again he does not dwell on the darker side of these reflections. He does not pursue, he does not even mention, the moral and political questions which they raise, any more than he mentions the reasons which he had elsewhere stated at length for rejecting the sanguine Enlightenment view that the benefits of control can be enjoyed without paying its price. He points out that many regions, North and South, flourish only because of men's collective labors, and he cites the very same examples as those which Montesquieu had cited in making the same point: China, Egypt, Persia, and the Low Countries (9[34], p. 271).[56] But whereas Montesquieu goes on to praise the policies that introduced these improvements, Rousseau does not. Instead, he goes on to describe the beginnings of peoples at the festivals by the fountains. These festivals evidently represent one privileged balance between natural scarcity and human excess and between natural laziness and civil busyness: men labor, but they labor collectively, without anyone's becoming irreversibly dependent on another, and without either repressing or inflaming the passions. This entire scene provides a standard, not in the sense of representing a—let alone the—simple and unqualified good, but in the sense of representing one possible, comparatively comprehensive and stable balance that can be achieved between equally urgent and valid but competing claims, and hence between nature on the one hand and art or convention on the other.

Throughout this discussion of "the first times," as indeed throughout the entire *Essay on the Origin of Languages*, Rousseau shows perhaps even more clearly and emphatically than he does in the *Second Discourse* that the disjunction between nature and art or convention, i.e., the disjunction nature/culture, is not and cannot be a disjunction between one state or matter of fact and another, but is and can only be a disjunction in and for thought. It should go without saying that this view is perfectly compatible with persevering in the quest for nature or for what is natural. Precisely because he understands nature in one of its senses as force and its law as that of the strongest, he for the most part understands nature in the sense of norm—and hence also natural "good" or "goodness"—as balance. Accordingly, here, as throughout the *Essay*, and indeed throughout all of his works, he is inquiring into the possible bases of comparatively comprehensive and stable balances. He will therefore view human contrivance—art, or convention, or culture—not so much in contrast to nature as either more or less in accordance with it. His discussion of the geography and history of the first times—the relations between the earth, its products, and cataclysms, between men's needs and labors, between "North" and "South"—throughout this middle section of the *Essay* reveals more clearly than does any other discussion of his how much his understanding of nature as balance is indebted to the Epicurean and Lucretian understanding of balance.[57]

NOTES

This essay originally appeared in the *Graduate Faculty Philosophy Journal,* vol. 11/2 (1986), pp. 123–46.

1. The current (1986) standard edition of the *Essay*, Jean-Jacques Rousseau, *Essai sur l'origine des langues, où il est parlé de la mélodie et de l'imitation musicale,* ed. Charles Porset (Bordeaux, 1970), served as the basis for the translation found in Rousseau, *The First and Second Discourses Together with the Replies to Critics,* and *Essay on the Origin of Languages,* ed. and tr. Victor Gourevitch, (New York, 1986). C. Porset, "'*L'inquiétante étrangeté' de l'Essai sur l'origine des langues:* Rousseau et ses exégètes," *Studies on Voltaire and the Eighteenth Century,* 154 (1976), pp. 1715–58, provides a comprehensive summary of the relevant secondary literature.

2. Otherwise unidentified references throughout the body of this essay indicate the relevant chapter and paragraph of the *Essay on the Origin of Languages*, followed by the page of the English edition cited in n. 1.

3. See also Rousseau, *First and Second Discourses*, Note XVII, p. 229.

4. Samuel Pufendorf, *Le droit de la nature et des gens* (Amsterdam, 1712), II, 3, sec. 2, who borrows the expression from Ovid, *Metamorphoses*, 1, 107.

5. Genesis 11: 10–27. They are also the times of dispersion in the weaker sense of men's living without fixed dwellings, among the animals (9[22], p. 266); also *Second Discourse* (1[3], 142); prior to the division of land, "peoples wander and disperse over grasslands or in forests. Marriage will not be as secure among them as among us, where it is fixed by residence, and where the wife keeps a house: they can therefore more readily change wives, have several of them, and sometimes mingle indifferently as beasts do." Montesquieu, *On the Spirit of Laws*, XVIII, 13.

6. Cf. Genesis 1: 6, 7: 11, 9: 11.

7. "And God blessed Noah and his sons and said unto them, be fruitful and multiply, and replenish the earth. And the fear of you and the dread of you shall be upon every beast of the earth, and upon every fowl of the air, upon all that moveth upon the earth, and upon all the fishes of the sea: into your hands are they delivered." Genesis 9: 1.2.

". . . Savage man, living dispersed amongst the animals and early finding himself in the position of having to measure himself against them, soon makes the comparison and, feeling that he surpasses them in skill more than they do him in strength, learns to fear them no more. Set a bear or a wolf against a Savage who is sturdy, agile, and courageous, as they all are, armed with stones and a good stick, and you will see that the danger will at the very least be mutual, and that after several such experiences, ferocious beasts, disinclined as they are to attack one another, will not readily attack man, whom they will have found to be just as ferocious as themselves" *Second Discourse* (1[6], p. 143).

8. Genesis 11: 1, 4, 6–8. Wherever the King James version translates "scatter," the seventeenth- and eighteenth-century French versions of this text read "disperse"; hence Rousseau's "dispersion."

9. Genesis 10: 5; cf. 10: 20, 31, 32.

10. Cf., for example, *Essay*, 9[30], p. 269, with its reference to Genesis 21: 25–32. It is striking how often the *Essay* explicitly refers to biblical stories. H. Grange, "*L'Essai sur l'origine des langues* dans ses rapports avec le *Discours sur l'origine de l'inégalité parmi les hommes,*" *Annales historiques de la révolution française*, 39 (1967), pp. 291–307, has called attention to this feature of the *Essay*. It is perhaps even more striking how often the *Essay* refers to the Bible implicitly: on nations being formed at wells (9[35], [36], p. 271 f.). Exodus 2: 16–22: on the first, i.e., post-deluvian men's carnivorousness (9[9],[10], p. 263), cf. Genesis 9:3; on giants (3[3], pp. 246 f.), cf. Genesis 6:4, Numbers 13:30–33, 14:30, 32:11,12: the list could be expanded considerably. These biblical echoes again remind us that Rousseau was thinking of publishing the *Essay on the Origin of Languages* together with the prose poem *The Levite of Ephraim*, in which he retells the story found at the end of the book of Judges.

11. Rousseau, *Discourse on Inequality*, in *First and Second Discourses,* ed. Gourevitch (E[5], p. 139).

12. Genesis 11: 9–17.

13. The device is as traditional as it is transparent; e.g., "Thus it is not the first men but their children who began to live in the State of Nature" (Pufendorf, *Le droit de la nature et des gens*, II, 2, sec. 4). So too Locke speaks of "the first Ages of the World . . . supposing a Man or Family in the state they were, at first peopling of the World by the children of *Adam* or *Noah*" (*Treatise*, II, v. section 36; see also II, vi, section 57). Condillac, *Essai sur l'origine des connaissances humaines*, II. 1 (Introduction); however consider also Plato, *Laws* III. 678a.

14. "The oldest of all societies, and the only one that is natural, is the family" (*Of the Social Contract*, I, 2).

15. Cf. *Discourse on Inequality*, II[10], p. 173; II[14], p. 174.

16. For a fuller discussion, see Victor Gourevitch, "Rousseau's 'Pure State of Nature,'" *Interpretation* 16 (1988), pp. 23–59.

17. Cf. Montesquieu, quoted in n. 5. Distinct verbal echoes of Pufendorf's discussion of primitive incest can be heard in Rousseau's remarks on the subject: *Le droit de la nature et des gens*, VI, 1, xxxiv; see also Hugo Grotius, *Le droit de la guerre et de la paix* tr. Barbeyrac (Amsterdam, 1724), II, v. sec. xiii, paragraphs 5, 6, 7; Richard Cumberland, *Traité philosophique des loix naturelles* tr. Barbeyrac (Amsterdam, 1744), VII. section 9; also, cf. Plato *Republic* V.460e–461e with *Laws* 838a–c.

18. *Discourse on Inequality*, II[11], p. 173.

19. On this transition see, for example, Aristotle *Politics*, 1.2.1252b 12–23; in *Of the Social Contract* Rousseau describes the transition as follows: "The oldest of all societies, and the only natural one, is that of the family. Still the children remain tied to the father only as long as they need him to preserve themselves. As soon as this need ceases, the natural tie is dissolved . . . if they continue to remain united, they no longer do so naturally but voluntarily, and the family itself maintains itself only by convention." I.2; see also *Discourse on Political Economy* [2] and [3], and *Fragments politiques* in *Oeuvres complètes,* ed. Pléiade, vol. 3. p. 487. On "families," see also Locke, *Treatises of Government* I. section 130, II. sections 77, 86, 110.

20. *Discourse on Inequality*, II[18], p. 172.

21. On pity the principle, see *Discourse on Inequality*, P[9], p. 132 I[35], p. 160; in animals, I[35]. p. 160 f.; a "Natural virtue," I[35], p. 160, "impulsion," I[34], p. 159, or "Natural pity," II[17], p. 176; the common attribute of all the virtues, I[37], p. 161 f.; a sentiment that is obscure and lively in Savage man, developed but weak in Civil man, I[37], p. 162; "repugnance," P[9], p. 132, I[35], pp. 160, 161, I[38], p. 163, and cf. II[17], p. 176.

22. Ibid., I[38], p. 162.

23. Ibid., I[35], p. 160, and Hobbes, *On the Citizen*, Preface to the Reader, ed. Howard Warrender (Oxford, 1983), p. 33 f.

24. *Discourse on Inequality*, I[35], p. 160.

25. Cf. ibid., I[6] (quoted in n. 7) and especially Rousseau, *Geneva Manuscript*, 1.2, in *Oeuvres complètes*, III, pp. 281–89; on ferociousness and cruelty, see n. 55.

26. On giants before the Flood, see Genesis 6: 4; after it, Numbers 13: 32–33, Deuteronomy 2:20, 21, I Samuel 17: 4, and the commentary by Robert Sacks, "The Lion and the Ass," *Interpretation* 9 (1980), pp. 1–82, esp. 13 ff. See also the references to the Cyclopes, *Essay*, 9[7], and cf. Plato, *Laws*, III, 680a–c, and Vico, *New Science*, secs. 121, 243, 338.

27. *Discourse on Inequality*, I[39], p. 163. The image is taken from Plato, who compares the conduct of soldiers despoiling their slain enemies to a dog's biting the stone that hit him: *Republic*, VI.469d–e; the passage is cited by Barbeyrac in a discussion of the right of burial which some ancient writers considered under the heading of "pity": Pufendorf, *Droit de la nature et des gens*, II. 3, sec. xxxiii, n. 9; Grotius, *Right of War and Peace*, II. 19, section i, paragraph 4.

28. Consider, for example, *Discourse on Inequality*, Preface [8], p. 132, and I[38], p. 162 f.

29. "The most inviolable law of nature is the law of the stronger." Rousseau, *Considérations sur le gouvernement de Pologne*, in *Oeuvres complètes*, III, p. 1013; trans. W. Kendall, p. 80; Benedict Spinoza, *Tractatus Theologico-Politicus*, chapter XVI.

30. Cf. *Discourse on Inequality*, Preface [12], p. 134, and Exordium [6], p. 140; also consider *Essay on the Origin of Languages*, 9[31], [32], p. 269 f., and *Discourse on Inequality*, I[3], p. 142.

31. *Discourse on Inequality*, I[21], p. 150 f.; Lucretius, II.1023–47, especially 1030–36; V.972–81; 1183–87; 1204–17: Cicero, *On the Nature of the Gods* II. xxxviii.96.

32. Rousseau, *Geneva Manuscript*, 1.2, in *Oeuvres complètes*, III, p. 288, citing Cicero, *Offices* I.12 and paraphrasing Grotius, *Le droit de la guerre et de la paix* II. xv. section v, paragraph 2; "Every partial society, when it is narrow and united, alientates itself from the great society. Every patriot is harsh to strangers; they are but men, they are nought in his eyes. The drawback is inevitable but it is weak. The essential thing is to be good to the people with whom one lives. . . . I distrust those cosmopolites who go to great lengths to find in their books duties which they fail to fulfill toward those around them. Some philosophers love the Tartars in order to be spared having to love their neighbors." Rousseau, *Emile*, in *Oeuvres complètes*, IV, p. 249, cf. p. 520 (trans. Bloom [New York, 1979], pp. 39, 233); also: "Es ist immer möglich eine grössere Menge von Menschen in Liebe aneinander zu binden, wenn nur andere für die Äusserung der Agression übrig bleiben." Freud, *Das Unbehagen in der Kultur*, V, in *Gesammelte Werke*, XIV, p. 473 and context *(Civilization and its Discontents*, trans. J. Strachey [W. W. Norton: New York, 1961], p. 68).

33. "As soon as one man was recognized by another as a sentient thinking Being, similar to himself the desire or the need to communicate to him his sentiments and thoughts made him seek the means to do so," *Essay*, I[2], p. 240. "Let man be as crudely structured as you please: no doubt he will acquire fewer ideas: but provided only that there is some means of communication between himself and his kind by which one man can act and the other feel, they will succeed in eventually communicating to one another all the ideas they have." *Essay*, I[12], p. 244. ". . . as soon as vocal signs strike your ear, they herald a being like yourself, they are, so to speak, the organs of the soul." *Essay* 12[7], p. 287.

34. "So that, in the first place, everything comes down to subsistence, and everything that surrounds man thus has a bearing on him. He depends on everything, and he becomes what everything he depends on forces him to be. The climate, the soil, the air, the water, the productions of the earth and the sea, form his temperament, his character, determine his tastes, his passions, his labors, his actions of every kind. If this is not strictly true regarding individuals, it is unquestionably so regarding peoples; and if fully formed men rose from the earth then, regardless of where this might take place, anyone who knew well the state of everything surrounding them could accurately ascertain what they will become." Rousseau, *Fragments politiques*, in *Oeuvres complètes*, III, p. 530.

35. "Although the earth, with a compass of three thousand leagues, is not an immense sphere, it so to speak expands its compass by the variety of its climates which, since they are the appropriate climate for different qualities of plants and animals, so to speak divide the earth into as many worlds whose inhabitants [are] restricted each one to his own world [and] cannot pass from one to the other. Only man and a few domestic animals subsist naturally everywhere, and can adopt as many ways of life as the diversity of climates and of their productions requires of them. Another diversity, which both increases and combines the preceding diversity, is that of the seasons. Their succession, by alternately bringing several climates to a single one, accustom the men who live in it to their diverse impressions, and so render them capable of growing and living in all the countries the temperature of which makes itself felt in their own. If the ecliptic had coincided with the equator, there might never have been any migration of peoples, and none might ever have left its native climate because it could not tolerate any other. To tilt the axis of the world with the finger or to say to man: Cover the earth and be sociable, was one of the same thing for Him who needs neither hand to act nor voice to speak," *Fragments politiques*, in *Oeuvres complètes*, III, p. 530 f.

36. See also *Discourse on Inequality*, Note IX [13], p. 212 f., and Montesquieu, *Of the Spirit of Laws*, XVIII, 1–4.

37. Cf. *Fragments politiques*, in *Oeuvres complètes*, III, p. 531 f.

38. *De rerum natura*, V.204f.; cf. Buffon, *Oeuvres philosophiques*, ed. Jean Piveteau, (Paris, 1954) pp. 34a–35b.

39. Abbé Du Bos had pointed out that "the Annals of Rome tell us that in the year 480 after its founding, the winter was so severe that the trees died. In Rome the Tiber froze, and snow remained on the ground for forty days. When Juvenal depicted the superstitious woman, he says that she had the ice on the Tiber broken up so that she might perform her ablutions in it," *Réflexions critiques sur la poésie et sur la peinture*, (Paris, 1770) II, 16. Reflecting on this passage and much other evidence from ancient writers, David Hume is led to ask, "Allowing, therefore, this remark to be just, that Europe is become warmer than formerly; how can we account for it? Plainly by no other method, than by supposing that the land is at present much better cultivated, and that the woods are cleared, which formerly threw a shade upon the earth, and kept the rays of the sun from penetrating to it. Our northern colonies in America become more temperate, in proportion as the woods are felled; but in general everyone may remark that cold is still much more severely felt both in North and in South America than in places under the same latitude in Europe." Hume, "Of the Populousness of Ancient Nations," *Essays, Moral and Political*, ed. T. H. Green and T. H. Grose (London, 1889), vol. 1, p. 434.

40. Montesquieu, *Of the Spirit of Laws*, XVIII, 3; so too Buffon, *Oeuvres philosophiques*, ed. Piveteau, p. 188a.

41. Ovid, *Metamorphoses*, I, 107; cf. Pufendorf, *Le droit de la nature et des gens*, II, 2, sec. 2; see also Lucretius, *De rerum natura*, V, 818 f.

42. See the article "Measure" in J.-J. Rousseau, *Dictionary of Music*, tr. W. Waring (London, 1779) paras. 3–5.

43. Montesquieu, *Of the Spirit of Laws*, XVIII, 3.

44. "In relation to the capital of Persia, Rome and Athens are northern cities"; Abbé Du Bos, *Réflexions critiques*, II, xvi. Regarding the migrations and mingling of peoples,

see also Rousseau, *Emile*, I, *Oeuvres complètes*, IV, p. 266 ff (Bloom translation, p. 52) and *Of the Social Contract*, III, 8.

45. See Hesiod, *Theogony*, 116, and Ovid, *Metamorphoses*, I.5–31, but also such successful contemporary productions as André Cardinal Destouches's 1721 ballet *Les éléments* and Jean Fery Rebel's 1737 ballet of the same name; however consider Lucretius II.673f., V.235–323, 380–415; and Descartes's "a chaos as confused as the poets might feign" *Discours de la méthode*, Gilson ed., p. 42: 23f.

46. Cf. "great accidents," *Essay*, 9[27], p. 268, and *Fragments politiques*, in *Oeuvres complètes*, III, p. 533.

47. Buffon, *Oeuvres philosophiques*, ed. Piveteau, "Le Boeuf" ("The Ox") (1753), pp. 358b6–359a 15; *Les animaux carnivores* (1758), pp. 366b25–367a29 and 373a32–377a44; and esp. *Le lièvre* (1765), pp. 363–65; consider also Le Roy's criticism of the *Second Discourse* with Rousseau's *Reply* [2], p. 238.

48. The permission to eat meat is post-Noahdic; see Genesis 9: 2–4.

49. "Lightning, a Volcano, or some happy accident acquainted them with fire, a new resource against the rigors of winter: They learned to conserve this element, then to reproduce it, and finally to prepare the meats they had previously devoured raw," *Discourse on Inequalily*, II[4], p. 171. "Neither man's stomach nor his intestines are made to digest raw meat. . . . With the possible single exception of the Eskimos . . . even savages grill their meats," *Essay on the Origin of Languages*, 9[29], p. 268.

"The Pongos gather around the fires lit by the Negroes, once these have left, and they in turn leave once the fire has died out; that is the fact; here, now, is the observer's commentary: *For although they are very skillful they have not sense enough to keep the fire going by adding wood to it.* I should like to fathom how Battel, or Purchas, his compiler, could have known that the Pongos' departure was an effect of their stupidity rather than of their will . . . it seems very strange that the Pongos, whose dexterity and strength is extolled, the Pongos who know how to bury their dead and how to make themselves roofs out of branches, should not know how to push embers into a fire. I remember having seen a monkey perform the same operation which it is claimed the Pongos cannot perform; it is true that, as my ideas were not at that time turned in that direction, I myself committed the mistake for which I reproach our travelers, and I neglected to examine whether it had indeed been the monkey's intention to keep the fire going, or whether it had simply been, as I believe, to imitate the action of a human being." *Discourse on Inequality*, Note X [5], p. 217. "Fire gives much pleasure to animals as well as to man, once they have become accustomed to its sight and felt its gentle warmth. Often it would even prove no less useful to them than to us, if only to warm their young. Yet no one has ever heard of any animal, wild or domestic, which, even by imitating us, has acquired the skills required to make fire. And these are the reasoning beings that are said to form an evanescent prehuman society, although their intelligence could not rise to the level of drawing sparks from a stone and catching them [on tinder] or at least of keeping some abandoned fire going! Upon my word, the philosophers quite openly mock us. Their writings clearly show that they indeed take us for beasts." *Essay on the Origin of Languages* 9[29]*, p. 268.

50. Cf. *Social Contract*, I, 6, paras. 1, 2.

51. Lucretius, *De rerum natura*, V, 855–77; cf. Plato, *Republic*, I, 343a–b.

52. *Discourse on Inequality*, II[29], p. 182; cf. II[15], p. 175, and II[18], p. 176.

53. See the texts cited in n. 39.

54. On the disruptiveness of man's accendancy, cf. Buffon, *Oeuvres philosophiques*, ed. Piveteau, p. 362 f., with p. 364; in this connection consider especially Rousseau's 1765 *Lettre à Voltaire* about the Lisbon earthquake, *Oeuvres complètes*, IV, pp. 1059–75. The *Essay's* silence regarding the Lisbon earthquake does not justify conclusions about the date of its composition or last revision.

55. See also *Discourse on Inequality*, I[6], p. 143, and Note IX[13], p. 212. "FEROCIOUS, adj. Epithet invented by man to designate in certain animals that share the earth

with him, a natural disposition to attack him, and which all animals would be fully justified to apply to him in return, if only they had language; for what animal in nature is more *ferocious* than man? Man has transferred this designation to the man who behaves toward his fellows [*ses semblables*] with the same violence and cruelty which the human species practices toward all sensible and living things. But if man is a *ferocious* animal that immolates the animals to itself, what kind of beast is the tyrant who devours men? It seems to me that there is this difference between *ferociousness* and *cruelty*, that since cruelty pertains to a reasoning being, it is specific to man; whereas *ferociousness*, since it pertains to a sensitive being, can be common to man and animal." Diderot, *Encyclopedia* article, "Féroce"; compare also Lucretius, *De rerum natura*, V.990–1000 with 1297–1349.

56. Montesquieu, *Of the Spirit of Laws*, XVIII, 6, 7.

57. Cf. Epicurus's *isonomia*, which Cicero renders *aequabilis tributio, On the Nature of the Gods,* I, xix, 50; Lucretius, *De rerum natura*, II, 67–79, 569–80, especially 573 f.; cf. *rerum summa novatur semper*, II, 75 f., with Bailey's note *ad loc.*

SEVENTEEN

In Search of the Political Object: Stoic and Aesthetic Political Philosophy

Frank Ankersmit

One of the most characteristic features of contemporary political philosophy is its apparent inability to define the domain of politics and the nature of the political object. We no longer seem to be able to demarcate the domain of politics from what lies before or beyond it. Take, for instance, the following statement by Fred Dallmayr in his rich and instructive *Polis and Praxis* (1984): "I would prefer to describe politics as a human practice, namely as the ongoing institution of the practice of friendship."[1] On the face of it, that is quite an attractive statement, and many will tend to agree with Dallmayr. However, if we link these three domains of politics, human practice, and friendship in this way, the result will inevitably be that political philosophy is no longer distinguishable from a philosophy of practice, nor from an encompassing philosophy of life that purports to deal with even the private world of our relations with friends. Following Freud and Norbert Elias, one might be prepared to take the ultimate step and assert that politics has even penetrated into the innermost recesses of our selves.

Politics now seems to be simply everywhere. But, as we all know, what is everywhere is, in practice, nowhere. We recognize that seventeenth-century theologians were quite justified in mistrusting Spinoza's pantheistic *Deus sive nature*. If God and politics are everywhere, they are nowhere. The Dutch historian E. H. Kossmann recently drew our attention to this curious Spinozistic dialectic of contemporary politics and political philosophy: "as soon as we accept that the State, the political factor, has become a natural part of our daily life, we no longer see them as problematic, we no longer notice them. Our existence is politicized to such a degree that we can no longer isolate the political factor and we feel no need to study it as a specific object of our attention."[2] Thus we witness today the disappearance of the political object, which came about precisely because of its omnipresence.

We can react in two ways. Of course we might acquiesce in or even applaud the gradual disappearance of the political object (and this course is recommended to us by all those who think that political problems are, in fact, socio-scientific problems). The alternative would be to start the search for the political object all over again. This is the strategy proposed by John Gunnell in an article entitled, just like this essay: "In Search of the Political Object." Gunnell admonishes us not to define politics in terms of the leftovers of epistemology or philosophy of science. However, for him there are no intrinsic political objects: "there are political objects, but the fact that they are political is predicational. It is a property, an attribute, or quality attached to certain instances of conventional objects."[3] In other words, it is convention that makes an object into a political object. This proposal has an immense plausibility if we bear in mind the variety of topics that have been politicized in the course of two and a half thousand years. But, as is so often the case with immensely plausible proposals, it is of little help in our present predicament. If present-day "convention" is such that we find it hard to define the political object, then an appeal to convention cannot contribute to a more accurate definition of what a political problem is. "Convention" can only result here in a restatement of our original difficulty.

In the first section of this essay I shall offer an explanation of why the political object has gradually lost its contours over the past three centuries. Next we shall see how this insight can lead to a resurrection of the political object. In the third and last section I shall investigate the nature of this new political object and of the political philosophy that has to study it.

Stoic Political Philosophy and the Disappearance of the Political Object

The gradual disappearance of the political object can be explained if we have recourse to the Stoic character of modern political philosophy since the seventeenth century; a Stoicism which, incidentally, has exercised its influence on many other areas of philosophical investigation as well. This *permanence du Stoicisme*, to quote M. Spanneut, has attracted relatively little attention,[4] probably because the all-pervasive Stoic character of modern Western philosophy since the seventeenth century could only be recognized from the point of view of the anti-Stoic, aesthetic philosophy gradually emerging today. The present-day owls of Minerva fly out in an aesthetic dusk.

When we think of the monism, the realism, or the rationalism of Stoicism or of its interest in logical and epistemological questions—when we consider its sympathy for a rationalist ethics or political philosophy (Cicero)—we find the same mood that has inspired most of modern Western thought about knowledge, science, and the sociopolitical order since the end of the sixteenth century. Whether we think of the Stoic intellectual faculties of συνκατάθεσις and διάνοια, our inner "forum" where true ideas are admitted to the mind, so obviously similar to Descartes's *idées claires et distinctes;* whether we think of the Stoic αἴσθητόν, that which is perceived by the senses; whether we think of the

Stoicist εἱμαρμένη, the equivalent of the modern idea of causality; whether we are reminded of the functionalism and the nominalism of the Stoics—everywhere we look we find evidence for the thesis that Western rationalism and empiricism since the seventeenth century have largely been a reenactment of and elaborations on Stoic conceptions.[5]

Of course, I do not wish to imply that modern philosophers in the rationalist and empiricist traditions have unwittingly been Stoics. My thesis merely is that Stoicism should be seen as a kind of master code that will enable us to give a new look to much of the history of Western philosophy. This thesis can be elucidated if we devote attention to the two related Stoic notions of οἰκειόωσις and the λόγοι σπερματικοί. Οἰκειόωσις (with its root οἶκος, "house") denotes the capacity of the human individual to identify both epistemically and morally with the rational, logical order of the universe. Such an identification is possible because the λόγοι σπερματικοί rule over two domains; according to Stoic panlogism, the ὀρθὸς λόγος, or *recta ratio*, in its manifestation of the λόγοι σπερματικοί, is operative on two levels. Reason rules both the world and the thought of rational man. Thus—and this is the crucial idea that determines a large part of my essay—the λόγοι σπερματικοί are, or embody, a common background; they embody a *tertium comparationis* in terms of which knowledge and the world can be compared to one another. There are not just two things—knowledge and the world—but we have *three* things: knowledge, the world, and a *tertium comparationis*, a hidden but ever-present background to both.

Our understanding of the Stoic master code can be deepened if we contrast Stoicism with its counterpart. The opposite of Stoicism is aestheticism, and it will function as such throughout this essay. Aestheticism rejects the *tertia comparationis* of Stoic philosophy, whatever its nature may be. It is so obvious as to be trivial that a rejection of such *tertia* is constitutive of the world of art (a rejection, I hasten to add, that has nothing to do with a rejection of metaphysics). Art knows neither *tertia* nor a common background for comparing the work of art with what it represents; what makes art interesting, "new," and aesthetically pleasing is precisely the fact that it successfully resists all mimetic (μίμησις not in the Aristotelian sense) attempts to reduce the work of art to reality by means of Stoic *tertia*. Thus Stoic philosophy should be contrasted with aesthetic philosophy, and because of the way this contrast has been formulated, there can be no doubt that these forms of philosophy formally and theoretically are mutually exclusive. More could be said, in the course of a close investigation, of what contemporary aestheticists have said concerning the artistic representation of reality, about how the rejection of the Stoic *tertia* has to result in aestheticism and vice versa.

From this perspective, a reinterpretation of several areas of Western philosophy is possible. It might be said that Kant's notion of the *Ding an sich* meant a decisive break with Stoic panlogism. However, Kant's idealist successors did everything they could to eliminate the anti-Stoic *Ding an sich* once again and, with the conflict between the Stoic master code and aestheticism in mind, we can now understand what their motivation was. More important, Kant himself and his neo-Kantian, positivist, empiricist, or analytical disciples have always tried to ignore the *Ding an sich* or to reduce it to a useless redundancy by concentrating on the epistemological links that tie language to the world and words to things. When seen in this way, all epistemology since Kant (including recent proposals like those of Putnam and Kripke to make theories of reference do what epistemology failed to achieve), is, in the final analysis, a reactionary attempt to undo the effects of Kant's Copernican revolution and, like all reactionary movements, bound to fail. For that which revolutions, whether they are intellectual or social revolutions, have once taken apart can never be put together again: all the distinctions that govern our lives have their origins in conceptual revolutions. Epistemology can never account for what we must now identify as the intrinsically aesthetic issues raised by the *Ding an sich*, and it is therefore the anti-Stoic, aesthetic path that we should follow once we have become aware of the intensely Stoic nature of so much of Western thought.

Because of its pronounced rationalism we are inclined to associate Stoicism primarily with epistemology, the philosophy of science, and, of course, the sciences themselves. However, with the exception of the Machiavellian, aesthetic tradition, most of our thinking about politics and the sociohistorical order (and its nature) is governed even more thoroughly by the Stoic *Weltanschauung*. And this should not surprise us. We all tend to agree with Vico's thoroughly Stoic insight that we can understand the sociohistorical world because we have made that world ourselves, whereas the physical world is not of our own making. That the sociohistorical world should contain something radically alien, something radically in- or unhuman, certainly is counterintuitive. Consequently, the Stoic notion of a *tertium comparationis* behind the individual human being or citizen and the sociohistorical world of state and political order has always seemed so obvious and self-evident that it has hardly been noticed. But its ubiquitous presence in much of contemporary and earlier philosophical thought cannot be doubted. Considering the contemporary scene, take for instance the twentieth-century phenomenological tradition that always strove for an unbroken continuum between the world of the individual and the social order; here *Lebenswelt* or interpretation form their common background. And social Stoicism reached an unexpected culmination in that brand of philosophy of action originally proposed by R. G. Collingwood and subsequently developed by W. H. Dray, G. A. von Wright, and many other proponents of intentional explanation. Surely, social Stoicism never found clearer expression than in Collingwood's re-enactment theory.[6]

Yet Collingwood's Stoicism is all the more astonishing if we recognize that the subject matter of his reflections—historiography—has arguably been the only discipline dealing with the sociohistorical world that has always demonstrated a remarkable resistance to Stoic seductions. This becomes clear if we remember that modern historiography has its origins in a rejection of both Stoic natural law theory and Stoic speculative philosophies of history. What Ranke, Burckhardt, and so many other historians found repulsive in the Hegelian system was the assumption that history is an essentially rational process in which

Reason, in its subjective form, ultimately recognizes itself in objective Reason—in short, the typical Stoic idea "daß die Vernunft die Welt beherrscht, daß es also in der Weltgeschichte vernünftig zugegangen ist."[7] Hegel historicized the Stoicism of classical natural law philosophy, but Reason preserved its function as the Stoic *tertium*; historiography, on the other hand, is anti-Stoic and aesthetic and the gap between speculative systems and historiography is therefore wider than is often believed these days.[8] It is, furthermore, interesting that nineteenth- and twentieth-century political philosophies with an historical orientation have always drawn their inspiration from Stoic speculative interpretations of the past and not from aesthetic historiography. Speculative systems were often seen as a morally acceptable basis for political ideologies, whereas historiography was thought to stimulate only Machiavellianism and *raison d'étât* thinking[9]—a typically Stoical way of seeing things. Next, we must note that the rejection by Popper, Mandelbaum, and many others of metaphysical, speculative interpretations of the past was always based on moral and epistemological, hence Stoic, arguments. This means that we should not see Stoicism as a kind of metaphysics—although under certain circumstances it may give rise to metaphysical systems. Nowhere does the debate about metaphysics transgress the borders of Stoicism: Stoicism may be just as easily be antimetaphysical as metaphysical. And that is what we might expect, since Stoicism was defined in terms of the *tertia* and not by speculations about the nature of reality. We must therefore distinguish strictly and clearly between the aesthetic rejection of speculative systems on the one hand and an antimetaphysical rejection of these systems on the other. The debate between Stoicism and aestheticism does *not* coincide with the debate about metaphysics.

What, then, about political philosophy? One may say that political philosophy has predominantly been of a Stoic nature and intent. Political philosophers have often attempted to explain, justify, or legitimate the state and the political order by deriving them from the (nature of the) individual citizen, the social order, or, as has become customary since the nineteenth century, from insights into a historical process embracing the citizen, the state, and the sociopolitical order. Taking the natural law tradition first, let us consider Hobbes and Rousseau. In that memorable chapter on representation in the *Leviathan*, Hobbes writes with respect to the representative (whom he designates as a *person artificiale*) that his actions are "owned" by those whom he represents.[10] The extremely close relationship of ownership between a person and the actions performed by him firmly ties together the citizen and the Hobbesian sovereign state and all the provocativeness of Hobbes's theory lies in his effort to make this link as strong as possible. Next, when Rousseau writes the famous words "enfin, chacun se donnant à tous ne se donne à personne; et comme il n'y a pas un associé sur lequel on n'acquièrt le même droit qu'on lui cède sur soi, on gagne l'équivalent de tout ce qu'on perd,"[11] the political order is presented to us as nothing but a convenient rearrangement of what was potentially already present in the prepolitical, natural order. And nowhere have the Stoic *tertia* found clearer or more influential expression than in the idea of popular sovereignty. This notion of popular sovereignty is a metaphor suggesting an idealized background against which we can move freely from the citizen to the state and vice versa.

For all their rhetoric against ahistorical natural law theories (or, perhaps, because of it), nineteenth- and twentieth-century ideologies have not abandoned the Stoic *tertia*, which here took the form of "history," in whatever way this word is understood. Consider, for instance, Marx's idea that the proletariat is, in our time, the designated maker of a new social order for no other reason than that the proletariat today is the substance of world history. Here the maker makes himself; he is his own actions and what is effected by them. This reads exactly like a historical adaptation of Hobbes's above-mentioned theory that the person represented "owns" the actions of the sovereign state and in both cases it is reliance upon a Stoic *tertium* that underlies the ideological short-cut.

Before entering upon a closer investigation of the Stoic *tertia* in Stoic political philosophy, we shall first proceed with the solution that can now be given for our initial problem: the disappearance of the political object. It should be observed here that it is precisely the purpose and logic inherent in the political *tertia* that in the end they should obliterate the political object and the clarity with which it stands out against a background. For it is the task of these *tertia* to make everything in the political universe maximally comparable, commensurable with everything else in this political universe. In other words, the *tertia* will naturally tend to suppress the generic differences between the citizen, the social order, and the state—in short, exactly that which is at stake in politics. And this tendency has been reinforced by the ideological debate which has been taking place over the past two centuries. It will need no clarification that most of this debate took, and had to take, the form of a debate about the nature of the *tertia*—about how the citizen, the sociohistorical order, and the state could be understood in terms of one another. Thus, and this is essential, ideological debate invited the *tertia* to surrender their modest, though influential, role in the background and to place themselves firmly at the foreground. It is this gradual movement from the background to the foreground on the part of the *tertia* that caused the political object's loss of identity and clear contours. This process was further stimulated by more prosaic factors, such as the growth and the alphabetization of the population, the tremendous increase in the power of the state and in interhuman contact, in the use of money (arguably the paradigmatic and most successful *tertium*) and, last but certainly not least, the revolution in the nineteenth and twentieth centuries in the means of communication. This communication revolution in particular effected a melting away of the sheer physical boundaries between ruler and ruled, between the state and the public and, therewith, of the political object. All in all, the Stoic *tertia* were responsible for the disappearance of the political object, and they made it disappear not by reducing several spheres one to the other—Stoicism is not necessarily reductionist—but by erasing the contours and the limits of these spheres.

This expiation of original political sin (as one might justifiably call it), this gradual evaporation of the political domain, has had some peculiar consequences. It has resulted in a depoliticization of politics and the state. To be more precise, politics and the state in its anti-Stoic or Machiavellianist form have come to be placed in a more or less transcendental position—in a position that, like the transcendental ego, can never be aware of itself. Politics and the state have become a negative presence, an empty arena never to be observed itself and whose existence can only be guessed at or inferred from its capacity to occasion what we, at present, call politics as well as the political science that studies this domesticated and denatured form of politics. Aesthetic political philosophy effects, as we shall see, an infinite number of smaller and larger rifts in the political order, rifts between the citizens mutually, between the citizens or social economic groups and the state, between the state and society, and so forth. By taking these rifts not as a *terminus ad quem* but instead as a *terminus a quo*, Stoic political philosophy and political science tended to explain away these rifts and by doing so succeeded in weaving the web that keeps the Stoic order together. In a word, by transcendentalizing and by marginalizing aesthetic politics, Stoic politics and political science have become possible and what has been made comparable and commensurable by Stoic political philosophy now has to be reaestheticized if we want to see politics as something more than the defective realization of Stoic schemata.

Political science is not the scientific study of political reality, since there is no such objective political reality outside political discourse—we shall deal with this in the next section. Political science, rather, is the socioscientific expression or reflection of Stoic political philosophy and is therefore our best guide if we want to know what practical effects the latter has. Contemporary political science demonstrates what the practical implications are of accepting Stoic political philosophy. In his recent and authoritative political theories of modern government, Peter Self concentrates on the two such implications he considers to be the most important: the fact that we can no longer distinguish between the state and society, and the growth of government bureaucracies. "It may pay both government and interest-group," Self writes, "to cooperate closely in policy-making and enforcement."[12] This close cooperation between the state and interest groups led, in the eyes of political scientists like Self, to a blurring of the contours of the state, and they therefore proposed the notions of the corporatist and the interventionist state in order to account for this gradual dissolution of the state in the social order.[13] However, we should note that the thesis of the dissolution of the state only makes sense against the background of Hobbesian or Rousseauist conceptions of the sovereign state. To put it bluntly, political science owes its existence to our unwitting attachment to the Stoic state, and it owes its field of investigation to the admittedly quite real gap existing between the Stoic state and the actual state. Thus Stocism produced a state that gradually dissolved into society and a political science giving us a detailed account of this evolution.

Nevertheless, I do not want to give the impression that political Stoicism is merely a matter of shadows chasing shadows. For Stoicism has undoubtedly been a powerful stimulus in the growth and development of government bureaucracy. In criticizing older theories on bureaucracy such as those of Max Weber and Woodrow Wilson—where bureaucracy is still seen as an instrument under the control of a centralized power—modern political scientists focus on the weakened capacity of the political leadership to direct and control bureaucracy from the top down.[14] Bureaucracy is a morbid growth that could attain its present proportions and complexity largely as the result of the characteristic Stoic unwillingness to acquiesce in the aesthetic rifts between the state on the one hand and the citizen and society on the other. Stoicism always strives for continuity, smoothness, and linearity, for a blurring of contours; it always experiences discontinuity, rifts, frictions, or interstices as challenges to itself, and this must, needless to say, strongly stimulate the growth of government bureaucracy. However, we can never eliminate the difference between a painting and the landscape that is represented by the painting; and for roughly similar reasons we can never eliminate these political rifts or frictions between the state and society, and our desperate efforts to achieve Stoic smoothness can only result here in an increasingly more complex bureaucracy.[15]

The result of Stoic political philosophy and its political practice has been succinctly summed up by Michael Walzer: "in contemporary Western societies power is dispersed, but not as democrats hoped to disperse it; not to citizens who argue and vote and so determine the politics of the central government. Citizenship and government alike have been superseded."[16] Stoic political philosophy has always aimed at putting an end to politics by means of its *tertia*, at "superseding" politics, and in a way it has succeeded. Political power, political issues, the political object have dissolved in the Stoic order like a drop of ink in a glass of water. How can this development be reversed? This is the question that will concern us in the next two sections.

The Resurrection of the Political Object in Aesthetic Political Philosophy

Until now I have refrained from saying anything specific about the nature of the *tertia*. Nevertheless, it may have become clear that they can be defined in many ways. Psychological characteristics of the individual human being, fear of death or injury or the wish to persist in one's personal existence, permitted Hobbes and Spinoza to argue from the individual to the state and the political order. Rousseau derived the political order from our better, moral selves, whereas Hegel, Marx, and their many disciples saw in history the *tertium comparationis*. And today we witness a remarkable renaissance of utilitarianism—that quantum theory of moral and political matter.

But by far the most obvious candidate for the *tertia* at present is language. And when I say language I mean any of the following specifications: "speech" as in the case of Hannah Arendt, "moral and political language" as meant by Oakeshott, "writing" if we wish to attribute to Derrida a political philosophy, "discourse" or even "truth" in the case of Foucault's speculations on power or "political vocabularies" as investigated by Pocock, the "speech-acts" discussed by Quentin Skinner, Habermas's "communicative action" and "ideal speech situation," or the "figurative language" as discussed by Hayden White.[17] The linguistic model of politics, though, is far from being a twentieth-century invention. Hobbes had seen the significance of language for politics[18] and at the end of the eighteenth century Herder made the ingenious suggestion that legislation should have language as its model. Language has a universalist dimension, because it enables people to communicate with one another; but language is also congenial to the individual, since it allows the individual to express his individuality. Thus the miracle wrought by language is that it reconciles the general with the individual; in language the general and the individual coexist in perfect harmony. If the law and the state are like language, our most urgent political problems must have been solved.[19] Although Oakeshott does not mention Herder, he has put forth a very similar idea.[20]

That language is relevant for politics has become more or less a platitude these days. Nevertheless, I must confess my inability to discover a common denominator in contemporary arguments to this effect.[21] After one has read Dallmayr's *Language and Politics* or Shapiro's volume with the same title, one is none the wiser in answering the question "Why does language matter to political philosophy?"[22] Admittedly, different answers to this question have been put forward, but insofar as there is any homogeneity to be observed, it seems to be purely accidental. What is more, a debate concerning the relative plausibility of these answers has never taken place. So if I suggest why language does matter to political philosophy, this is not a reconstruction but an objective account of the present state of affairs in the debate.

The political domain of contemporary Western democracies, whether defined Stocially or aesthetically, is the domain of political action, of citizens choosing their representatives and of these representatives acting on behalf of the electorate. The crucial political question is therefore "Who acts?" According to liberalism, individual citizens or politicians should be seen as political agents; according to Marxism, economic groups or interests fulfill this role. And in both cases we are dealing with entities existing *outside* (political) language. The transition from the liberal to the Marxist proposal was made mainly because the Marxist proposal was supposed to be more in accordance with political reality itself and with how this reality should be explained. Thus the perspective of explanation (and, as we shall find out in a moment, that of political legitimacy) stimulated a process of decentering that moved the real political agent ever further away from the liberal, enlightened individual who can still believe to be in complete control of his actions. Explanation and legitimacy functioned as a *vis a tergo* that pushed the political agent deeper and deeper into (explanatory) language. In this way the Stoic emphasis on explanation and on legitimacy effected the absorption of the political agent into language. Obviously, the final stage in this evolution had to be to designate language as the true political agent. And indeed, whether we think of Freudian psychoanalysis as interpreted by Lacan or of Gadamer's, Foucault's, or Derrida's speculations about who the author of the text is, in all cases what is outside language (the individual, the social or the historical group) has had to give way to language as the true agent. The traditional *tertia* of ideological political philosophy, which were always referentially defined, thereby lost their plausibility—language, speech, or discourse, being nonreferential *tertia*, ultimately took their place. And this must be the end of the evolution in question, for precisely because of its nonreferentiality the linguistic *tertium* can no longer be replaced by an even more perfect one. The referential nature of the *tertia* always evoked the idea of a more fundamental *tertium* that should be situated between itself and the level of language. Explanation (and legitimacy) naturally tended to absorb sociopolitical reality into language. However, with language, speech, or discourse—as these terms are understood at present—this movement has come to an end: linguistic political philosophy truly is the last and the highest stage of Stoic political philosophy.

Linguistic political philosophy as the logical outcome of three hundred years of Stoicism must awaken in the mind of the political philosopher an intense feeling of despair and hopelessness. Language is so ubiquitous, has such a Protean nature, knows so infinitely many usages, is such an elusive cultural phenomenon, is both so strong and so weak, so hard and so pliable, that political philosophers must feel at a loss regarding both their goals and their instruments. What can they expect from a political philosophy that respects no *de hors texte* and is even reluctant to recognize the existence of individual human beings and of social groups? To be more concrete, what seems to be left but the unpalatable choice between, on the one hand, a quietist acceptance of existing political language and institutions and, on the other hand, Orwellian attempts to tamper with this language? It may seem that we witness here the death of political philosophy.

It was Frank Lentricchia who, in an impressive and eloquent essay, accused linguistic political philosophy of political quietism, of what he called "political acedia."[23] His target was Paul de Man, whose literary criticism clearly entails a political philosophy. An absolute forgetting, an absolute disregard of what is and has been, appears to be, for De Man, the prerequisite for true political action, and because of the rejection by linguistic political philosophy of any referential or ontological anchor, this is what we might have expected. Someone who does not know where to begin to repair a broken watch had better throw it away and buy a new one. Thus nothing short of total revolution can be considered meaningful political change, and the inevitable result is, according to Lentricchia, "a paralysis of praxis" and "the inculcation of a matrix of despair, resignation, futility, frustration, cynicism and hopelessness."[24] As is well known, the same kind of accusation can be brought against Foucault. To take just one of the many examples, when Walzer speaks of the "catastrophic weakness" of Foucault's political philosophy[25] he has in mind Foucault's all too apparent inability to steer a reasonable middle course between a conservative acceptance of the powers that be and a total revolution reducing the Stalinist and the Maoist revolutions to mere child's play. And, exactly as in the case of De Man, the net result can only be an acceptance of what exists: "Foucault isn't a good revolutionary because he doesn't believe in the sovereign state of the ruling class. . . . There can't be a seizure of power if there is nothing at the center to seize."[26]

Stoic political philosophy in its ultimate, linguistic form can only help us to understand political practice (that is where Foucault's true genius as a historian lies); and from its beginnings in the days of Hobbes, Stoic philosophy has always remained quite close to the explanatory perspective. It explained what it legitimated and vice versa. The close alliance of legitimation and of the explanatory perspective has proved to be a formidable one, since it succeeded in creating the quasi-transparent Stoic political order we presently live in. What obscured the Stoic order could be put aside by the alliance as illegitimate, could thereby be pushed outside the political domain—think of the rejection of history by seventeenth-century rationalists or of morality by Hegel—and was placed beyond the grasp of politics. The alliance of explanation and legitimation thus produced a peculiar dialectics within which the political domain itself became smooth, transparent, and lacked any veritable point of application for political action, while such points of application as there were came to fall outside the political domain. Stoic political philosophy attempted and succeeded in creating for itself an *ideal* world in which it would be able to move freely from the citizen or the social group to the state and vice versa. However—and this marks the turning point in this essay—what *looks* ideal often turns out in practice to be exactly the reverse. This familiar but thought-compelling truth with its direct corollary has been formulated by Wittgenstein: "we have got onto the slippery ice where there is no friction and so in a certain sense the conditions are ideal, but also, just because of that we are unable to walk. We want to walk: so we need friction. Back to the rough ground!"[27]

So friction is what we need. And after the above diagnosis given of the Stoic disease we have some indications as to where we should look for friction. First, linguistic political philosophy is the highest stage of Stoicism and should therefore be our point of departure. Next, and this is crucial, if we look for friction we shall have to look *within* language, speech, discourse, or truth. We should not concentrate on language, speech, etc., *as such* but look where it breaks off or comes into contact with something outside it. This has been Foucault's (and perhaps De Man's) shortcoming. Foucault merely reversed Stocism: what the Stoic explanatory light of discourse was able to clarify was thereby legitimate for the Stoic, while Foucault would reject it for exactly the same reason. But we should avoid both forms of totalitarianism. Instead, in our search for friction and the political object, we now have to concentrate upon where language, speech, etc.—upon where the ultimate *tertium* of the Stoic tradition can no longer fulfill its role as *tertium*, that is, where it shows breaks, discontinuities, and anomalies within itself. We have to discover where language is no longer the continuum that, as a satisfactory Stoic *tertium*, it ought to be; we have to find out where language, speech, and discourse are no longer *un et indivisible* like that Stoic republic of the French revolutionaries.

The epochal significance of Derrida is, in my opinion, that his writings suggest a radical departure from Stoic conceptions of language. With Derrida it is not just that different texts are incommensurable if compared with one another, for this would leave the plausibility of the Stoic *tertia* merely suspended, but that texts have now become incommensurable with themselves—and that is decisive for the fate of language as Stoic *tertium*. When reading the text, Derrida tells us, "we must proceed using a double gesture, according to a unity that is both systematic and in and of itself divided, that is, a writing that is in and of itself multiple. . . . We must traverse a phase of overturning . . . , we are not dealing with the peaceful coexistence of a *vis à vis*, but rather with a violent hierarchy. One of the two terms governs the other (axiologically, logically, etc.) or has the upper hand. To deconstruct the opposition, first of all, is to overturn the hierarchy at a given moment."[28] Language or the text is always a palimpsest on which another counterlanguage or countertext is inscribed. And surely we are dealing here rather with a countertext or counterlanguage than with a metalanguage since there is an element of both proximity and opposition that a metalanguage could never contain. In spite of its proximity, this counterlanguage does not express something that was already present or remained hidden in the text. Derrida's "exorbitant," as he calls it, way of reading should be associated with dissemination rather than with polysemy. Polysemy is only intrinsic to the text and therefore still Stoic; dissemination, on the other hand, if we think for instance of what Derrida does with Rousseau's notion of the "supplement," is both intrinsic and extrinsic to the text.[29] Language and counterlanguage are related here as the front and the back of an infinitely thin piece of paper, and it is in their being different while in the closest proximity to each other that we discover the anti-Stoic "friction" of which Wittgenstein made us aware.

Even more revealing of Derrida's break with Stoic conceptions of language than a sustained exposition of his reading of texts here could be is Derrida's suspicion of spatial and ocular metaphors. Obviously, spatial metaphors are often used by philosophers in order to visualize their theories, and it is even likely that such metaphors do not determine the content any less than the exposition of these theories. Take for instance the plane on which we project the Fregean or Saussurean scheme of sign, extension, and intention; it is the very idea of this plane that has stimulated all kinds of theories of reference. Without it we would be far less sure about what we are looking for. It will need no clarification that in this case the plane is a spatial metaphor that functions as a *tertium comparationis* for the terms that are at issue in the philosophical date. And all the problems which theories of references as such may give rise to become visible as soon as we try to think away, or to do without, the spatial metaphor. Spatial metaphors (or visual metaphors) are typically Stoic, and resistance to them is a condition for anti-Stoic aesthetic philosophy.

But undoubtedly we need something more concrete than this for political philosophy. So let us have a look at the philosophy of history, that *trait d'union* between the philosophy of language and political philosophy. In the previous section we have seen that modern historiography was born out of a rejection of Stoic speculative philosophies of history. This anti-Stoic nature of historiography has become a central issue in the so-called narrativist philosophy of history. A point of departure has been Louis O. Mink's succinct statement "stories are not lived but told,"[30] the statement according to which there is an unbridgeable gap between life and narrative, between the past and its narrative representation, between what was said and written in the past and the historian's account of it. Mink's statement has been attacked by David Carr, who, in accordance with phenomenology, the most consistently Stoic social philosophy today, argued for the continuity between life and narrative: "Louis Mink was thus operating with a totally false distinction when he said that stories are not lived but told. They are told in being lived and lived in being told."[31] True, in our speech and in our writing, life and narrative may come infinitely close to each other, and in this sense stories can be part of our lives. However, living, speaking, or writing is *not* following a story, and the decisive argument is, as Mink pointed out, the fact that life, or the past, is not an "untold story" to which our narratives approximate as much as possible.[32] Narrative is not a mimesis or a copy of life. The whole raison d'être of all writing of history lies in historiography's transcendence of life, and what one might call "the historical object" only comes into being thanks to the difference between life and history despite their contiguity. The phenomenological philosopher who, like Carr or Paul Ricoeur, [33] obliterates this difference which exists despite contiguity throws us back into some indiscriminate, primeval philosophical chaos in which both the historical and the political object will be lost forever. If there is to be a resurrection of the political and the historical object, it can only take place on the graves of phenomenology and its intellectual scions.

We should even go one step further than Mink did. For we cannot fail to notice that the wedge driven between life and narrative is also present on the level of historical language itself. This is suggested by Mink's own argument concerning the role of chronological time in history. It is the task of the historian, wrote Mink, to achieve in narrative interpretation "a synoptic seeing together" of what took place in the past in chronological order.[34] This order of chronological time is truly "deconstructed," in the Derridean sense of the word, as this chronological order is first destructed and then replaced by a new, interpretative order. However, and this Mink did not point out, this chronological order must somehow be present on the narrative level itself as well. For chronological order is the point of departure for the historical narrative, even though it may be the precise purpose of the historian to overturn this order as much as possible in order to achieve a maximum of narrative coherence. Narrative coherence is achieved *in* and *by* a successful deconstruction of time. The anti-Stoic play of language and counterlanguage, of time-bound life and its narrativist deconstruction, is therefore a crucial dimension of and within the historian's use of language itself. Surely it is difficult to imagine a more complete reversal of Carr's and Ricoeur's Stoic position.

But there is an even more important side to the play of language and counterlanguage in historiography. In his last book, Hayden White proposed a so-called semiological reading of texts, which need not necessarily be historiographical texts. He describes the semiological perspective as follows: "a semiological perspective, on the other hand, treats the text less as an effect of causes more basic or as a reflection, however refracted, of a structure more fundamental than as a complex mediation between various codes by which reality is to be assigned possible meanings. It seeks, first of all, to identify the hierarchy of codes that is established in the process of the text's elaboration, in which one or more emerge as seemingly self-evident, obvious, natural ways of making sense of the world."[35] The suggestion is, clearly, that the text is a hierarchy of codes, while the interplay between these codes gives rise to "seemingly self-evident, natural ways of making sense of the world," or, to use Roland Barthes's phraseology, to an *effet du réel,* a "reality effect," that is, to a definition of the nature of the sociohistorical reality we live in. In his previous writings White had frequently emphasized that historical reality is not a reality "out there" but should be seen rather as a kind of shadow accompanying our narrative interpretations or language. What *is* "out there" are historical documents, artifacts, etc., and naive historical realism always drew its inspiration from our constant inclination to equate historical reality with historical evidence. While in his earlier views the break with Stoicism was less conspicuously present, White's more recent emphasis on the hierarchies and rifts within historical language itself brings him closer to a "deconstructivist" anti-Stoicism, according to which the nature of sociohistorical reality is defined by those hierarchies, rifts, "aporias," or "undecidabilities" within the historical text itself. Historical language is like a prism: by refracting the light coming from historical evidence, it gives us historical reality.

The political implications of all this will be obvious. For is not he who has both the right and the duty to define the nature of sociohistorical reality—the historian, the social scientist, the philosopher—the politician par excellence? Politicians, as we know them, only administer what is created in and by historical or socioscientific discourse. The fate of the historical object is clearly related to that of the political object: both owe their origin to the frictions within narrative language. Let me explain it differently. Is not reality our supreme authority? Revolutionaries, too, have to recognize the authority of the reality they wish to change and, even more, that of the future reality that inspires their revolutionary élan. Every meaningful political standpoint, whether reactionary or revolutionary, has above all to recognize the authority of political reality; only the dreamer can afford to be disrespectful of reality's authority. However, as Derrida and White have suggested, sociopolitical reality should not be conceived of as a passive, objective deadweight "out there." Political reality is not a *de hors texte*; rather, it is a shadow accompanying the texts written by historians, social scientists, philosophers, and, last but not least, novelists. *They* are the real politicians; they do not passively reproduce a sociopolitical view of reality created by politicians. On the contrary, they define the space in which the political game will be played. And the definition of this space, of the political field, originates in the frictions and tensions arising from the interplay of linguistic codes and tropes that have been discussed by White since his *Metahistory.* Thus not only are these frictions and tensions between codes, semantic hierarchies, and tropes of importance to the historian or to the philosopher of history, but they also determine what the content and purpose of political debate will be.

It must be emphasized that this political reality is a reality precisely because it is, in a certain sense, beyond our control. What is within the scope of conscious (Stoic) control has no objective existence. But the political reality meant here has its origin in the free and intersubjective play of frictions both within and between historical texts. It is, so to speak, the result of a kind of "invisible hand" that no historian or social scientist can claim is his own. Two consequences follow from this. First, since historical texts create these frictions freely, whereas the social scientist, at least in theory, tends to distrust and avoid them, historiography must be our natural focus of interest if we wish to discuss the origins of sociopolitical reality. Second, we may agree with Hans Kellner's statement that "for twenty years the thrust of White's inquiry into the nature of historical thinking has been to single out the moral and aesthetic . . . values in the choices underlying historical images."[36] Nevertheless, we must take exception to the term *moral* and replace it by the term *political*: the term *moral* suggests a dimension of conscious (Stoic) rule-guided deliberation that is in defiance of the nature of sociopolitical reality as presented here. Aesthetic political philosophy is certainly not an annex of moral philosophy.[37]

To round off this section I shall formulate the conclusions that can be derived from what has been said, especially insofar as these conclusions are of relevance for the next section. Stoic political philosophy ultimately opted for language as the *tertium comparationis.* Without a further specification of political language—to be more precise, if language is either explicitly or implicitly still seen as a smooth, transparent medium—language will effect the disappearance of the political object and linguistic political philosophy will then mean the death of political philosophy. However, White's investigations of historical language have made clear to us that language *does* have the capacity to restore the political object to us. The condition is that we must recognize the opacity of language (historical and political) and the presence in it of Derridian rifts and frictions. Narrativist philosophy of history as proposed by White must therefore be the key if we wish to develop a new aesthetic political philosophy. In the next section we shall see how friction in (political) language is constitutive of political reality and of political power. The aesthetic political philosophy to be expounded could thus best be seen as a translation of narrativist philosophy of history into political philosophy.

The Aesthetic Education of the State

In this section I shall give a rough draft of what an aesthetic political philosophy might be. The conclusions from the previous paragraph provide us with a matrix for such a philosophy. This matrix can be summed up in the following six points.

First, political philosophy should not be referential or ideological in the sense that extralinguistic entities such as individual citizens and social groups serve as the foundation for political philosophy. Aesthetic political philosophy is consistently antifoundationalist, and extralinguistic political reality does not *precede* political language but is *derivative* from it.[38] The polemical sting of this thesis is, of course, that it implies the rejection of each attempt to found political philosophy on the social, rational, etc., character of the human individual, or on any other extralinguistic property of either the individual or society. Aesthetic political philosophy is ruthlessly formalist and nominalist.

Second, this antifoundationalism implies for political philosophy a rejection of the reassuring perspectives of explanation and legitimacy for political philosophy. These two closely related perspectives always presupposed the existence of a given outside and prior to political philosophy itself. Both perspectives are suggestive of a reductive attitude that has always severely handicapped traditional political philosophy when it has tried to come to terms with the highly creative political administrations of contemporary Western democracies. The permanent "newness" of the state renders it irreducible to the "is" and the "ought" of the explanatory and legitimating perspective. This does not mean that state and political order should be seen as inexplicable and illegitimate; rather, that explanation and legitimacy are of little use if we want to define ourselves politically in our present predicament.

Three, aesthetic political philosophy has language as its model and its point of departure. It seems likely that Shapiro is correct when he suggests that Saussure's semiotics will prove useful in elaborating this model.[39] And because language, knowledge, communication, and information are the most powerful determinants of contemporary Western societies, the linguistic model of necessity *is* virtually inescapable in our time.

Four, and this will be the leitmotiv of this section, our attention within this linguistic model should be directed more toward frictions, differences, uncertainties, and ambivalences than toward continuity, smoothness, and transparency. The emphasis here is clearly different from that of Foucault. In his speculations on knowledge and power, Foucault most often followed the transparent Stoic gaze until it met the opacity of a radically alien discourse, that of the madman, the homosexual, or the delinquent. Within the less dramatic Derridean model proposed here, friction arises not only at the extremities of Stoic language but, more important, within it. Politics thus leaves the periphery where Foucault tended to concentrate it and, by doing so, radicalized it unnecessarily.

Five, the political world of aesthetic political philosophy is, in striking contrast to the Stoic tradition since Hobbes and even Marx,[40] an irrevocably broken world. Aestheticism destroys all *tertia* in terms of which a (re)integration or (re)unification of the political world had always been attempted within the Stoic tradition. The aesthetic political world is an alienated world. The aesthetic philosophy proposed here is therefore opposed to that of Schiller. When Schiller looked for an aesthetic motivation for ethical behavior, aestheticism was, in his eyes, the best instrument to fight the alienation he considered to be so characteristic of his own age. His reluctance to break free from the Kantian categorical imperative—a Stoic *tertium* if ever there was one—undoubtedly caused Schiller to associate aestheticism with unification rather than with friction and alienation. For the aesthetic political philosophy proposed here, alienation is something positive, the true mark of political freedom and autonomy. Perhaps we should distinguish between two kinds of alienation: the alienation from the self suffered if one has to conform to some Stoic order versus the alienation from a Stoic order if the limitations of this order become visible from an aesthetic point of view. Schiller, the left-Hegelians and the romantic *schöne Seelen* of this century and the last undoubtedly had the former kind of alienation in mind. But the latter kind of alienation as conceived of here can be seen as the origin of freedom, since it emancipates us from the "horizontal" social chain where the gains and the joys of the one are intrinsically related to the losses and the sorrows of the other. A "vertical" dimension is revealed in which we can express ourselves socially and politically without intruding upon the spheres of others. John Caputo obviously had this "vertical" or "aesthetic" dimension in mind when he defined his so-called "ethics of dissemination" as follows: "an ethics of dissemination is an ethics of otherness aimed at giving what is other as big a break as possible."[41] Within this vertical dimension we do certainly form a community, but this is a community to which we belong precisely because of our "difference" from others. If this sounds vague and imprecise, I'd like to draw a parallel between the political community and the world of culture. The truly great works of art, literature, and the history of Western culture undisputedly do belong to one cultural community and yet they do not stand in the way of one another; on the contrary, the greater their diversity, their "alienation" from one another, the richer the cultural and aesthetic universe that is defined by them. In one word, to deplore alienation is to deplore both culture and politics.

Six, we should not look with too much despair upon this world of moral confusion depicted so convincingly by A. MacIntyre in *After Virtue*.[42] Rather, this moral confusion should be seen to reflect the fact that we have outgrown the several Stoic determinations of social reality that have been proposed over the centuries. I personally find the spectacle of this moral diversity rather pleasing and certainly less menacing than those sudden upsurges of Stoic consensus that have so much disfigured the face of Western history. What is, for example, so wonderful about the Reformation is that no party won this religious battle and the first major friction or rift was thus introduced in the European mind. In our time there certainly is no longer room for nostalgia, for the kind of Stoic οἰκειώσις that inspired *After Virtue*.

If frictions, ambiguities, and the play of language and counterlanguage are to be the leitmotiv for aesthetic political philosophy, two tasks lie before us. First, we have to trace the locus of these frictions; this will give us the political object. Second, we have to develop a political language that is appropriate for dealing with this political object both in political philosophy and in political practice. The first task is not difficult to carry out. The destabilization or breaking up of the Stoic political universe by aesthetic political philosophy undoubtedly will cause frictions at numerous places: everywhere the clear contours required by Stoic political philosophy will tend to give way to ambiguity and uncertainty because of a dialectic proper to Stoic political philosophy itself. The Stoic wish for clarity ultimately resulted in a blurring of the contours of the objects of the political universe. But nowhere has this destabilization been more conspicuous than in the case of the state. As we have seen in the first section, the (notion of the) state has been the most prominent victim of this Stoic dialectic entailed by the Stoic's confidence in the *tertia*—and for that very same reason the state also has to be the most prominent candidate to function as the political object of aesthetic political philosophy.

However, the following qualification should be added at once. Within the Stoic tradition, the term *the state* called to mind something massive, solid, blocklike. On the other hand, because of the differential character of the state of aesthetic political philosophy, we ought not to conceive of the state as a coherent unity. The state is no longer—and this happens to be in accordance with actual political reality that has become aestheticist of its own accord—a political institution that has crystallized around a well-defined center, a center of supreme political authority or of political sovereignty. There is no longer a sole subject of political power, embodied in either the monarch of absolutism or the parliaments of contemporary Western democracies.[43] To put it metaphorically, the state and political power have gradually moved from the center to the periphery, to where the state and what is not the state come into contact. And, as we shall see, we have to accept what this centrifugal movement entails—the fact that "the center" no longer exists. All the traditional Stoic metaphors proposing that the state be seen as a (unitary) body or, more specifically, as a ship that is set on a certain course and has to be "steered," now have to be abandoned.[44] Our predicament has been aptly characterized by Holton as follows: the state is like "the labyrinth with the empty center, where the investigator only meets his own shadow,"[45] his own "Stoic" shadow, I should like to add. The state has become a mosaic of institutions and, just as in the case of a mosaic, the unity it has does not lie in itself but is in the eyes of the beholder.

If we are looking for a sociological specification of this aesthetic model of the state and of the political order, we are well advised to recall that the term *politics* is derived from the word πόλις. Whether we think of classical political philosophy, of Hannah Arendt's admiration for this tradition, of Rousseau's lifelong affinity for Geneva—and we can add to this list—in all these cases the city is the sociological model for politics. If, then, the village or the small, surveyable city has been the obvious model for Stoic politics, the modern metropolis has to be the model for aesthetic politics. Life in the modern *Großstadt*, life in the Asphalt Jungle, was the subject of a number of novels in the 1920s. Take, for instance, Alfred Doblin's *Berlin Alexanderplatz* (1929), Hans Fallada's *Kleiner Mann was nun?* (1932), Bernhard Kellerman's *Der 9. November* (1920), or John Dos Passos's *Manhattan Transfer* (1925) or, to take painting, the expressionism of Conrad Felixmuller.[46] Authors like Doblin and Dos Passos had the striking insight that one could only be an insider of the *Großstadt* by being an outsider. In a paradoxical way one can only become a true citizen of the *Großstadt* after abandoning the desire to be part of it. One is excluded from the *Großstadt* if one tries to endow it with a certain essence with which one wants to identify oneself. For attempts to identify with the *Großstadt* invariably meet with an emptiness, a hollowness, a nothingness, and it is precisely this experience that one has to accept if one is to become a real citizen of the *Großstadt*. Similarly, we should no longer strive to identify ourselves with an ideological center or essence of the state; the state manifests itself now in an infinity of small apparently insignificant encounters with the public.

Such insight has, of course, been common enough since Foucault drew our attention to the "capillaries of power" and to the fact that we still need to cut off the king's head.[47] What is a great deal less obvious is how we should react to this situation. Stoics will regret the loss of clarity and insist upon a redefinition of the state and of its relation to the public. Aesthetics, on the other hand, will see this situation not as the result of an evolution we have lost control of and which has to be reversed but rather as the point of departure for a new definition of political philosophy and political practice. The main task of this new political philosophy must be to indicate how contact between the public and this dispersed, "disseminated" state should be regulated. One thing is clear, however. Stoicism culminated in linguistic political philosophy; in language, therefore, lies the key for solving our problem. This, then, brings me to the second topic of this section: the question of what language we should use in political philosophy and political practice.

The most obvious answer to this question is aesthetic language. I shall enumerate the virtues of this proposal. Aesthetic political language characterizes the relation between the state and the public correctly, since it expresses the fact that there are no ultimate *tertia* in terms of which this relation can be defined. This has an important consequence. If neither the state itself nor its political actions are ever completely reducible to the public or the electorate by means of some *tertium*, the rift or difference between state and public is inescapable. In this simple datum lies the origin of the state's political power. For Stoics this power of the state must be illegitimate, since by its very nature it cannot be an extension or implementation of the political will of the public. Aesthetic political philosophy can accept this power for both a theoretical and a practical reason. From a theoretical point of view, it can be pointed out that the Stoic's condemnation of the political power in question is like condemning the work of art for not being identical to the reality represented in it. But anyone who requires the work of art to be identical to the reality represented in it simply rejects art; similarly, the Stoic's insistence on the identity of the political will of the public and that of the state in fact rejects politics and government. Speaking from a more practical point of view, we may say that the rift between the public and the state, from which political power originates, is covered by political representation: the representative is both the master and the slave of those whom he represents. This strongly suggests that political representation, the procedure by which the public chooses its representatives who act on its behalf and are responsive to the public, must be the heart of all politics. The political object can only articulate itself in the non-Stoic openness that is created by aesthetic political representation. Here the rifts and frictions referred to in the previous section find their origin and permanence.[48]

On the other hand, the proposal to use the language of aesthetics has two disadvantages. We are inclined to use aesthetic language with regard to the aesthetic object as such rather than with regard to its relation to the reality represented in it, which seems to rule out the possibility of an interaction between the two—and no one will doubt that the interaction between the state and the public is essential for all politics. Next, even if we maintain the relational character of aesthetic representation, another difficulty remains. Aesthetic language is an object-language in that it talks about aesthetic objects and their relation to the world but does not absorb this relation into itself. It therefore lacks the "performative force" that political language should possess. So the notion of aesthetic language has to be supplemented by another. To this end I propose educational language. Intuitively we believe that the child and the adult belong to different worlds in the sense that there is no shared background of either meaning or social practice against which the child can define the words used by the parent in its presence. One might say that education, the play of the adult's language and the counterlanguage of the child, has as its purpose the constitution of such a shared background. And education comes to an end when such a background is available; from that time on, the dictionary will suffice to solve the child's semantic problems. This intuition is confirmed by what psychologists are saying about meaning acquisition by the child. Psychologists such as Susan Carey and John MacNamara have demonstrated that there are no *tertia*, as we could call them, that determine the process of meaning acquisition by the child.[49] The process is, therefore, aesthetic in the sense meant here. However, in the context in which language is used by both the child and the adult, the interaction we missed in the case of purely aesthetic language will be prominently present. Moreover, language, meaning itself, is at stake here. So what we might refer to as educational language is free from the limitations of aesthetic language. It is possible that other kinds of language or contexts of the use of language would also be suitable, but I consider it superfluous to continue our search.

Consequently, the anti-Stoic political language we have been looking for can be defined as aesthetic, educational language that aims at the aesthetic education of the state. Friedrich Schiller was the first *Bildung* philosopher to use this concept of aesthetic education. However, in his *Letters on Aesthetic Education* Schiller spoke of the aesthetic education of man, not of the state.[50] Schiller even said that he could not conceive of the aesthetic state before "die Trennung in dem innern Menschen wieder aufgehoben und seine Natur vollständig genug entwickelt ist, um selbst die Künstlerin zu sein und der politischen Schöpfung der Vernunft ihre Realität zu verbürgern."[51] Schiller seems to require here a kind of congruence between the aesthetic state and the aesthetically formed individual: they should have a microcosm-macrocosm relationship to each other. It goes without saying that there can be no room here for a Stoic intuition such as this. For Schiller attempts to reduce the relation between public (or man) and the state to one Stoic axis again. In contrast to this, aesthetic education as meant here requires the relation between the public and the state to be aesthetic itself, and the aesthetic education of the state takes place in the "space" or "field" that has come into being thanks to the enforcement of the aesthetic difference between public and state contrary to all Stoic intuitions. Schiller firmly locked the aesthetic dimension within the sphere of the individual and that of the state and kept it out of the relation between them—but that is precisely where we need it.

If we allow ourselves to speak of the aesthetic education of the state and bear in mind where it differs from Schiller's, we obtain a new view of the Stoic state and of how it contrasts with the aesthetic state. The Stoic model could be compared with a tree. The public or the electorate forms the roots of the tree. The trunk of the tree is where the citizens are brought together and are made politically commensurable; this is where all the traditional liberal notions of the *Rechtsstaat* of popular sovereignty and of the continuity between the citizen and the state originate. The tree branches out in the different government departments that reach down again to the citizen thanks to bureaucratic interpretation of government decision. We go up with popular sovereignty and down again with bureaucracy—and that demonstrates once again how much these two need, stimulate, and depend upon each other. The Stoic continuity between the state and the public finds its expression in both bureaucracy and the notion of popular sovereignty. The aesthetic, educational model drives a wedge in this unitary system. Therefore it has instead the form of a square, with the public and the state at the top and the bottom and two educational processes as the sides. On the one side we find the aesthetic education of the state by the public, on the other the education of the citizen by the state. The crucial difference, then, between this and the tree model is that the two educational processes, if they are to function properly, should never come *together* in a common trunk but should always be kept *as far apart* as possible. In contrast to Schiller's view, the aesthetic education of the state and that of man should never be cast in the same mold. To the degree that they move closer together their educational value will be reduced accordingly. With the latter model in mind we have every reason to agree with Jürgen Habermas when he condemns what he calls "die Verrechtlichung des Schul- und Familienrechts"[52] as follows: "der Rechtsschutz von Schülern und Eltern . . . wird mit einer tief in die Lehr- und Lernvorgänge eingreifenden Justizialisierung und Bürokratisierung erkauft."[53] This tendency is described by Habermas as "dysfunctional,"[54] but it is, of course, highly functional from the perspective of the state, since this will diminish the gap between the two educational processes. One educational process thus gradually gets infected by the language, the vocabulary, and the social practice belonging to the other and its function is reduced accordingly. For roughly similar reasons, both education in school and political preference should always go beyond what falls within the scope of science (or what is *seen* as science). The crucial fact here is that science *is* taught at schools and universities and *is* invoked for gaining the support of the public for government policies. Being, therefore, the common denominator of *both* educational processes, an excessive emphasis on science also endangers the independence of both educational processes. Anti-Stoic disciplines such as art, literature, and history form, from this perspective, an essential part of the curriculum at schools and universities.

No political philosophy without demonstrable consequences for political practice deserves to be taken seriously. So we must now ask ourselves what the purpose of the aesthetic education of the state could be. We spoke of the differential relation between the language and counterlanguage of the public and of the state. From this we can derive a definition of political evil. Not the abuse of power but a failure to accept the instruments offered by aesthetic education, an acquiescence in misunderstanding, is the paramount evil in contemporary Western democracies. This paradigm of political evil was poignantly described by Richard Brown: "this is why we feel so estranged when trying to communicate with either schizophrenics or with bureaucrats: in each case we encounter a world of perfect rationality which is so abstracted and disconnected from shared experience as to be false and unreal."[55] Kafkaesque experiences such as these exemplify the kind of frictions that Stoic political philosophy always sought to ignore or, at best, to interpret as regrettable lapses from Stoic unity that have to be, and in principle *can be*, corrected. Aesthetic political philosophy, on the other hand, recognizes the inevitability of these frictions.

However, by taking these frictions more seriously than Stoicism did, aesthetic political philosophy has a better chance of dealing with them effectively. Aesthetic political philosophy can point out that we have political representation to combat Kafkaesque misunderstandings. And it would certainly help to replace bureaucracy, wherever possible, by representation. But, more important, the idea of the aesthetic education of the state is also valuable here. Contemporary aestheticists like Gombrich, Danto, and Gadamer recognize that the work of art, if it represents a person or a landscape, also presents *itself* in its representation.[56] The work of art has an opacity, an element of self-referentiality, in which it differs from a *trompe l'oeuil*. As Danto has demonstrated, it is this self-referentiality or "intentionality" of the work of art that we naturally associate with its style.[57] If we transpose this insight of political philosophy, we may conclude that what is radically alien, that is, what can never be understood from the Stoic perspective of the state, is the style of the state. Stoicism can only ascertain that there is or is not, or that there is only to a certain degree, a congruence between what the state does and the political wishes of the public; but the style of the state must always remain an *arcanum imperii* within the Stoic tradition. Style is never reducible to Stoic *tertia*, however subtle these may become. On the other hand, aesthetic political philosophy, by leaving room for the autonomy of the state with respect to the public (and its political wishes), creates room for the concept of the style of the state. More than that, for aesthetic political philosophy the state should preferably be understood in stylistic terms. To paraphrase Buffon: *le style, c'est l'état même.*

Now that we have this concept in our possession we can grasp what hitherto was beyond our reach. For with the introduction of the notion of the style of the state, the otherness of the state remains intact, the aesthetic divide between the state and the public is not ignored but respected, the double educational process we discussed above is not conflated into a single one, yet we now have the possibility of recognizing what lies on the other side of the aesthetic divide.

Both the public and the politician now have an additional instrument at their disposal for reducing the (stylistic) conflicts between the state and the public. True, this aesthetic divide can never be completely closed; aesthetic political philosophy is not a kind of super-Stoicism that will succeed where Stoicism failed. Nevertheless, the aesthetic concept of the style of the state and of politics will clarify much to which Stocisim of necessity remained blind. And this new insight will undoubtly contribute to a more satisfactory political practice. We shall have to abandon the ideals of Stoicism for the realities of aesthetic political philosophy. Similarly, we can make better use of a car if we recognize that it is not a ship, even if this means that we shall now have to abandon the hope of crossing the oceans in it. To put it in a single formula: the notion of the style of the state permits us to bridge the gap between the state and the public while surrendering the hope of closing it altogether. And this is in accordance with what political practice is like and has always been like and, moreover, with the present interest in the non-Stoic aspects of (political) language: rhetorics, figurative language, and literary style. I can therefore wholeheartedly agree with John Nelson, who wrote: "at a minimum, it seems to follow for the historical moment that political theory and political interpretation should concentrate on politics as style and style as politics."[58] What threatens to escape our political grasp in this Indian summer of Stoic political philosophy becomes a suitable topic for political theory and interpretation if understood as political style.

We should be interested not so much in what the state does or does not do, but rather in its behavior. "Doing" is suggestive of an ideological, Stoic identification with the state, of a transgressing of the aesthetic divide between state and public and of the possibility of having access to what Collingwood referred to as the "inside" of an action. Behavior and style, on the other hand, are consonant with the oblique "metropolitan" gaze we cast on the state; we see only its outside, as it were—from the aesthetic point of view the state only *has* an outside. I would like to emphasize that this does not mean a marginalization of the role and function of aesthetic politics. Since Goodman and Quine we have known that no clear distinction can be made between style and content and that much that is initially perceived of as a matter of substance or content can be shown to be a matter of style. This can be clarified if we consider a few examples of political style. The state may be lenient or strict, active or standoffish, proud or modest, and we can speak of the minimal state or of the welfare state and so on, for the repertory of ideologies is very limited compared with the abundance of political styles. However, as these examples of political styles must have suggested already, in many cases the issues of ideological political philosophy can easily be translated into the terminology of political style.

Apart from returning to us what we shall lose with Stoic political philosophy and practice, political style has one more advantage that needs mentioning. As both the public and the politician should realize, changes in political style can be effected more or less from one day to the other, whereas ideological changes may take years to achieve, and even then they may easily fall victim to such contingencies as social unrest and economic crises. Moreover, stylistic changes can be effected relatively easily for the totality of the government apparatus. Stoic political philosophy, with its predilection for continuity and linearity, offers little hope of changing the mentality of the middle levels of bureaucracy. But style can embrace all levels of government bureaucracy; here bureaucracy no longer has the opportunity to disappear from sight by appealing to bureaucratic hierarchy. This is like an "opening up" of the state. Thus political style may revivify what tends to become fossilized in the highly complex bureaucracies of contemporary Western societies. There is a category of political issues (like the allocation of financial means to different government departments) that can be found exclusively on the state's side of the aesthetic divide and that, therefore, by their very nature can only be conceived of stylistically. In a word, style may make visible again what tends to be obscured by Stoic political practice—admittedly an obvious conclusion if we recall that aesthetic political philosophy creates rifts and frictions where Stoicism strove for continuity and smoothness.[59]

Conclusion

This essay was an attempt to deconstruct traditional ideological and Stoic political philosophy. I have tried to show that Stoic political philosophy always wished to explain or to legitimate the state in terms of a *tertium* embracing both the state as the political object and the public, society, or whatever else is seen as the foundation of the state. However, a secret and hidden countermovement was discernible in all these attempts to define the political object, a countermovement that would ultimately result in the evaporation of the political object into language. The political object can be restored to life if an aesthetic rift is introduced into Stoic political language itself. This rift creates both political power and political reality—terms which for aesthetic political philosophy are interchangeable. The self-destruction of Stoic political philosophy could be checked by placing these aesthetic rifts in the foreground. In political practice this means a plea in favor of the aesthetic education of the state. The two closely related notions of political representation and political style indicate where and how this aesthetic education can take place. In political representation we encounter the "opening" in which the state can develop its style. In this aesthetic "opening" the aesthetic education of the state also takes place, an education in a political style that can never come to a (Stoic) end, since the presence of this "opening" is the very condition for the education of the state. Politics will never come to an end; but we can be sure of better and more efficient political practice if we decide to do more with this notion of political style.

NOTES

1. F. R. Dallmayr, *Polis and Praxis* (Cambridge, 1984), p. 42.

2. E. H. Kossmann, "Veertig Jaren," in Kossmann, *Politieke theorie en geschiedenis* (Amsterdam, 1987).

3. J. G. Gunnell, "In Search of the Political Object: Beyond Methodology and Transcendentalism," in J. Nelson, ed., *What Should Political Theory Be Now?* (Albany, 1983), p. 42.

4. See M. Spanneut, *Permanence du Stoïcisme: De Zenon à Malraux* (Gembloux, 1973). The number of authors who have stressed the importance of the Stoic legacy is relatively small; examples are P. Barth, M. Pohlenz, R. M. Wenley, and the Polish logician J. Lukasiewicz.

5. See, for a more detailed exposition of these Stoic concepts, Spanneut, esp. chaps. I, II, and III; and M. van Straaten, *Kerngedachten van de Stoa* (Roermond, 1969).

6. Surely Collingwood's requirement that "the historian must re-enact the past in his own mind" is the most Stoic statement made by any twentieth-century philosopher. See R. G. Collingwood, *The Idea of History* (Oxford, 1970), p. 282. See also W. H. Dray, *Laws and Explanation in History* (Oxford, 1970), and G. H. von Wright, *Explanation and Understanding* (London, 1971). The amount of Stoic literature on intentional explanation is immense.

7. G. W. F. Hegel, *Vorlesungen über die Philosophie der Weltgeschichte. Band I. Die Vernunft in der Geschichte* (Hamburg, 1955), p. 28.

8. For the continuity between the natural law tradition and Hegel, see B. Croce, "La naissance de l'historisme," *Revue de métaphysique et de morale* (1937), p. 606 ff. Remarkably, this article is not discussed in D. D. Roberts, *Benedetto Croce and the Uses of Historicism* (Berkeley, 1987). For a forceful attempt to close the gap between speculative systems and historiography, see H. Fain, *Between Philosophy and History* (Princeton, 1973). The same tendency is present in H. White, *Metahistory: The Historical Imagination in Nineteenth-Century Europe* (Baltimore, 1973) and in P. Munz, *The Shapes of Time* (Middletown, 1978).

9. The *locus classicus* for all problems concerning the Machiavellianist implication of historiography is F. Meinecke, *Die Idee der Staatsräson in der neueren Geschichte* (Munich, 1957).

10. T. Hobbes, *Leviathan* (London, 1970, Everyman's Library), pp. 90, 84.

11. J. J. Rousseau, *Du contrat social* (Paris, 1962, Classiques Garnier), p. 244.

12. P. Self, *Political Theories of Modern Government: Its Role and Reform* (London, 1985), p. 111.

13. The two concepts of the corporatist and the interventionist state are closely related: if the state is an institution that can claim no more than to be a *primus inter pares* if compared with other institutions, the term *intervention* nicely defines the limits of its power. See J. W. de Beus and J. A. A. van Doorn, *De interventiestaat* (Meppel, 1984).

14. Self, p.141.

15. See F. R. Ankersmit, "Politieke representatie: Betoog over de esthetische Staat," *Bijdragen en mededelingen betreffende de geschiedenis der Nederlanden*, 102 (1987), pp. 358–79.

16. M. Walzer, "The Politics of Michel Foucault," in D. C. Hoy, ed., *Foucault: A Critical Reader* (Oxford, 1986), p. 53.

17. See, for example, H. Arendt, *The Human Condition* (Chicago, 1958), p. 4; M. Oakeshott, *On Human Conduct* (Oxford, 1975), p. 63 ff; J. Derrida, "Préjuges—devant la loi," *La faculté de juger* (Paris, 1985); M. Foucault, *Power/Knowledge* (New York, 1980); J. G. A. Pocock, "Verbalizing a Political Act," in M. Shapiro, ed., *Language and Politics* (Oxford, 1984), and "Languages and Their Implications: The Transformation of the Study of Political Thought," *Politics, Language and Time* (New York, 1973); Q. Skinner, "Meaning and Understanding in the History of Ideas," *History and Theory*, 8 (1969), p. 3 ff., and "Conventions and the Understanding of Speech Acts," in P. King, ed., *The History of Ideas* (London, 1983), p. 259 ff.; H. V. White, *Tropics of Discourse* (Baltimore, 1978), and *The Content of the Form* (Baltimore, 1987). Representative of linguistic political philosophy are the essays in J. Nelson, ed., *What Should Political Theory Be Now?* (Albany, 1983), and J. Habermas, *Theorie des kommunikativen Handelns*, vol. 2 (Frankfurt, 1982).

18. Hobbes, p. 369; J. W. Danford, *Wittgenstein and Political Philosophy* (Chicago, 1978), pp. 16–73.

19. F. M. Barnard, *Herder's Social and Political Thought* (Oxford, 1965), chap. 3.

20. According to Oakeshott, moral and political pracatice "compose a vernacular language of colloquial intercourse" (Oakshott, p. 63). Just like Herder, Oakeshott endows moral and political language with the capacity both to achieve moral and political communication and to constitute ourselves as moral and political beings. The former capacity is called by Oakeshott "self-disclosure" and the latter "self-enactment."

21. When discussing the relation between language and philosophy from a political perspective, it is necessary to distinguish between two kinds of linguistic political philosophy: a political philosophy dealing with the language (or representation) of politics and a political philosophy dealing with the politics of language (or of representation). See, e.g., White, *Content*, p. 58. In contrast to the latter kind, the former kind of political philosophy need not necessarily imply a break with political philosophy as we know it. The perspective of the language of politics merely suggests a new context for traditional topics such as the nature of justice, of the state, or of legitimacy. The perspective of the politics of language raises a set of really new issues within political philosophy. If one considers the essays in the volumes edited by Nelson and Shapiro that were mentioned in n. 17, there seems to be no consensus as to why a political philosophy investigating the politics of language should be pursued; more than that, this lack of consensus has stimulated remarkably little discussion. This is all the more regrettable since, owing to the absence of debate, ambiguities remain. These ambiguities can be mapped on the ambiguity inherent in Gadamer's statement "Sein das verstanden werden kann, ist Sprache"; see H. G. Gadamer, *Wahrheit und Methode* (Tübingen, 1960), p. 450. Can Being be understood only insofar as it is language, or is Being language because only language can be understood? The latter, more radical option inspires the present essay.

22. F. Dallmayr, *Language and Politics: Why Does Language Matter to Political Philosophy?* (London, 1984); of relevance also is F. Dallmayr, *Twilight of Subjectivity: Contributions to a Postindividualist Theory* (Amherst, 1981). For Shapiro's volume, see n. 17.

23. F. Lentricchia, *Criticism and Social Change* (Chicago, 1983), p. 43; see also p. 51.

24. Ibid., p. 49.

25. Walzer, p. 67.

26. Ibid., p. 55.

27. L. Wittgenstein, *Philosophical Investigations* (Oxford, 1974), sec. 107.

28. J. Derrida, *Positions* (London, 1987), p. 41.

29. J. Derrida, *Of Grammatology* (Baltimore, 1976), pp. 152–65.

30. L. O. Mink, "Narrative Form as a Cognitive Instrument," in H. Kozicki and R. Canary, eds., *The Writing of History* (Madison, 1978), p. 145.

31. D. Carr, "Narrative and the Real World: An Argument for Continuity," *History and Theory, 25* (1986), pp. 125, 126.

32. Mink, p. 148.

33. The relation between what Ricoeur refers to as "mimesis^1," "mimesis^2," and "mimesis^3," a relation within which the one automatically develops into the other, is characteristic of the Stoic's perennial resistance to the kind of frictions meant here; see P. Ricoeur, *Time and Narrative* (Chicago, 1984–88). The Stoic exaggerations in Ricoeur's oeuvre have been pitilessly exposed by J. Hillis Miller, "But Are Things as We Think They Are?" *Times Literary Supplement*, October 9–15, 1987, p. 1104.

34. L. O. Mink, "The Autonomy of Historical Understanding," in W. H. Dray, ed., *Philosophical Analysis and History* (New York, 1966), p. 184 ff.

35. White, *Content*, p. 202.

36. H. Kellner, "Narrativity in History," *History and Theory*, 26 (1987), p. 25.

37. For a tentative translation of the aesthetic rejection of Stoic *tertia* for the sphere of ethics (and political philosophy?), see B. Williams, *Ethics and the Limits of Justice*

(London, 1985). However, Williams discards the aesthetic frictions with an appeal to a set of prejudices that forms the background for ethical debate. In general, in phenomenology and practical philosophy prejudice (*Vorverständnis*) has always been the favored candidate to function as Stoic *tertium*; aesthetic political philosophy is, therefore, a philosophy going beyond prejudice. A rejection of the *tertia* in aesthetics can be found in E. H. Gombrich, "Meditations on a Hobbyhorse," in M. Philipson and P. J. Gudel, eds., *Aesthetics Today* (New York, 1980); A. C. Danto, *The Transfiguration of the Commonplace* (Cambridge, 1983); H. G. Gadamer, *The Relevance of the Beautiful* (Cambridge, 1986); see esp. chaps. 5, 7, and 8).

38. This statement should be qualified. I do not wish to suggest that there is a political language and a political reality that is derived from it. This is a tactless way of putting things and should be avoided. For understanding what is language and what is reality can only be the result of a philosophical debate. Asking what the relation is between language and reality is asking for the sake of asking. Therefore the only legitimate way to discuss the relation between language and reality is never to use these terms in the course of the philosophical discussion but merely to *suggest* (as the result of the discussion) a way of using them or to suggest what the nature is of the regime that determines their relation. Dealing with the relation between language and reality is like a courtship: everything is spoiled if one goes straight for one's goal.

39. See Jameson's brilliant essay on Saussure: F. Jameson, "The Linguistic Model," in M. Shapiro, ed., *Language and Politics* (Oxford, 1984). Apparently the political implications of Saussure's semiotics are so obvious to Shapiro that he considers it superfluous to explain in his introduction why this essay on semiotics is included in the volume on politics. But undoubtedly he is correct.

40. Surely the Marxist economic world that is ruled by the dialectic conflict between *Produktivkräfte* and *Produktionsverhältnisse* is also a broken world. It was, however, Marx's intention to develop a perspective from which this broken world could be reintegrated.

41. J. D. Caputo, *Radical Hermeneutics: Repetition, Deconstruction, and the Hermeneutic Project* (Bloomington, 1987), p. 260.

42. A. MacIntyre, *After Virtue* (London, 1982); see esp. chaps. 1 and 2.

43. For an interesting analysis of this development in the Netherlands, see H. D. Tjeenk Willink, *Berichten regeringscommissaris reorganisatie rijksdienst* (1985).

44. M. A. P. Bovens and W. J. Witteveen, eds., *Het schip van staat* (Zwolle, 1985).

45. Quoted in C. C. Lemert, *Sociology and the Twilight of Man* (Carbondale, 1979), p. 227.

46. I rely here on the unpublished doctoral dissertation by D. A. Buiskool.

47. M. Foucault, *Power/Knowledge* (New York, 1980), pp. 96, 121.

48. For an aesthetic interpretation of political representation, see H. F. Pitkin, *The Concept of Representation* (Berkeley, 1967), chap. 4, esp. pp. 66, 67. Also see K. Burke, *The Philosophy of Literary Form: Studies in Symbolic Action* (Berkeley, 1973), p. 26, and F. R. Ankersmit, "Politieke representatie: Betoog over de esthetische Staat," *Bijdragen en mededelingen betreffende de geschiedenis der Nederlanden*, 102 (1987), pp. 358–79.

49. Until some ten years ago psychologists accepted what has been called the "component by component" theory of language acquisition; see S. Carey, "Semantic Development: The State of the Art," in E. Wanner and L. R. Gleitman, eds., *Language Acquisition: The State of the Art* (Cambridge, 1983), p. 347. The idea is that the meaning of concepts should be seen as the sum of its semantic components. Gradually, according to this theory, all the components of the adult's definition of a word will be included in the child's. See Carey, p. 350. It has been pointed out by MacNamara that this somewhat simplistic model for language acquisition does commit one "to an innate language in which ideas can be expressed"; see J. MacNamara, "Problems about Concepts," in MacNamara, *Language Learning and Thought* (New York, 1977), p. 143. The semantic structure of meanings is here supposed to be present in the minds of both the child and

the adult—a very Stoic conception, of course. The model was falsified empirically. It was found, for example, that children learn the pair big/little before the closely related pairs long/short, deep/shallow, and thick/thin, although the latter pairs are componentially less complex than the former. See Carey, p. 365 ff. Carey's conclusion is worth quoting: "we are left with no theory of lexical acquisition beyond the basic framework principles in terms of which the research problem is set," p. 371.

50. For an evaluation of Schiller's contribution to the development of the idea of aesthetic education, see K. S. Richter-Reichenbach, *Bildungstheorie und ästhetische Erziehung heute* (Darmstadt, 1983), and the excellent G. Buck, *Rückweg aus der Entfremdung* (Paderborn, 1984).

51. F. von Schiller, *Schillers sämtliche Werke in zwölf Bänden*, XII (Stuttgart), p. 21.

52. J. Habermas, *Theorie des kommunikativen Handelns*, (Frankfurt, 1982), p. 540.

53. Ibid., p. 545.

54. Ibid., p. 547.

55. R. H. Brown, *Society as Text: Essays on Rhetoric, Reason and Reality* (Chicago, 1987), pp. 54, 55.

56. This is the recurring theme in Gombrich's numerous writings. The idea can also be found in Danto's *Transfiguration*, in my opinion the best and most stimulating study of aesthetics presently available.

57. The insight is elaborated both brilliantly and convincingly by Danto, chap. 7.

58. J. Nelson, "Political Theory and Political Rhetorics," in J. Nelson, ed., *What Should Political Theory Be Now?* (Albany, 1983), p. 229.

59. In additon to a renewed emphasis on political representation and the introduction of the concept of political style, aesthetic political philosophy entails many other deviations from accepted Stoic political theory and practice. First, because of the central role played by the notion of "difference," aesthetic political philosophy will leave little room for liberalist and socialist egalitariansim; second, because of the disappearance of the Stoic ideological heart of the state, we must expect a shift in emphasis from the legislative to the executive power; third, what can be decentralized must now be decentralized; fourth, because the state and the public are separated by the aesthetic divide, their contacts will become less juridical and more "Machiavellianist"; fifth, politics should not be identified exclusively with the citizen's choice either in favor of or against a certain representative but instead with the contacts between the citizen and the state, and this—in its turn—requires bureaucrats to see themselves as representatives of the public rather than as executors of government policies; sixth, because of the disappearance of Stoic ideologies as schemata of political form, political practice can no longer be hidden behind lofty but multi-interpretable political ideals (and politics will take a new directness); seventh, because aesthetic political philosophy has as its point of departure these aesthetic rifts regardless of their theoretical, Stoic interpretation, aesthetic politics will be more practical than Stoic politics; eighth, because of the linguistic or intellectualist nature of these aesthetic rifts, political debate caused by these rifts will be intellectualist rather than practical; ninth, whereas Stoic political philosophy was "practical" about "theoretical" matters, aesthetic political philosophy will hence be "theoretical" or "intellectualist" about "practical" matters; tenth, the need to identify these rifts wherever they are greatly increases the political significance of the independent media and that of schools and universities even more; eleventh, because of the "semanticization" of political debate, "intellectual capital" will reassert itself in respect of economic capital. Numerous other items could be added to this list. However, the political issues raised by these changes in political theory and political practice are quite complex, and discussing them would require more space than I have here. I shall deal with them elsewhere.

EIGHTEEN

Death and Nothingness in Literature

Heinrich Mohr

Christian Concepts of Death and the Hereafter

The subject of this essay expresses the distance separating our views from the tradition of Christian reflection and meditation on death, a tradition that has dominated the West for at least one and a half millennia and shows no sign of disappearing to this day, let alone of becoming obsolete; obsolescence is an impossible concept as far as a subject like the one I have chosen is concerned. Only prattlers imagine they might claim the opposite.

Nonetheless, notions of death inspired by the Bible no longer dominate today, at least not in philosophy and literature. On the other hand, they are the background against which the many approaches to death in European thought become clear, and it is for this reason that I wish to outline them first, at no greater length than necessary, in a simplified, as it were, skeletal form.

To the announcement of the names of those who have recently died, Christian churches sometimes add a biblical quotation: "So teach us to number our days: that we may apply our hearts unto wisdom."[1] Death as Mentor is a basic image in Christian thought. Certain death—we say "dead certain" in English and German—points to an existence beyond the grave: this is eternal, whereas earthly life is transient. One would be wise to live one's life in this world by the standards of the next. Transience by the standards of eternity. Death itself is the passage from a known to an unknown state, over which, however, the living do have partial control. For this very reason they should be wise. Beyond this passage, after the apocalypse moreover, there waits, according at least to most, though not all, of the pronouncements of the New Testament, a judge, the Last Judgment.

"He hath shewed thee, O man, what is good; and what doth the Lord require of thee, but to do justly, and to love mercy, and to walk humbly with thy God?"[2] Man is, however, unable to do what is required of him. Incapable of good, injured to the core by original sin, he needs redemption. This is accorded him through the mercy of God, who becomes man in Christ, expunges the sin through His sacrificial death and breaks the power of death for all those who confess Him and follow Him. "For the wages of sin is death; but the gift of God is eternal life through Jesus Christ our Lord."[3] In the Mass and Holy Communion the faithful celebrate the gift of redemption and assure themselves of it.

The two concepts, those of judgment and redemption, do not contradict each other, but there is nonetheless a tension between them that cannot be totally resolved. The Bible is not a system, and every systematic theology has been, and always will be, thoroughly worsted in the encounter with it.

Christian concepts of death and the hereafter have found almost endless articulation in art and literature. *Memento mori* in all its variations suffuses theology and moral philosophy and inspires fine art and literature. The man with the scythe, the skeleton making his approach, foreseen by none, in the dance of death, the hourglass, *any* clock, with its threatening inscription, "*una ex his*" and the skull at the very scene of happiness, "*et in arcadia ego.*" The imagination has taken hold of the hereafter, above all the abhorrent hereafter: hell, the scene of eternal torment, invites depiction, less so the splendor of the "heavenly Jerusalem," which is preferably discussed in metaphors.

Taking an abstract approach, it is possible to sketch reasonably briefly the effect on the living of Christian notions of death, despite their many nuances and inconsistencies. The Last Judgment is simultaneously a threat and a promise. A threat, first of all, to all who have power and wealth on earth and misuse them, who break God's law and place themselves in His position, who, in other words, are full of pride. This is discussed and criticized by the prophets of the Old Testament. For those who suffer injustice God's judgment means promise and comfort, although it is the stalling promise of justice hereafter, of, as it were, reparation after death. This procrastinatory function has rightly often been discussed critically as an instrument of discipline with a wide range of applications.

Let it be said in passing that there is also in opposition to this a heterodox tradition of biblical exegesis which imposes divine justice as a duty for this life on the faithful, who are called upon to realize the kingdom of God here and now; a tradition that continues in the liberation theology of our own day.

Redemption is a mystery. "Work out your own salvation with fear and trembling. For it is God which worketh in you both to will and to do this good pleasure."[4] This is the way Paul formulates the paradox. The theological doctrine of predestination, that is, of an eternally fixed divine election, is the intellectually forced resolution of the paradox. It has gained acceptance only among Calvinists; among the remaining Christian churches it remains a will-o'-the-wisp of varying significance. The practice of the churches is disposed differently. In the sacrament of the Mass or Holy Communion the mystery of redemption is celebrated ever anew. The sacrament addresses the individual directly in a process but excludes completely any mediation. At the same time it is through such a radical individualization that the church as an institution gains its power, essentially as a custodian of these very sacraments. This sketch should suffice. If one is at all versed in the history of European culture, one will know that and in how many varied ways the comments of the Old and

New Testaments and their exegesis have inspired literature and art. This inspiration lives on to the present day. But it has, especially since the second half of the eighteenth century, lost its dominance—its "cultural hegemony," we would say today.

Pantheism—Dea Natura

Long before Nietzsche declared in a flourish of trumpets that "God is dead," the God of the Bible had ceased generally to dominate the consciousness of people. More and more had escaped from Him. A long process, without end, of course; a process of fundamental influence on the modern era in Europe.

Nature was rediscovered, no longer as creation but as a living unity in its own right, timeless and without a hereafter. Life is eternal. Death disappears into life. Late classical notions were resuscitated: *Dea Natura* celebrates a triumphant resurrection in pantheism.[5] Let us consider an outstanding text, one attributed to Goethe, the hymn "Die Natur" ("Nature"): "Die Natur. Wir sind von ihr umgeben und umschlungen; unvermögend aus ihr herauszutreten und unvermögend tiefer in sie hineinzukommen. . . . Es ist ein ewiges Leben, Werden und Bewegen in ihr und doch rückt sie nicht weiter. Sie verwandelt sich ewig und ist kein Moment Stillestehn in ihr. . . . Ihr Schauspiel ist immer neu, weil sie immer neue Zuschauer schafft. Leben ist ihre schönste Erfindung, und der Tod ist ihr Kunstgriff, viel Leben zu haben. (Nature: We are surrounded and embraced by her; incapable of withdrawing from her and incapable of entering her more deeply. . . . In her there is eternal life, growth and movement, yet she does not move further. She is constantly changing and there is no moment of standstill in her. . . . Her spectacle is ever new, because she is always creating new spectators. Life is her most beautiful discovery, and death her stratagem to enable there to be much life.)"[6] Death is merely change. Dissolution in the all-embracing life of divine nature.

This erotic and religious view of the world had a remarkably fruitful effect on literature. It made possible diverse new experiences and a new way of speaking about and with a nature which had only just come alive, with one's own soul, in a state of love. This latter was celebrated as the very center of life; of both the individual and all-embracing nature. It also became the most important and preferred path for the nonconformer: love, achievable not at all or only partially within the bounds and constraints of society, could hope to find in the transcending of individuation a more perfect fulfillment and the comfort of dissolution, of neutralization in the organic whole: the longing and instinct for death as a desire "for more life." Goethe's Werther hopes for salvation in death, but not at all in the Christian sense: in a high-handed gesture he kills himself on Christmas Eve, on the anniversary of the birth of the Redeemer, an all-too-obvious contrast. Hölderlin's Empedokles throws himself into Mount Etna: death as marriage.

The central issue is the suffering felt through isolation and the lures of a death newly interpreted as an access to all-embracing life. Rapture and ecstasy—later drug-induced—are excursions on the edge of the life and often inspire one to cross over it. The concept of the love-death is not new. The lovers mean everything to each other. The energy of their souls may lead them to cross the boundaries of their individuality, in the same way that they experience a hint of self-dissolution in the orgasm: *la petite mort*, as a popular French saying has it. Tristan and Isolde acknowledge their love as an *ewigliches Sterben* (everlasting death). The early romantic Friedrich Schlegel was inclined to regard death as *Selbstauflösung* (self-dissolution), as the extreme intensification of the experience of love. "Die Wollust ist vollendet, wenn sie bis zur Ahndung des Todes wird, und so der Tod, wenn er Lust wird. . . . Die mystische Synthesis der Individuen in der Liebe besteht im Zusammensterben; das ist das Geheimnis des Todes (Bliss is perfect when it leads to the premonition of death, and similarly death, when it becomes joy. . . . The mystical syntheses of individuals within love consists in their dying together; this is the mystery of death)."[7]

In the late eighteenth century the visual representations of death also changed. The hourglass, the man with the scythe, the skeleton are grim images rejected by the new consciousness. Instead we have the guardian angel with the lowered torch or even the gentle and soothing reference to the *Todesschlaf* (sleep of death). "Death is an eternal sleep"—so decreed the Jacobin Fouché on a cemetery gate.

A modest question, though: what happens to the ego that finds such congenial rest? It is noticeable that at the same time some of the same authors make attempts to rescue their unique individuality. Lessing pleads for the transmigration of souls, Goethe for entelechy:

> Und keine Zeit und keine Macht zerstückelt
> Gepragte Form, die lebend sich entwickelt
>
> (Neither time nor power fragments
> Moulded form that evolves full of life).[8]

The soul should wander active through time, its entelechy through the cosmos.

This raises a question which certainly touches our subject and which we wish to indicate, even if in attempting an answer we have to admit defeat. *Dea Natura*—all-embracing life—may be a supreme form of life in which, as we have seen, death, as it were, disappears. It is merely a *Kunstgriff, viel Leben zu haben* (a stratagem to enable there to be much life). But what of the individual? With however much joy and ecstasy it conceives of its own dissolution, as an individual, at all events, it ceases to exist; it is destroyed, becomes nothing. Might not, indeed must not, all-embracing life also appear to it as a disguised form of nothingness?

Death and Killing

The most sinister and profoundest figure in early German romanticism was Novalis. It was left to him to wander the borders of life on a polydimensional level and indirectly become a model for many. He longed for death in the hope of finding his deceased fiancée again. But in the workings of his mind she had been transformed into divine wisdom: Sophie into *sofia*, his desire to recover his betrothed transformed into a pursuit of the *unio mystica* with the godhead. It became the purpose of the erotic craving for death dominating him to enter into a spiritual life on a higher plane. "Religion" is what he called the urge to transcend, to be delivered from *individuation*. An appetite for death is, however, also an appetite for killing. This is what is sinister and new about him. "Es ist sonderbar, daß nicht längst die Assoziation von Wollust, Religion und Grausamkeit die Menschen aufmerksam auf ihre innige Verwandtschaft und ihre gemeinschaftiche Tendenz gemacht hat (It is strange that the association of sensual pleasure, religion, and cruelty has not long since drawn the attention of people to their profound affinity and their common tendency)."[9] He notes down for himself, "Todeslust ist Kriegergeist (An appetite for death is the true spirit of the warrior)"[10]—most ambiguously, because there is no distinction between the craving for death and the urge to kill. Extremely sinister is the way that here under the guise or in the context of a backward-looking catholicizing piety profoundly anti-Christian and antihuman ideas are articulated, ideas with the most evil of futures. In the words of a writer—von Loeben—following in Novalis's footsteps: "Im Krieg wird der Tod bis zur höchsten Wollust und der Haß zur heiligen Andacht getrieben (In war death is raised to the level of supreme pleasure and hatred becomes an act of religious devotion)."[11] One hundred years later Hanns Johst—on its strength he became one of Adolf Hitler's court poets—wrote: "Es ist eine rasende Wollust jung zu sein und von den Entzückungen des Todes zu wissen (It is a heady rapture to be young and know the ecstasies of death)."[12]

What is all this about? It is the seduction of empty transcendence. Crossing the frontier of life is conceived as an erotic adventure with a dual form: killing and dying—Nietzsche's *Tod als Fest* (Death as Celebration) in the language of a confused bourgeois intelligentsia unable to come to terms with either itself or social reality.

It is well known that at the outbreak of the First World War enthusiasm for the war rampaged through many places in Europe as a type of mass hysteria. War was a collective breakout from the limiting and unsatisfying normality of life: "Da hatte uns der Krieg gepackt wie ein Rausch. In einem Regen von Blumen waren wir hinausgezogen in einer trunkenen Stimmung von Rosen und Blut (The war had taken hold of us as if we were intoxicated. We had marched away in a rain of flowers, in a drunken euphoria of roses and blood)."[13] It is Ernst Jünger who has probably articulated most impressively—to reverse Novalis—what the spirit of the warrior means in terms of an appetite for death. The struggle is experienced as a *blutiges Fest* (bloody celebration),[14] the attack as a period of intoxication, and both are simultaneously perceived as an *Übermaß an Glück* (excess of happiness).[15] "Die ungeheure Ballung der Kräfte in der Schicksalsstunde . . . hatten mich zum ersten Male in die Tiefen überpersönlicher Bereiche geführt . . . es war eine Einweihung (The immense concentration of powers at the fateful moment. . . had led me for the first time to the depths of suprapersonal areas . . . it was an initiation)."[16] It should be stressed that nothing, absolutely nothing, is said about the character of the suprapersonal powers. We discover just as little about the contents of the initiation. Quite clearly it is an empty transcendence touching on the ecstasy of the warrior spirit. It is—obviously without admitting as much—nothingness against which the warrior, drunk with ecstasy, brushes. Destruction is his aim; in many variations Jünger describes an urge to kill that is erotically determined through and through. This is also found elsewhere. What is rare is that Jünger also depicts the approach of his own death as a happy fate. The will to destroy is also directed against his own self. The perfect warrior is a double sex-killer: murderer and suicide in one. "Wir übersprangen einige Schützenlöcher . . . Gerade als ich mich mitten im Sprung befand, riß mich ein durchdringender Stoß vor die Brust wie ein Flugwild aus der Luft. Mit einem lauten Schrei, mit dessen Gellen die Lebensluft auszuströmen schien, wirbelte ich um die Achse und klirrte zu Boden. Nun hatte es mich endlich erwischt. Gleichzeitig mit der Wahrnehmung des Treffers fühlte ich, wie das Geschoß ins Leben schnitt. Schon an der Straße vor Mory hatte ich die Hand des Todes gespürt—diesmal griff er fester und deutlicher zu. Als ich schwer auf die Sohle des Grabens schlug, hatte ich die Überzeugung, daß es unwiderruflich zu Ende war. Und seltsamerweise gehört dieser Augenblick zu den ganz wenigen, von denen ich sagen kann, daß sie wirklich glücklich gewesen sind. In ihm begriff ich, wie durch einen Blitz erleuchtet, mein Leben in seiner innersten Gestalt. Ich spürte ein unglaubliches Erstaunen darüber, daß es gerade hier zu Ende sein sollte, aber dieses Erstaunen war von sehr heiterer Art (We jumped across some foxholes. Just as I was in the middle of jumping a penetrating blow to the chest tore me like a game bird from the air. With a loud cry in which my life's breath seemed to stream away, I spun completely round and crashed to the ground. I had finally caught it. At the same time as registering the hit I felt the bullet cutting into my life. I had already felt the hand of death on the road to Mory—this time its grasp was firmer and clearer. As I collapsed to the bottom of the ditch I was convinced that I was irrevocably done for. And strangely this moment is one of the very few of which I can say were truly happy. In it I understood, as if illuminated in a flash of lightning, the innermost contours of my life. I felt an unbelievable astonishment that it should all be over right here, but this astonishment was a very happy kind)."[17]

Death in Marxist Thinking

In Marxist ideology death and nothingness are regarded explicitly and without prevarication as identical. Ernst Bloch has therefore celebrated the "red hero": "Alle nehmen frühere Blumen ins Grab. . . . Nur eine Art Menschen kommt auf dem Weg zum Tod fast ohne überkommenen Trost aus: der rote Held. Indem er bis zur Ermordung die Sache bekennt, für die er gelebt hat, geht er klar, kalt, bewußt in das Nichts. . . . Das macht: er hatte vorher schon aufgehört, sein Ich so wichtig zu nehmen, er hatte Klassenbewußtsein. . . . Diese Gewißheit des Klassenbewußtseins . . . ist in der Tat ein Novum gegen den Tod (Everyone takes former flowers to the grave. . . . Only one sort of person manages without traditional consolation on the road to death: the red hero. Since up to his murder he bears witness to the cause for which he has lived, he enters nothingness clearly, coldly, consciously. . . . This is owing to his already having ceased to attach so much importance to his own ego, he has class-consciousness. . . . This certainty of class-consciousness is . . . indeed something new in the fight against death)."[18] It is "solidarity" that supports the new hero, the sense of being linked with the past and the future in the emacipatory struggle of mankind, "das Untötbare des revolutionär-solidarischen Bewußtseins. . . . Geborgenheit ohne alle Mythologie (the indestructible in the consciousness of revolutionary solidarity . . . security without any mythology)."[19] The dead find a haven in the memories and deeds of the living "eingeschreint im Herzen der Arbeiterklasse (enshrined in the hearts of the working class),"[20] as the great philosopher but bad poet puts it. For humanity after its liberation Bloch predicts a new understanding of death. This lies still in the future of a "kommunistische Kosmologie . . . einer dialektischen Vermittlung des Menschen und seiner Arbeit mit dem möglichen Subjekt der Natur (a communist cosmology of a dialectical mediation of man and work with the potential subject of Nature)."[21] Some of Bloch's ideas are less new and unique than he thinks and, above all, have associations that are embarrassing. Thus fascist and National Socialist ideologues celebrate the *Volksgemeinschaft* (folk community)—sometimes without any religious or metaphysical embellishment. Here the dead, in the first instance those killed in action, are gathered up like the red hero in the hearts of the working class. It is in their lives that his life's work will continue. The revolting phrase "Der Toten Tatenruhm (the glory of the deeds of the dead)" was used frequently during the Third Reich, both beforehand and sometimes also subsequently, and writers labored zealously to draw a pleasant veil of this sort over nothingness.

The Ever-present Nothingness

The reader of contemporary German literature is for the most part spared such things. However different and varied the landscape of literature in German is, I can see it is true with one important exception: no celebration of death. Ernst Jünger is still alive, admittedly, but as a writer he is dead—despite the scandalous award of the Goethe prize to him in 1982. This goes at least for Germany: in France Jünger continues to play an important and well-respected role.

Postwar and contemporary German literature is, all in all, not in an ecstatic mood. Death appears without splendor; it is not an eloquent seducer, and it lacks the magic of exotic and mysterious beauty. The mermaids of Romanticism and all their relatives have disappeared, and Hofmannsthal's often-quoted verses from "Der Tor und der Tod" ("Death and the Fool") have an alien ring today. In them the *fin-de-siècle* aesthetic cult of death and Friedrich Schlegel's vaunted

Kunstsinn für den Tod (artistic sense of death) are poetically articulated. Death declares:

> Steh auf, wirf dies ererbte Graun von Dir!
> Ich bin nicht schauerlich, bin kein Gerippe!
> Aus des Dionysos, der Venus Sippe,
> Ein großer Gott der Seele steht vor Dir.
>
> (Arise, and cast off thy inherited fear!
> I am not horrible, I am no skeleton!
> Born of the stem of Dionysos, of Venus,
> I stand, a great God of the soul before thee.)[22]

Death appears in contemporary literature as the void that forces its way into life, that can be, as it were, everywhere and constantly seen, heard, smelled. "Es riecht nach Kadaver (It smells of corpse)," so said Max Frisch, more or less, in a recent interview rather angrily and without any particular application. But he refers altogether more accurately to a specifically contemporary feeling about life: the void seems to have become ever-present—and, what is more, without a mask, without a fancy costume. Life may be experienced by the individual as something without meaning, as tribulation and torment, as a burden of which one should like to be free. In these circumstances death can be the *promise* more than the *threat* of nothingness.

Todesarten (Forms of death) is a variant title of Ingeborg Bachmann's *Malina*.[23] It is truly a significant title, not least because the right direction is the one that it does not point to. For its subject in many variations is the inability to live and love: the death wish is the result of this inability. *Sterbensarten* (Forms of dying) would be the more accurate title.

More intensively and monomaniacally than all others, Thomas Bernhard has made death the supremely dominant theme of his writing: life is a fatal disease, and nowhere else is it described thus in so astonishing a variety of terms. Such writing has two sides: the text points with self-indulgent luxuriance to different forms of disease. But at the same time this writing is an assertion of life directed *against* his theme. Life appears in all its ambivalence. There is reference to the ridiculousness of life, as it is indeed nothing more than a disease leading inevitably to death. "Der in so vielen Gestalten . . . auftretende noch jedem alle möglichen Vorschläge machende Tod (Death appearing in so many forms and making every possible suggestion to everyone.)"[24] And at the same time the author confesses: "Der Schatten des Todes, der begleitet mich natürlich immer, und den lieb ich dadurch, weil er mir den Ernst garantiert (The shadow of death naturally accompanies me constantly and I cherish it for this reason, since it ensures my seriousness)."[25]

One of Bernhard's early stories begins with the phrase "Nach dem Selbstmord unserer Eltern (after our parents' suicide)" and refers in expansive gestures to "dem Entschluß unserer Eltern . . . zum Selbstmord und der Ausführung ihres Selbstmords . . . [über] unsere Einübung in den Selbstmord (the decision of our parents . . . to commit suicide and to the implementation thereof . . . to our experience of suicide)."[26] Sketches are presented of an "unertraglich gewordenen Welt (a world that has become intolerable)."[27] "Warum wir noch leben müssen (Why we have to go on living)"[28] is the central question of the narrator and his brother, who have both survived the family suicide by accident. A sense of unhappiness is presented and localized in a specific time and place—Austria, Salzburg, Innsbruck—a very special way of feeling at home. "Und gerade hier, auf diesem mir angeborenen Todesboden, bin ich zuhause und mehr in dieser tödlichen Stadt und in dieser tödlichen Gegend zu Hause als andere. . . . Ich und die Stadt sind eine lebenslängliche untrennbare, wenn auch fürchterliche Beziehung (And it is on this very spot, on this, the deadly ground to which I am born, that I am at home, and in this deadly city and in this deadly region at home more than others are. . . . The city and I are involved in a lifelong, indissoluble, if also terrifying, love affair)."[29] We need not pursue this line. As far as a longing for death is concerned, Bernhard is the most radical of contemporary German writers; but there are many standing at his side, speaking in different ways and with other voices. But we shall not concern ourselves with them further.

Contempt for Death—*Der Todfeind* (The Enemy of Death)

It is Elias Canetti, defiantly hanging on in a quite isolated position, who provides the denunciation of every form of longing for or obsession with death or even merely its tired and resigned acceptance. "Deine einzige Rechtfertigung ist dein unerschütterter Haß gegen den Tod (Your only justification is your unshaken hostility toward death)."[30] *Todfeind* (The Enemy of Death) was to have been the name of the central figure of a projected novel.[31] In his (thus far) last sketches, Canetti observes: "Es könnte aber sein, daß die Jungen bei dir Hilfe gegen die Todesseuche in der Literatur suchen. Als einer, der den Tod mit jedem Jahr mehr verachtet, bist du von Nutzen (It may be, however, that the young seek in you assistance against the obsession with death in literature. As one who scorns death more with every year that passes you may be of use)."[32]

It is not easy to interpret Canetti's denunciation. One's first thought is to approach it from the standpoint of the French existentialists Sartre and Camus. Death as something alien, as the epitome of all that is hideous in the fate of the individual. The absurdity which has to be endured, in the revolt against which man creates himself. Sartre polemicizes against Heidegger, who in *Sein und Zeit* declares life to be *Sein zum Tode* (being toward death) and perceives in this very feature its *Eigentlichkeit* (authenticity). According to Heidegger the individual achieves independence and self-determination through the intellectual anticipation of his *eigenen Tod* (own death). One wins the *Freiheit zum Tod* (freedom to die).

Canetti's words are, of course, a rejection of Heidegger. But his views are not identical with those of Sartre or Camus either. As far as I can see, his words stand as a personal and independent statement. They are directed not primarily toward life but against death. It is not difficult to see in Canetti a Don Quixote tilting at windmills. This octogenarian writes: "Alles tust du, das Bewußtsein des Todes zu verstärken. . . . Nie darf dein Wissen vom Schrecklichen sich ausruhen. Was aber gewinnst du durch die unaufhörliche Wachheit dieses Bewußtseins vom Tode? . . . Die Wahrheit ist, daß du noch nicht gefunden hast, was die richtige, die gültige, den Menschen nützliche Haltung wäre. Du hast es nicht weiter gebracht als dazu nein zu sagen (You do everything to strengthen the awareness of death. . . . Your knowledge of the horrible may never relax. But what do you gain from being constantly consciously aware of death? . . . The truth is that you have not yet discovered what would be the correct, the valid attitude most useful to mankind. You have not got beyond saying no to it)."[33]

In the very next lines Canetti provides his own answer, not solving anything intellectually but articulating very clearly his desperate position. "Aber ich verfluche den Tod, ich kann nicht anders, und wenn ich darüber blind werden sollte, ich kann nicht anders, ich stoße den Tod zurück. Würde ich ihn anerkennen, ich wäre ein Mörder (But I curse death, I can do no other, even if I go blind in the process, I can do no other. I reject death. If I recognized it, I should be a murderer)."[34]

What is the meaning of this? The primal gesture of power, as Canetti has repeatedly argued, is that of a dead body beneath the foot of a living person: the victor and the vanquished. The threat of power destroys freedom; it oppresses. This is exactly what Canetti also applies to natural death: if it is tolerated and accepted it is able through its oppressiveness to determine life, to form it, deform it, whether it be the life of an individual or a whole society. This is his idea. Of course he remains helpless. Canetti is a *wütiger* (angry) writer. "Bevor er zur Auflösung wird, ist der Tod Konfrontation (before becoming dissolution, death is confrontation)." He demands "Mut, sich ihm zu stellen, jeder Vergeblichkeit zum Trotz. Mut, dem Tod ins Gesicht zu spucken (courage to stand up to it, despite the futility; courage to spit in death's face)."[35]

On the Comfort of Nothingness

Nothingness can shock, attract, but it can also be experienced "simply" as a comfort. I quote a late poem of Brecht's, which takes up ancient ideas, already formulated by Epicurus, and presents them as simply as it does personally.

Als ich in weißem Krankenzimmer der Charité
Aufwachte gegen Morgen zu
Und die Amsel hörte, wußte ich
Es besser. Schon seit geraumer Zeit
Hatte ich keine Todesfurcht mehr. Da ja nichts
Mir je fehlen kann, vorausgesetzt
Ich selber fehle. Jetzt
Gelang es mir, mich zu freuen
Alles Amselgesanges nach mir auch.

(When, in the white ward of the Charity,
I woke up toward morning

And heard the blackbird, I knew
Better. For some time now
I had no fear of death. For after all
I cannot ever want for anything as long
As I myself am wanting. Thus
I succeeded in enjoying
The song of all blackbirds, even the ones coming after me.)[36]

Death as a Productive Force

Brecht's most significant sucessor, even if not his direct pupil, is Heiner Müller. He is regarded generally as the most important dramatist in the German language at present. He *cannot* and *may* not be disregarded here because it is he above all who stands as an imposing foreign body in the landscape of contemporary German literature.

Müller's central theme is revolution. In the texts, stage productions, and interviews of the past two decades, Müller has mythicized this theme more and more. In the process—and this is astonishing enough—he has been strongly influenced by Nietzsche and the philosophy of life. This is the way in which the utopia of the revolution is to be rescued,[37] in the very face of experience, in the very face of history and the insights which it imposes. Death is a function of life; it is productive. The precondition of such an idea is that one shifts one's view away from the individual toward the collective. "Der Tod . . . eine Funktion des Lebens, das als Produktion gefaßt wird, eine Arbeit unter anderem, vom Kollektiv organisiert und das Kollektiv organisierend. Damit etwas kommt, muß etwas gehen. Die erste Gestalt der Hoffnung ist die Furcht, die erste Erscheinung des Neuen, der Schrecken (Death . . . a function of life understood as production, a piece of work among many, organized by and organizing the collective. For something to come, something must go. Hope first appears as fear, the new as a nightmare)."[39]

Enlightenment and humanity have failed, are played out, finished. Rebarbarization is the order of the day. True enough, Müller does not conjure up the *lachenden Löwen* (laughing lions) from *Also sprach Zarathustra (Thus Spake Zarathustra)*;[40] but his exemplars, taken from mythology and literature, are much clearer. For instance, Medea: dismembering her children and killing her rival, she emerges from suppression and becomes a beast of prey and thereby suitable as a revolutionary subject. The dog must become a wolf, so it says. The old world has to be torn apart if the new is ever to have a chance of being born. I quote from the end of "Hamletmaschine" what is doubtlessly the message of the text. Ophelia is speaking as Electra, the victim as the avenger. "Hier spricht Elektra. Im Herzen der Finsternis. Unter der Sonne der Folter. An die Metropolen der Welt. Im Namen der Opfer. Ich stoße allen Samen aus, den ich empfangen habe. Ich verwandle die Milch meiner Brüste in tödliches Gift. Ich nehme die Welt zurück, die ich geboren habe. Ich ersticke die Welt, die ich geboren habe, zwischen meine Schenkeln. Ich begrabe sie in meiner Scham. Nieder mit dem Glück der Unterwerfung. Es lebe der Haß, die Verachtung, der Aufstand, der Tod. Wenn sie mit Fleischermessern durch eure Schlafzimmer geht, werdet ihr die Wahrheit wissen (This is Electra talking. In the heart of the darkness. Under the sun of torture. To the metropolises of the world in the name of the victims. I expel all the semen I have received. I turn the milk of my breasts into deadly poison. I take back the world I have born. I suffocate the world I have borne between my thighs. I bury it in my womb. Down with the happiness of subjection. Long live hatred, scorn, rebellion, death. When it comes through your bedroom with butchers' knives, you'll know the truth)."[41]

Müller's references to Nietzsche and the philosophy of life in the service of a poetry of world revolution are strange enough—and, if I am not mistaken, unique. As far as our theme is concerned, however, Müller points only to the dual possibility of avoidance or denial. Death is canceled out in the life of the collective, and nothingness continues to be ignored, since his view is concentrated on change and utopia.

Auschwitz and Hiroshima

The Holocaust produced an experience unique in history. There are no analogues. The words of the preacher Solomon "And there is nothing new thing under the sun"[42] have been shown to be incorrect. Auschwitz, the factory of death, was something new—and we Germans introduced it into history. A collection of essays edited by Dan Diner bears the title *Zivilisationsbruch: Denken nach Auschwitz (The Breaching of Civilization: Thinking after Auschwitz)*.[43] The breaching of civilization refers to something having become reality that was considered unthinkable, that seemed simply inconceivable within the scope of human civilization. The writer Günter Kunert speaks for many when referring to a destroyed *Weltvertrauen* (trust in the world) and a lost *Daseinssinn* (meaning of existence) as a consequence.[44] Hannah Arendt has described the incomprehension of Jewish emigrants, especially on hearing the first news of the extermination camps: "Schock. . . . Das war wirklich, als ob der Abgrund sich öffnet. Weil man die Vorstellung gehabt hat, alles andere hätte irgendwie noch einmal gut gemacht werden können. Dies nicht. Dies hätte nie geschehen dürfen. . . . Ich meine die Fabrikation der Leichen (Shock. . . . It really was as if the abyss was opening up. Because people had the feeling that somehow everything else could be put right again. But not this. This should never have been allowed to happen. . . . I mean the manufacture of corpses)."[45] The study of the Holocaust is not our theme, not even the biographical, autobiographical, and fictional texts dealing with the extermination camps. Our theme does, however, oblige us to ask whether writers in the face of something horrifically new speak in new ways about death and nothingness.

> Schwarze Milch der Frühe wir trinken sie abends
> wir trinken sie mittags und morgens wir trinken sie nachts
> wir trinken und trinken
> wir schaufeln ein Grab in den Lüften da liegt man nicht eng

(Black milk of dawn we drink it in the evenings
we drink it at noon and in the mornings we drink it at night
we drink and drink
we dig a grave in the airs so people do not lie close together).[46]

This text, Paul Celan's "Todesfuge (Fugue of death)," is probably the best-known Auschwitz poem in the German language. As we know, it persuaded Adorno to revise his view that poetry was impossible after Auschwitz. The poet gazes on horror; in the absolute metaphor *schwarze Milch* (black milk), which defies definite interpretation, language surrenders to the abyss. It is life faced with death, with very close death, which here becomes language. In no sense is it an interpretation of death.

This is also the case, in my opinion, with the poetry of Nelly Sachs, which revolves around the holocaust. "O ihr Schornsteine, o ihr Finger, Und Israels Leib im Rauch durch die Luft (Oh you chimneys, oh you fingers, and Israel's body in smoke through the air)."[47] The horrific is made present in the language of the lyric, and where interpretations are hazarded they center on the area of Jewish literature and history and the mysticism of the Cabala. It would probably have seemed arrogant, or quite simply inappropriate, to the poet, for someone to have expected new interpretations of death or statements about nothingness.

Mass extermination as the writing on the wall of our civilization. With greater emphasis than many who think like him, Günter Anders has linked Auschwitz and Hiroshima and taken the universal Hiroshima, the end of mankind as a species, as his central theme: the philosophy of catastrophe and the apocalyptic, the *Apokalypse ohne Reich* (apocalypse without a kingdom)[48]—the reference is to the messianic kingdom—compel him to think, but as an urgent warning rather than as a fatalistic statement: "Hiroshima, da wie ein Blitz die Einsicht in mich einschlug, daß wir vielleicht, oder sogar wahrscheinlich, einem Nicht-Mehr entgegen treiben. Das war das Ende meines Messianismus (Hiroshima, the place where the recognition struck me like a lightning bolt that we are perhaps, or even probably, drifting toward a no-more. That was the end of my messianism)."[49]

Anders demands *ohne Hoffnung zu leben* (a life without hope); but he *predigt* (preaches), he, the unbeliever, and is of the opinion that the prophets of the Old Testament are whispering *Warnungsworte* (words of warning) to him. He speaks in Japan on the anniversary of Hiroshima, pointing to the threatening universal Hiroshima, and urges "daß es an uns allen läge, dieses Ende abzuwenden: daß wir, die gleichermaßen Bedrohten, gleich wo wir lebten, gleich was wir glaubten oder nicht glaubten, daß wir alle 'proximi,' 'Nächste,' geworden seien; daß was alle treffen könne, auch alle betreffen müsse (that it is up to us all to avert this end: that we, all equally threatened, wherever we live, whatever we believe or do not believe, have all become *proximi,* 'neighbors'; that what could affect us all should concern us all)."[50] The quotation speaks for itself and renders interpretation superfluous.

The thought of the universal Hiroshima, the demise of the species, does not lead to a new meditation on death: it leads to an appeal to the living.

Conclusion

Spinoza is convinced that "Homo liber de nulla re minus quam de morte cogitat; et eius sapientia non mortis, sed vitae meditatio est (the free man thinks about nothing less than about death. His wisdom derives from thinking about life, not death)."[51] Spinoza is referring to a free person whose thoughts dwell on the accessible, on the space in which he or she can act and work. Thinking about the inaccessible leads to bondage. Montaigne wrote: "Life is in itself neither a good nor an evil. It is the space for good or evil, depending on what you place in it."[52]

Let us attempt to establish a link with our initial observations, with the Christian notions of death and the hereafter. They do not necessarily contradict a secular ethical system, be it ever so radical. In the twenty-fifth chapter of Matthew, Jesus refers to the Last Judgment. The son of man will gather all before him and separate them; the righteous to his right, the damned to his left. "And these shall go away into everlasting punishment: but the righteous into life eternal." The righteous, however—and this is of interest to us here—do not know why they are the righteous. The judge has to tell them: "For I was an hungred, and ye gave me meat; I was thirsty, and ye gave me drink; I was a stranger, and ye took me in; naked and ye clothed me; I was sick, and ye visited me; I was in prison and ye came unto me." But the righteous still do not understand: "Lord, when saw we thee an hungred, and fed thee? or thirsty, and gave thee drink? When saw we thee a stranger, and took thee in? or naked, and clothed thee? Or when saw we thee sick, or in prison, and came unto thee?" The answer: "Verily I say unto you, inasmuch as ye have done it unto one of the least of these my brethren, ye have done it unto me."

The text admits of no doubt. The righteous thought neither of righteousness, nor of God, nor of any kind of hereafter. They gave love where there was need. Their thoughts were directed solely to the suffering and did not go beyond concrete help. They made use of freedom to do good independently of any compulsion or promise or any kind of hope. Paradoxical is the fact that and the manner in which the response to this very worldly and secular exercise of love is the gift of eternity and the world to come.

It is an agreeable paradox. It could encourage us to turn our backs on the all-too-tricky intellectual acrobatics of theology and to resist attempts to find, beyond the confines of the accessible, in death and nothingness enlightenment on the individual and insights into life.

NOTES

1. Psalms 90: 12.
2. Micah 6: 8.

3. Romans 6: 23.

4. Philippians 2: 12–13.

5. *On Dea Natura*, see Ernst Robert Curtius, *Europäische Literatur und lateinisches Mittelalter* (Bern/Munich, 1961), ch. 6.

6. Goethe, *Werke* (Hamburger Ausgabe), vol. 13, p. 45 f. Not Goethe, who decades after believed himself to have been the author, but Tobler, a Zürich theologian and pupil of Lavater, was the writer of the prose hymn "Die Natur." Tobler was at that time living in Weimar and belonged to Goethe's inner circle of acquaintances. The hymn is typical of its time and generation, enthusiastic pantheism being to a large extent the common property of the spiritual and literary avant-garde of the time.

7. Quoted from Walther Rehm, *Der Todesgedanke in der deutschen Dichtung vom Mittelalter bis zur Romantik* (Halle, 1928, 2d ed. 1967), pp. 392, 393.

8. Goethe, *Werke* (Hamburger Ausgabe), vol. 1, p. 359.

9. Novalis, *Schriften*, vol. 3, ed. R. Samuel (Stuttgart, 1960), p. 568. Similarly he writes: "Sonderbar, daß der eigentliche Grund der Grausamkeit Wollust ist (It is strange that sensual pleasure is the very base of cruelty)," p. 655.

10. Ibid., p. 677.

11. Quoted from Rehm, p. 430.

12. Ibid., p. 468.

13. Ernst Jünger, *In Stahlgewittern* (Stuttgart, 1983), p. 7. The earlier editions, which in part differ quite substantially from the (so far) latest edition, have been ignored here.

14. Ibid., p. 315.

15. Ibid., p. 261.

16. Ibid., p. 289.

17. Ibid., p. 316.

18. Ernst Bloch, *Das Prinzip Hoffnung* (Frankfurt, 1973), p. 1378 ff.

19. Ibid., p. 1381.

20. Ibid., p. 1379.

21. Ibid., p. 1383.

22. Hugo von Hofmannsthal, *Gedichte und kleine Dramen* (Frankfurt, 1966), p. 83.

23. Ingeborg Bachmann, *Malina* (Frankfurt, 1974).

24. Thomas Bernhard, *Amras* (Frankfurt, 1964), p. 91.

25. Thomas Bernhard, *Monologe aus Mallorca* (Bochum, 1981), p. 8.

26. Bernhard, *Amras*, p. 10.

27. Ibid., p. 9.

28. Ibid., p. 15.

29. Thomas Bernhard, *Die Ursache: Eine Andeutung* (Salzburg, 1975), p. 14.

30. Elias Canetti, *Die Provinz des Menschen: Aufzeichnungen 1942–1972* (Munich, 1973), p. 211.

31. Ibid., p. 52.

32. Elias Canetti, *Das Geheimherz der Uhr: Aufzeichnungen 1973–1985* (Darmstadt, 1987), p. 32.

33. Ibid., p. 199 f.

34. Ibid., p. 200.

35. Ibid., p. 147.

36. Bertolt Brecht, *Gesammelte Werke*, vol. 10, Werkausgabe ed. (Frankfurt, 1967), p. 1031.

37. On this theme, see Horst Domdey, "Mit Nietzsche gegen Utopieverlust: Zur 'Hamletmaschine' und Heiner Müllers Rezeption in West und Ost," in Gert Joachim Glaeßner, ed., *Die DDR in der Ära Honecker: Politik-Kultur-Gesellschaft: Festschrift fur Hartmut Zimmermann,* (Opladen, 1988), pp. 674–89. Domdey's studies on Müller are in my opinion the most perceptive and intelligent interpretations of this author.

39. Heiner Müller, *Mauser* (Berlin, 1978), p. 88 f.

40. Friedrich Nietzsche, *Also sprach Zarathustra*, in Nietzsche, *Sämtliche Werke. Kristische Studienausgabe*, vol. 4 (Munich, 1980), p. 351.

41. Müller, p. 97.

42. Ecclesiastes 1: 9.

43. Dan Diner, ed., *Zivilisationsbruch: Denken nach Auschwitz* (Frankfurt, 1988).

44. Günter Kunert: "Atempause," in *Die neue Gesellschaft*, 36, no. 8 (August 1989), p. 729.

45. H. Reif, ed., *Gespräche mit Hannah Arendt*, quoted in Diner, p. 7.

46. Paul Celan, *Ausgewälte Gedichte* (Frankfurt, 1970), p. 22.

47. Nelly Sachs, *Ausgewählte Gedichte* (Frankfurt, 1966), p. 9.

48. Günter Anders, in Hans Jürgen Schulz, ed., *Mein Judentum* (Munich, 1987), p. 60.

49. Ibid., p. 59.

50. Ibid., p. 53.

51. Baruch de Spinoza, *Ethik*, part 4, theorem 67.

52. Quoted after Rehm, p. 180.

NINETEEN

Postnormative Subjectivity

James Mensch

We seen to be at the end of an age. We are no longer moderns, but rather post-moderns. A sign of this is the pluralism which has spread across our culture. In the arts, every style is acceptable, from abstract expressionism to photographic realism. Traditional harmonies reappear in music, often alongside the most severe atonalities. "Postmodern" architects, who coined the term *postmodernism* some thirty years ago, feel free to use an often bewildering variety of architectural styles. Even in philosophy, where once a rigid dogmatism reigned, "doing philosophy" is no longer limited to a set of particular problems or methodologies. Here, too, postmodernism implies pluralism with its corresponding lack of determining norms. The postmodern period is thus postnormative. By contrast, the modern period was preeminently normative. In philosophy, its birth was announced by Descartes's *Rules for the Direction of the Mind*, prescribing a set of norms for correct thinking. Since then, it has produced rules for practically everything. From the Kantian conditions for the possibility of experience to the Marxian laws of dialectical materialism to our century's various guides on everything from sexuality to accounting, modernity has been intent on declaring *in advance* how things must be. In this essay, I look at the roots of modernity in order to sketch how this attitude came about. I then look at a few of the implications of the shift from the modern to the post-modern with regard to subjectivity. My goal is to advance a proposal for a postmodern philosophy.

The Origin of Modernity

Philosophical modernity has some unlikely sources. Its immediate impulses came from reports on cannibals and dreams. Montaigne, in his essay "Of Cannibals," declares that "we have no other criterion of truth and reason than the example and pattern of the opinions and customs of the country wherein we live."[1] After praising the virtues of the cannibals and finding them in no wit inferior to those of sixteenth-century France, he laughingly concludes: "But hold on! They don't wear breeches."[2] Pants alone make Europe superior. A similar but much more penetrating relativism is advanced by Cervantes in *Don Quixote*, the international bestseller of the seventeenth century. For Cervantes's hero, dreams have the force of reality. Any evidence to the contrary is explained by the "enchanters [who] have persecuted, are persecuting, and will continue to persecute me."[3] Evil and all-powerful, they make it impossible to decide on what precisely is real, what is a dream and what not. Indeed, on one level, the whole book can be considered as a meditation on the impregnability of Don Quixote's argument. It exposes the bankruptcy of contemporary claims regarding reality and illusion.

Modernity in philosophy begins with Descartes's response to this. The first of Descartes's Meditations considers the possibilities that everything we now sense and experience is actually a dream and that "an evil genius, as clever and deceitful as he is powerful" prevents us from realizing this.[4] To banish this enchanter, Descartes searches for something that is absolutely certain, something that he cannot doubt. He finds it in the "I" or subject of the "I think." Even if we doubt every object of this subject's thought, we cannot doubt it. It becomes the *ens certissimum*, the being whose certainty is such that it can stand as a norm, a standard against which to judge all other claims to knowledge. This norm is mediated through the concepts of clarity and distinctness. To the point that our perceptions and thoughts of other objects approach the clarity and distinctness of our grasp of the subject, to that point we can be equally certain of the reality of their objects.

This positioning of the subject or self as normative has worked for hundreds of years. In fact, in a broad sense, modernity is this appeal to subjectivity. Descartes's argument, however, for all its apparent force, has a fateful contradiction. The subject to whom he appeals is not an object like other objects. It is a subject who thinks objects, who doubts or sensuously perceives them as the case may be. Descartes argues that all the objects of its attention can be doubted; what cannot be doubted is simply the attending itself. Qua attending, however, the subject is not an object, but rather that which directs itself to objects. As such, Descartes's attempt to turn it into a "thinking thing"—an entity whose perception can stand as a norm for the perception of other objects—is highly problematical.

This point may be put in terms of the abstraction which Descartes is compelled to make in order to make the subject indubitable. What cannot be doubted is not myself as having a "face, hands, arms, and this entire mechanism of bodily members." It is not the self that perceives through its bodily organs. It is rather the self that doubts whether any of this pertains to it. Such a self, then, is "only a thing that thinks." Its "essence," he asserts, "consists in this alone."[5] As such, it is completely nonextended. If I am, then, only what I can be certain of, it follows for Descartes "that I am truly distinct from my body." Indeed, reduced to what I can be certain of, it follows that "I can exist without [this body]."[6] The distinction between mind and body here is deceptively simple. Bodies are divisible and, hence, extended; the self or mind by contrast is a thoroughgoing unity. Thus, as Descartes argues, "it is one and the same mind that wills, senses, and understands . . . [while] no corporeal or extended thing can be thought of by me that I did not easily in thought divide into parts."[7] Since I cannot say I am a different mind when I will or understand or sense, as I often perform these activities simultaneously, I cannot be divided and, hence, cannot be taken as something extended. In fact, as later philosophers were to point out, insofar as I persist as I pass from one form of mental activity to another, I cannot be identified with any of them. Not only am I nonextended, I am also not my sensing or my willing or my understanding, but only a sort of unity of apperception underlying these and all other conscious states.

With this we come to the classic modern problem: how can this nonextended subject interact with the body? The body is extended while the mind or soul is a unity. As Descartes writes in *The Passions of the Soul*, "we have two eyes, two hands, two ears," etc., yet "we have but one solitary and simple thought of one particular thing at one and the same time."[8] There must then be "a place" where the impressions "can unite before arriving at the soul,"[9] this being the "little gland" (the pineal) which alone of the brain's structures is not bifurcated. Body and soul communicate by moving this little gland. In Descartes's words, the soul "possesses as many diverse perceptions as there are diverse movements in this gland," such movements being caused by the "impressions" made on the sense organs. "Reciprocally, . . . this gland is diversely moved by the soul," which thereby communicates through it to "the machine of the body."[10] How a nonextended substance is to move something extended, even if it is just a "little" gland suspended in "animal spirits," is not explained. Given that between the extended and nonextended there can be no point of physical contact, the failure of this attempt was to become paradigmatic, echoing down the centuries in the characteristic mind-body dualism of modernity.

When we recall the motive for positing subjectivity as nonextended, which is that of making it normative, there is more than a little irony here. The perceived failure of ancient philosophy involved its inability to relate its standard of certainty, the ideas, or εἴδη, to the physical world. In the premodern period, the failure to solve what was called "the problem of the universals" led to the nominalism and relativism which set the climate for Descartes's reaction. With Descartes, the problem reappears as that of the reduced subject's relation to the world. The otherworldliness of the Platonic norms is matched by a similar otherworldliness of the normative subject. As this brief reading of intellectual history indicates, the key to this dualism is the attempt to make subjectivity normative. This is what requires the abstraction which makes it nonextended.

Synthesis and the Crisis of Modernity

Kant, Descartes's greatest successor, took up the Cartesian project with his typical thoroughness. The subject, he asserts, is a "thoroughgoing identity."[11] When we regard it, "nothing multiple is given."[12] As Kant explains, I am always "conscious of the self as identical with respect to the multitude of the representations which are given to me in an intuition."[13] Whatever I represent myself as experiencing or doing, I am always conscious of myself as the same. This unitary self is also normative. Indeed, for Kant, without it "there would be no nature, i.e., no synthetic unity of the multiplicity of appearances according to rules." Taken as a "unity of apperception," it is, in fact, "the transcendental ground of the necessary lawfulness of appearances composing an experience."[14]

Kant does more than simply reaffirm the normativity and unity of subjectivity. It was his genius to unite these two insights in a radical manner. For Descartes, subjectivity was normative in the sense of providing the most certain object we could perceive. Its perception was supposed to set the standard for clarity and distinctness. Kant asks what we mean by "clarity and distinctness," and as a prior question, what is meant by the perceptual process itself. His answer is that the process is one of synthesis, of connecting perception with perception so that, through their ordering, we can have an extended intuition of a unitary object. Clarity and distinctness involve following the rules of this ordering. To the point that such rules are violated, the object fails to appear. Such rules, in other words, are viewed as "conditions for the possibility of experience." They determine in advance how the object can appear. Thus, in the Kantian view, subjectivity is normative insofar as it is seen as constitutive, through its synthesis of perceptions, of the appearing of the world. The norms we draw from it, those of the synthetic a priori judgments, are those based on the "universal and necessary connection of the given perceptions," a connection which is required if we are to intuit a unified, self-consistent world.[15] Thus, instead of Plato's forms, we have synthetic a priori judgments, and behind these we have the rules for connecting or synthesizing our perceptions, which must be followed if objects are to appear. The step from this to the unitary subject is simplicity itself. It occurs once we admit that synthesis requires a synthesizer. As Kant expresses this deduction, there is "an action of the understanding which we may name with the general title of *synthesis* in order, thereby, to draw attention to the fact that we cannot represent to ourselves anything as combined in the *object* without ourselves first having combined it and that combination . . . can only be performed *by the subject itself* since it is an act of its selfhood."[16] The deduction, then, is from the givenness of the *action of synthesis* to the necessity of the subject as an *active synthesizer*. Now, admitting that all combination requires a combiner, this subject must be uncombined. Otherwise it would be the result rather than the ground of combination. In Kant's words, given that it is what "first makes possible the concept of combination," this self must be an absolute unity.[17] If it were not a unity, it would be combined, but then there would have to be another self behind it acting as *its* combiner.

Ingenious as this analysis is, it sharpens rather than solves the problem of the subject's relation to the world. Given that appearing is a result of the synthesis (or combination) of perceptions, the subject taken as a cause of synthesis (and hence of appearing) cannot appear. If it did, it would be a result rather than a cause of synthesis. In Kant's terms, this means that the subject, taken as an uncombined combiner, must be a *noumenal* rather than a *phenomenal* subject. None of the categories which we draw from experience can apply to it. Indeed, given that the action of synthesis is that of placing its perceptions in time, even the categories of temporality fall away. Not only is it nonextended; it is out of time. Its relation to the world, in particular, its relation to the "transcendent affection," by which the world provides it with the material of its synthesis, cannot be known.

With Kant the mind-body dualism becomes explicitly that of self and world. Strictly speaking, neither of these poles is knowable "in itself." The noumenal self is matched by the noumenal world. This last is the world that remains once we abstract from its notion all the categories (all the rules of synthesis) the self imposes upon it to make it intuitable. Now a dualism in which both sides are unknown is, as Fichte noted, inherently unstable. Once we think it through, it requires that we choose between two incompatible alternatives. Either we embrace a thoroughgoing idealism and assert that the ego produces the world, positing itself as finite within it, or else, taking the opposite "dogmatic" stance, we "construe the self merely as a product of things, an accident of the world."[18] Fichte asks, "which of the two [self or world] should we take as primary? Given that both are inherently unknown, we cannot decide. As Fichte says, "reason provides no principle of choice." It cannot because what is at issue is not "a link in the change of reasoning," but rather "the beginning of the whole chain."[19] In other words, what is at issue is the ground of reason itself.

With this we come to the special crisis of modernity. The Cartesian attempt to ground reason in subjectivity by making the latter normative ultimately results in a kind of philosophic split personality. Either we embrace an idealism which ultimately positions subjectivity as an unknowable, nonrational ground of the rational or else turn and place this ground in the world. The subject, then, becomes an accident of the world in the sense of being contingent on such nonsubjective factors as the particulars of its biology, chemistry, and physics.

The scientific attempt to work out this second alternative displays an instructive circularity. To explain how the physical structure of the subject determines the nature of its perception and thought, science, as it must, uses this perception and thought to investigate this structure. Such perception and thought give us our general knowledge of anatomy, chemistry, and physics. We use this to examine the brain—with the object of ultimately knowing how the brain determines such knowledge. Thus our knowledge is explained by the structure of the brain and the operation of this structure is itself explained by our knowledge—i.e., by the scientific laws we discover through our perception and thought. Given that the structure of the brain is contingent—i.e., is something which in the course of evolution could have been different—science finds itself in the unpleasant situation of relativizing itself. Since it can never know whether the brain is so structured that it gets the world as it is in itself, it is, like its idealist alternative, reduced to a level of sheer appearance. Beyond the appearing world lies the "in itself," the unknown, nonrational ground of the rational. Although it is not to our purposes to explore this further, we cannot help mentioning that Nietzsche's discovery and exploration of this fact marks the culmination and end of modernity.[20]

Overcoming Modernity

If the above is correct, the failure of modernity is the failure of its central project. This is to make subjectivity normative, in broad terms, to make it serve as a substitute for the ideas or forms of ancient philosophy. The forms were to be reinterpreted as rules for synthesis while the synthesizing subject was to be seen as the most certain, the most clear and distinct, of the objects we could grasp. In this way, it would serve as a new foundation of knowledge, one whose openness to inspection would be its bulwark against the skepticism of a Montaigne. Subjectivity, however, was not up to the task. The history of modernity in the account we have given is, unfortunately, the story of its disappearance under the weight of the requirements placed upon it.

The fault here lies not with any of the philosophers who pursued the modern project, but rather with subjectivity itself. Whatever it is, it is an openness to the world. Capable of becoming anything in the peculiar identity that mind has with its objects, it is, "in itself," nothing but this openness. As Aristotle puts this, "before it thinks," that is, before it grasps an object, "mind has no actual existence."[21] It is "potentially identical with the objects of its thought," indeed, this potentiality is its openness. But as Aristotle immediately adds, it "is actually nothing until it thinks."[22] This means that it has no inherent content, all such content being derived from the objects which it thinks. If Aristotle is right, then the attempt to grasp the subject as an object is bound to fail. It cannot be an object, for to be such demands a definite, distinguishing content. But a subject has content only in its temporary identity with what is not itself. (This, incidentally, is the curse of psychology. Infinitely adaptable, the subject in its content seems to support every form of analysis, from the Freudian to the cognitive). Given this, the subject is the last place we should look to for normative structures. It is open to such structures. As we shall see, it can take them on in its identity with its objects. This very openness, however, signifies its lack of any *inherent* normative structures or laws. Sartre, incidentally, puts this point rather nicely when he asserts: "there is no law of consciousness, but rather a consciousness of law."[23] You cannot, he notes, have both; you cannot make consciousness an openness and require from it a set of normatively prescriptive laws. Such laws make it "opaque" rather than open. As our account of Kant indicates, they ultimately conceal rather than reveal what is not consciousness. Here, we must add that this does not mean that we shall ever encounter consciousness without its manifesting laws. These laws, however, come not from itself, but rather from its identity with its objects.

The best way to express this point is in terms of temporalization. As Kant observed, all "our representations . . . are subject to time, the formal condition of inner sense. Time is that in which they must be ordered, connected and brought into relation."[24] On the level of "inner sense," the sense by which we grasp subjective processes, we are, formally regarded, simply a series of temporal relations. We say "temporal," as opposed to "spatial," since it makes no sense to say that one representation is so many feet from another or is a certain size. We can, however, talk about one being before or after another and, indeed, about the processes by which we grasp this. This insight allows us to see why the subject cannot have any inherent content. Time per se is capable of exhibiting every sort of content precisely because it *lacks any content of its own*. Its moments are, as it were, empty containers—or rather, place holders—of possible contents. Indeed, it is this very lack of any inherent, distinguishing content which undercuts the notion of discrete moments. It is a correlative of the continuity of time. Granting this openness of time, if subjectivity is a field of temporal relations, any content it has must come from its objects. Its being as such a field *is*, in other words, *its openness* to what is not itself.

It is possible to draw a radical conclusion from the above. If we really hold that subjectivity is temporality, then the implication is that it has as many forms as time has. This means we can speak of subjectivity as sheer nowness, subjectivity as temporal flowing, subjectivity as the form of objective synthesis, subjectivity as our being-there in and through other persons, and even of subjectivity as the unidirectional flow of objective causality (the flow that allows us to suppose that our own inner relations are subject to causal laws). Each corresponds to a different sort of object. When I grasp a mathematical relation (when at the moment of insight I am no longer conditioned by the before and after of time), then I exhibit the first form of subjectivity. I exhibit a very different form playing with others as a member of an ensemble. In none of these manifestations are specific contents suggested. Subjectivity so conceived is silent on the nature of nowness, on the contents which might occupy its temporal stream, on the nature of its relations with other subjects, or on the type of causal laws it might assume it is subject to. As a sheer openness, it has a perfect plasticity. It simply provides a place for different types of objects to appear.

Post-Normative Subjectivity and Temporalization

To arrive at this notion of subjectivity a crucial transformation of the modern view of temporalization is required. Since the seventeenth century, subjectivity has been normative by virtue of serving as the ultimate focal point for the constitution of experience. For this, it must, as Kant saw, involve itself in temporalization. Its universal and necessary rules for connecting perceptions are normative in the sense that they are what first make experience possible. They perform this function by being rules for temporalization, i.e., rules for inserting experiences in the before and after of time. In other words, subjectivity is normative because time is what we bring to the data of experience to make objective experience possible. If this is right, then *the reversal of the normativity of subjectivity is the reversal of this temporalization.* The object must time the subject. It must be what inserts it in the before and after of time.

To see how this is possible requires something more than the description of the mechanics of the process. The process, to be comprehensible, requires a shift in the metaphysics which underlies modernity. This metaphysics can be summed up in a single sentence: the whole notion of the constitution of reality by the subjective act of temporalization assumes the dependence of reality on temporalization. In other words, "modernity" presupposes the dependence of being on time.[25] A "postmodern" metaphysics would assert the reverse. It would claim that time was dependent on being.

Its starting point, then, would be the fact that we have no sense of time as a flow of moments without sense of change. It would interpret this by saying that the presence which characterizes the "now" of time *is* the presence of the entity.

The continuity of time would be interpreted in terms of this continuity, this lack of any gaps in the entity's presence. It would be registered as the now in which we always dwell. The fact that we experience this now as flowing, as maintaining its presence by shifting its relation to the before and after, would be similarly interpreted in terms of the entity's motion. Moving, it remains the same while shifting its relation to its environment. Our registering this fact is its timing us, the result being that we experience ourselves as dwelling in what Husserl called the "stationary streaming" of the present. This is the present that appears to remain now by advancing from one momentary present to the next. If we are right, this streaming is simply the result of the advance of the entity, it is our registering *its* shift with regard to its environment.

To flesh out the details of this we would have to take account of the one subjective capacity which it presupposes: that of retention. This is our ability to retain (or, as Kant would say, "reproduce" in the present), the impressions an entity makes on us. Husserl's early work on retention, particularly his account of how we are timed through it, is of particular value here. A great part of his *Phenomenology of Internal Time Consciousness* can be read not as describing how we time the world but rather as describing how we are *placed in time* by the world.

Post-Modern Philosophy

Rather than getting further into the mechanics of this process, I want to conclude with a general description of postnormative subjectivity and the philosophy it implies. Here, several points can be made. The first is that such subjectivity is not epiphenomenal. In spite of its being determined, both in its laws and its content, by the world, it is not an "accident of the world." It is rather an openness that lets the world be. Such "letting be" is not to be conceived in the Heideggerian sense of letting the world reveal itself through *our* projects, goals, or criteria for being.[26] "Letting be" in the postnormative sense means letting the world temporalize itself in and through an apprehending subject. This subject times the world not by being the origin of time but by letting itself be timed by it. In the process, it lets the world be by letting the world set the laws of its appearing. In itself, it is simply an openness to these laws. We say essentially the same thing when we assert that its "laws," if such we wish to call them, are basically those by which it maintains and preserves its openness to beings.

Such openness is its "nothingness" and its receptivity. Both are a result of its being as a temporal form (essentially that of retention), which allows it to be timed by the different forms of motion surrounding it. So timed, this subject *is always on the level of ontological identity* with its object. It is inherently pluralistic. Attentive to mathematical objects, it has one form of being; attentive to another (e.g., to another musician playing in a quartet), it has another form of being. For Kant, of course, a similar kind of ontological identity held between the subject and its appearing objects, but only because the subject, through its syntheses, set the laws for the latter. When we reverse this determination, the identity continues to hold, but it does lose its normative component. There are, as we said, as many forms of subjective being as there are forms of time, such forms being determined by the way objects come to presence.

An example will help us understand this reversal. As I walk through a forest, the trees that surround me unfold themselves in perspectival patterns. Those that are nearer do so more quickly. Those on a distant hillside hardly seem to move. All this is correlative to my having a finite standpoint, more particularly, to my being an embodied perceiver. Such unfolding requires that I have a finite "here," one which I can, through my bodily motion, continuously shift. In a word, my openness to finite beings seems to rest on my own embodied finitude. A "modern" standpoint would take such finitude as constitutive of the presence of the finite things which surround me. My body (and its motion) would be taken as part of the way I "time" the world so as to apprehend finite beings. The postmodern perspective would reverse this. It would assert that it is by virtue of finite things timing me that my subjectivity displays the features of embodiment. It is through my registering their motion, including especially the motion of my own limbs, that I become finite, i.e., become a subject capable of being definitely described by a here and a now. The laws which are applicable to me as such a subject are those of my openness to finite beings.

Because these laws of openness have a foundational character, there is here a possibility of an ethical standpoint. Briefly put, its moral ideal would be that of "fullness of being," something which would be achieved by maximizing the possibilities of the subject's openness to being. Radical evil, in the sense of that which cuts things off at their roots, would consist of actions which permanently foreclose possibilities of openness. The sexual abuse of children is one example of this. It seems to structure the subject so as to close off the possibilities of its being open to others on certain fundamental levels of sexual intimacy. The key point here is the open acknowledgment of the vulnerability of the subject. As constituted in and through its world, it is capable of suffering all sorts of indignities, of having its possibilities prematurely and permanently foreclosed.[27] A moral concern for the subject begins, I believe, with this acknowledgment of its vulnerability. From this comes the sense that actions can have permanent consequences, that there are things which we can do which cannot be undone, words which, once spoken, cannot be unsaid.

Kant announced his new philosophy as a "Copernican revolution," one which reverses the view that knowledge must conform itself to objects. It is objects, he asserted, which must conform themselves to knowledge—that is, to the subjective conditions by which we know them.[28] In fact, his revolution, in making the subject the active, determining center of the world, might properly be called Ptolemaic. It was after all Ptolemy who put our earth and ourselves at the center of things. Kant claims that only through his reversal is a priori knowledge of objects possible. Does our reversal, which involves a genuine Copernican shift of standpoint, imply the abandonment of this possibility? Do we relativize truth when we assert that the subject is constituted by the world? The objection, I think, is based on a misunderstanding. Relativism in the classic sense presupposes a subject to which things are relative. Its assertion is that different subjects imply different truths. What is true for me (or for my clan, race, epoch, etc.) is not true for you, for we are differently constituting subjects (or subjective collectivities). Our position, however, makes the subject relative to the world. Where subjects agree, the world is the focus of this agreement. We thus can accept Kant's correspondence between universal and objective validity. We can say that there would be no reason for subjects to "universally" agree with one another if there were no object to which their judgments refer and with which they all agree.[29] The object mediates their agreement with one another. Is such "universal agreement" a priori in the Kantian sense? For us it cannot be, since subjectivity is posterior to the world. For Kant it can be, since the appearing object is constituted by the subjects and the necessary and universal connections of such constitution make possible *in advance* universal validity. This does not mean that we cannot speak of an a priori but only that, following our own Copernican revolution, we must reverse its sense. All a prioris must be taken from those conditions by which the world constitutes the subject. Thus it is perfectly possible for us to affirm regional ontologies with their corresponding universal truths. Their root is the constitution *by* the world of a particular openness of the subject. Indeed, there may even be nonregional, formal ontologies which would be rooted in the world's constitution of the subject in its openness as such. None of this implies the traditional notion of relativism, which is based on the notion of subjective constitution. "True for me" does not signify a private, subjective claim, but rather one of a certain correspondence to the world.

With this, the "weight" of normativity is placed on the one object that can bear it: the world itself. That the world supports a plurality of overlapping norms is simply a reflection of its containing a plurality of types of being. In its postmodern interpretation, the world simply does not permit any metaphysical monism, any appeal to an exclusive standard of what being must be. Needless to say, postmodernism is equally hostile to any form of reductionism. Given that from its perspective the subject is always on a level of identity with its object, it is in the curious position of offering us epistemological certainty without ontological normativity—the normativity of one form of being to the exclusion of others. Here, of course, we have to add that such certainty is never absolute, but only that *appropriate to its object*.[30] It is the object rather than the subject which sets its limits. Once we disengage philosophy from its task of laying down subjective norms (a task which in subtle and not so subtle ways allowed it to serve as an organ of central political control), we can also permit it another ancient truth. For the first time in many centuries, we can affirm with good conscience that "being can be said in many ways."[31]

NOTES

1. Montaigne, *Selected Essays* (New York, 1949), pp. 77–78.
2. Ibid., p. 89.

3. Cervantes, *Don Quixote* (New York, 1949), p. 722.

4. Descartes, *Meditations on First Philosophy*, tr. D. Cress (Indianapolis, 1980), p. 60.

5. Ibid., p. 93.

6. Ibid.

7. Ibid., pp. 97–98.

8. *Philosophical Works of Descartes*, vol. I, tr. Elizabeth S. Haldane and G. R. T. Ross (Cambridge, 1955), p. 346.

9. Ibid.

10. Ibid., p. 347.

11. I. Kant, *Kritik der reinen Vernunft*, A 116.

12. Ibid., B 135.

13. Ibid.

14. Ibid., A 127.

15. I. Kant, "Prolegomena," §19 in *Kants Schriften*, vol. IV (Berlin, 1911), p. 298. See also §21a; IV, 304.

16. Kant, *Kritik der reinen Vernunft*, B 130.

17. Ibid., B 131.

18. J. G. Fichte, "First Introduction . . . ," §5, in *The Science of Knowledge*, tr. P. Heath and J. Lachs (Cambridge, 1982), p. 13.

19. Ibid.

20. Nietzsche writes, "We wished to awaken the feeling of man's sovereignty by showing his divine birth: this path is now forbidden, since a monkey stands at the entrance," *The Dawn of the Day* (New York, 1974), no. 49.

21. Aristotle, *De anima*, 429a 24.

22. Ibid., 429a 24.

23. J.-P Sartre, "Consciousness of Self and Knowledge of Self," in *Readings in Existential Phenomenology* (Englewood Cliffs, 1967), p. 136.

24. Kant, *Kritik der reinen Vernunft*, A 99.

25. Given that the definition is prescriptive, not every post-Cartesian philosopher is necessarily "modern" in the sense that we use. Only those who share in the modern project and in its accompanying metaphysical commitment are.

26. Such projects would still be our norms, our modes of constituting the world's appearance. Heidegger's notion of this "pragmatic" disclosure is largely derived from William James. James writes that in disclosing an entity, "I am always unjust, always partial, always exclusive. My excuse is necessity—the necessity which my finite and practical nature lays upon me. My thinking is first and last and always for the sake of my doing, and I can only do one thing at a time." From this, it follows that "the essence of a thing is that one of its properties is so important for my interest that in comparison with it I may neglect the rest" (Reasoning," *Psychology, Briefer Course* [New York, 1948], pp. 355, 257). The interest, then, is the subjective norm for disclosure.

27. For a more extended discussion of the notion of radical evil, see J. R. Mensch, *Intersubjectivity and Transcendental Idealism* (Albany, 1988), pp. 385–88, and "Radical Evil and the Ontological Difference between Being and Beings," in *Philosophy and Culture*, ed. Venant Cauchy (Montreal, 1988), pp. 487–94.

28. Kant, *Kritik der reinen Vernunft*, B xvii.

29. "Prolegomena," §18, *Kants Schriften* IV, p. 298.

30. See Aristotle's *Nicomachean Ethics*, I, ii. 1094b 25.

31. Aristotle, *Metaphysics* 1003a 33.

Contributors

GIORGIO AGAMBEN is Professor of Foreign Language and Literature at the University of Verona. His works include *Infancy and History, Stanzas, The Coming Community,* and *Language and Death.*

FRANK ANKERSMIT is Professor of Intellectual History and Historical Theory at the University of Groningen, the Netherlands. His publications include *Narrative Logic, Denken over geschiedenis, De navel van de geschiedenis,* and *History and Tropology.*

RÉMI BRAGUE is Professor of Philosophy at the University of Paris I (Panthéon-Sorbonne). His publications include *Aristote et la question du monde, Europe, la voie romaine,* and numerous articles in the history of philosophy.

RÜDIGER BUBNER is Professor of Philosophy at the University of Tübingen. His publications include *Essays in Hermeneutics and Critical Theory, Modern German Philosophy, Handlung, Sprache und Vernunft,* and *Wiederkehr der Geschichte?*

CORNELIUS CASTORIADIS is Professor of Philosophy at Ecole des hautes études, Paris. His publications include *Crossroads in the Labyrinth, The Imaginary Institution of Society,* and *Philosophy, Politics, Autonomy.*

VICTOR GOUREVITCH is Professor of Philosophy at Wesleyan University. His publications include *The First and Second Discourses of Jean-Jacques Rousseau* (tr. and ed.) and Leo Strauss's *On Tyranny* (co-ed.).

WOLFGANG HARDTWIG is Professor of Modern History at Humboldt University, Berlin. His publications include *Geschichtskultur und Wissenschaft, Über das Studium der Geschichte, Deutschlands Weg in die Moderne. Politik, Gesellschaft und Kultur im 19. Jahrhundert,* and *Nationalismus und Bürgerkultur in Deutschland.*

KLAUS HELD is Professor of Philosophy at the Bergische University, Wuppertal, Germany. His publications include *Lebendige Gegenwart. Die Frage nach der Seinsweise des transzendentalen Ich bei Edmund Husserl, Heraklit, Parmenides und der Anfang von Philosophie und Wissenchaft. Eine Phänomenologische Besinnung,* and "Stato, interessi e mondi vitali" in *Per una fenomenologia della politica,* ed. Antonio Ponsetto.

REINHART KOSELLECK is Professor of Philosophy at the University of Bielefeld. His publications include *Studien zur Beginn der modernen Welt, Critique and Crisis,* and *Futures Past.*

REGINALD LILLY is Assistant Professor of Philosophy at Skidmore College. His publications include translations of Martin Heidegger's *Principle of Reason*, Michel Haar's *Song of the Earth,* and Werner Marx's *Is There a Measure on Earth?* as well as numerous articles in nineteenth- and twentieth-century European philosophy.

JEAN-LUC MARION is Professor of Philosophy at the University of Paris X (Nanterre) and Visiting Professor at the University of Chicago. His publications include *God without Being, Réduction et donation,* and *L'idole et la distance.*

CHRISTIAN MEIER is Professor of History in the Institute for Ancient History at the University of Munich. His publications include *The Greek Discovery of Politics, Entstehung des Begriffs Demokratie,* and *The Political Art of Greek Tragedy.*

JAMES MENSCH is Professor of Philosophy at St. Francis Xavier University in Antigonish, Nova Scotia. His publications include two forthcoming books: *Knowing and Being: A Post-Modern Reversal* and *After Modernity: Husserlian Reflections on a Philosophical Tradition.* He also authored *The Beginning of the Gospel of St. John: Philosophical Perspectives, Intersubjectivity and Transcendental Idealism* and *The Question of Being in Husserl's Logical Investigations.*

HEINRICH MOHR is Professor of Literature and the Social History of Literature at the University of Ösnabrück, Germany. His publications include *Wilhelm Heinse. Das erotisch-religiöse Weltbild und seine naturphilosophischen Grundlagen* as well as numerous articles on literature and society in East Germany.

PAUL RICOEUR is Professor Emeritus at the University of Paris and the University of Chicago. His publications include *Freud and Philosophy, The Conflict of Interpretations, The Rule of Metaphor, Time and Narrative I, II, III,* and *Oneself as Another.*

MANFRED RIEDEL is Professor of Philosophy at the University of Halle–Wittenberg, Germany. His publications include *Hegel und die antike Dialektik* (ed.), *Between Tradition and Revolution, Metaphysik und Politik,* and *Urteilskraft und Vernunft.*

JOHN SALLIS is Professor of Philosophy at Pennsylvania State University. He is editor of *Research in Phenomenology*, and his publications include *Being and Logos: The Way of Platonic Dialogue, The Gathering of Reason, Delimitations, Echoes,* and *Double Truth.*

JACQUES TAMINIAUX is Professor of Philosophy at Louvain-la-Neuve, Belgium, and Boston College. He is editor of *Etudes Phénoménologiques* and author of *La Nostalgie de la Grèce à l'aube de l'idéalisme allemand, Recoupments, Dialectic and Difference, Heidegger and the Project of Fundamental Ontology,* and *Poetics, Speculation and Judgment.*

Index